The
Family Life
of
Black People

EDITED BY

Charles V. Wi...

Syracuse University

713205

Charles E. Merrill Publishing Company
A Bell & Howell Company
Columbus, Ohio

Merrill Sociology Series

Under the editorship of

Richard L. Simpson
University of North Carolina,
at Chapel Hill

ISBN: 0-675-09297-3

Library of Congress Catalog Card Number: 79-127082

1   2   3   4   5   6   7   8   9   10 — 77   76   75   74   73   72   71   70

Printed in the United States of America

This book is dedicated to:

my friend and teacher,
the late Doctor Walter R. Chivers,
of Morehouse College;

my family of procreation,
Mary Sue, my wife;
Sarah Susannah, Martin Charles and James Theodore,
my children;
Theodore L. and Isabel Conklin, my parents-in-law;
Elizabeth, my sister-in-law;

my family of orientation,
Louis James and Carrie Sykes Willie, my parents;
Louis, Joseph, Alfred and Mary, my brothers and sister.

Preface

NOT SINCE THE MONUMENTAL WORK OF THE LATE E. FRANKLIN FRAZIER, of Howard University, has there been a comprehensive study of the family life of black people in the United States. Professor Frazier's studies were conducted during the 1930's and have been continuously referred to as a primary source of information.

An updated view of the family life of black people is now needed. It would be most difficult, however, for a single scholar to do this in a comprehensive way today. The task of this book, therefore, is to assemble a series of articles prepared by competent social scientists which describe and analyze the many variations and adaptations which characterize the family life of black people. I am particularly interested in presenting contributions from black and white scholars, who study middle class as well as lower class styles of life, and who deal with both pathological and nonpathological conditions in the Negro family. This book will approach the study of the family life of black people as an integrative, adaptive, functional system rather than as a social problem or as an illustration of deviance.

Twenty-six articles have been assembled and arranged in a way that effectively deals with the issue of stability and instability in family life and the question of whether or not there is a breakdown in the Negro family. These articles are written by scholars who identify with the disciplines of sociology, psychology, anthropology, political science, demography, psychiatry and social work. An outstanding feature is the recent publication of these articles: all since 1960, nearly 90 percent since 1964, and about 30 percent as late as, or after, 1968. Moreover, approximately 20 percent of the articles will be published for the first time in this volume.

I call attention to the fact that black and Negro are used interchangeably. None is used pejoratively, no ulterior motive is present. The technique of using both words interchangeably is simply the adaptation of an editor over 40 to the language preference of his readers, many of whom are under 30. Indeed this book is prepared for use as a supplementary text in courses in the family and in racial and ethnic minorities, as well as for use as a basic text in Black Studies. The general public will find several articles in this volume of value, particularly articles which provide answers to some of the issues raised in the Moynihan Report on "The Negro Family."

I am most grateful to the authors and publishers who permitted their work to appear in this volume. Acknowledged with appreciation is the fine assistance rendered by Donald Reed, James O'Hair and Mrs. Dorothy J. Walker, who served as research assistants. A special word of thanks goes to Roger Ratliff, sociology editor of Charles E. Merrill Publishing Company, for his patience and perseverance as this project carefully unfolded in its own time and slowly moved toward fruition. The editor is also deeply indebted to his family of procreation and his family of orientation whose comfort and care have sustained him over the years and have given him the audacious courage to contemplate preparation of a book on the Negro family, about which disagreement is certain considering what is included and what is omitted.

Charles V. Willie
Professor and Chairman
Department of Sociology
Syracuse University
Syracuse, New York
1970

Contents

Contributors

ALMA BEMAN	Rice University, Houston, Texas
ZENA SMITH BLAU	Northwestern University, Evanston, Illinois and Institute for Juvenile Research, Chicago, Illinois
ROBERT COLES	Harvard University, Cambridge, Massachusetts
JAMES E. CONYERS	Indiana State University, Terre Haute, Indiana
BEVERLY DUNCAN	University of Michigan, Ann Arbor, Michigan
OTIS DUDLEY DUNCAN	University of Michigan, Ann Arbor, Michigan
REYNOLDS FARLEY	University of Michigan, Ann Arbor, Michigan
WILLIAM J. FARMAR	Federation of Southern Co-operatives, Atlanta, Georgia
JOE R. FEAGIN	University of Texas, Austin, Texas
MYRNA E. FRANK	Health Insurance Plan of Greater New York, New York, New York
PAUL C. GLICK	United States Department of Commerce, Bureau of Census, Washington, D.C.
MARY ELLEN GOODMAN	(deceased)
ELIZABETH HERZOG	Social Research Group (G.W.U.), 2401 Virginia Avenue, N.W., Washington, D.C.
HELEN MACGILL HUGHES	Sociological Resources for Social Studies, 27 Shepard Street, Cambridge, Massachusetts
CAMILLE JEFFERS	Child Service and Family Counseling Center, Model Cities Program, Atlanta, Georgia
CLYDE V. KISER	Milbank Memorial Fund, New York, New York
LOUIS KRIESBERG	Syracuse University, Syracuse, New York
WILLIAM LADD	Associate Director, Center for Urban Studies, University of Michigan—Dearborn Campus, Dearborn, Michigan
MARTIN L. LEVIN	Emory University, Atlanta, Georgia
RUSSELL MIDDLETON	University of Wisconsin, Madison, Wisconsin
DANIEL P. MOYNIHAN	The White House, Washington, D.C.

EVA MUELLER	University of Michigan, Ann Arbor, Michigan
MOLLIE ORSHANSKY	United States Department of Health, Education and Welfare, Washington, D.C.
SNELL PUTNEY	San Jose College, San Jose, California
WILLIAM B. ROTHNEY	New England Medical Center, Boston, Massachusetts
DAVID A. SCHULZ	University of Delaware, Newark, Delaware
J. RICHARD UDRY	University of North Carolina, Chapel Hill, North Carolina
UNITED STATES DEPARTMENT OF COMMERCE	Bureau of Census, Washington, D.C.
HERBERT L. WASSERMAN	New England Medical Center, Boston, Massachusetts
LEWIS G. WATTS	(deceased)
JANET WEINANDY	Child and Family Service, Syracuse, New York
CHARLES V. WILLIE	Syracuse University, Syracuse, New York

Introduction

THE PREPARATION OF THIS BOOK WAS STIMULATED BY THE NATIONAL controversy that followed publication of a report entitled "The Negro Family, a Case for National Action." The report was prepared by the United States Labor Department and Daniel Patrick Moynihan was its chief author. It soon became known as the Moynihan Report.

The Moynihan Report quickly became the eye of a stormy contro versy. The controversy whirled with acrimonious debate all the way from inner-city black ghettoes of the nation to the White House and had a devastating impact on the White House Conference on Civil Rights.

In a Howard University speech in 1965, the President promised to convene a White House Conference which would have as a major objective discovering ways to help the American Negro people to move beyond opportunity to achievement. The words of the President in that speech sounded similar to the phrases in the Moynihan Report which suggested that poverty might be perpetuated among black people in the United States largely because of their unstable family structures. Moynihan, of course, did not rule out increasing the economic resources of the Negro family as a way of contributing to its viability; but it is clear that the social integration of family members should receive priority attention, according to his analysis.

Many black ghetto dwellers and some social scientists disagreed with this assertion and assessment. The reason for the continuing poverty and unequal opportunity of black people in America, they said, was a blocked opportunity system, blocked largely because of racial discrimination.

Supporters of the Moynihan point of view, which included many white suburbanites and some social scientists, argued that the demand for equal opportunities inevitably would be linked with the demand for equal results. They were not attempting to deny the presence of racial discrimination and its effects upon the way of life of black people. They were pointing beyond the present in their analysis, suggesting that even an open system would be an empty victory of limited value if black peo-

1

ple were unable to take advantage of the new opportunities and could not produce equally with whites.

Leaders in the black communities and particularly leaders of religious organizations warned that if conclusions about the Negro family in the Moynihan Report were used as a basis for a national policy, the Freedom Movement would suffer a major setback. As preparation for the White House Conference on Civil Rights (actually named the White House Conference "To Fulfill These Rights") continued, many black leaders believed that the Conference was an effort by the Administration to refocus the Freedom Movement from court cases, street demonstrations, legislative lobbying and concern with *changing institutions* and *systems* which deny opportunities to concern with *changing individuals* and *families* of limited achievement. The White House Conference was held in June of 1966. Because of the intense controversy which was sparked by the Moynihan Report published a year earlier, the participants were divided on the goals which they wished to achieve. The gathering which was billed as the conference of the century to hammer out a blueprint for action became nothing more than a fading ritual low in vitality and confused in purpose.

Yet controversy surrounding the Moynihan Report on the Negro Family did not fade as several chapters in this book indicate. The controversy continued unabated almost as a polemical debate or an adversary proceeding with advocates revealing or concealing information helpful or harmful to their side. Such a process, of course, is alien to science in which all data are admissable.

Although stimulated by the national debate about the Negro family, this book is not intended as a rebuttal to the Moynihan Report. It is a social science document which attempts to go beyond the polemics of debate by drawing together the findings of basic research. A few chapters are interpretative works which synthesize the ideas of different scholars. Most of the chapters, however, are reports of field studies conducted by social scientists who have used rigorous research methods in their investigations.

Although analytical rather than polemical, this book is not without a point of view. A theme running throughout its pages is that the family of black people continues to exist. Data in support of and data which qualify this theme are brought together in this document, including a thorough and thoughtful chapter by Daniel Patrick Moynihan on the "Ordeal of the Negro Family" which was prepared after the original report was published. Careful reading of this book could lead to a new understanding of the Negro family.

A comparative perspective was an important aid to the editor in selecting chapters. The structure and process of family life among black people is compared with the family life among white people, and brown people, such as Mexican-Americans, and other populations in the United States. Comparative contributions included in this volume are those which control social-class variables in the study design or analysis. Failure to deal adequately with differential economic strata within or between racial and ethnic groups has been a major limitation of many investigations. At times spurious conclusions have emerged from some of these studies in which effects attributed to race and ethnicity could be consequences of social class.

Central in the development of this book is the issue of stability and instability in the family life of black people. After a background section on the social facts of family life which, for the most part, includes historical, demographic and ecological data, a series of chapters is presented which discuss (1) how marital stability can be used as a social indicator; (2) historical trends in marital status among black people; and (3) variations in marital stability by income, occupation, education and race. Thus, the first two parts of this book provide conclusive evidence for determining whether or not there is breakdown in the Negro family.

Beyond the issue of social breakdown, exploration of the Negro family could be an enriching experience. This book, therefore, carries on with a discussion of the multitudinous variations and adaptations which have been observed among black people in America and the consequences for children who have experienced these varying conditions of existence. In general, these chapters tell how poor black families have coped with their circumstances, sometimes failing but often prevailing. Both strengths and weaknesses in the family structure are revealed.

These studies also are contributions to social science theory about innovations, adaptations, social change, social contextual and situational responses. The third and fourth parts of this book provide information of general value to the social sciences over and above the contribution which analysis of the Negro family makes to the understanding of social problems.

Finally, the book is concluded by returning to the initial question. Is the black family in contemporary America crumbling? In the past, this question has been answered affimatively or negatively in a partisan way. Coming at the end of the volume as it does, the question now can be answered on the basis of evidence presented, including evidence presented by Daniel Patrick Moynihan.

An interesting feature about the final part of this book is that it casts doubt upon the hypothesis of social breakdown but then goes on to indicate conditions under which it might or might not occur in different racial populations. The editor, for example, states in a chapter which he authored that the Moynihan thesis about family instability in the end may be a more appropriate explanation for the presence of poverty among whites than blacks. This idea was not necessarily saved as a surprise ending. Actually, this is usually the outcome: that an increased understanding of white people in America tends to flow from an honest, unbiased and conscientious study and understanding of black people in America. This outcome is seldom experienced because many studies of black people are offensively critical or defensively apologetic, with justification rather than explanation as their primary goal. This book attempts to overcome these distortions by including material prepared by black and white scholars, representing a diversity of disciplines, who studied different racial and ethnic groups of varying economic circumstances and whose families exhibited strengths and weaknesses. This book neither exhalts nor condemns. Its task is to understand the black family — an understanding which could provide a modest clue for better understanding the family life of all people.

Part 1

Social Facts and Family Life

We the Black People of the United States

WE ARE BLACK

We are the black people of the United States. The 1960 census counted 18.8 million of us and the current estimate is 22 million; 10.5 million males and 11.5 million females. We make up 11 percent of the total population and that percentage should continue to increase because 15 percent of the children under five are black. Birthrates have been declining for both races since 1957; however, while the birthrate was 16.7 babies per thousand population for whites in 1967, it was 25.9 for blacks.

When the country was smaller, early in its history, we represented a bigger chunk of the population than the present 11 percent. The first census in 1790 counted nearly 700,000 black people, about one in every five Americans. In 1860 we were about one in seven.

When America stopped importing slaves, births became the basis of our population growth. Africans didn't voluntarily rush to America's shores as the white European immigrants did. So the white population grew faster than the black, forcing our earlier high percentage to decline.

WHERE WE LIVE

In the days of slavery and for many years afterward, most of us lived on farms. At the turn of the century 80 percent of our people still were in the rural areas. But farming changed. Machines began to replace people on the farms. We had to move to new places, to new kinds of work. By 1940 only about a third of us lived on farms; by 1960 the proportion was down to 8 percent. Now it is about 7 percent, about the same percentage as for the white population.

Where did we go? Most of us, perhaps after several moves, wound up in the cities — in the big cities. From 1950 to 1968, the total black

Reprinted by permission of The United States Department of Commerce, Bureau of The Census (1969).

City	Negro Population 1960	National Rank, 1960 Negro	National Rank, 1960 Total	Percent Negro 1960	Percent Negro 1965*
New York	1,087,931	1	1	14%	18%
Chicago	812,637	2	2	23	28
Philadelphia	529,240	3	4	26	31
Detroit	482,223	4	5	29	34
Washington, D.C.	411,737	5	9	54	66
Los Angeles	334,916	6	3	14	17
Baltimore	325,589	7	6	35	38
Cleveland	250,818	8	8	29	34
New Orleans	233,514	9	15	37	41
Houston	215,037	10	7	23	23
St. Louis	214,377	11	10	29	36
Atlanta	186,464	12	24	38	44
Memphis	184,320	13	22	37	40
Newark	138,035	14	30	34	47
Birmingham	135,113	15	36	40	x
Dallas	129,242	16	14	19	21
Cincinnati	108,754	17	21	22	24
Pittsburgh	100,692	18	16	17	20
Indianapolis	98,049	19	26	21	23
Richmond	91,972	20	52	42	x
Oakland	83,618	21	33	23	x
Kansas City, Mo.	83,146	22	27	18	22
Jacksonville	82,525	23	61	41	x
Norfolk	78,806	24	41	26	x
Columbus	77,140	25	28	16	18
San Francisco	74,383	26	12	10	12
Buffalo	70,904	27	20	13	17
Louisville	70,075	28	31	18	x
Gary	69,123	29	70	39	x
Mobile	65,619	30	58	32	x
Miami	65,213	31	44	22	x
Nashville	64,570	32	73	38	x
Boston	63,165	33	13	9	13
Milwaukee	62,458	34	11	8	11

(x indicates no estimate was made for 1965)
*Census Bureau estimate

Population Distribution by Location 1960-1968 (Percent)

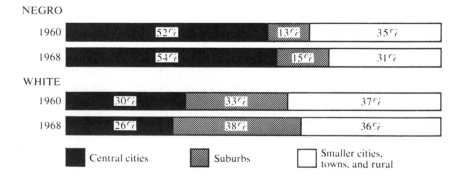

NEGRO

1960 — 52% Central cities, 13% Suburbs, 35% Smaller cities, towns, and rural
1968 — 54% Central cities, 15% Suburbs, 31% Smaller cities, towns, and rural

WHITE

1960 — 30% Central cities, 33% Suburbs, 37% Smaller cities, towns, and rural
1968 — 26% Central cities, 38% Suburbs, 36% Smaller cities, towns, and rural

Central cities | Suburbs | Smaller cities, towns, and rural

Distribution of the Black Population by Region

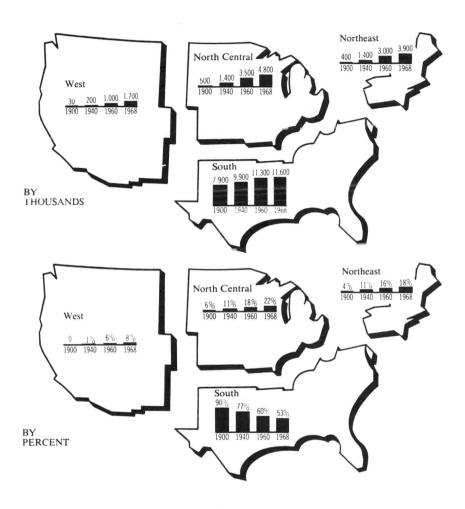

Northeast
| 400 | 1,400 | 3,000 | 3,900 |
| 1900 | 1940 | 1960 | 1968 |

North Central
| 500 | 1,400 | 3,500 | 4,800 |
| 1900 | 1940 | 1960 | 1968 |

West
| 30 | 200 | 1,000 | 1,700 |
| 1900 | 1940 | 1960 | 1968 |

South
| 7,900 | 9,900 | 11,300 | 11,600 |
| 1900 | 1940 | 1960 | 1968 |

BY THOUSANDS

Northeast
| 4% | 11% | 16% | 18% |
| 1900 | 1940 | 1960 | 1968 |

North Central
| 6% | 11% | 18% | 22% |
| 1900 | 1940 | 1960 | 1968 |

West
| 0 | 1% | 6% | 8% |
| 1900 | 1940 | 1960 | 1968 |

South
| 90% | 77% | 60% | 53% |
| 1900 | 1940 | 1960 | 1968 |

BY PERCENT

population increased by 7 million, and 5 million of the increase was in the central cities of our metropolitan areas. More than half (54 percent) of us now live inside the central cities. So, starting out as "farm" people, we have now become "big-city" people.

The whites, too, moved from farms to the cities, and then on to the suburbs. Considering only the metropolitan areas, most of the blacks are in the central cities and most of the whites are in the suburbs. The most recent figures indicate an increase in the number of Negroes in the central cities and a slight increase in our suburban population since 1960.

OUR MIGRATION PATTERNS

Let's take another look at our long-term movement. As we moved from the farm to the city, we also moved from the South to the North and West. In 1860, our population was 4½ million including 4 million slaves. At that time 92 percent of all black Americans lived in the South. In 1900, 90 percent of us were still there. But then we began to spread out. By 1940 the census showed just 77 percent of us in the South. By 1960 this figure was down to 60 percent and the 1968 estimate is 53 percent. The Census Bureau counts Maryland, Delaware, Kentucky, Oklahoma, West Virginia and the District of Columbia as "South," along with the States of the old Confederacy.

Our percentage in the South is dropping and the black population there would also show a decline in actual numbers if it were not for new babies, fewer infant deaths, and better care for the aged. Millions of our people have left the South for new homes in the North and West. More than four million moved away between 1940 and 1960.

WHAT WE EARN

The average black family earns less money than the average white family, although the average black family is larger. Nine percent of the families in the United States are black, but we receive only 5 percent of the national income. Our pay is lowest in the South and highest in the West and Midwest. The income gap between whites and blacks follows the

Median* Family Income in 1967

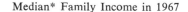
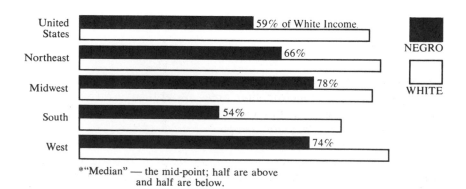

*"Median" — the mid-point; half are above
and half are below.

same pattern . . . widest in the South and narrower in the West and the Midwest.

Negro median income was 59 percent of the median income for white families in 1967, the highest percentage ever. One reason our incomes are low is that black families are 5 times as likely to be headed by a woman as white families. The earning power of the black worker is lower than that of the white even when they have both had the same amount of schooling.

Median Income for Men 25 Years Old and Over, 1966

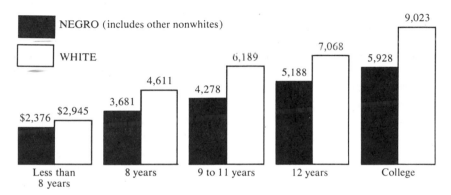

HIGHEST GRADE OF SCHOOL COMPLETED

OUR JOBS

Finally, our low income level is caused by our having so many low-paying jobs. About two of every five black men and more than half of all black women who work are service workers, laborers, or farm workers.

But we are growing away from these low-paying jobs. A comparison of 1960 and 1967 employment figures shows that 169,000 fewer Negroes worked in household service, 70,000 fewer were laborers, and 453,000 fewer worked on farms in 1967. At the same time, the number of black professional, technical, and crafts workers increased by more than 2 million.

Still, black representation in the professions and in some skill areas remains proportionately small. Black men represent 8.4 percent of the employed males in this country, but only 2 percent of the doctors, 2.5 percent of the dentists, 1.5 percent of the insurance brokers, 3.3 percent of the plumbers, 1.5 percent of the electricians, and 0.5 percent of the engineers. Black women represent 11.6 percent of the employed women

EMPLOYMENT BY OCCUPATION AND SEX, 1967
Percent of Employed Labor Force*

	MALE		FEMALE	
	Black	White	Black	White
Professional, managerial, technical, clerical, sales workers.	41%	46%	30%	63%
Skilled blue-collar. (Carpenters, construction craftsmen, mechanics, factory workers, drivers, etc.)	21	40	17	16
Service, labor, farm.	38	14	53	21

*Does not include the armed forces

but only 2.4 percent of the lawyers, 5.6 percent of the professional nurses, 6.5 percent of the medical technicians, 2.4 percent of the telephone operators, 1.5 percent of the secretaries, and 8.8 percent of elementary school teachers.

We have our full share of some jobs including clergymen, social workers, cosmetologists, and dietitians. And we have more than our share of mail carriers, masons, metal workers, plasterers, service station attendants, furnace men, laundry workers, packers, taxi-drivers, elevator operators, and practical nurses.

Some of us are self-employed: 200,000 with farms, 1,200 with clothing stores, 400 with furniture stores, 300 with household appliance stores, 2,600 with gasoline and service stations, over 8,000 with trucking services, 4,000 in wholesale trade, 13,000 with food and dairy stores, 15,000 with eating and drinking places, and 1,700 with other retail stores of various kinds.

There is some black ownership of almost every conceivable kind of enterprise from hotels and radio stations to banks, management consultant firms, and super markets.

PEOPLE WITHOUT JOBS

Although the employment statistics are more encouraging now than in earlier years, unemployment is still a major problem for Negro Americans. An estimated 654 thousand blacks were unemployed in 1967. This included more than 107 thousand married men. Compared with white workers, we are twice as likely to be out of work.

Our total unemployment rate declined slightly from 7.3 in 1967 to 6.8 for the first 6 months of 1968.

In ghetto areas the problem is much worse, with one out of every three available black workers either unemployed or seriously underemployed, that is, working for substandard pay or working only part-time. Nationally, 14 percent of our people are on welfare, compared with 3 percent of the whites.

UNEMPLOYMENT RATES 1967
Percent of available workers who are without jobs

	Negro	White
Total	7.3%	3.3%
Adult men	4.5	2.1
Adult women	6.9	3.7
Teenagers(16-19)	26.4	10.2

HOW WE LIVE

About 38 percent of our families own their homes — an increase from 24 percent in 1940. However, much of the housing we live in is substandard. Three of every ten dwellings occupied by black families are dilapidated or lack hot water, toilet, tub or shower.

Almost half (46 percent) of the black people in the South and 16 percent of those in the North and West live in such housing. Slowly these substandard housing units are disappearing. The number of black-occupied housing units described as dilapidated or lacking basic plumbing declined from 2.2 million in 1960 to 1.7 million in 1966. (For whites the decline was from 6.2 million to 4 million.)

Using the yardstick of one person per room, one fourth of our housing in the cities is overcrowded; in rural areas, two fifths.

We are buying more and more automobiles and appliances. About 52 percent of our families have at least one car; 10 percent own two or more. Eighty-three percent own black-and-white television sets, and 6 percent have color sets. (Percentages for whites are 86 for black-and-white sets and 17 for color.) Seventy-six percent of us have refrigerators or freezers, 4 percent have dishwashers, and 8 percent own room air conditioners.

OUR SCHOOLING IS IMPROVING

Our educational record looks better every year, with fewer "drop-outs" and more high school graduates and college students. Only 77 percent of our young men and women aged 16 and 17 were enrolled in school in 1960. In 1966 that figure had risen to 83 percent.

The proportion of young adults who have completed high school continues to rise for both races, although there is still a gap between black and white.

Percent of Males and Females 25-29 Who Have Completed High School

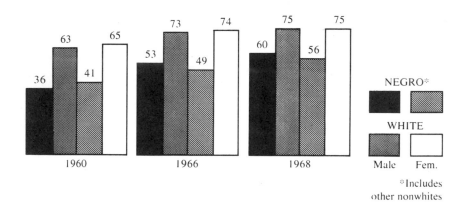

These tables also compare male and female graduates, with our young men showing the larger percentage gains.

Percent of Negroes 25-34 Who Have Completed 4 Years of College

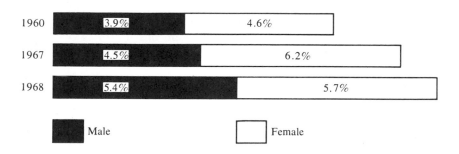

OUR VOTING RECORD

Fifty-eight percent of our voting age population voted in the 1968 Presidential election. For whites, 69 percent voted. A higher percentage of Negroes in the North and West voted than in the South.

In the 1964 Presidential election, 59 percent of the eligible black voters cast ballots, compared with 71 percent of the whites. In the 1966 Congressional election, the comparison was 42 percent to 57 percent.

Most, but not all of those who did not vote were not registered. Registration in the South still lags behind the North and West.

PRESIDENTIAL ELECTION VOTERS, 1968		
	BLACK	WHITE
Number of voting age	10,935,000	104,521,000
Percent who voted: U.S.	58%	69%
North and West	65	72
South	52	62

PERCENT OF NEGROES OF VOTING AGE WHO WERE REGISTERED		
	1968	1966
North and West	72	69
South	62	53

Seventy-one percent of the whites in the South and 77 percent in the North and West were registered in 1968.

LOOKING AHEAD

Looking to the future, the Census Bureau says that there probably will be about 28 million black Americans by 1980 and more than 35 million by 1990. We will account for 12.4 percent of the total population in 1980 and 13.6 percent by 1990.

The black labor force is expected to increase by almost 4 million from 1965 to 1980 while the total labor force will be adding 23 million. The nation will need to find an additional 4 jobs for every 10 held by blacks in 1965.

. . .

We, the Black People of the United States, know these things about ourselves because the Census Bureau has asked us questions and totaled up the answers.

Dominance in Decisions in the Family, Race and Class Differences

RUSSELL MIDDLETON AND SNELL PUTNEY

THE LOCUS OF POWER WITHIN THE FAMILY IS AN IMPORTANT VARIABLE in family structure, an indication of which is dominance in making decisions. Idiosyncratic factors affect dominance in any individual couple, but among a group of families cultural or subcultural influences establish typical patterns. Thus, for example, it is reported that in Navaho culture the wife generally dominates in decisions, whereas among the Mormons it is the husband.[1]

The making of decisions in a family may be conceptualized along a continuum from the matriarchal, through the equalitarian, to the patriarchal. The question of where the typical American family would be located on it has been the subject of considerable speculation but of comparatively little systematic research. Particularly lacking is research explicitly relating to differences in marital dominance among the subcultures in American society, for example, racial and social class groupings. The available literature — much of it impressionistic — suggests that the American Negro family tends to be matriarchal because of the important economic role of the wife and the family insta-

---

[1] Fred L. Strodtbeck, "Husband-Wife Interaction over Revealed Differences," *American Sociological Review*, XVI (August, 1951), 468-73.

[2] Maurice Davie, *Negroes in American Society* (New York: McGraw-Hill Book Co., 1949), pp. 207-9; St. Clair Drake and Horace R. Clayton, *Black Metropolis* (New York: Harcourt, Brace & Co., 1945), pp. 582-83; E. Franklin Frazier, *The Negro Family in the United States* (Chicago: University of Chicago Press, 1939), pp. 125-45, 438-40; Charles S. Johnson, *Growing Up in the Black Belt* (Washington, D.C.: American Council on Education, 1941), pp. 59, 80; Charles E. King, "The Negro Maternal Family: A Product of an Economic and a Culture System," *Social Forces*, XXIV (October, 1945), 100-104; Hortense Powdermaker, *After Freedom* (New York: Viking Press, 1939), pp. 145-46; and Frances J. Woods, *Cultural Values of American Ethnic Groups* (New York: Harper & Bros., 1956), pp. 242-45.

Reprinted by permission of the publisher and author from *The American Journal of Sociology*, LXV (May 1960), 60⁵-9.

bility, traditional since slavery times.[2] White families, on the other hand, have a patriarchal tradition deriving from Europe. There is some evidence within both racial groups that the middle-class families have shifted to equalitarianism and that the working-class families remain closer to tradition.[3]

On the basis of the literature, then, we would expect to find that families of professionals, whether white or Negro, would reflect their middle-class orientation by being generally equalitarian in decisions. Workers, somewhat more removed from middle-class values, might be expected to remain closer to their traditions — matriarchal among Negro workers and patriarchal among white workers.

This paper reports a research project designed to determine whether or not these groups differ in dominance in family decisions, as predicted from the literature. College professors were selected to represent the professional middle class, and skilled workers to represent the working class.

We chose to observe dominance in the making of decisions rather than to rely upon self-appraisals. For both practical and theoretical reasons minor decisions of daily life, rather than crises, were selected for study.[4] In order to observe dominance in the making of minor decisions, a modification of the technique used by Strodtbeck was developed.[5] A questionnaire seeking opinions on subjects of common family interest was filled out by each husband and wife individually. Included were questions such as the following: "Should toilet-training for a child begin before he is one year old?" "Should a couple that is getting married ask their friends for silver as wedding gifts or practical things, such as towels, sheets, and dishes?" "When friends come over to your house in the evening would you prefer to watch television or just sit and talk?" "If it becomes necessary to speak to your neighbors about their child's behavior, is it better for the husband or the wife to do it?" The questionnaire included fifteen questions in each of four areas: child care, purchases and living standards, recreation, and role attitudes; the items were selected following a pretest to determine those most likely to elicit disagreement.

---

[3]Frazier, *op. cit.*, p. 439.

[4]Many of the questions on which the subjects reached joint decisions were related to major problems. For example, "If you were buying a house, would you prefer to buy a small new house or a larger but older house costing the same amount?" However, deciding what their joint answer to this question will be in the experiment, as opposed to real life, is a minor decision comparable to many daily decisions.

[5]Strodtbeck, *op. cit.*

After husband and wife had filled out the questionnaire individually, they were requested to fill it out a second time jointly, giving opinions "as a family." The number of disagreements on the individual questionnaires was then tabulated, and the proportion of the disagreements which were resolved in favor of the position originally taken by the husband was computed. This proportion was taken as a measure of position along the continuum between matriarchy and patriarchy.

In Strodtbeck's original technique there was some possibility that the partner with the most information would appear dominant regardless of the usual pattern of interaction.[6] In order to avoid this danger, all our questions concerned judgments of value or preference rather than matters of fact on which one partner might have more information.

Forty couples served as subjects for the study, ten from each of the following: white college professors, Negro college professors, white skilled workers, and Negro skilled workers. The subjects were brought together in homogeneous groups to promote a relaxed atmosphere and sense of anonymity. Each couple was paid a small sum.

The selection of subjects began with construction of four mailing lists, as far as possible random selections from the universes defined by the study. Final selection of subjects was made from those who responded to the mailed invitation. All subjects selected were American-born, had at least one child, had been married at least two years, were between the ages of twenty-five and forty-nine in the case of males and twenty and forty-four in the case of females, and were residents of the same small southern city. In addition, the groups were matched

TABLE 1

CHARACTERISTICS OF THE SAMPLE

Sample Group	Mean Years of Marriage	Mean Age of Husband	Mean Age of Wife
White professors	9.5	37.0	32.0
White workers	9.2	35.3	29.2
Negro professors	9.3	34.7	30.2
Negro workers	9.6	33.0	30.1
All couples	9.4	35.0	30.4
No. of couples	40.0	40.0	40.0

[6]Strodtbeck's subjects were instructed to pick which of three families with whom they were acquainted was most ambitious, had the happiest children, etc. The danger is that one partner may be less well acquainted with the other couple and hence may defer to the other partner's greater knowledge even though he is ordinarily dominant.

on mean years of marriage, mean age of husband, and mean age of wife. The matching was designed to control variables independent of race and class (Table 1).[7] The only statistically significant difference among the samples is between the mean ages of husbands for white professors and Negro skilled workers.[8]

Statistical significance of the differences in dominance among the four groups was tested with the Mann-Whitney *U* Test.[9] The procedure involves ranking the couples along the continuum of dominance and testing the null hypothesis that the two groups being compared have the same distribution.

RACIAL AND OCCUPATIONAL DIFFERENCES

Contrary to the expectation that the racial and occupational groups would occupy different points along the continuum from matriarchy to patriarchy, no differences significant at the .05 level were discovered among the four samples, or between all whites compared to all Negroes, or between all professors compared to all skilled workers (Table 2). Although the probability of β error cannot be computed, a relatively powerful statistical test was used on the small differences observed,

TABLE 2

DOMINANCE IN DECISIONS BY RACE AND OCCUPATION

	PERCENTAGE OF COUPLES				
PERCENTAGE OF DECISIONS WON BY HUSBANDS	White Professors	White Workers	Negro Professors	Negro Workers	Total
0-32 (matriarchal)	20	20	......	20	15
33-67 (equalitarian)	60	70	90	80	75
68-100 (patriarchal)	20	10	10	......	10
Total	100	100	100	100	100
No. of couples	10	10	10	10	40

[7]Other characteristics such as number of children, employment of wife, and education were not matched, since these variables are not independent of socioeconomic position.

[8]Although the resulting samples suffer the disadvantages of self-selection and partial matching, they may be assumed to be considerably more representative than the samples used in typical small-group research.

[9]The *t* test was not used, since it cannot be justified with a measuring instrument which yields only ordinal measurement. The Mann-Whitney *U* Test is approximately as powerful for moderate or larger samples, with the advantage of being non-parametric and appropriate for use with ordinal measurement (see Sidney Siegel, *Nonparametric Statistics for the Behavioral Sciences* [New York: McGraw-Hill Book Co., 1956], pp. 116-27).

TABLE 3

PERCENTAGE OF DECISIONS WON BY HUSBAND,
BY RACE, OCCUPATION, AND PROBLEM

Problem Area	White Professors	White Workers	Negro Professors	Negro Workers	Total
Child care	35.6	48.1	56.6	48.8	47.7
Purchases and living standards	64.1	53.8	41.0	46.0	50.9
Recreation	58.6	40.0	54.7	57.1	53.8
Role attitudes	47.4	38.1	58.7	54.5	49.7
Total	50.3	45.6	53.4	51.4	50.4
No. of decisions	151	160	191	175	677

and it is probably safe to conclude that the null hypothesis should be accepted. Thus we find no evidence that whites and Negroes, professors and skilled workers, differ as to which spouse dominates in the making of daily decisions. Contrary to the literature, our data suggest that all these groups are predominantly equalitarian. In view of this, it would be interesting to conduct further investigations with lower-class whites and Negroes to see whether they deviated from the predominant equalitarian pattern.

The pattern of equalitarianism is essentially unchanged when the disagreements are broken down into the four areas of the questionnaire (Table 3). The proportion of disagreements won by the husband was not greater than .64 or less than .36 in any area or for any group. Only one of these differences is significant at the .05 level: the tendency of the families of white professors to be more patriarchal in making decisions concerning purchases and living standards than the families of Negro professors.[10] Thus, although over-all differences were lacking, there is some evidence of specific differences. This gives some support to the original hypothesis of racial differences, although the difference was observed in only one area and between white and Negro professionals rather than white and Negro workers. But this lone significant difference should be interpreted with caution. Of the twenty-four tests of significance computed, at least one could have been expected to reach significance and the .05 level by pure chance. Nevertheless, the differences are larger when the data are broken down into separate areas. Therefore there is a greater possibility of β error in accepting the

---

[10]The difference between all whites and all Negroes was also significant at the .05 level in this area, but, since the difference between the white and Negro skilled workers was small, this result may be attributed to the difference between the two groups of professors rather than the racial differences.

null hypothesis that dominance in the four samples does not differ in specific areas. Further research might be made on the hypothesis that, although, in general, there may be no differences in dominance among white and Negro professors and skilled workers, differences may exist between them in specific areas. The present study, however, does not support the hypothesis that differences exist.

THE WORKING WIFE

Previous research has suggested that the employment of the wife increases her importance in family decisions.[11] Our data permit a comparison of the relative dominance in decisions of working and non-working wives among the forty couples;[12] 65 per cent of the wives were employed outside the home, and 35 percent were not (Table 4). The difference in dominance between working wives and non-working wives is significant well beyond the .05 level, but in a surprising direction: families in which the wife works are significantly *more* patriarchal in decisions than those in which the wife does not work in direct contradiction to findings of previous studies.

If the data are again broken down into the four areas in which questions were asked, the working wives are found to be significantly less dominant, at the .05 level, in three of the four — child-rearing, recreation, and role attitudes. They do not differ significantly from the non-working wives in decisions about purchases and living standards, where a difference might be expected, since the working wife contributes to the family income. In the other three areas the working wives are less dominant than the non-working wives.

---

[11]Robert O. Blood, Jr., and Robert L. Hamblin, "The Effect of the Wife's Employment on the Family Power Structure," *Social Forces*, XXXVI (May, 1958), 347-52; David M. Heer, "Dominance and the Working Wife," *Social Forces* XXXVI (May, 1958), 341-47.

[12]The four samples were not matched on proportion of working wives. Had they been, atypical groups would have been selected. Employment of the wife, our sample lists indicated, is simply a characteristic of the families of Negro professors —at least in the Deep South. It would have been very difficult to generalize to this group from a sample which had been selected to match the much lower rate of wife employment among the white professors. Thus generalization of the findings was facilitated by leaving employment of wives uncontrolled. The assessment of the relative importance of variables such as a race and the employment of the wife in determining patterns of dominance was, however, more difficult. It is entirely possible that subcultural differences between the races might introduce a predisposition toward matriarchy, for example, which was canceled out by a predisposition toward patriarchy related to the employment of wives. Our samples were too small to permit partialing in an effort to investigate such possibilities. But the intent of the study was to investigate whether or not the subcultural groups, as they actually are, differed in dominance, and the sample was designed toward this end.

Since the difference between families with working wives and those with non-working wives was clearly significant when other differences were not, it is unlikely that this is a spurious result arising from other differences between the groups. However, it is difficult to interpret. It is worth noting that previous studies were based on the subjects' statements rather than observation of their behavior. Perhaps we have here another example of people saying one thing and doing another.

A possible interpretation of our findings would be that husbands whose wives do not work tend to leave minor family decisions largely to the wife. Husbands of working wives, on the other hand, almost necessarily participate to a much greater degree in home life and

TABLE 4

DOMINANCE IN DECISIONS
BY EMPLOYMENT OF WIFE

PERCENTAGE OF DECISIONS WON BY HUSBAND	PERCENTAGE OF COUPLES		
	Wife Employed	Wife Not Employed	Total
0-32 (matriarchal)	7.7	28.6	15.0
33-67 (equalitarian)	76.9	71.4	75.0
68-100 (patriarchal)	15.4	....	10.0
Total	100.0	100.0	100.0
No. of couples	26	14	40

might, therefore, be expected to play a greater role in minor family decisions. Further research might investigate the validity of this post factum interpretation.

Black Women
in the American Work Force

JOE R. FEAGIN

INTRODUCTION

U. S. SOCIETY IS STRATIFIED ALONG NUMEROUS DIMENSIONS — AGE,
sex, race, occupation, income, to mention some of the more important
stratification variables. Each of these variables is reflected in a class
system, with the classes in each system differing in the allocation of
power, status, and privilege. Three of these important dimensions
intersect in a socially distinguishable group of Americans — black
women in the labor force.

* * *

A major purpose of this paper is to examine occupation and to determine the effect of being black and female on the position of black
women workers in the occupational system. The related issues of
extent of labor force participation by black women and the relationship
of such participation to income and family characteristics will also
be analyzed.

EXTENT OF LABOR FORCE PARTICIPATION

In March 1966 there were over 3 million black women in the U. S.
civilian labor force, comprising 12.1 percent of the total female
work force.[1]

* * *

In 1900 and in 1960 the proportion of black women who partici-
pated in the labor force was roughly the same — about four in ten.[2]
In the intervening years the pattern was one of a slight decline in the
participation rate from 1900 to 1950, with a rise from 1950 to 1960.
Recent 1966 data indicate that the proportion of black women in

---

Published by permission of the author.

the labor force is apparently still increasing, to the point that one half of black women over the age of 18 years now work, compared to 39 percent of white women, a percentage which is also still on the increase. The apparent rise in the participation rate for black women since 1950 may be due in part to the same factors usually adduced to explain the rising white rate: rising family aspirations for a higher standard of living and the liberation of women from housework to pursue meaningful careers outside the home. Some evidence for this interpretation can be seen in the rising proportion of black women who work as one moves up the family income scale, a phenomenon examined later in this paper.

THE OCCUPATIONAL SYSTEM

Where have black women workers been located in the American occupational structure? . . . Around the turn of the century (1890-1900) their position in the occupational structure was, in terms of power and privilege, at the bottom; 96 percent were either farm workers or domestics, a pattern which had not changed in many ways since the early days of slavery.[3] A significant shift from farm work did occur with the great northward and westward migration out of the South to the cities between 1900 and the present, but the placement of black women at the bottom of the occupational ladder was in general unchanged even by 1940. By 1940 only 6 percent of black women workers were in white-collar jobs, compared to just over one half of all white women workers.[4] Doubtless many, if not most, of these black, white-collar workers were teachers concentrated in segregated Southern and Northern ghetto schools. Moreover, 72 percent of the black women workers were in unskilled blue-collar jobs (not including those in farm jobs), these being predominantly "private household positions", a Census euphemism for "maids and servants." Less than one quarter of white women workers were in similar unskilled blue-collar positions. Thus in 1940 black women were still a major source of domestic household help. And not just in the South. Whereas middle-class wives in the North and West in the early decades of the twentieth century had been able to find white immigrant girls to clean their houses, by the 1930's and 1940's black and other nonwhite women were coming to be a major source of domestic help.[5] In this case the need of the United States economy for cheap domestic labor was filled by black women migrating out of the South.

The war years brought some significant improvements in the employment opportunities for black men and women, particularly in the war industries and in the federal government. Between 1940 and 1950 the proportion of black women workers in white-collar positions doubled, rising from 6 percent to 12 percent. A similar doubling occurred in regard to the semi-skilled blue-collar category (from 7 percent to 15 percent). And the proportion of black women workers in unskilled blue-collar jobs dropped somewhat to 63 percent by 1950. This upward trend in the number and proportion of white-collar workers continued into the decade of the fifties. By 1960 the white-collar proportion was up another six percentage points to 18 percent, while the unskilled blue-collar percentage remained approximately the same. Yet over the same twenty-year period the proportion of white women in the white-collar category also increased, if less dramatically, so that even in 1960 the proportion of white women in *white-collar* jobs was roughly the same as the proportion of black women in *unskilled blue-collar* jobs (about six in ten).

Recent 1966 figures for employed black women 18 years of age and over break down as follows:[6]

White-color — 23%
Unskilled blue-collar — 60%

These figures do not take into account working women aged 14-17 or the experienced unemployed. . . . Nevertheless, they do suggest somewhat of an improvement since 1960 in the area of white-collar jobs, the proportion rising from 18 percent to 23 percent. Conspicuous too is the fact that the proportion of black women in unskilled blue-collar jobs has not decreased significantly in this same six-year period. . . . The shift since 1940 in the proportion of black women holding white-collar jobs has provoked numerous optimistic comments about the present and the future of black women in the occupational system. Some authors have spoken eloquently of "significant breakthroughs in recent years" for black women.[7] And Moynihan in his now famous report claimed that

> . . . Negro females have established a strong position for themselves in white-collar and professional employment, precisely the areas of the economy which are growing most rapidly, and to which the highest prestige is accorded.[8]

No one can deny the element of truth in such assertions; occupational gains have been made by some black women in recent decades.

But a less optimistic assessment of the occupational situation seems warranted by several additional considerations. In the first place, the white-collar gains made by black women have been primarily in the fields in which women have traditionally held a significant number of positions: teaching, nursing, social work, clerical work, counter sales work, and similar employment fields. Although some black women have been crashing the barrier of race discrimination, most of these have then found themselves confronting sex discrimination. Secondly, there is evidence that black women hold lower-status jobs even within certain important white-collar occupational categories. For example, in 1960 nearly a quarter of all white women workers in the Census "clerical" category held jobs with the title of "secretary", compared to one in ten among black "clerical" workers. Black women were about twice as likely as whites to be in the lower status position of "typist".[9] Moreover, a fair number of the lower-grade clerical jobs now opening up to black women, such as key-punch operator positions, seem likely to be eradicated by automation in the not-too-distant future.[10] A third and perhaps more important limitation on the optimistic assessments of the future of black women workers in the American occupational system is the very pace of the trend which we have examined. Although extrapolating present trends into the future is a tricky business, even a crude projection of the proportion of black women in white-collar positions on the basis of the present rate of change indicates that parity between white and black women in this critical job category is likely to take three or four generations — at least — to attain.[11]

INCOME

Given the fact that black women, both in the past and in the present, have found themselves on the lower rungs of the occupational ladder, a logical question arises: What have they earned for their efforts? . . . The median income for full-time, year-round women workers, white and nonwhite, has grown dramatically since 1939, even taking into account inflation.[12] In 1939 the median income of white women workers was $1,840, compared to $697 for nonwhite workers. By 1965 the medians had increased to $3,744 for whites and $2,642 for non-whites, with the most dramatic gains again occurring in the World War II period. Looking at relative changes over the last few decades, we can see that the white/nonwhite income ratio also improved significantly from 1939 to 1960, moving downward from 2.64 to 1.44. However, in the first half of the decade of the 1960's, the white/nonwhite income ratio has fluctuated up and down but has not dropped lower than 1.42, the 1965 ratio. In this respect — a slackening of relative gains — the income situation of nonwhite women workers has been similar in recent years to that of nonwhite men workers.

How can one account for these persisting income differentials? The obvious explanation is that black women workers have long been concentrated in characteristically low-paying jobs at the bottom of the occupational ladder. A very large proportion have traditionally found themselves in job categories which have not been unionized to a significant degree, and even in the nineteen-sixties this non-unionized condition persists for many black women workers. Moreover, many hold jobs which are still exempted from the minimum wage regulations of the Fair Labor Standards Act. According to recent estimates approximately six nonwhite women workers in ten arc still not covered by federal minimum wage regulations, not even by the new regulations established by the 1966 amendments to that Act. When one reflects on the fact that a very large percentage of black women workers hold "private household" positions, jobs extremely unlikely to be unionized or covered by either federal or state minimum wage legislation, the low-income situation of these black women workers becomes readily explainable.[13]

BLACK WOMEN AND THEIR FAMILIES: RECENT DATA

Many discussions touching on the participation of black women in the American work force focus on the effect of such participation on black families. Although this emphasis is too often the predominant one, with other critical questions remaining undiscussed, it is certainly important. According to a recent Census survey the labor force participation rates for black women in key child-bearing age brackets were quite high. In March 1967, 60 percent of nonwhite women 35 to 44 years of age were in the work force, compared to 46 percent of white women of the same age.[14] This differential of 14 percentage points was exceeded only by the 16 percent difference between white and nonwhite women 25 to 34 years of age. In that age bracket 55 percent of nonwhite women were working or looking for work, compared to 39 percent of white women. Just over half of the women 20 to 24 years of age, white and nonwhite, were in the work force. These age brackets cover the most important child-bearing years.

Given such information, one might well predict that black wives and mothers would be more likely to be in the labor force than their white counterparts. The data generally substantiate this prediction. According to March 1967 Bureau of Labor Statistics figures, nonwhite wives were more likely to be in the labor force than white wives (48 percent versus 36 percent). Further corroborating data from the same source, for white and nonwhite mothers, are presented in Table 1.

Looking at the categories including both husband-absent and husband-present mothers, one sees that 50 percent of nonwhite mothers with children under 18 years of age were in the labor force in March 1967, compared to 37 percent of white mothers. The nonwhite/white differential was greater in the case of mothers with children from 6 to 17 years of age. However within these groups of mothers there were two important subcategories, mothers with husbands present and mothers with husbands absent. For both nonwhite and white women, in each "age of child" category, the proportion of women in the labor force was greater for those mothers with husbands absent(because of divorce, separation, or death) than for those with husbands present. Moreover, in each of the white/nonwhite comparisons for mothers with husbands absent the proportion of white women working exceeds that of nonwhite women. Of white husband-absent mothers with children under the age of 18 years, 67 percent were in the work force in March 1967, compared to 56 percent of comparable nonwhite mothers, a differential of 11 percentage points. The differential was substantially greater in the case of husband-absent mothers with children 6 to 17 years of age, and substantially smaller for husband-absent mothers with children 5 years old or less.

TABLE 1

PROPORTION OF MOTHERS IN THE LABOR FORCE, BY AGE OF CHILDREN, COLOR, AND MARITAL STATUS
(March 1967)

| | PROPORTION IN THE LABOR FORCE | | |
	Nonwhite	White	Differential
(1) Mothers with children under 6	44%	27%	+17%
Married, husband present	42	25	+17
Other women ever married	49	52	− 3
(2) Mothers with children 6 to 17	58	48	+10
Married, husband present	55	44	+11
Other women ever married	63	80	−17
(3) Mothers with children under 18	50	37	+13
Married, husband present	47	34	+13
Other women ever married	56	67	−11

Source: Bureau of Labor Statistics, Department of Labor, *Marital and Family Characteristics of Workers*, March 1967, Special Labor Force Report No. 94.

Such participation differentials indicate that black mothers taken as a group are more likely to be away from their children for employment reasons than white mothers, particularly when their children are very young. . . . Research on children with working mothers, of both school and pre-school age, generally has found no meaningful differences between them and children of nonworking mothers. Although some as yet inconclusive research has turned up a relationship between juvenile delinquency and maternal employment for middle-class children, for lower-class and blue-collar children no deterimental effects of maternal employment have been demonstrated.[15] The only hard-and-fast conclusion one can draw from existing research is that much additional research on this maternal employment issue is needed before firm generalizations can be made.

One important idea has been suggested by Alice Rossi: It is not maternal employment *per se* which is the critical variable, but the character of the care which the child receives, an argument she buttresses by allusion to the research to kibbutz-reared toddlers.[16] What kind of child care is actually provided by black working mothers? One recent government survey revealed that a very small percentage of the children of both white and nonwhite working mothers were left in group facilities such as day care centers: about 2 percent of the children in each group.[17] Well over half of the children, white and nonwhite, were left in the care of relatives or were attended by the mothers themselves while they worked. White and black mothers relied most heavily on relatives to take care of their children while they work; there were no dramatic differences between the two groups in the character of child care arrangements. . . .

There has been much comment in both the popular and social science literature, particularly after the publication of the "Moynihan Report", on the effects of labor force participation by wives on the structure of black families. A major point frequently made is that in many male-headed black families the woman is the primary wage earner; Moynihan says that this is true of one fourth of all male-headed black families, the suggestion being that in such families the woman makes the important decisions, that the family structure is matriarchal.[18] Numerous other commentators have suggested or implied that the black woman often earns more than her husband. The available data indicate that the contribution of working wives to family income has been grossly exaggerated.[19] Of those nonwhite wives with work experience, only 12 percent contributed to 1966 family income to the extent of 50 percent or more. The figure for white wives was similar, approximately 10 percent. The median percentage of family income accounted for by the earnings of black wives was 25 percent, only slightly higher than the median figure for white wives (23 percent). At the low end of the contribution continuum, approximately one fifth of both groups of working wives contributed earnings comprising less than 5 percent of family income. This perhaps unexpectedly low level of contribution can be explained by several salient facts. Black women, like white women, are much more likely to be working part-time, or full-time for only part of the year, than black men or white men. Moreover, those black women who are full-time, year-round workers average substantially lower incomes than full-time black men workers.[20]

Although the earnings of black working wives usually account for substantially less than half of their family incomes, in many cases such earnings do enable black families to pull themselves above the $3,000 poverty line. Economic necessity has long forced black wives into the job market. . . . The data show that black husband-wife families without working wives were twice as likely to be below the $3,000 poverty line as black families with working wives.[21] These statistics clearly suggest that tens of thousands of black families were above the poverty line because of the wife's labor force participation. Some analysts, moreover, consider the income range a thousand or so dollars above this $3,000 poverty level as a "deprivation" range, since such incomes seldom allow families to purchase any luxuries. When husband's income is in this "deprivation" range, black wives are somewhat more likely to be in the labor force than when husband's income is lower.[22] . . .

Nor should one neglect the significance of wife's income for black middle-income families. According to 1966 Bureau of the Census data the black wives most likely to be in the labor force had husbands earning from $5,000 to $7,000 a year.[23] The effect of such participation is a total family income approaching the level of affluence. While only one quarter of the wives in families with family incomes under $2,000 were in the work force, fully three quarters of the wives in families with incomes over $9,000 were working. Clearly, the richer the black family, the more likely a wife was to be in the labor force. For these families wife's participation in the work force is more than a matter of dire economic necessity. Her participation may well be a function of traditional values in regard to women working plus a desire to move closer to the symbols and substance of an affluent way of life.

SUMMARY AND CONCLUSION

The existing literature on women in the American labor force, literature which has been on the increase in recent years, gives insufficient attention to the participation and position of black women in that work force. Such an oversight has led some commentators to discuss the rising rate of white female participation in the work force as though it were really new for large groups of American women to work outside the home. This kind of emphasis overlooks the traditional labor force participation of black women. From the data examined in this paper, it is evident that black women have played an important part in America's labor force in the twentieth century, as they had in previous centuries. Four black women in ten were in the labor force in 1900, comprising fully one quarter of the female work force in that period. In 1960 the proportion in the job market was roughly the same, and since 1960 the proportion of black women working or looking for work appears to have risen somewhat.

Today black women are still over-represented, given their proportion in the population, in the female work force, although the growing number of white women seeking work is gradually altering that situation. According to recent Bureau of Labor Statistics projections, between 1970 and 1980 the proportion of nonwhite women in the labor force will not change substantially from the levels of the 1960's, hovering around 45-50 percent. The proportion of white women working is expected to continue its upward climb until it comes within a few percentage points of the nonwhite rate by the 1980's,[24] Such projections are based on the assumptions that the already high nonwhite rate is approaching an absolute maximum and that expected economic improvements in the condition of nonwhite men will bring about a leveling off of the participation rate of nonwhite women. However it may well be that increased socioeconomic status will send many middle-class nonwhite women into the work force, as seems to be the case for increasing numbers of middle-class white women, more than replacing black women who have quit work because their earnings are no longer a necessity for family survival.

In past decades the twin barriers of racial and sex discrimination have relegated black women to unskilled blue-collar positions, most typically in private households. Even in the 1960's a majority of black women who work still find themselves in low-paying, blue-collar positions, though many have educational attainments which theoretically qualify them for higher-status positions. In the last three decades significant, if gradual, gains have occurred in the white-collar area, but neither the character of these gains nor the pace of change is such as to generate much optimism about the future. Although some black women have moved up into higher-status, white-collar categories, all too frequently the new positions are lower-status ones within these categories, some of which may soon fall under the sharp axe of automation. Moreover, extrapolations based on the present slow rate of change in the occupational distribution indicate that parity between white and black women in the critical area of white-collar jobs is likely to take at least several generations to attain.

Given the past and present positioning of black women workers at the bottom of the occupational ladder, with little minimum wage coverage or unionization, one might well expect significant white/black differentials in earnings. In our examination of the incomes of black women workers over the last three decades, we found that black women earned substantially less than white women workers in 1939 and in 1965, and in the years in between. . . .

When one examines the marital and family characteristics of black women workers in the 1960's, he finds that large numbers of black wives and mothers are in the labor force. Black wives and mothers are significantly more likely to be in the labor force than white wives and mothers. This has apparently been true for many decades. Some observers, noting the growing number of *white* women entering the American work force, have argued that the traditional role of the American woman as wife and mother, with an emphasis on securing self-fulfillment in exclusive devotion to marriage and motherhood, is changing in the direction of combined roles of wife and worker, or wife, mother, and worker. Although such an assessment does seem a reasonable one, it should not obscure the fact that for many decades black wives and mothers have had to adopt, usually out of economic necessity, the role and self-image of wife-worker or wife-mother-worker. It might well be argued that black (and other nonwhite) women pioneered these combined role-sets long before large proportions of white women began to enter the work force.

•   •   •

Data on wife's contribution to family income brings into question arguments to the effect that black working women in husband-wife families economically dominate their families. Most do not in fact contribute even 50 percent of family income. Yet this fact should not obscure the additional point that black women frequently do, with substantial contributions to family income, keep their families above the poverty level. And for many not-so-poor black families, the wife's contribution to family income enables them to move farther up the ladder of affluence than would otherwise be possible for them strictly on the basis of husband's income.

Given the current spectacle of black wives and mothers — in large numbers — leaving their own homes to labor either in the homes of white wives and mothers or in the hotels, laundries, and restaurants of white men, and given the present slow rate of change in the occupational distribution, one might well predict continuing, perhaps growing, discontent with American society among black women. One concrete measure of this discontent can already be seen in the participation of black women in the ghetto revolts of the 1960's. Black women have certainly been under-represented among the rioters, but they have been present, comprising between one tenth and one quarter of those rioting.[25] Other black women, moreover, are participating in unions and strikes to a degree not seen before in American history. With such growing discontent, and the societal turmoil fed by it, it seems unlikely to this observer that the skewed occupational and income structure of this society can long endure in its present form.

NOTES

[1] U. S. Bureau of the Census, *Current Population Reports*, series P-20, no. 168 (December 22, 1967), p. 32. Figures in this report are based on sample survey data. In the general analytical discussions in this paper the terms "black", "Negro", and "nonwhite" are used interchangeably, since black Americans comprise about 93 percent of "nonwhites" as counted by governmental agencies. However in statements quoting data specifically referring to Negroes the terms "black" or "Negro" will be used for the reader's information; where the data used are for the broader category of nonwhites, sentences quoting the data will use the term "nonwhite".

[2] The labor force participation rates cited in this paragraph are taken from the following U.S. Bureau of the Census publications: (1) *Thirteenth Census of the United States: 1910*, Vol. IV, *Occupation* (1914), pp. 64-65; (2) *Negro Population, 1790-1915* (Washington D.C.: Government Printing Office, 1918), p. 504; (3) *Fifteenth Census of the United States: 1930,* Vol. V. *General Report on Occupations* (1933), pp. 74-75; (4) *Sixteenth Census of the United States 1940,* Vol. III, *The Labor Force*, pt. 1, United States Summary (1943), p. 18; (5) *United States Census of Population: 1950*, Vol. IV, *Special Reports*, pt. 3 Ch. 8, Nonwhite Population by Race (1953), p. 27; (6) *United States Census of Population: 1960*, Subject Reports, PC(2)-6A, Employment Status and Work Experience (1963), pp. 16, 101, 214; 1966 figures are taken from U.S. Women's Bureau, *Negro Women in the Population and in the Labor Force* (Washington, D.C.: Government Printing Office, 1967), p. 23. Data for 1900-1930 refer to "gainfully employed" women as a percentage of the total female population 10 years and older; data for 1940 to 1960 refer to women "in the labor force" as a proportion of the total female population 14 years and older; data for 1966 refer to women "in the labor force" as a proportion of the total female population 18 years and older. To a certain extent the changing aspects of the definitions cancel each other out; yet the decade by decade comparisons remain crude.

[3] Bureau of the Census, *Negro Population,* 1790-1915, pp. 526-527.

[4] The data on occupational distributions are taken from the following U.S. Bureau of the Census publications: (1) *Sixteenth Census of the United States: 1940*, Vol. III, *The Labor Force*, pt. 1, United States Summary, (1943), p. 90ff; (2) *United States Census of Population: 1950*, Vol. IV, *Special Reports*, pt. 1 Ch. B, Occupational Characteristics (1956), p. 29ff; (3) *United States Census of Population: 1960, Subject Reports*, PC(2)-7A, Occupational Characteristics (1963), p. 21ff. The "experienced civilian labor force" includes all employed persons plus the experienced unemployed. In recent years nonwhite women workers have been somewhat less likely than white women to hold full-time, year-round jobs.

[5]Cf. Alice S. Rossi, "Equality Between the Sexes: An Immodest Proposal," *Daedalus*, XCII (Spring, 1964), 630.

[6]Bureau of the Census, *Current Population Reports*, p. 33. These figures also exclude the "not reporting" category.

[7]E.g., National Manpower Council, *Work in the Lives of Married Women*, (New York: Columbia University Press, 1958), p. 87.

[8]Daniel P. Moynihan, "The Negro Family: The Case for National Action", in *The Moynihan Report and the Politics of Controversy*, ed. L. Rainwater and W. L. Yancey (Cambridge: MIT Press, 1967), p. 78.

[9]Bureau of the Census, *United States Census of Population: 1960,* Occupational Characteristics, p. 21ff. This pattern also appears within blue-collar occupational categories. In the "operatives" Census category black women were six times more likely than whites to be laundry and dry-cleaning workers; even in the "service workers" category, one heavily dominated by black women, black women were much more likely than whites to be maids and much less likely to be waitresses. In the "farm laborer" category a majority of whites were actually unpaid family workers on a family farm, while the overwhelming proportion of black women in this category were wage laborers.

[10]*Vide* the comments of one governmental personnel official in Elizabeth F. Barker, *Technology and Woman's Work* (New York: Columbia University Press, 1964), p. 234.

[11]One additional variable, recent variations in which also do not generate optimism, is the unemployment rate. According to comments made publicly by Bureau of Labor Statistics officials recent increases in the U.S. unemployment rate reflect an increasing proportion of black women who are jobless. Women's Bureau data going back to 1954 indicate that the unemployment rate for nonwhite women has been double, or nearly double, that of white women in the years since that year. In 1966 the nonwhite unemployment rate was 6.6 percent, compared to 3.3 percent for white women, 4.9 percent for nonwhite men, and 2.2 percent for white men. Women's Bureau, *Negro Women in the Population and in the Labor Force*, p. 38.

[12]*Ibid.*, p. 40. Figures are expressed in 1960 constant dollars.

[13]Because of difficulties involved in measuring the quality of black educational attainments, and thus in comparing white and black education figures, I have omitted a detailed analysis of education in this paper. However the extant data do suggest the following intriguing hypothesis for further research: Black women have to be more than equal to white women educationally to get into higher-status, particularly white-collar, job categories. Evidence for this can be seen in the tabulations coming out of the 1960 Census. In 1960 nonwhite females employed in professional-technical, clerical, sales and operatives categories had higher median educational attainment than "all females" working in those same categories. Bureau of the Census, *United States Census of Population: 1960*, Occupational Characteristics, p. 130ff.

[14]Bureau of Labor Statistics, Department of Labor, *Marital and Family Characteristics of Workers*, March 1967, Special Labor Force Report No. 94.

[15]Gerald R. Leslie, *The Family in Social Context* (New York: Oxford University Press, 1967), pp. 569ff.

[16]Rossi, "Equality between the Sexes: An Immodest Proposal," pp. 618-619.

[17]Women's Bureau, *Negro Women in the Population and in the Labor Force*, pp. 32-33.

[18]Moynihan, "The Negro Family", p. 78.

[19]Bureau of Labor Statistics, *Marital and Family Characteristics of Workers*, March, 1967.

[20]Some might argue that black families have earners other than husband or wife and that, though black working wives average only 25 percent of family income, that might be larger than the husband's share of family income. Doubtless this is true in some cases, but what limited data are available show that the contributions of other family members to black family incomes are usually quite small; apparently in most black husband-wife families there are no full-time workers except husband and/or wife. *Ibid.*

[21]Bureau of the Census, Department of Commerce, *Negro Population: March 1966, Current Population Reports*, P-20, No. 168; and Women's Bureau, *Negro Women in the Population and in the Labor Force*, December, 1967.

[22]Women's Bureau, *Negro Women in the Population and in the Labor Force*, p. 28.

[23]*Ibid.*

[24]Bureau of Labor Statistics, Department of Labor, *Labor Force Projections by Color, 1970-1980*, Special Labor Force Report No. 73.

[25]Robert M. Fogelson and Robert B. Hill, "Who Riots? A study of participation in the 1967 riots", in *Supplemental Studies for the National Advisory Commission on Civil Disorders* (Washington, D.C.: Government Printing Office, 1968), p. 245

Factors Associated with the Low Fertility of Nonwhite Women of College Attainment

CLYDE V. KISER AND MYRNA E. FRANK

THE CO-EXISTENCE OF POVERTY, ILLITERACY AND HIGH FERTILITY IS A familiar problem to persons attempting to improve levels of living in the underdeveloped areas of the world. Although much less intense and less pervasive in this country, it is familiar enough in rural and urban slums, particularly among the nonwhites in these areas.

In a general way this paper is concerned with the interrelation of color, fertility and socioeconomic status in this country. This relationship is frequently studied by comparing the socioeconomic differentials in fertility among the whites with that among the nonwhites. This paper, however, is concerned mainly with the differentials in fertility by *color* at different socioeconomic levels. It focuses upon comparisons of the fertility of nonwhites and whites at upper socioeconomic levels and particularly upon factors associated with the low fertility of nonwhite women reporting one or more years of college attendance.

Most of the past studies have correctly explained the comparatively high fertility of nonwhites in terms of the relative poverty and absence of family planning. Few studies have focused attention upon the fertility of the minority of nonwhites of upper socioeconomic status. Yet more precise knowledge in ˙this area is important. Data on this question, derived mainly from the 1960 census, may provide some indication of the potential demographic effect of socioeconomic advance of the nonwhites in this country.

It should be acknowledged at the outset that the people classified as nonwhites in this country are ethnically diverse. However, the great majority are Negroes. Approximately 92 per cent of either the nonwhite women or ever-married women, 15-49 years old, in the 1960 census were Negro.[1]

Reprinted by permission of the publisher and authors from *Milbank Memorial Fund Quarterly*, LXV (October 1967), 427-49.

TABLE 1

EXCESS OF FERTILITY OF EVER-MARRIED NONWHITES OVER THAT OF WHITES
BY AGE AND TYPE OF RESIDENCE, AND BY REGION[12]

Type of Residence and Region	AGE						
	15-19 %	20-24 %	25-29 %	30-34 %	35-39 %	40-44 %	45-49 %
United States	72.0	45.9	27.6	23.9	19.5	18.6	19.7
Urbanized areas	75.6	47.4	25.2	14.6	9.1	4.0	6.0
Other urban	74.7	52.6	32.9	31.8	26.3	27.7	21.4
Rural nonfarm	63.3	47.3	41.1	17.7	47.7	50.5	46.6
Rural farm	70.5	58.8	48.2	62.7	68.9	71.8	67.3
Northeast	61.8	37.7	16.6	3.3	−0.2	−9.9	−4.5
North Central	78.7	39.6	18.5	8.9	−0.9	−6.4	−9.4
South	77.6	56.3	41.5	40.7	36.5	33.0	27.1
West	50.5	19.7	5.7	6.2	7.7	15.2	22.0

According to the 1960 census data, age-specific fertility rates of ever-married women in the United States as a whole were at that time consistently higher for nonwhites than for whites (Table 1). For women 25 years of age or older the percentage excess of the fertility of non-whites over that of whites tended to be higher in rural than in urban areas. For women of all ages it was higher in the South than in other regions of the country. For women under 30 years old, the percentage *excess* was lowest in the West. For women, 35-49 years old, the non-whites had *lower* fertility than whites in the Northeastern and North Central regions. The percentage excess in the fertility of nonwhites over that of whites tended to be inversely associated with age of wife and socioeconomic status. It tended to be larger for the younger than for the older women and larger for women of low than of middle socioeconomic status. Stated in another manner, at lower socioeconomic levels the fertility of nonwhites tended to exceed that of whites and the percentage excess was inversely related to age. At higher socioeconomic levels the fertility of nonwhites tended to fall below that of whites at ages 25 and over.

The tendency toward lower fertility of nonwhites than of whites at upper socioeconomic levels holds for a variety of criteria of socioeconomic status. By occupation group of the husband in 1960, the lower fertility of nonwhites than of whites was found for wives of professional men (Table 2). By income of the husband it was found for wives of men reporting $10,000 per year or more in 1959 (Table 3).

Table 4 is of interest in that it introduces "presence of all of a specified list of housing characteristics" along with number of housing units in structure, and occupation group and income of the husband as

Factors Associated with Low Fertility

TABLE 2

EXCESS OF AVERAGE NUMBER OF CHILDREN EVER BORN TO NONWHITE WOMEN
OVER THAT OF WHITE WOMEN, MARRIED AND HUSBAND PRESENT, BY AGE OF
WOMEN AND MAJOR OCCUPATION GROUP OF HUSBAND, URBAN AREAS,
1960 AND 1950.[13]

Year and Major Occupation Group	AGE						
	15-19 %	20-24 %	25-29 %	30-34 %	35-39 %	40-44 %	45-49 %
1960							
Professional, technical and kindred workers	108.3	21.8	−16.8	−11.9	−11.2	−8.8	−2.4
Managers, officials and proprietors, except farm	*	32.4	6.2	10.2	1.3	4.4	14.4
Clerical, sales and kindred workers	78.3	38.6	11.3	5.6	2.9	−1.2	−0.1
Craftsmen, foremen and kindred workers	54.5	36.3	20.7	17.0	14.6	5.8	10.5
Operatives and kindred workers	65.1	34.2	22.1	19.9	15.1	5.7	1.3
Service workers including private household	64.5	34.0	21.6	15.5	8.9	5.6	0.6
Laborers except farm and mine	70.7	43.1	25.7	20.7	13.1	6.4	−3.3
1950							
Professional, technical and kindred workers	*	*	0.6	−9.5	−20.5	−3.6	*
Managers, officials and proprietors, except farm	*	*	−16.0	3.7	−8.9	14.9	21.7
Clerical, sales and kindred workers	*	56.3	21.7	−2.9	5.5	−7.7	−7.9
Craftsmen, foremen and kindred workers	100.4	34.8	2.6	6.8	11.0	9.7	10.4
Operatives and kindred workers	62.0	28.6	14.3	5.3	1.6	7.1	1.4
Service workers including private household	59.0	40.8	3.6	−8.8	−12.3	−3.5	−0.8
Laborers except farm and mine	56.6	40.0	8.0	−9.0	−7.6	−15.2	−14.6

*Rate not shown if based on fewer than 1,000 women in 1960; 4,000 in 1950.

criteria of socioeconomic status. The "specified list" includes direct access, kitchen or cooking equipment, sound (as opposed to deteriorating) condition of the structure, flush toilet and bath for exclusive use, hot piped water and less than 1.01 persons per room. Among women 35-44 years old, married and husband present, living in homes in urbanized areas *with all the specified housing characteristics,* the fertility rates tended to be lower for nonwhites than for whites at all occupation and income levels except for service workers of low income and except for wives of professional men in structures with five or more housing units. Among those living in houses lacking one or more of the

TABLE 3

EXCESS FERTILITY OF NONWHITES OVER THAT OF WHITES FOR WOMEN MARRIED
AND HUSBAND PRESENT BY AGE OF WOMAN AND INCOME OF HUSBAND IN 1959
FOR THE UNITED STATES AND URBAN AREAS, 1960.[14]

Income of Husband in 1959	AGE OF WIFE						
	15-19 %	20-24 %	25-29 %	30-34 %	35-39 %	40-41 %	45-49 %
United States							
$15,000 and over	*	*	*	3.4	−2.2	−2.7	6.4
10,000-14,999	⫲	⁎	−1.1	0.8	−6.8	−5.1	26.3
7,000-9,999	*	10.4	1.1	7.6	9.6	2.6	5.3
5,000-6,999	49.1	28.5	10.7	11.5	8.8	5.0	0.2
4,000-4,999	68.9	37.0	22.0	15.5	8.7	3.8	−2.0
3,000-3,999	73.5	44.4	23.3	16.5	12.5	4.4	0.0
2,000-2,999	79.0	58.1	35.4	24.1	15.6	12.9	9.7
1-1,999 or less	103.4	86.9	44.6	38.1	35.5	29.2	24.6
None	56.1	49.8	33.3	31.9	19.5	39.0	18.8
Urban areas							
$15,000 and over	*	*	*	7.5	−8.7	−4.3	7.1
10,000-14,999	⫲	⁎	−3.7	0.5	−11.2	−3.1	20.2
7,000-9,999	*	11.2	1.7	7.1	9.1	0.3	3.8
5,000-6,999	51.0	30.2	13.3	12.8	10.3	8.2	1.7
4,000-4,999	73.2	42.9	27.1	20.3	11.3	7.1	1.1
3,000-3,999	81.6	51.5	28.9	19.1	16.6	6.2	1.0
2,000-2,999	87.2	68.8	40.4	24.1	16.2	9.1	7.1
1-1,999 or less	112.7	101.1	42.9	23.8	11.9	6.3	7.3
None	63.0	46.9	28.5	17.9	4.6	0.1	−0.6

*Rate not shown where base is fewer than 1,000 women.

amenities mentioned above, the cases of lower fertility of nonwhites than of whites were restricted to white-collar workers living in structures with only one housing unit and to one group of service workers. The results in Table 4 may connote a more rigid selection of childless and small families among the nonwhites than among whites who can afford to live in homes with all the specified housing characteristics.

As indicated above, the chief aim of this paper is an exploration of the nature of and reasons for the lower fertility of nonwhite than of white women who reported one or more years of college education. By age, the lower fertility rates of nonwhite than of white women of some or complete college education was restricted to women 25 years of age and over (Table 5). At younger ages the higher fertility of nonwhites than of whites was found at all educational levels. It should be emphasized at once that this type of difference between women under 25 and over 25 is not to be interpreted as an omen of a new trend. Similar situations existed in 1950 and 1940. In 1950, fertility rates for women of college 1-3 and college 4+ status tended to be higher for nonwhites

TABLE 4.

EXCESS OF NONWHITE OVER WHITE FERTILITY AMONG WOMEN 35-44 YEARS OLD,
MARRIED AND HUSBAND PRESENT, ACCORDING TO PRESENCE OF ALL OF A
SPECIFIED LIST OF HOUSING CHARACTERISTICS, BY NUMBER OF
HOUSING UNITS IN STRUCTURE AND BY OCCUPATION
GROUP AND 1959 INCOME OF THE HUSBAND,
URBANIZED AREAS, 1960.[15]

Number of Housing Units in Structure and Husband's Income	Pro-fessional	Pro-prietors	Other White Collar	Crafts-men	Operatives and Laborers	Service Workers
			With all Specified Characteristics			
	%	%	%	%	%	%
1 Housing unit	−17.3	−10.4	−13.9	−14.8	−16.4	−22.3
$1-$2,999 or Less	*	−37.3	−12.2	−28.0	−17.4	−21.6
3,000-6,999	−14.7	1.1	− 9.8	−11.4	−16.2	−19.2
7,000 and over	−13.1	−8.9	−7.1	−7.6	−1.9	*
2-4 Housing units	−11.5	−5.0	−19.0	−20.8	−26.4	−23.4
$1-$2,999 or Less	*	*	*	*	−34.6	14.7
3,000-6,999	−13.7	−2.2	−18.3	−21.7	−23.0	−29.8
7,000 and over	*	*	*	*	−33.6	*
5 or more Housing units	20.3	−1.2	−13.0	−9.2	−14.1	1.5
$1-$2,999 or Less	*	*	*	*	−20.0	14.1
3,000-6,999	*	*	−13.7	−0.6	−13.8	−1.2
7,000 and over	*	*	*	*	*	*
			Lacking one or More Characteristics			
1 Housing unit	−7.6	−14.4	−3.8	0.7	0.5	0.4
2-4 Housing units	*	*	9.2	3.3	0.3	−16.2
5 or more Housing units	*	5.6	25.7	14.6	11.2	4.5

*Per cent not shown in categories with fewer than 1,250 nonwhite women.

than whites at ages under 25 and lower at later ages. A corresponding situation existed in available comparisons for Negro women and native-white women in 1940.[2] The chief difference between 1960 and 1950 was that at the earlier date the lower fertility of nonwhite than of white women extended to high school 4 and lower educational levels to a greater extent than in 1960.

The white-nonwhite comparisons of fertility at different ages and educational levels hold for urban areas as well as for all areas combined. They hold for women regardless of marital status as well as for ever-married women.

An inconsistency in the data for women under 25 years old should be mentioned. Among ever-married urban women 20-24 years old in 1960, the percentage excess in fertility of nonwhite over that of whites tended to be *directly* related to educational attainment of the women. The excess was 41 per cent for urban ever-married women at the college

TABLE 5.

Excess of Average Number of Children Ever Born to Ever-Married
Nonwhite Women over that of Ever-Married White Women, by
Age and Education, United States, 1960, 1950, 1940,
Urban Areas 1960 and 1950[16]

Area, Year and Educational Attainment of Woman	Age						
	15-19 %	20-24 %	25-29 %	30-34 %	35-39 %	40-44 %	45-49 %
United States							
1960							
College: 4 or more	†	38.1	−11.5	−25.2	−26.5	−29.3	−32.3
1-3	106.3	32.2	0.6	−1.9	−10.1	−8.9	−7.0
High school: 4	95.1	27.3	9.0	5.7	0.3	−1.0	0.4
1-3	54.2	26.9	23.0	21.5	16.5	11.9	12.7
None or elementary	42.2	30.6	28.2	25.4	18.6	13.7	9.5
1950							
College: 4 or more	†	39.3	−14.2	−30.1	−34.5	−16.8	−13.5
1-3	†	35.2	−5.7	−19.9	−21.7	−10.3	14.4
High school: 4	72.7	32.1	−3.8	−12.1	−11.4	−0.5	8.7
1-3	33.6	20.0	7.3	1.7	0.1	5.9	10.1
None or elementary	38.2	19.6	6.0	3.1	1.4	0.2	2.6
1940*							
College: 4 or more	†	†	−4.8	−22.7	−24.6	−15.0	†
1-3	†	32.7	−1.0	−5.2	−1.7	−0.3	−32.3
High school: 4	44.7	27.5	6.3	−2.1	2.1	12.3	9.9
1-3	23.7	10.3	7.9	−0.4	−4.5	2.0	7.9
None or elementary	13.1	5.3	3.9	−0.6	−2.6	−0.6	2.3
Urban areas							
1960							
College: 4 or more	†	41.1	−10.2	−25.5	−27.2	−28.9	−33.3
1-3	113.6	36.8	2.0	−2.7	−9.9	−8.5	−9.4
High school: 4	109.3	31.6	11.1	5.3	0.6	−1.4	1.0
1-3	56.5	29.5	23.1	20.2	14.2	8.5	9.5
None or elementary	45.8	28.4	24.1	17.1	9.4	2.3	−0.4
1950							
College: 4 or more	†	56.6	−17.3	−31.3	−38.0	−25.0	−10.2
1-3	†	49.5	−4.9	−17.9	−26.6	−17.5	21.5
High school: 4	94.7	39.9	−1.4	−13.3	−12.8	−3.2	9.7
1-3	64.1	26.7	8.7	1.1	−6.0	4.4	9.1
None or elementary	46.5	15.9	−0.2	−8.2	−9.8	−10.0	−10.2

*1940 data relate to native-white and Negro women instead of white and nonwhite women.

†Per cent excess not shown where base is fewer than 1,000 women in 1960, 4,000 in 1950 and 3,000 in 1940.

4+ level and 28 per cent at the "none or elementary school level." In classifications of urban women 20-24 years old, married and husband present, by major occupation group of the husband the percentage excess of the fertility of nonwhites over that of whites tended to be *inversely* related to occupational status of the husband. The excess was about 22 per cent for wives of professional men and 43 per cent for wives of unskilled laborers (except farm or mine). This type of inconsistency was found for 1950 as well as for 1960. As for reasons, in the first place, despite a real tendency toward assortive mating, college women are not necessarily married to professional men and professional men do not always choose college-trained women as wives. Possibly the extent of assortive mating differs by color.[3] Whereas the college-trained women considered here include all who were "ever-married," the wives of professional men are those described as "married and husband present." This probably makes some difference even for wives 20-24 because of the factor of absence of husbands for military service. Whatever may be the reason for this type of inconsistency of the relation of nonwhite to white fertility to education and occupation at the young ages, the data by occupation resemble those by education in that 1. among women under 25, fertility rates for all classes tended to be higher

TABLE 6.

NUMBER OF CHILDREN EVER BORN PER 1,000 WOMEN AND EVER-MARRIED WOMEN OF THE 1915-1919 BIRTH COHORT AT THREE POINTS IN THEIR REPRODUCTIVE LIVES, BY COLOR AND EDUCATION, UNITED STATES.[17]

Education and Age	Year Reached Age	ALL WOMEN			EVER-MARRIED WOMEN		
		Children Ever Born per 1,000 Women		Per Cent Excess Nonwhite Over White	Children Ever Born per 1,000 Women		Per Cent Excess Nonwhite Over White
		White	Nonwhite		White	Nonwhite	
College 4 or more							
20-24	1940*	65	126	93.8	319	†	†
30-34	1950	1,285	916	−28.7	1,601	1,119	−30.1
40-44	1960	1,871	1,387	−25.9	2,195	1,552	−29.3
College 1-3							
20-24	1940*	122	165	35.2	493	654	32.7
30-34	1950	1,518	1,223	−19.4	1,718	1,372	−20.1
40-44	1960	2,126	1,920	−9.7	2,279	2,077	−8.9
High school 4							
20-24	1940*	280	388	38.6	698	890	27.5
30-34	1950	1,634	1,417	−13.3	1,798	1,580	−12.1
40-44	1960	2,148	2,117	−1.5	2,275	2,252	−1.0
High school 1-3							
20-24	1940*	650	699	7.5	1,073	1,184	10.3
30-34	1950	1,986	1,988	0.1	2,112	2,148	1.7
40-44	1960	2,438	2,688	10.3	2,539	2,842	11.9
Elementary or none							
20-24	1940*	810	917	13.2	1,338	1,409	5.3
30-34	1950	2,311	2,403	4.0	2,519	2,598	3.1
40-44	1960	2,830	3,198	13.0	3,011	3,424	13.7

*1940 data relate to native whites and Negroes instead of whites and nonwhites.
†Rate not shown for women 20-24 in 1940 where base is fewer than 3,000 women.

for nonwhites than for whites and 2. among women 25 and over the fertility rates for wives of professional men, like those for women of college attainment, tended to be lower for nonwhites than for whites. In scattered cases the fertility of nonwhites tended to fall below that of whites at the proprietary and clerical levels on the basis of husbands' occupation in much the same manner as did those for women reporting high school 4 status.

The fact that the data for 1940, 1950 and 1960 all indicate higher fertility of nonwhites than of whites among college-trained women at ages under 25 and the reverse situation at ages 25 and over, leads one to ask whether this change in pattern with advancing age is inherent in cohort fertility. An affirmative answer seems to be given in Table 6, derived from comparisons of fertility rates for white and nonwhite women in the 1915-1919 birth cohorts.

For women born during 1915-19, and of college 4+, college 1-3, and high school 4 attainment the fertility rates of nonwhites surpassed those of whites at the ages of 20-24 (reached in 1940),[4] but fell below those of whites at ages 30-34 (reached in 1950) and 40-44 (reached in 1960). A similar situation is found for ever-married women. The use of data in this fashion for ever-married women does some violence to the idea of birth cohorts because many new recruits are added after age 20-24 through marriage at later ages. Nevertheless, the data are shown since they provide some suggestion that the patterns observed for the total cohorts do not arise from differential proportions married. It seems rather clear that nonwhite women of college or even complete high school attainment get an earlier start in family growth than do white women of similar educational attainment. It seems likely that they are less prone to postpone first births. At later ages, perhaps for some of the reasons discussed later in this paper, the fertility of the whites of college attainment surpasses that of the nonwhites of similar education, and the fertility of whites of high school 4 attainment tends to be approximately the same as, if not higher than, that of nonwhites of similar education.

Whelpton, Campbell and Patterson, at one point in their study,[5] compare actual and expected fertility of nonwhite women in their sample with that of a matched group of white women and that of total white women. For both actual and expected fertility of women who had gone to college the nonwhites had the lowest rates, the "matched whites" were in intermediate position and "all whites" had the highest rates. The average number of expected births per woman was 2.4 for nonwhites, 2.8 for "matched whites" and 3.0 for "all whites." Therefore, for whatever reason, the nonwhite women who had completed

Factors Associated with Low Fertility

TABLE 7.

Excess of Fertility of Nonwhite over White Women, Married and
Husband Present, by Age of Woman and Education of Husband
and Wife, United States and Urbanized Areas, 1960.[18]

| EDUCATION | | UNITED STATES | | URBANIZED AREAS | |
| Wife | Husband | 35-44 | 45-54 | 35-44 | 45-54 |
		%	%	%	%
College: 4 or more	College: 4 or more	−28.7	−31.6	−26.9	−30.8
College: 4 or more	College: 1-3	−23.1	−28.7	−19.5	−35.7
College: 1-3	College: 4 or more	−18.8	−16.4	−18.7	−11.1
College: 1-3	College: 1-3	−7.1	11.7	−6.8	7.9
College: 4 or more	High school: 4	−18.9	−20.7	−20.0	−24.9
High school: 4	College: 4 or more	−3.9	16.2	−4.7	15.3
College: 1-3	High school: 4	−8.1	−2.9	−7.3	−1.5
High school: 4	College: 1-3	4.2	−0.6	3.1	2.3
High school: 4	High school: 4	−1.1	4.7	−2.3	3.3
College: 4 or more	High school: 1-3	−24.7	−24.6	−22.6	−30.0
High school: 1-3	College: 4 or more	7.3	12.1	−3.5	*
College: 1-3	High school: 1-3	10.1	−13.4	6.7	−9.8
High school: 1-3	College: 1-3	8.4	3.0	8.6	−0.2
High school: 1-3	High school: 1-3	16.3	19.7	11.7	13.0
College: 4 or more	Elementary: 8	−7.2	−12.3	−16.1	−18.7
Elementary: 8	College: 4 or more	*	*	*	*
College: 1-3	Elementary: 8	−18.2	−7.2	−8.8	−3.0
Elementary: 8	College: 1-3	−11.2	−0.5	−11.9	−1.2
Elementary: 8	Elementary: 8	3.4	3.9	8.6	9.3
College: 4 or more	Elementary: <8	0.0	−7.2	4.6	−16.9
Elementary: <8	College: 4 or more	*	*	*	*
College: 1-3	Elementary: <8	4.8	−5.5	2.6	−5.1
Elementary: <8	College: 1-3	9.7	−10.6	5.9	−7.5
Elementary: <8	Elementary: <8	13.5	0.9	−4.5	−12.3

*Per cent not shown where base for nonwhites is fewer than 1,000.

one or more years of college had fewer children on the average than
white women of similar education and age (25 and over). Nonwhite
college-trained married women 18-39 years old also *expected* a smaller
completed family than did white women of similar age and education.[5]

It may be noted that the college education of the wife contributes
more to lower fertility of nonwhites than of whites than does college
education of the husband. This is brought out in the data in Table
7 relating to fertility by the jointly considered educational attainment of the wife and husband. For instance, among couples in which
the wife had completed four or more years of college and the husband was of high school 4 status, the fertility of the nonwhites fell
below that of whites by nearly 19 per cent. In contrast, among couples
in which the husband had completed four or more years of college
and the wife was of high school 4 status, the fertility rate for nonwhites fell below that of whites by less than four per cent.

FACTORS CONSIDERED

Age at Marriage

What are the factors that lead to a lower fertility rate among nonwhite than among white women of college attainment? Since both groups have approximately the same education, other variables must intervene. It is known that age at marriage, marriage stability, labor force status and occupation all have association with fertility. The first hypothesis considered is that lower fertility rates of nonwhite than of white college-trained women were due in part to a later age at marriage among the nonwhites. Two types of data may be adduced. First the median ages at marriage for white and nonwhite women of similar age and educational attainment may be compared. As indicated in

TABLE 8.

AGE AT FIRST MARRIAGE FOR EVER-MARRIED WOMEN 35-54 YEARS OLD, UNITED STATES AND URBANIZED AREAS, 1960[19]

| Age and Education of the Woman | MEDIAN AGE AT FIRST MARRIAGE | | | |
| | United States | | Urbanized Areas | |
	White	*Nonwhite*	*White*	*Nonwhite*
35-44	21.4	21.0	23.0	21.4
College: 4 or more	24.2	24.5	24.2	24.6
1-3	22.6	23.0	22.8	23.0
High school: 4	21.8	22.0	22.8	22.1
1-3	20.1	20.6	20.8	20.7
Elementary: 8	20.4	20.4	21.1	20.7
5-7	19.7	19.9	20.6	20.5
0-4	20.0	20.1	21.4	20.8
45-54	21.9	21.2	22.5	21.7
College: 4 or more	26.0	26.1	26.1	26.2
1-3	23.9	23.6	24.1	23.7
High school: 4	22.8	22.8	23.2	22.8
1-3	21.0	21.3	21.6	21.5
Elementary: 8	20.9	20.9	21.5	21.2
5-7	20.0	20.5	20.7	20.9
0-4	20.0	20.5	20.8	21.1

Table 8, little difference was seen in median age at marriage by color among women reporting some college attendance and especially among those reporting four or more years of college.[6] The attendance of college and especially the completion of college by women rather automatically means delay of marriage.

Next, data may be derived from the 1960 census relating to fertility by color for two age-at-marriage groups (14-21 and 22 and over) and by education, occupation and income of the husband. The fertility rates for these groups are shown in Tables 9 and 10 respectively for

TABLE 9.

CHILDREN EVER BORN PER 1,000 WHITE WOMEN, 35-44 YEARS OLD, MARRIED ONCE
HUSBAND PRESENT, BY AGE AT MARRIAGE OF WOMAN AND OCCUPATION,
EDUCATION AND INCOME OF HUSBAND, FOR UNITED STATES,
1960.[20]

Education and Income in 1959 of Husband	Profes- sional	Pro- pri- etors	Cler- ical	Crafts- men	Opera- tives	Service Work- ers	Labor- ers except Farm and Mine	Farm- ers and Farm Labor- ers
			WIVES MARRIED AT AGES 14-21					
Total	2,691	2,688	2,615	2,940	3,135	2,935	3,569	3,609
College 1+	2,701	2,684	2,620	2,736	2,820	2,744	3,107	3,083
$10,000 and over	2,780	2,746	2,754	2,878	2,857	2,906	*	2,837
7,000-9,999	2,667	2,661	2,623	2,638	2,897	2,767	*	2,798
4,000-6,999	2,614	2,556	2,562	2,757	2,771	2,750	3,115	3,312
2,000-3,999	2,583	2,685	2,434	2,690	2,748	2,763	*	3,156
High school 1-4	2,621	2,640	2,569	2,798	2,884	2,771	3,096	3,173
$7,000-9,999	2,592	2,657	2,567	2,770	2,885	2,732	3,195	3,050
4,000-6,999	2,610	2,641	2,567	2,791	2,842	2,793	2,989	3,331
2,000-3,999	2,925	2,574	2,561	2,897	2,984	2,694	3,271	3,183
1-1,999 or less	2,780	2,485	2,659	2,902	3,254	2,993	3,373	3,082
No High school	3,058	2,869	2,805	3,207	3,405	3,205	3,842	3,960
$7,000-9,999	2,775	2,877	2,831	2,974	3,110	2,737	3,216	3,664
4,000-6,999	2,924	2,894	2,707	3,125	3,262	2,986	3,538	3,906
2,000-3,999	3,274	2,840	2,943	3,490	3,558	3,376	3,990	3,974
1-1,999 or less	*	3,102	2,995	3,684	4,315	3,711	4,547	4,014
			WIVES MARRIED AT AGES 22 AND OVER					
Total	2,314	2,260	2,145	2,215	2,204	2,107	2,272	2,783
College 1+	2,367	2,371	2,253	2,276	2,193	2,209	2,123	2,705
$10,000 and over	2,589	2,504	2,495	2,502	2,453	2,438	*	2,842
7,000-9,999	2,292	2,322	2,317	2,292	2,383	2,406	*	2,873
4,000-6,999	2,153	2,188	2,131	2,181	2,189	2,237	2,150	2,777
2,000-3,999	2,017	2,054	1,845	1,966	1,654	2,003	*	2,596
High school 1-4	2,106	2,169	2,096	2,204	2,167	2,123	2,174	2,626
$7,000-9,999	2,217	2,246	2,298	2,349	2,337	2,452	2,410	2,734
4,000-6,999	2,003	2,100	2,052	2,165	2,153	2,163	2,173	2,922
2,000-3,999	1,834	1,922	1,765	1,967	2,016	1,868	2,109	2,630
1-1,999 or less	1,939	1,857	1,754	1,824	1,957	1,600	1,827	2,257
No High school	2,083	2,175	2,040	2,219	2,259	2,044	2,365	2,949
$7,000-9,999	2,224	2,157	2,056	2,257	2,431	2,246	2,492	3,392
4,000-6,999	2,126	2,195	2,073	2,188	2,217	2,084	2,217	3,186
2,000-3,999	2,112	2,239	1,927	2,257	2,236	1,989	2,488	2,954
1-1,999 or less	*	1,973	1,919	2,194	2,492	1,926	2,664	2,760

Rate not shown where base is fewer than 1,000 women.

white and nonwhite women aged 35-44 in the United States. Table
11 shows the per cent excess of the rates for nonwhites over those of
whites, computed from the preceding tables.

The tendency for fertility of nonwhites to fall below that of whites
was much greater among women married at age 22 and over than

TABLE 10.

CHILDREN EVER BORN PER 1,000 NONWHITE WOMEN, 35-44 YEARS OLD, MARRIED ONCE HUSBAND PRESENT, BY AGE AT MARRIAGE OF WOMAN AND OCCUPATION, EDUCATION AND INCOME OF HUSBAND FOR UNITED STATES, 1960.[21]

Education and Income in 1959 of Husband	Professional	Proprietors	Clerical	Craftsmen	Operatives	Service Workers	Laborers except Farm and Mine	Farmers and Farm Laborers
	WIVES MARRIED AT AGES 14-21							
Total	3,018	3,373	3,195	3,896	4,054	3,646	4,543	6,463
College 1+	2,712	2,645	2,756	3,248	3,356	3,037	*	*
$10,000 and over	*	*	*	*	*	*	*	*
7,000-9,999	2,418	*	*	*	*	*	*	*
4,000-6,999	2,733	*	2,856	*	3,338	*	*	*
2,000-3,999	*	*	*	*	*	*	*	*
High school 1-4	3,328	3,220	2,992	3,491	3,572	3,319	4,056	5,126
$7,000-9,999	*	*	*	3,052	3,701	*	*	*
4,000-6,999	*	3,079	2,840	3,500	3,450	3,079	3,545	*
2,000-3,999	*	*	3,121	3,502	3,624	3,360	4,495	*
1-1,999 or less	*	*	*	4,122	4,109	3,346	4,567	5,971
No High school	*	3,893	3,889	4,206	4,294	3,916	4,682	6,632
$7,000-9,999	*	*	*	*	3,883	*	*	*
4,000-6,999	*	*	3,761	3,797	3,736	4,068	4,159	5,823
2,000-3,999	*	4,309	3,951	4,268	4,302	3,896	4,451	6,484
1-1,999 or less	*	*	*	4,737	5,236	3,859	5,550	6,681
	WIVES MARRIED AT AGES 22 AND OVER							
Total	1,897	2,035	1,995	2,236	2,392	1,980	2,570	3,685
College 1+	1,886	2,054	1,872	2,046	1,864	2,101	2,093	*
$10,000 and over	2,129	*	*	*	*	*	*	*
7,000-9,999	2,131	*	*	*	*	*	*	*
4,000-6,999	1,698	2,192	1,787	2,106	1,915	2,097	*	*
2,000-3,999	1,770	*	*	*	*	*	*	*
High school 1-4	1,824	1,956	1,974	2,144	2,070	1,911	2,178	2,881
$7,000-9,999	*	*	*	2,042	2,290	*	*	*
4,000-6,999	1,785	2,066	1,977	2,174	2,016	2,047	2,141	*
2,000-3,999	*	*	1,980	2,129	2,086	1,826	1,962	2,985
1-1,999 or less	*	*	*	*	2,207	1,957	2,817	3,193
No High school	*	2,138	2,210	2,359	2,633	2,022	2,732	3,937
$7,000-9,999	*	*	*	*	2,065	*	*	*
4,000-6,999	*	*	1,889	2,224	2,355	2,051	2,430	*
2,000-3,999	*	1,975	2,515	2,382	2,618	2,010	2,739	3,252
1-1,999 or less	*	*	*	2,754	3,240	2,040	2,995	4,021

*Rate not shown where base is fewer than 1,000 women.

among those married at younger ages. Stated in another manner the tendency for the fertility rate of nonwhites to fall below that of whites was virtually restricted to wives of husbands reporting one or more years of college if the wife married at an age younger than 22. The lower fertility of nonwhites than of whites was found even for wives of husbands reporting one to four years of high school or even less

Factors Associated with Low Fertility

education among women who married at ages 22 and over. The data for women 45-54 and for those of both age groups in urbanized areas give essentially similar results. Therefore, although the variation was

TABLE 11.

Excess of Average Number of Children ever Born to Nonwhite Women over that of White Women, Married Once and Husband Present, Aged 35-44, by Age at Marriage of Woman and by Occupation Group, Education and Income in 1959 of Husband, for the United States, 1960.[22]

Education and Income in 1959 of the Husband	Professional %	Proprietors %	Clerical %	Craftsmen %	Operatives %	Service Workers %	Laborers except Farm and Mine %	Farmers and Farm Laborers %
	WIVES MARRIED AT AGES 14-21							
Total	12.2	25.5	22.2	32.5	29.3	24.2	27.3	79.1
College 1+	0.4	−1.5	5.2	18.7	19.0	10.6	*	*
$10,000 and over	*	*	*	*	*	*	*	*
7,000-9,999	−9.3	*	*	*	*	*	*	*
4,000-6,999	5.3	*	11.5	*	20.5	*	*	*
2,000-3,999	*	*	*	*	*	*	*	*
High school 1-4	27.0	22.0	16.5	24.8	23.9	19.8	31.0	61.6
$7,000-9,999	*	*	*	10.2	28.3	*	*	*
4,000-6,999	*	16.6	10.6	25.4	21.4	10.2	18.6	*
2,000-3,999	*	*	21.9	20.9	21.4	25.0	37.4	*
1-1,999 or less	*	*	*	42.0	26.3	11.8	35.4	96.9
No High school	*	35.7	38.6	31.2	26.1	22.2	21.9	67.5
$7,000-9,999	*	*	*	*	24.9	*	*	*
4,000-6,999	*	*	38.9	21.5	14.5	36.2	17.6	49.1
2,000-3,999	*	51.7	34.3	22.3	20.9	15.4	11.6	63.2
1-1,999 or less	*	*	*	28.6	21.3	4.0	22.1	66.4
	WIVES MARRIED AT AGES 22 AND OVER							
Total	−18.0	−10.0	−7.0	0.9	8.5	−6.0	13.1	32.4
College 1+	−20.3	−13.4	−16.9	−10.1	−15.0	−4.9	−1.4	*
$10,000 and over	−17.8	*	*	*	*	*	*	*
8,000-9,999	−7.1	*	*	*	*	*	*	*
4,000-6,999	−21.1	0.2	−16.2	−3.4	−12.5	−6.3	*	*
2,000-3,999	−12.3	*	*	*	*	*	*	*
High school 1-4	−13.4	−9.8	−5.8	−2.7	−4.5	−10.0	0.2	9.7
$7,000-9,999	*	*	*	−13.1	−2.0	*	*	*
4,000-6,999	−10.9	−1.6	−3.7	0.4	−6.4	−5.4	−1.5	*
2,000-3,999	*	*	12.2	8.2	3.5	−2.3	−7.0	13.5
1-1,999 or less	*	*	*	*	12.8	22.3	54.2	41.5
No High school	*	−1.7	8.3	6.3	16.6	−1.1	15.5	33.5
$7,000-9,999	*	*	*	*	−15.1	*	*	*
4,000-6,999	*	*	−8.9	1.6	6.2	−1.6	9.6	*
2,000-3,999	*	−11.8	30.5	5.5	17.1	1.1	10.1	10.1
1-1,999 or less	*	*	*	25.5	30.0	5.9	12.4	45.7

*Per cent not shown in categories with fewer than 1,000 nonwhite women.

small in median age at marriage among women who completed college, the delay in marriage necessitated by college attendance seemed to have more impact on the fertility of nonwhites than of whites.

Furthermore, age at marriage is a critical factor in the direction of *socioeconomic differentials* in fertility of white women. The direct relation of fertility to socioeconomic status occurred much more frequently among white women marrying at age 22 and over than among those marrying at age 14-21. This is apparent from the data in Table 9, giving number of children ever born among white women married and husband present according to age at marriage of the wife, and occupation, education and income of the husband.

Stability of Marriage

A second hypothesis is that differences in stability of marriage contribute appreciably to the lower fertility of nonwhite than of white ever-married women of upper socioeconomic status. The 1960 data indicate that for both white and nonwhite ever-married women the proportion of those in unbroken first marriages (married once and husband present) was directly related to socioeconomic status. Nevertheless, among women 35-44 years old reporting four or more years of college, the proportion of ever-married women classified as "married once and husband present" was 85.2 per cent for whites and 67.5 per cent for nonwhites (Table 12). In the older age group (45-54) the percentages were lower because of increased widowhood and longer time for other types of marriage disruptions, but the differential by color was marked. For women reporting four or more years of college the percentages were 76 per cent for whites and 56 per cent for nonwhites.

Although stable marriages tend to be more fertile than unstable marriages and although instability of marriage is more frequent among nonwhite than white women of college attainment, this factor does not account for much of the lower fertility of nonwhites of the college level. Within each detailed marital status category of college-trained women the fertility of the nonwhites was lower than that of whites. If the fertility rates of nonwhites are adjusted to the distributions of the whites by detailed marital status the fertility rates of the nonwhite women of college status are increased by about four per cent for each age group.[7]

Employment Status

A third hypothesis is that differences in employment status of women partially account for the lower fertility of nonwhite than of white

TABLE 12.

DISTRIBUTION OF WOMEN AND CHILDREN EVER BORN PER 1,000 WHITE AND
NONWHITE WOMEN 35-44 YEARS OF AGE, BY MARITAL STATUS AND
COLLEGE ATTENDANCE, UNITED STATES, 1960.[23]

Marital Status	COLLEGE 4 OR MORE YEARS				COLLEGE 1-3 YEARS			
	Per Cent		Children Ever Born per 1,000 Women		Per Cent		Children Ever Born per 1,000 Women	
	White	Non-white	White	Non-white	White	Non-white	White	Non-white
Ever married	100.0	100.0	2,277	1,651	100.0	100.0	2,373	2,149
Married once	92.5	85.3	2,314	1,685	87.7	80.2	2,418	2,214
Married more than once	7.4	14.6	1,814	1,452	12.2	19.8	2,046	1,887
Married husband present	91.5	77.6	2,345	1,736	90.5	74.3	2,435	2,263
Married once	85.2	67.5	2,380	1,773	80.2	60.2	2,479	2,344
Married more than once	6.3	10.3	1,880	1,494	10.3	14.0	2,097	1,913
Married husband absent	2.3	10.8	1,801	1,481	2.6	13.0	2,123	2,103
Married once	2.0	8.8	1,841	1,477	2.0	10.6	2,136	2,064
Married more than once	0.3	2.0	1,555	*	0.6	2.4	2,079	2,271
Separated	0.9	5.2	1,605	1,520	1.1	8.7	2,035	2,210
Married once	0.7	4.3	1,643	1,490	0.8	7.2	1,991	2,160
Married more than once	0.1	0.9	*	*	0.3	1.5	2,148	*
Other	1.5	5.6	1,916	1,444	1.5	4.3	2,184	1,885
Married once	1.3	4.5	1,955	1,465	1.2	3.4	2,226	1,864
Married more than once	0.2	1.1	1,662	*	0.3	0.9	2,013	*
Widowed	2.3	4.0	1,661	1,420	2.4	4.5	1,924	1,752
Married once	2.1	3.6	1,689	1,405	2.1	3.6	1,947	1,672
Married more than once	0.2	0.4	1,385	*	0.3	1.0	1,764	*
Divorced	3.9	7.4	1,307	1,130	4.5	8.2	1,498	1,416
Married once	3.3	5.5	1,291	1,119	3.5	5.8	1,476	1,471
Married more than once	0.6	1.9	1,396	*	1.0	2.4	1,576	1,284

*Rate not shown where base is fewer than 1,000.

college women. Women who work tend to have fewer children than those who do not. For all women and for those classified as "married and husband present," the percentage in the labor force among those 22-44 years old reporting one to three or four or more years of college was considerably higher among nonwhite than among white women. Thus at ages 25-29 the proportions in the labor force among women "married and husband present" and reporting four or more years of college were 35 per cent for whites and 66 per cent for nonwhites. The data also throw light on the reason why fertility of nonwhite college women surpasses that of white college women at ages under 25. It will be noted that at age 20-21 the proportion of women in the

TABLE 13.

PER CENT OF WOMEN 20-44 YEARS OLD IN THE LABOR FORCE BY AGE, COLOR,
MARITAL STATUS AND YEARS OF COLLEGE COMPLETED, UNITED STATES, 1960.[24]

Marital Status and Age of Woman	COLLEGE 4 OR MORE YEARS		COLLEGE 1-3 YEARS	
	White %	Nonwhite %	White %	Nonwhite %
All women				
20-21	72.8	72.4	51.7	42.9
22-24	71.7	80.2	51.1	56.2
25-29	48.5	75.8	37.2	57.9
30-34	39.6	74.8	33.9	58.6
35-44	50.7	80.1	42.9	62.1
Married husband present				
20-21	61.4	46.8	44.3	35.2
22-24	56.8	68.8	36.4	47.5
25-29	35.0	65.7	27.3	48.1
30-34	28.2	68.5	26.3	50.4
35-44	40.1	76.0	35.9	56.3
Other marital status				
20-21	79.5	78.6	54.3	44.7
22-24	89.1	85.7	78.2	62.7
25-29	90.7	89.9	82.6	74.5
30-34	88.5	88.1	81.5	77.2
35-44	89.1	89.1	81.6	76.8

TABLE 14.

NUMBER OF CHILDREN EVER BORN PER 1,000 EVER-MARRIED EMPLOYED WOMEN
35-44 AND 45-54 YEARS OLD, BY COLOR, AND PER CENT EXCESS OF NONWHITE
OVER WHITE FERTILITY, BY MAJOR OCCUPATION GROUP OF THE WOMAN,
UNITED STATES, 1960.[25]

Occupation Group	35-44			45-54		
	White	Non-white	Per Cent Excess Nonwhite Over White	White	Non-white	Per Cent Excess Nonwhite Over White
Professional, technical, etc.	1,973	1,627	−17.5	1,702	1,308	−23.2
Managers, proprietors, etc.	1,879	1,897	1.0	1,733	2,018	16.4
Clerical	1,787	1,747	−2.2	1,595	1,606	0.7
Sales workers	2,206	2,111	−4.3	1,997	1,970	−1.4
Craftsmen	1,959	1,884	−3.8	1,838	1,968	7.1
Operatives and kindred workers	2,309	2,161	−6.4	2,307	2,156	−6.6
Private household workers	2,836	2,864	1.0	2,846	2,546	−10.6
Service, exc. priv. household	2,545	2,567	0.9	2,544	2,355	−7.4
Laborers, exc. farm and mine	2,496	2,584	3.5	2,585	2,181	−15.6
Farmers	3,017	5,296	75.5	2,841	5,153	81.4
Farm laborers	3,165	5,001	58.0	3,086	4,436	43.7

labor force was lower for nonwhites than for whites among those
reporting one to three or four years of college. At ages 22-24 the

difference was in the other direction but the gap was not so wide as at ages 25 and over. Among college-trained women of "other marital status" (including the single) not much difference by color occurred in the high proportions in the labor force (Table 13).

Unfortunately, fertility rates are not available by education and labor force status simultaneously considered. However, when the fertility rates of ever-married nonwhite women, regardless of education, were adjusted to the labor force status of white women of corresponding age, the fertility rates of nonwhites were increased by about seven per cent at ages 30-39, six per cent at ages 40-44 and four per cent at ages 45-49.[8]

The increases at ages 35-44 are somewhat larger than those previously observed by standardizing for marital stability. The decreases in the percentages with increasing age may reflect a greater tendency for white women to have children and to re-enter the labor force after the family is completed.

Occupation of Employed Women

Although fertility rates are not available for employed women by education *and* occupation,[9] they are presented in Table 14 by color and broad occupation group and they are available for selected specific occupations. First of all, among ever-married women 35-44 years old and employed as "professional, technical and kindred workers," the average number of children ever born was 17.5 per cent lower for nonwhites than for whites. It will be recalled that among women married to professional men the fertility was only about 11 per cent lower for nonwhites than for whites at ages 35-39 and nine per cent lower at ages 40-44 (Table 2). Just as the gap by color was larger for ever-married women who had completed college themselves than for those whose husbands had completed college, so also was the gap by color wider for ever-married women who were themselves employed as professional workers than for those whose husbands were of professional status.

It is particularly noteworthy that the specific occupation of teaching was relatively more important among nonwhite than among white employed women of professional status. The proportion was about 41 per cent for whites and 55 per cent for nonwhites at ages 35-44, and 52 per cent for whites and 63 per cent for nonwhites at ages 45-54. Furthermore, the nonwhite teachers were characterized by especially low fertility in relation to that of whites and in relation to that of nonwhites in other professional pursuits.[10]

As for the low fertility of nonwhite teachers, the number of children ever born per 1,000 ever-married nonwhite women 35-44 years old was 1,523 for those employed as elementary teachers, 1,437 for those employed as secondary school teachers and 1,456 for the relatively few labeled as "teachers, not elsewhere classified." These rates are respectively approximately 25, 25 and 30 per cent below those of comparable white teachers. On the other hand, the fertility rate was 1,833 per 1,000 ever-married nonwhite women employed as professional nurses — only about 15 per cent below that for comparable white nurses. The fertility rate was 1,941 for ever-married nonwhite women employed as medical and dental technicians, a rate about seven per cent *higher* than that for comparable white medical and dental technicians.[11] Probably relatively few of these technicians attended college. Whatever this situation may be it seems likely that the relatively low fertility of nonwhite women of college attainment is due in appreciable part to the low fertility of nonwhite teachers.

SUMMARY

Among married women 25 years of age and over the fertility of nonwhites tends to surpass that of whites in the United States except at upper socioeconomic levels. Among women under 25 the fertility of nonwhites tends to surpass that of whites at the upper as well as other socioeconomic levels.

In seeking the reasons for the lower fertility of nonwhite than of white women of college education, the authors examined available data from the 1960 census and other sources relating to three possible factors: age at marriage, marriage stability and the employment status of women.

Little difference was found between white and nonwhite women of college attainment with respect to age of wife at marriage. However, the delay in marriage occasioned by college attendance appears to have more impact on the fertility of nonwhite than of white married women. Among women marrying at ages under 22 the cases of lower fertility of nonwhite than of white women were virtually restricted to those whose husbands had attended college. Among women marrying at age 22 and over the fertility of whites frequently surpassed that of nonwhites even at lower educational levels.

Differences in marital stability, i.e., proportions of ever-married women classified as "married once and husband present," contributed in a modest manner to the lower fertility of nonwhite than of white married women. Standardization of the fertility rates of nonwhites to the detailed marital status of whites raise the fertility rates of ever-married women of college status 35-44 or 45-54 years old by about four per cent.

The higher proportion of nonwhite than of white women in the labor force apparently also has relevance to the relatively low fertility of nonwhite women of college attainment. Standardization of the fertility rates of nonwhites to the labor force status of the white ever-married women raised the fertility rates of the nonwhites by about seven per cent. Of particular importance is the fact that among employed professional women, teachers formed a higher proportion among nonwhites than among whites. Furthermore, the nonwhite teachers were characterized by lower fertility rates than those of white teachers and lower than those of nonwhite women in other professional pursuits.

REFERENCES

[1]More specifically, of the nonwhite ever-married women 15-49 years old in the 1960 Census of the United States, 92.2 per cent were designated as Negro, 2.2 per cent as American Indian, 2.9 per cent as Japanese, 1.1 per cent as Chinese and 1.6 per cent as "other races." *See* United States Bureau of the Census, 1960 CENSUS OF POPULATION: WOMEN BY NUMBER OF CHILDREN EVER BORN, PC(2)-3A, Washington, United States Government Printing Office, 1964, Table 8.

[2]Although the data for 1940 related to native-white women and those for 1950 and 1960 to white women, this introduces no appreciable incomparability. Approximately 96 per cent of all white women or all ever-married white women 15-49 years old in 1960 were native white.

[3]Among professional men who in 1940 were husbands of native-white women 20-24 years old in urban areas, married once and husband present, 36.8 per cent of the wives had attended college and an additional 42.9 per cent had completed high school. Conversely among all native-white urban women 20-24 years old who had attended college and were reported as "married once and husband present" in the 1940 census, 22.1 per cent of the husbands were professional men, an additional 16.1 per cent were proprietors and 29.3 per cent were clerical workers, a total of 67.5 per cent in the "white-collar" classes. Derived from United States Bureau of the Census, 1940 CENSUS OF POPULATION, WOMEN BY NUMBER OF CHILDREN UNDER 5 YEARS OLD, Washington, United States Government Printing Office, 1945, Table 58.

[4]The data for 1940 relate to native-white and Negro women rather than to white and nonwhite.

[5]Whelpton, Pascal K., Campbell, Arthur A. and Patterson, John E., FERTILITY AND FAMILY PLANNING IN THE UNITED STATES, Princeton, Princeton University Press, 1966, p. 339.

[6]The median age at first marriage was 24.2 years for whites and 24.5 for nonwhite ever-married women 35-44 years of age in the United States reporting four or more years of college. The median ages of ever-married women 45-54 years of age and reporting four or more years of college were 26.0 and 26.1 respectively for whites and nonwhites. The median ages at marriage for those with one to three years

of college were respectively 22.6 and 23.0 years for whites and nonwhites 35-44 years old, and 23.9 and 23.6 for whites and nonwhites 45-54 years old.

[7]The computed increases by age and educational attainment are as follows:

Women 35-44 (regardless of education)		4.7 per cent
Women 35-44	College 1-3	4.0 per cent
Women 35-44	College 4+	3.9 per cent
Women 45-54 (regardless of education)		5.7 per cent
Women 45-54	College 1-3	3.9 per cent
Women 45-54	College 4+	4.5 per cent

[8]Derived from United States Bureau of the Census, 1960 CENSUS OF POPULATION, WOMEN BY NUMBER OF CHILDREN EVER BORN, *op cit.*, Table 30.

[9]Cross classifications of employed women by education and broad occupation group are available from the 1960 census by age and color, but regardless of marital status. These were examined to ascertain whether the proportions of employed women of college attainment *engaged in professional pursuits* were higher among nonwhites than among whites. It was thought that if this were the case it might help to account for the relatively low fertility of nonwhite women of college attainment. However, the results were not uniform at the different levels of college attainment. For instance, among employed women 35-44 years old, reporting one to three years of college, the proportion classified as "professional, technical, and kindred workers" was *lower* for nonwhites (17 per cent) than for whites (26 per cent), Among those reporting four years of college the proportion was *higher* (74 per cent) for nonwhites than for whites (67 per cent). The proportion was approximately the same (85 for nonwhites and 83 for whites) for those reporting five or more years of college.

Among the employed college women 35-44 years old mentioned above the proportion of graduates and postgraduates was higher among the nonwhites than among the whites. Among the nonwhites about 48 per cent reported one to three years of college, 31 per cent reported four years and 21 per cent reported five or more years. Among the whites the comparable proportions were 57, 27 and 16.

Derived from United States Bureau of the Census, 1960 CENSUS OF POPULATION, EDUCATIONAL ATTAINMENT, PC(2)-5B, Washington, United States Government Printing Office, 1963, Table 8.

[10]Derived from United States Bureau of the Census, 1960 CENSUS OF POPULATION, WOMEN BY NUMBER OF CHILDREN EVER BORN, *op. cit.*, Tables 35 and 36.

[11]*Ibid.*

[12]*Ibid.*, Table 1, pp. 1-5.

[13]United States Bureau of the Census, *op. cit.*, Tables 31-32, pp. 147-164; Grabill, Wilson H., Kiser, Clyde C. and Whelpton, Pascal K., THE FERTILITY OF AMERICAN WOMEN, New York: John Wiley & Sons, Inc., 1958, Tables 54 and 55, pp. 131-132 and 145-146.

[14]United States Bureau of the Census, *op. cit.*, Table 37, pp. 181-183.

[15]*Ibid.*, Table 44.

[16]United States Bureau of the Census, *op. cit.*, Table 25; Grabill, Kiser and Whelpton, *op. cit.*, Tables 76 and 77.

[17]United States Bureau of the Census, *op. cit.*, Table 25; Grabill, Kiser and Whelpton, *op. cit.*, Tables 75 and 77.

[18]United States Bureau of the Census, *op. cit.*, Tables 26-27, pp. 109-110 and 113-114.

[19]*Ibid.*, Table 9, pp. 112-120.

[20]*Ibid.*, Table 39, pp. 109-202.

[21]*Ibid.*, Table 40, pp. 223-226.

[22]*Ibid.*, Tables 39 and 40, pp. 109-202 and 223-226.

[23]*Ibid.*, Tables 28 and 29, pp. 117-118 and 129-130.

[24]United States Bureau of the Census, 1960 CENSUS OF POPULATION: EDUCATIONAL ATTAINMENT, PC(2)-5B, Washington, United States Government Printing Office, 1963, Table 5.

[25]United States Bureau of the Census, 1960 CENSUS OF POPULATION: WOMEN BY NUMBER OF CHILDREN EVER BORN, *op. cit.*, Tables 35 and 36.

Racial, Ethnic, and Income Factors in the Epidemiology of Neonatal Mortality

CHARLES V. WILLIE AND WILLIAM B. ROTHNEY

EVIDENCE ON THE DIFFERENCE IN INFANT MORTALITY RATES BETWEEN white and nonwhite populations is inconclusive. For example, a report of the National Office of Vital Statistics (from 1949 to 1951 which include the first two years of this study) indicates that the infant mortality rate of 45.5 per 1,000 live births in the nonwhite population is 65 per cent greater than the infant mortality rate of 27.7 in the white population of the United States.[1] However, Alfred Yankauer in a 1947 study of the New York City population found that in neighborhoods where more than 75 per cent of nonwhite parents reside the neonatal mortality rate of 52.7 per 1,000 live births among nonwhite persons is less than two points greater than the rate of 51.0 among white persons who reside in the same neighborhoods.[2] Clearly, discrepancy exists in the findings of these reports. This discrepancy has not been resolved because studies of variation in infant mortality rates between racial and ethnic populations seldom control adequately for socio-economic status.

The purpose of this study is to determine whether infant mortality rates, particularly neonatal mortality rates, vary by racial and by ethnic neighborhoods when socio-economic status is held constant.

Also, the distribution of neonatal mortality is studied in relationship to the distribution of families of varying income levels within racial and ethnic neighborhoods and within the total city. In a previous report, it was pointed out (1) that the distribution of median family income, by census tracts, had only a modest association, intercorrelating at .53, with the distribution of socio-economic status (consisting of occupation,

---

[1]National Office of Vital Statistics, "Infant Mortality, United States, 1915-50," *Vital Statistics Special Reports*, 45 (July 27, 1956), p. 13.

[2]Alfred Yankauer, Jr., "The Relationship of Fetal and Infant Mortality to Residential Segregation," *American Sociological Review*, 15 (October, 1950), p. 645.

Reprinted by permission of the publisher and author from *The American Sociological Review*, XXVII (August 1962), 522-26.

education and housing items) and, (2) that family income correlated significantly with the distribution of neonatal mortality rates, by census tracts, while the socio-economic status index did not.[3] Thus, it would seem that socio-economic status as subsequently defined in this study and family income are not interchangeable variables. This study is designed to hold socio-economic status constant. However, it cannot be assumed that family income is also held constant. A secondary consideration in this investigation, then, is the three-way association, if any, between neonatal mortality, racial or ethnic neighborhood, and family income.

DATA AND METHOD

The study area is Syracuse, New York, an industrial city of approximately 25 square miles, with a population of 220,583 persons in 1950. Because of the small numbers of infant deaths that occur during a single year, it is necessary to combine several years. The study utilized data for the years 1950 through 1956 and is limited to the neonatal period, since 80 per cent of all infant deaths (excluding still births) occur during the first month of life.

The study includes four racial and ethnic populations in Syracuse — Negro, Native White, Italian, and Polish — that have neighborhoods in the lowest socio-economic area of the city. The study is limited to these groups that have significant populations in Area VI, lowest in the hierarchy of residential areas according to an ecological investigation,[4] so that socio-economic status and age of parents are held relatively constant.

Median age of women in the child-bearing years, 20 to 44, is, computed for each racial and ethnic neighborhood. Medians for Negro, Native White, Italian, and Polish populations are 30, 31, 30, and 31 years, respectively. Thus, age of mother appears to be constant for the four neighborhoods and cannot account for variations, if any, in neonatal mortality rates.

Census tracts are the basic units of analysis. A socio-economic status score, derived for each census tract, is a composite of five factors representing occupation, education, and housing characteristics of the population. Specifically, the variables are (1) percentage of persons in

---

[3]Charles V. Willie, "A Research Note on the Changing Association Between Infant Mortality and Socio-Economic Status," *Social Forces*, 37 (March, 1959), pp. 222-225.

[4]Charles V. Willie, *Socio-Economic and Ethnic Areas in Syracuse, New York,* unpublished Ph.D. thesis, Syracuse University, 1957, pp. 167-222.

the combined occupational categories of operatives, service workers and laborers; (2) median school year completed by the adult population over 25 years of age; (3) average monthly rental; (4) average market value of own homes; and (5) percent of single-family dwelling units. (The first factor is inverted so that it will vary directly with the other four.) All factors in the socio-economic index, except one indicating house-type, intercorrelate with each other at .80 and above. The Pearsonian correlation coefficients between per cent of single-family dwelling units and the other four factors range from .59 to .70. Thus, a significant and high association exists between all variables in the socio-economic status index. Distributions of all variables are converted into standard scores with assigned means of 100 and assigned standard deviations of 10. Standard scores for the five factors are averaged into a composite socio-economic score for each census tract, and tracts with similar standard scores are combined into a single socio-economic area. Six areas incorporating several neighborhoods are delineated; they range from Area I, high in socio-economic status, to Area VI, low in socio-economic status. Composite index scores, for individual census tracts, range from 85 to 123. The average socio-economic status score for the four racial and ethnic neighborhoods is 92, well below the city assigned mean of 100. A difference of five between the highest and lowest average score of the four neighborhoods, is, of course, not statistically significant at the five per cent level of confidence. Thus, socio-economic status is held constant for all four neighborhoods.

Racial and ethnic neighborhoods are delineated by a method similar to one used by Shevky and Williams to measure ethnic segregation.[5] When the percentage of a racial or ethnic population in a census tract is three or more times greater than the percentage of that population in the total city, a census tract is designated as part of the racial or ethnic neighborhood. This is the method used to identify neighborhoods with high proportions of Italian and Polish foreign born. Data on foreign born only are available in census publications for determining the boundaries of the two ethnic neighborhoods. Because of the high degree of segregation of the Italian and Polish populations (40 to 50 per cent of their foreign born are concentrated in identifiable neighborhoods), it is assumed that many second and third generations of these families also lived near their foreign-born kinsmen.[6] The same method

---

[5] Eshref Shevky and Marilyn Williams, *The Social Areas in Los Angeles,* Berkeley: University of California Press, 1949, pp. 47-57.

[6] Charles V. Willie, *Socio-Economic and Ethnic Areas in Syracuse, New York, op. cit.,* pp. 223-269.

is used to delineate the Negro neighborhood. However, the total Negro population is included. The Native White neighborhood consists of those census tracts in socio-economic Area VI, with few Negroes and few foreign born, in which the percentage of Native White is greater than that in the total city population; more than 90 per cent of the residents in these census tracts are native born and white.

A few census tracts are eliminated from the study because they are neighborhoods that include two or more racial or ethnic populations in significant numbers. The final study area consists of 15 census tracts,

TABLE 1.

NEONATAL MORTALITY RATE PER 1,000 LIVE BIRTHS AND SOCIO-ECONOMIC
STATUS BY RACIAL AND ETHNIC NEIGHBORHOODS
SYRACUSE, 1950-56

Neighborhood	Live Births	Neonatal Deaths	Mortality Rate	Average Socio-Economic Score[a]
Negro	1,442	46	32	96
Native White[b]	1,749	52	30	91
Italian	3,226	66	20	90
Polish	2,208	33	15	91
Total	8,626	197	23	92

[a]The average socio-economic status score for the total city is 100. Socio-economic status is derived from a composite standard score of five variables reflecting occupation, education and housing characteristics of the population. The composite score ranges from 85 in the census tract of lowest status to 123 in the tract of highest status.

[b]That portion of the neighborhood in the lowest socio-economic area.

two in the Negro neighborhood, three in the Native White Neighborhood, and five each in the Italian and Polish neighborhoods. There are 52,497 persons in these tracts, about one-fourth of all persons in the city. The final study population consists of 8,626 live births and 197 neonatal deaths.

Unless otherwise stated, associations resulting from the statistical analysis are considered significant if they would occur by chance less than 5 times out of 100.

FINDINGS

For the total city, principal causes of death during the neonatal period are congenital malformations, complications associated with prematurity, and injuries at birth.[7] There are 34,700 live births and 658 neonatal

[7]Syracuse Department of Health, *Annual Report of the Bureau of Vital Statistics,* 1956. (typewritten).

deaths in the total city for the seven-year study period, resulting in a neonatal mortality rate of 19 per 1,000 live births.

As seen in Table 1, socio-economic status is fairly similar for all neighborhoods. The neonatal mortality rate for the four racial and ethnic neighborhoods combined is only slightly higher at 23 than the total city rate. By individual neighborhoods, however, there is great variation with the Negro and Native White rates of 32 and 30 respectively, being signicantly higher than the rates of 20 and 15, and in that order, in the Italian and Polish neighborhoods. It should be noted that Negro and Native White neighborhoods consisting of two different racial populations have similar, almost identical, rates. At the same time, the neonatal mortality rate in the Native White neighborhood contrasts with and differs significantly from the mortality rates found in neighborhoods populated by white persons of Italian and Polish ancestry.

The analysis, thus far, demonstrates that Negro and Native White populations, though different racially, have similar neonatal mortality rates when socio-economic status is held constant. Also, it demonstrates that the neonatal mortality rate of white native-born persons in a lower socio-economic neighborhood differs from rates of other Caucasian populations in neighborhoods of similar socio-economic status. Because the Native White and Negro neighborhoods with different racial populations have similar rates, and because the neighborhoods of white native born and white foreign born have different rates, though racially similar, doubt is cast upon any hypothesis that racial factors directly contribute to variations in the distribution of neonatal mortality by residential neighborhoods.

Since socio-economic status as defined in this study and family income are not interchangeable variables, the family finance factor is introduced into the analysis at this point to see if it helps to explain

TABLE 2.

ANNUAL MEDIAN INCOME OF FAMILY BY RACIAL AND ETHNIC
NEIGHBORHOOD, SYRACUSE, 1950-56

Neighborhood	Median Family Income
Negro	$1,584
Native White[a]	2,101
Italian	2,676
Polish	3,121

[a]That portion of the neighborhood in the lowest socio-economic area.

the wide variations in neonatal mortality rates among different neighborhoods. Family income data are reported by census tracts and include
the total earnings of all family members in one household for a single
year. As seen in Table 2, income is unequally distributed among the
racial and ethnic populations included in this study. Median family
income varies from a low of $1,584 in the Negro neighborhood to a
high of $3,121 in the Polish neighborhood. The Italian and Native
White populations are second and third, respectively, following the
Polish in the hierarchy of annual family income by racial and ethnic
neighborhoods.

Using all 15 census tracts in the racial and ethnic neighborhoods,
a Spearman rank correlation coefficient was computed because of the
small numbers of units in the analysis. For the variables, median
family income and neonatal mortality rates, a correlation coefficient
of −.75 gave definite evidence of a significant negative association.
As median family incomes decrease neonatal mortality rates increase.
The Negro and Native White populations in the lowest socio-economic
area of the city have similar high neonatal mortality rates notwith-
standing their racial difference. It would appear that the similarities
in high neonatal mortality rates is explained by the low-income status

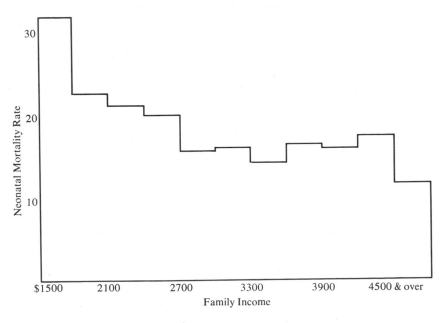

FIGURE 1.   Median Annual Family Income and Neonatal Mortality Rate per
1,000 Live Births, By Census Tracts, Syracuse, N. Y., 1950-56

of families that populate these two neighborhoods. More than half of the families in the combined census tracts of these two neighborhoods received less than $40 per week in 1950. As a contrast, the Polish neighborhood has a low infant mortality rate of 15 and a median family income of $3,121, indicating that half of its families received incomes of $60 per week or more in 1950.

The high association between family income and neonatal mortality found to exist in some neighborhoods of the lowest socio-economic area is quite different from the association between these two variables throughout the entire city. When family income and neonatal mortality rates were intercorrelated for the remaining 42 census tracts not included in the racial and ethnic neighborhood analysis, the Pearsonian correlation coefficient of −.06 was small and obviously not statistically significant. This finding corresponds with a conclusion arrived at in an earlier investigation that the historical association between infant mortality and economic conditions of life is diminishing.[8]

Nevertheless, a highly significant association exists between neonatal mortality and family income in part of the city, indicating that a critical income level must exist at some point along the continuum of family finances above which there is little, if any, association and below which there is significant association between neonatal mortality and this economic variable. To determine that critical level, a histogram was constructed as seen in Figure 1. By median family income, census tracts were grouped into 11 income intervals ranging from $1,500 to $4,500 and over. By inspection, it is seen that $2,700 is the critical level below which there is a regular increase in neonatal mortality rates as the median incomes of families decrease. Above $2,700 fluctuations in the distribution of family income and neonatal mortality rates by census tracts is irregular and insignificant. Illustrating the very definite association between low-income status and neonatal mortality, two census tracts in which half of the families earned less than $1,600 a year in 1950 have mortality rates of 40 or above; these are twice as great as the neonatal mortality rate for the total city.

CONCLUSIONS

Under the conditions of this analysis, it may be concluded: (1) that Negro and Native White populations have similar neonatal mortality rates when socio-economic status is held constant; (2) that Native White populations in lower-income neighborhoods have neonatal mor-

---

[8]Charles V. Willie, *Social Forces, op. cit.,* pp. 225-227.

tality rates greater than the rates of white populations in higher income neighborhoods; (3) that neonatal mortality rates are inter-correlated with family income in neighborhoods where at least half of the households receive less than $2,700 per year; and (4) that no association exists between the distribution of neonatal mortality by neighborhoods and family financial status above the critical median income level of $2,700 per year.

The association between infant mortality and economic circumstances of life is diminishing. As with all generalizations, however, the conditions under which a phenomenon will or will not occur should be specified. Our data refine this generalization by indicating that the probability of death during the neonatal period is heightened in neighborhoods where at least half of the families have incomes of less than $2,700 per year. The specific income level, below which the occurrence of neonatal mortality is significantly increased, may vary in time and by region. But the principle of a *critical income level* should persist as long as poverty exists.

While better care of premature children and more skillful handling of mother and child in the delivery room might further reduce the neonatal death rate, the importance of medically attended pregnancies cannot be over-emphasized. Although our data do not indicate this, it is quite possible that part of the increased incidence of neonatal mortality among families below the critical income level of $2,700 is due to inadequate prenatal care experienced by pregnant women in these families. A nationwide family survey sponsored by the Health Information Foundation in 1953 discovered that "medical skills were utilized less fully in families with annual incomes of less than $3,000. . . . One out of seven mothers in this group did not see a physician during pregnancy, and approximately two thirds had fewer than seven prenatal physician visits."[9] In Rochester, New York in 1951, Alfred Yankauer and associates found that difference in the neonatal mortality rate between two populations of women in the lowest social class "was related to the amount of prenatal care sought."[10]

Why pregnant women in lower-income families do not seek prenatal care, even when it may be available without charge, is a sociological problem worthy of further research and study. One possibility is that lower-income people are constricted in their ability to reach out to

---

[9]Health Information Foundation, "Maternity Care and Its Costs in the United States," *Progress in Health Services*, 6 (January, 1957), p. 4.

[10]Alfred Yankauer, Jr., Kenneth G. Goss and Salvator M. Romeo, "An Evaluation of Prenatal Care and Its relationship to Social Class and Social Disorganization," *American Journal of Public Health*, 43 (August, 1953), p. 1003.

community health and welfare services for help. Were this hypothesis confirmed it would indicate the importance of professional workers in health and welfare seeking out the poor rather than waiting for community services to be sought. A second possibility is that many lower-income women do not know what services are available. A third possibility is that variations in the use of medical services during pregnancy may be a function of variation in cultural values of different populations of people. As stated by Odin Anderson, "the next steps in research in infant mortality which may yield useful information . . . should be directed toward relationships between infant mortality . . . and *mothercraft,* specific infant-care customs and practices. . . ." (Italics added)[11] As the total rate decreases, the proportion of infant deaths attributable to different causes may increase. Thus, several hypotheses should be studied.

---

[11]Odin W. Anderson, "Infant Mortality and Social and Cultural Factors," in E. Gartly Jaco, editor, *Patients, Physicians and Illness,* Glencoe: The Free Press, 1958, p. 23.

Black Youth in a Southern Metropolis

JAMES E. CONYERS, WILLIAM F. FARMAR
AND MARTIN L. LEVIN

THIS PAPER WAS ORIGINALLY CONCEIVED AS A STUDY OF NEGRO delinquency with implications and suggestions for correction and reform. Although this idea has not been completely abandoned, it was felt to be far too narrow in its conception to have practical or theoretical significance for understanding black youth in a southern metropolis. Stating the problem of black youth in terms of the many factors impinging upon their existence and known to affect their behavior would seem to have more relevance to delinquency than merely requesting information about delinquent acts, *per se.*

The most crucial aspects of reform partake of more than mere delinquent acts. The objective conditions in which the Negro youth of America exist are the materials out of which meaningful reform and correction must grow.

It is an unfortunate fact that action programs for social change, delinquency prevention projects, the on-going programs of social service agencies, and other efforts to meet the challenges presented by youth are all too often designed, implemented, and administered by individuals who lack any kind of practical or theoretical understanding of the attitudes, aspirations, and perceived needs of the people whom the projects are designed to assist. More often than not, the problems to which youth programs must respond are stated in quasistructural terms, but the treatment is directed toward individual pathology. The "Alice in Wonderland" quality of such programs is essentially the reason why the application of social welfare agency services on an individual basis has not thus far produced significant change.

In Atlanta, as elsewhere, there is need for a reasonably objective statement of the opinions and attitudes of youth toward themselves, their communities, their leaders and their city, as Negroes, and not

Reprinted by permission of the publisher and the author from *Black Youth in a Southern Metropolis* (Atlanta, Georgia: Southern Regional Council, January 1968), pp. 3-20.

merely as victims of deprivation, as potential delinquents, incipient rioters, or members of the various categories of "otherness" under which they are usually subsumed.

In view of the above considerations, the staff broadened the research objectives to include: (1) social and background factors of Negro youth in Atlanta; (2) neighborhood evaluation and problems; (3) attitudes toward the city of Atlanta; (4) self-concept, level of aspiration, and significant reference group symbols and patterns of identification; (5) attitudes about Negro-white relations, civil rights approaches and organizations, and (6) religious attitudes and participation.

In the 1940's the American Council on Education conducted a series of studies in different sections of the United States to explore the types of distinctive problems Negro youth face in their development as individual personalities. The principal works which came from this endeavor were:

In a Minor Key: Negro Youth in Story and Fact, by Ira De A. Reid.

Children of Bondage: The Personality Development of Negro Youth in the Urban South, by Allison Davis and John Dillard.

Negro Youth at the Crossways: Their Personality Development in the Middle States, by E. Franklin Frazier.

Growing Up in the Black Belt: Negro Youth in the Rural South, by Charles S. Johnson.

Color and Human Nature: Negro Personality in a Northern City, by W. Lloyd Warner, Burford H. Juner, and Walter A. Adams.

Since most of these studies were of a pioneering sort, their present value is primarily historical. This is true partly because the changes brought about by the civil rights movement in recent years have altered the emphasis on, if not the substance of, the problem, and partly because modern scientific developments demand more than these qualitatively oriented studies were able to give.

THE SAMPLE

Methodology and Data Collection

The reader of this report should be cautioned that this is not a study of all Negro youth. As a matter of convenience in data collection, only high school students were chosen. This means that youth below the high school level, in college, or in military service are not included.

The present study used as respondents 688 Negro high school students selected from five predominantly Negro high schools in Atlanta, Georgia. The high schools (and the number of students they contributed to our sample) were: Harper (121 students); Howard (146 students); Booker T. Washington (150 students); Archer (159 students); and Price (112 students). These schools are composed of practically all-Negro student bodies comprising the overwhelming majority of Negro high school students in Atlanta.

The questionnaires were distributed by teachers and counselors at the high schools. Every attempt was made to obtain as representative a cross-sectional sample as resources would permit. The questionnaires were self-administered. Their relative completeness was an indication to the research staff that students had little difficulty in interpreting the questions.

Confidence in the representative nature of the sample is supported by the fact that about 25 per cent of the sample came from each of the schools' grades, 9th through 12th. The sex composition in the sample favored females, who comprised about 60 per cent of the total. About 94 per cent of the students in the sample were between 14 and 18 years of age.

Social Characteristics

This section treats some of the social characteristics of the 688 high school students comprising the study group, particularly in terms of place of birth, length of residence in Atlanta, and family characteristics.

The respondents are indigenous to the South. (Only 12 of the students in our sample were born outside of the region.) Most of the respondents were born in Atlanta (about 80 per cent), while an additional 10 per cent were born in Georgia, but not in Atlanta.

In a separate question relating to length of residence in Atlanta, only 24 respondents (3 per cent) indicated that they had lived in Atlanta less than three years, while about 19 percent reported living in the city for more than three years, and about 78 per cent stated that they had resided in Atlanta all their lives. It is clear from these statistics that our respondents are not "outsiders," but are largely Atlanta-born youth looking at themselves, their neighborhoods, and the city which contains them.

When asked "With whom do you live?" 58 per cent of the respondents reported residence with both parents, while the remaining 42 per cent reported living under the following arrangements: 32 per cent with the mother only; 2 per cent with the father only; and 8 per cent with neither parent. In the latter category, residence was divided among the following, in descending order of magnitude: older sister, grandmother, older brother, aunt, grandfather, and uncle.

. . .

When 40 per cent of a group live in family situations which are socially perceived as "abnormal," the whole question of what constitutes a normal family, at least for that group, might well require re-evaluation. Furthermore, it would seem to follow from this that attempts to alter society's view of normative family structure might be a more fruitful approach to social integration (i.e., creating an environment in which black people would assume appropriate roles with relative ease) than is the current approach which emphasizes the need for Negro families to conform to white models.

In response to a question about the main source of family income, only 43 per cent of the sample reported father's income as their principal means of support, 23 per cent indicated mother's income, and 18 per cent stated that both parents' incomes were of equal importance. Small percentages of the students stated that social security (8 per cent), welfare (3 per cent), and "other," such as brother's salary, uncle's salary, etc. (5 per cent), were the family unit's primary source of economic support.

In terms of parental employment patterns, it was found that a higher percentage of the responding students' fathers than mothers were employed, 96 per cent vs. 66 per cent. The data further suggest that of employed parents, mothers were more frequently employed in *low status* occupations than fathers, 67 per cent vs. 56 per cent. (*Low status* occupations were defined, in a most general sense, to include operatives, service workers, domestic workers, common laborers, etc.) Employed fathers were more likely to be in *medium status* occupations than were employed mothers, 32 per cent vs. 16 per cent. (*Medium status* occupations were defined to include clerical, sales, craft, and skilled workers, etc.) Occupations of a *high status* (professional, technical, managerial, etc.) favored employed mothers over employed fathers, 17 per cent vs. 12 per cent.

When asked whether the persons with whom they lived owned (or were buying) their home, 49 per cent of respondents answered in the affirmative, while 51 per cent indicated that their place of residence was being rented. This tends to support our earlier observations concerning the relative stability of the sample population since this percentage of owner-occupied dwellings significantly exceeds the percentage for the non-white population of Atlanta as a whole (which is 38%).

The Neighborhood

We wanted to know how Negro youth evaluate their neighborhoods. A list of facilities and services of concern to every neighborhood was presented to the respondents. They were asked to evaluate the quality of each item on a four-point scale, indicating each as either *very poor, needing some improvement, pretty good, or don't know.*

The responses *very poor* and *needing some improvement* were combined into a single category and considered as a negative evaluation. The facilities and services shown in Table 1 were negatively evaluated by at least one-third of the respondents.

TABLE 1.

NEIGHBORHOOD FACILITIES OR SERVICES EVALUATED AS POOR OR NEEDING IMPROVEMENT BY AT LEAST ONE-THIRD OF THE RESPONDENTS.

Facility or Service	Per cent of respondents indicating facility or service is poor or needs improvement
Recreational facilities	62%
Police protection	52%
Condition of sidewalks	50%
Garbage and trash collection	47%
Cleanliness and appearance	46%
Quality of schools	43%
Condition of streets	43%
Sewers	41%
Crowded conditions	40%
Street lights	35%
Bus service	35%
Parking facilities	34%

. . .

This level of negative reaction to those services, facilities, and conditions which comprise the basic circumstances in which the respondents live would seem to bode ill for the future. Indeed, it is those very conditions which receive least approbation which have appeared to precipitate civil disturbances most frequently in recent years.

. . .

How Negro youth view the entire city is of particular importance to this study for two obvious reasons: (1) Atlanta prides itself on having a very positive image, particularly in the area of race relations; and (2) the Atlanta Negro population is now 45 per cent of the total population of the city and growing steadily. In view of the limited scope of the sample, the responses of the youth in this study may be seen as a moderate forecast of the views of the majority of the future adult population of Atlanta; therefore, their evaluation of the city is both strategic and informative.

A list of 14 aspects of life in the Atlanta community was presented to the respondents. They were asked to rate each on a four-point scale: *poor, fair, good,* or *very good.* Combining the *poor* and *fair* categories, and the *good* and *very good* categories, it was found that the respondents evaluated more items positively than negatively. The per cent of *very good* evaluations was particularly high in regard to the following aspects of the city's life: (1) sports; (2) colleges and universities; (3) moral and religious climate; and (4) public schools.

A more crucial concern to city planning might be the question of what aspects of city life were negatively evaluated by the respondents. Four items were evaluated as *poor* or *fair* by more than 50 per cent of the respondents, the most negatively evaluated in rank order being: (1) race relations, (2) housing, (3) recreation, and (4) police officers. That race relations would be so evaluated by the respondents of this study seems to contradict widely held assumptions about the city's good race relations and the view of Atlanta as "a city too busy to hate." Evidently, these students feel that good race relations are built on more than the *idea* of good race relations.

• • •

How Negro youth view themselves, whether they want to change themselves, their educational aspirations, whom they turn to for advice, and what leadership figures they are familiar with or identify with are important facets of their sub-culture, all having implications for patterns of action and social planning.

Self-Image

In an attempt to assess the respondents' satisfaction with their self-images, they were asked to check, from among four statements, the one which came closest to their feelings about themselves. The statements were:

1. I don't like myself the way I am; I'd like to change completely.
2. There are many things I'd like to change; but not all.
3. There are a few things I'd like to change; but not too many.
4. I'd like to stay very much the same; there is almost nothing I would like to change.

Combining responses to statements 1 and 2 as an index of persons desiring substantial changes in their self-images, and responses to statements 3 and 4 as an indication of respondents desiring few or changes, it was found that 26 per cent of the respondents desired complete or substantial changes in their self-images, while 74 per cent would make few or no changes. Males felt the need for substantial change in their self-images more often than did females, 30 per cent vs. 24 per cent. . . .

Qualities for "Getting Ahead in Life"

What one believes are important qualities for "getting ahead" in life are often clues to his personality and orientation. . . . The respondents were asked, "How important is each of the following items in helping one to 'get ahead' in life?: pleasant personality; family background; good clothes; good looks; being a white person; ability; high ideals; proper morals; friendliness; athletic ability; high grades in school; luck;

TABLE 2.

RESPONSES TO THE QUESTION: "HOW IMPORTANT IS EACH OF THE FOLLOWING QUALITIES IN HELPING ONE TO GET AHEAD IN LIFE?

| | PER CENT OF RESPONDENTS WHO RATED EACH QUALITY AS: | | | | TOTAL | |
Quality	Very Important	Fairly Important	Not too Important	Don't Know	N	%
Pleasant personality	89	6	2	3	664	100
Ability	86	10	3	1	664	"
Friendliness	78	15	5	2	656	"
Proper morals	65	22	7	6	655	"
Grades in school	63	26	8	3	662	"
High ideals	62	26	8	4	661	"
Personal ambition	61	21	13	5	649	"
Family background	37	28	32	3	667	"
Good clothes	20	39	39	2	668	"
Athletic ability	17	25	53	5	655	"
Luck	13	23	58	6	652	"
Being a white person	12	9	69	10	655	"
Good looks	10	19	68	3	662	"
Being "slick"	5	7	73	15	650	"

personal ambition, and being 'slick.' " They were asked to respond on a four-point scale of *very important, fairly important, not too important,* and *don't know.* The response patterns shown in Table 2 are ranked on the basis of the frequency with which each quality was rated as *very important.*

It can be seen that the first seven items were rated as *very important* by 60 per cent or more of the respondents (pleasant personality, 89 per cent; ability, 86 per cent; friendliness, 78 per cent; proper morals, 65 per cent; high grades, 63 per cent; high ideals, 61 per cent; and personal ambition, 61 per cent). Then there is a sudden drop in qualities rated as *very important* with being "slick," good looks, being a white person, luck, and athletic ability assigned relatively low priority. With the exception of personality and reputational concerns, the magnitude of assessment and ranking of items contrasts vividly with similar items endorsed by students in Coleman's *Adolescent Society,* where athletic ability, good looks, and family were important attributes. . . .

Females were more inclined to assign higher priority to proper morals, personal ambition, high ideals, friendliness, and pleasant personality than were males. While males were somewhat more likely to place a higher premium on good clothes, good looks, and athletic ability, it is particularly significant that these latter attributes, frequently assumed to be most highly valued in the youth culture of the ghetto, were consistently rated very low even by the male respondents.

Educational Aspiration

Commonly assumed, but frequently questioned, is the notion that Negro youth have low aspirational levels in terms of education and success orientations. The previous question on qualities *very important* in "getting ahead" indicated that Negro youth rated ability, grades in school, and personal ambition as highly significant priorities in achievement. In this vein, respondents were asked, "Do you plan to go to school after you get out of high school?"

Responses to the above questions suggest a high level of personal aspiration among the respondents: 96 per cent indicated intentions of staying in high school until graduation. Eighty-six per cent of these expect to continue their education beyond high school with nearly half planning to attend college, and the rest to attend various kinds of vocational training institutions. These data suggest that there is nothing lacking in the intentions and aspirations of Negro youth. They have, to borrow a phrase, "Great Expectations." The difficulties in actual achievement must be sought among other realities of the social system; e.g., economic organization, reference group support, opportunity structures, etc.

Sources of Advice and Identification

To whom does one turn for advice? With whom does one identify? These are important factors in anyone's patterns of orientation; they provide cues to action, commitment, and personal anchorage for ideological and economic support and comfort.

In response to the question, "Whom do you usually turn to for advice?" "mother" and "friend(s) of same age" were most frequently cited. (See Table 3.) These were followed in frequency by both par-

TABLE 3.

RESPONSES TO THE QUESTION: "TO WHOM DO YOU USUALLY TURN
FOR ADVICE," BY SEX.

Source of Advice	PER CENT OF RESPONDENTS WHO REPORTED SEEKING ADVICE FROM EACH SOURCE*		
	All respondents (%)	Male (%)	Female (%)
Mother	57	53	60
Personal Friend(s) of same age	45	33	52
Both parents	31	36	27
Older friend(s)	29	26	31
School personnel	29	33	26
Other relatives	29	26	30
Father	12	17	9
Minister	12	14	11

*Percentages do not total 100% because respondents were asked to report as many sources of advice as were appropriate.

ents, older friend(s), school personnel, other relative(s), father, and minister. The dominance of the mother figure as a source of advice should not lead one to assume that this is simply due to the matricentric nature of the Negro family, though nearly a third of the respondents live with mother only. Given the expressive nature of her role, we would expect the mother to be a principal source of advice in many two-parent families. The position of "friend(s) of same age" likewise should not be interpreted along racial lines, but is consistent with the notion that a youth sub-culture exists in which support and comfort from one's peer group are important components.

In addition to the fact that mothers and personal friends were the most frequently cited sources of advice, and fathers and ministers were the least cited sources, some interesting variations by sex of respondents were found. Male respondents more frequently indicated a wider range of sources of advice than did females. Also, a higher per cent of males than females cited "father," "both parents," "school personnel," and "minister" as sources of advice, whereas a higher per cent of females cited "friend(s) of same age," "mother," and "older friend(s)."

The attitudes of youth in America might turn out to be the most crucial predictor for the nature and direction of social change. Many of the recent reform and revolutionary movements in the world have heavily involved youth, who have often been among the principal architects and initiators of change. Youth are now receiving a type of exposure and recognition which has no direct counterpart in earlier periods of history. They are being heard in popular art, the "hippie" movement, peace politics, and civil rights. The latter aspect of contemporary change and the attitudes of Negro youth toward it is the principal concern of this report, for it is here that Negro youth have made their presence felt most strongly.

Racial Attitudes

Respondents were asked to express agreement or disagreement with a number of statements assessing their attitudes toward certain problems of race and race-related behavior, shown in Table 4.

. . .

A separatist philosophy does not appear to be the dominant theme for the respondents. Most of them are not strong believers in "black power," nor do they think the situation would be improved if Negroes were more separated from whites. The fact that 21 per cent of the respondents felt that "sometimes Negroes ought to carry guns when protesting," and 22 per cent felt that "civil rights demonstrations do not accomplish anything," might suggest that Negro youth opinion is in a transitional phase and that, all else being equal, a similar question in the future might well elicit more militant views. However, the extent to which the respondents reported willingness to participate in a riot is still comparatively small, about 8 per cent. This figure is smaller than that reported by William Brink and Louis Harris, where 15 per cent of the total rank and file of the Negro population "would join a riot."[1]

Responses to the statement, "White people can usually be trusted," are a partial index of the limited extent to which black youth have faith in whites. Whereas 30 per cent responded "don't know," 45 per cent of the respondents do *not* feel that whites can usually be trusted. Upper class Negroes fare much better in this regard, as indicated by

---

[1]William Brink and Louis Harris, *Black and White* (New York: Simon and Schuster, 1966), p. 67.

the fact that only 15 per cent of the respondents believed that they "usually cannot be trusted."

•   •   •

The possibility of future disturbances of a riotous nature is suggested by 53 per cent of the respondents, who agreed with the statement, "If things don't get better in Atlanta, there will be riots." Similar conclusions are being reached in a number of other American cities.

An analysis by sex categories of the responses to the statements in Table 4 revealed that the younger male respondent is more militant

TABLE 4.

RESPONSES TO STATEMENTS CONCERNING SELECTED PROBLEMATIC ASPECTS OF RACE AND RACE-RELATED BEHAVIOR.

Statements Concerning Race-Related Problems and Behavior	REACTION OF RESPONDENTS BY PER CENT EXPRESSING:			TOTAL	
	(%) Disagreement	(%) Agreement	(%) No Opinion	N	%
1. The more Negroes are separated from whites the better	76	12	12	664	100
2. I am a strong believer in "Black Power"	73	11	16	667	"
3. I would participate in a riot	69	8	23	672	"
4. Sometimes Negroes ought to carry guns when protesting	63	21	16	674	"
5. Civil Rights demonstrations do not accomplish anything	58	22	20	678	"
6. "Upper class" Negroes are usually not to be trusted	56	15	29	678	"
7. Black Americans should be proud to be fighting in Vietnam	49	31	20	669	"
8. White people can usually be trusted	45	25	30	675	"
9. I blame whites for riots in Atlanta	40	25	35	672	"
10. I blame Negro agitators for riots in Atlanta	39	25	36	667	"
11. I blame police brutality for riots in Atlanta	33	35	32	677	"
12. Non-violence is always the best approach for Negroes to use	30	51	19	675	"
13. I blame poor economic and social conditions of Negroes as cause of riots in Atlanta	25	48	27	669	"
14. I blame bad race relations for riots in Atlanta	19	64	17	665	"
15. If things don't get better in Atlanta, there will be riots	19	53	28	676	"

and separatist in his racial stance than older males or females. Since this was not the dominant stance for the total group, and since the significance of the maturation process in this regard is unmeasured, implications for future orientations of Negro youth cannot be determined by this study, however provocative the data may seem.

. . .

The dominant approaches to the problems faced by Negroes are still educational, legalistic and nonviolent, with a third or more of the respondents also endorsing more dramatic forms of activity, such as street demonstrations, sit-ins, economic boycotts, and rent strikes. The least favorably endorsed approach or idea was riots (12 per cent).

. . .

SOME RELIGIOUS CONCERNS

No questions were asked about the religious affiliation of the respondents. Traditional evidence and the number and type of Negro churches in the Atlanta community would tend to suggest that the respondents are likely to have Baptist or Methodist affiliations.

. . .

The respondents were also asked to react to statements about the church and religion. Many of the statements were drawn from current controversies in church circles, i.e., "Is the church on the decline?"; "Is God dead?"; "Is the church too old-fashioned?" etc.

Responses to these statements suggest that the church is still a powerful personal force in the lives of Negro youth; however, the respondents believe that "the church ought to be more concerned about social problems."

Some ambivalence was noted in responses to a question about the decline of the church as indicated by the fact that an equal number of respondents stated that they *agree, disagree,* and *don't know* that the influence of the church in America is on the wane. Similarly, the majority of respondents did not know whether the white man takes his religion seriously or not; but when asked to react to the statement, "The Negro does not take his religion seriously," a majority of the respondents disagreed (54 per cent).

Evaluated in a negative sense were the statements which read, "The church is too old-fashioned for me" (91 per cent disagreeing); "Sometimes I feel God is dead" (83 per cent disagreeing); "When I have a problem my pastor is one of the first persons I turn to" (76 per cent disagreeing); and "I am neither for nor against the church" (70 per cent disagreeing).

From the above statements, it would appear that the respondents are fairly religious; yet, they do not feel that the pastor is a principal source of advice, an attitude indicated by the earlier findings on personal sources of advice.

The data may suggest the existence of a certain amount of ambivalence in the students' feelings toward the church, especially in light of the fact that statements expressing general positive attitudes about God and religion tended to be accepted more readily than statements relating to the institutional church or to clergymen.

SUMMARY

This study has attempted to assess the attitudes, values and opinions of Negro youth in a wide range of areas. While a more narrowly focused study would have permitted a fuller evaluation of any given aspect, the remarkable dearth of information available made a general survey seem imperative. Additionally, the unusually crucial role played by young people in the development and elaboration of normative values in our society and the high correlation which exists among seemingly disparate elements of our culture effectively preclude the possibility of concentrating attention on isolated factors.

This study, then, not only presents data relating to concerns of particularly timely interest, such as perception of the urban environment, evaluation of racial problems, attitudes toward civil rights organizations and approaches, and deviant behavior, but also attempts to assess other crucial dimensions of the subculture of Negro youth; e.g., religious concerns, self-images, aspirations, and sources of advice and identification.

The Aged Negro and His Income

MOLLIE ORSHANSKY

IN OUR WORK-ORIENTED SOCIETY THE AGED, AS A GROUP NO LONGER earning their living, suffer much lower income status than do the rest of us. So too, but for other reasons, does the population of nonwhite persons, whatever their age. The aged Negro, thus doubly disadvantaged, has resources far below the high levels generally prevailing in our affluent economy. On the other hand, thanks to old-age, survivors, and disability insurance and other public programs that help support so many persons aged 65 or more, the Negro in his old age may find his income more closely approximating that of his white fellow American than often was the case during his working years.

Public programs are administered without respect to race and, though limited in what they pay, are relatively more generous to the aged whose previous earnings were lowest or whose current need is greatest. In contrast, earned income of young families is not balanced, nor is there yet adequate public provision for those who may be in need — not even to the limited extent that there is for the aged. Accordingly the Negro family, though larger than the white, generally must get along on little better than half as much income. The Negro man earns little more than half the employed white worker, even when both work full time. Among those aged 65 and older, however, the nonwhite couples average two-thirds as much income as do the white couples and nonmarried nonwhite persons about three-fourths the income of white persons. By and large, racial differences in income are less among aged persons drawing old-age, survivors, and disability insurance benefits than among those not benefiting from this income-support program.

To be sure, the Negro in old age does not lose the underprivileged economic status of his younger years: Simply because he fares somewhat better, he does not fare well. It is perhaps not so much that his

Reprinted by permission of the publisher and author from *Social Security Bulletin* (February 1964), pp. 3-13.

lot improves as that the income of the generally more fortunate drops proportionately more in retirement than does his own.

Like all persons with low lifetime earnings the Negro enters upon retirement with little savings, more often than not without an owned home, and with little else in the way of private pensions or other resources to add to any public program benefits to which he is entitled. Indeed, for the aged Negro as for many white persons, his poverty does not come upon him newly as an affliction of later life except for special exigencies, such as an increased need for medical care. Rather, he brings it with him as a logical sequence of what has gone before. And while an expanded social insurance program increasingly operates to afford him an opportunity equal with that of the white worker to qualify for an old-age, survivors, and disability insurance benefit, this program alone cannot cancel the long-standing wage and employment differences that result in a smaller benefit. He is accordingly three times as likely as the aged white American to receive public assistance — an assistance incidentally not so readily available in younger years at times of even greater need.

What the social insurance program can and does do is to give the lower-paid worker — and consequently the Negro — benefits representing a larger portion of earlier earnings.

The income of the average white worker is more sharply reduced in retirement than the income of the Negro worker, thus drawing the two groups closer together in the common bond of stringency.

THE AGED NONWHITE POPULATION

At the end of 1962, persons aged 65 or older in the United States numbered about 17½ million, of whom nearly 1½ million or 8 percent were nonwhite. Although in a few States the majority of these nonwhite persons were of Japanese, Indian, or other minority races, for the country as a whole and in most geographic areas more than 90 percent of the nonwhite population was Negro. Most of the statistics cited in this article apply to the total nonwhite population rather than to the Negro population alone. (Unless otherwise indicated the terms Negro and nonwhite are used here interchangeably.)

Because of their shorter life expectancy and a considerably higher marriage disruption rate, fewer Negroes aged 65 and over than white persons of that age are still married and living with a spouse. The differences are particularly striking among the women (table 1). Considerably more of the Negro women have no husband's income to count on in old age, just as many more of them than of white women —

according to other data — have earlier lacked a husband's income while raising their children. Because of their inferior earning capacity, more Negro men than white men never marry and so face retirement and old age alone, with no possibility of turning to a wife or grown children to ease health care or financial stress.

INCOME OF AGED NONWHITE POPULATION

Data are only now becoming available from the 1963 Survey of the Aged made by the Social Security Administration. They show that half the nonwhite married couples aged 65 or older had money income in 1962 totaling less than $1,960. This median represented two-thirds that of white couples. Among nonmarried persons — that is, persons widowed, separated, divorced, or never married — median income of nonwhite persons was four-fifths that of the white population among men and three-fourths among women (table 2).

These incomes are not large. Only among the white couples could a majority be said to have an amount sufficient for independent living in terms of a "modest but adequate" level of living as defined by the Bureau of Labor Statistics: for an elderly couple about $2,500 a year

TABLE 1

MARITAL STATUS OF POPULATION AGED 65 OR OVER, BY
RACE AND SEX, MARCH 1962

Marital status	MEN		WOMEN	
	White	Nonwhite	White	Nonwhite
Number (in thousands)	7,087	623	8,818	702
Total percent	100	100	100	100
Never-married	6	9	7	3
Married, spouse present	72	55	37	24
Widowed	18	31	52	65
Separated, divorced, other	4	4	3	7

Source: Bureau of the Census, *Current Population Reports*, Series P-20, No. 122, March 1963.

and for an aged person without a spouse about $1,800, even with allowance for the reduced costs resulting from home ownership and the somewhat lower cost of living in the smaller communities in which many older persons live. Almost none of the non-married Negro women not getting old-age, survivors, and disability insurance benefits and only 1 in 8 of those who did receive such benefits could be considered economically independent by this standard.

TABLE 2

TOTAL MONEY INCOME IN 1962 OF POPULATION AGED 65 AND OVER: PERCENTAGE DISTRIBUTION OF INCOME OF OASDI BENEFICIARIES AND NONBENEFICIARIES, BY RACE, SEX, AND MARITAL STATUS

White

Total money income	MARRIED COUPLES			NONMARRIED MEN			NONMARRIED WOMEN		
	Total[1]	OASDI beneficiaries[2]	Non-beneficiaries	Total	OASDI beneficiaries[2]	Non-beneficiaries	Total	OASDI beneficiaries[2]	Non-beneficiaries
Total number (in thousands)	5,023	3,496	993	2,132	1,361	677	5,857	3,213	2,298
Number reporting income	4,333	3,062	820	1,930	1,266	574	5,075	2,819	1,952
Percent	100.0	100.0	100.0	100.0	100.0	100.0	100.0	100.0	100.0
Under $1,000	4.4	3.9	7.8	30.0	25.1	43.7	47.4	38.5	63.0
$1,000-1,999	21.6	23.3	20.1	37.7	45.0	24.0	33.9	41.8	21.9
2,000-2,999	25.0	29.5	11.3	16.9	20.1	10.3	10.4	12.0	7.4
3,000-3,999	16.1	16.1	11.6	5.5	5.6	4.4	3.3	2.9	3.1
4,000-4,999	10.9	11.0	9.9	3.2	2.0	4.0	1.5	1.5	1.5
5,000-9,999	16.4	12.9	26.7	5.7	1.7	12.5	3.1	2.9	2.7
10,000 and over	5.6	3.3	12.7	.7	.5	1.4	.4	.4	.4
Median income	$2,955	$2,765	$3,920	$1,390	$1,390	$1,240	$1,060	$1,275	$775

Total number (in thousands)	422	247	127	270	129	126	472	201	245
Number reporting income	386	227	112	243	119	1-1	461	195	240
Percent	100.0	100.0	100.0	100.0	100.0	100.0	100.0	100.0	100.0
Under $1,000	10.1	6.2	22.3	45.7	37.8	60.4	68.5	52.3	85.0
1,000-1,999	41.2	39.2	43.8	30.9	49.6	14.4	28.0	41.0	15.0
2,000-2,999	22.3	33.5	3.6	10.3	11.8	5.4	2.8	5.6	0
3,000-3,999	13.0	10.1	15.2	5.8	1.7	5.4	.4	1.0	0
4,000-4,999	8.0	4.8	11.6	2.5	0	5.4	0	0	0
5,000 and over	5.2	5.7	3.6	4.5	0	9.0	0	0	0
Median income:									
Amount	$1,960	$2,105	$1,500	$1,100	$1,180	$865	$795	$956	$665
As percent of median for white aged	66	76	38	79	85	70	75	75	86

[1] Includes two groups not shown separately—all beneficiaries whose benefits started during 1962, and a small number with benefits starting earlier who had entitled children or whose own entitlement was as the parent of a deceased worker.

[2] Benefits starting before 1962. Among married couples, either or both spouses may have received benefits.

Source: Social Security Administration, 1963 Survey of the Aged.

83

What is striking about the figures, however, is not that the Negro incomes are so low but that they are relatively high. Data obtained by the Bureau of the Census in its annual income survey for the same year indicate a median income for all non-white families only half that observed among white families — a ratio that has prevailed for several years. For persons living alone or with nonrelatives — most of them nonmarried and nearly 40 percent aged 65 or older — the nonwhite group has a median income two-thirds that of white persons.[1]

What do these differences imply? When the aged generally have incomes lower than the rest of the population, how is it that the nonwhite aged seem better off in relation to white aged persons than the total nonwhite population is in comparison with the white?

Available data supply one answer. With his lower educational attainment and the ensuing occupational stricture, with a discrimination in the marketplace that leaves him earning less than his fellow American even when educational levels are the same, and subjected to greater risk of unemployment throughout a lifetime, the Negro and his family must suffer relatively low-income status as long as they depend on earnings for their main source of support.

As tables 2-4 show, it is among the aged for whom earnings are still the main source of income that the relative position of the Negro is least favorable. It is in the groups relying largely on some type of public program that the Negro does best.

Among all nonbeneficiary couples, for example, 3 out of 5 had a member working some time during 1962. Payments from assistance, veterans', and other public programs made up a fifth of total income for the white couples and a third for the nonwhite couples not receiving old-age, survivors, and disability insurance benefits. Earnings accounted for substantially more than three-fifths of income for both groups. The nonwhite couples had on the average, however, earnings equal to only 35 percent of the amount earned by the white couples, and their median total income ($1,500) was only 38 percent of that for white couples.

By contrast, for nonmarried men who were old-age, survivors, and disability insurance beneficiaries it was not earnings but their benefits — together with payments from other programs — that were the chief source of support. Only 1 in 4 reported earnings of any kind, and earnings accounted, all told, for only about a seventh of their income.

---

[1]Bureau of the Census, *Current Population Reports*, Series P-60, No. 41, October 1963.

The median income of the nonwhite beneficiaries in this group was $1,180 or 85 percent of that for the white beneficiaries.

As members of yet another aged group for whom earnings are commonly not the primary resource, nonwhite nonmarried women who were not beneficiaries also achieved a high degree of income parity; their median income was 86 percent of that for white women in a similar situation. To be sure, neither group had very much; half the white women had less than $775, and half the nonwhite women less than $665. Altogether, only a fourth of the total money income of the white group and an eighth of that of the nonwhite came from employment. Public assistance alone accounted for 70 percent of the income received by nonwhite married women, who seldom owned any income-producing assets. Among white women, assets produced about a fourth of the year's income, and public assistance an almost equal share.

Nonmarried women generally relied much more heavily on public assistance than other aged persons, and the nonwhite aged, regardless of marital status or beneficiary status under old-age, survivors, and disability insurance, relied more heavily on public assistance for support than did the white aged (table 3). Among nonmarried Negro women, every other one received assistance at some time during the year. For those with no old-age, survivors, and disability benefits, the number receiving assistance rose to 3 out of 5, but even among the insurance beneficiaries 1 in 3 required some supplementation of benefits.

The effect of chronic low income on capacity for self-support in old age is indicated also by the relatively few Negroes who had assets from which they derived income. About a fourth of the couples and a sixth of the nonmarried persons received income in the form of interest, dividends, or rents. Among the white aged, two-thirds of the couples and about half the nonmarried reported such income.

Data on homeownership and living arrangements from the survey are not yet available by race. But it will come as no surprise that the *Decennial Census of* 1960 shows relatively fewer of the Negro aged enjoying the benefit of homeownership and relatively more living in housing units needing repair or without adequate facilities. Among all white households with an aged head, 70 percent owned their home, compared with 54 percent of the nonwhite households. More than a fourth of the units rented by nonwhite households and almost a fifth of those owned were described as dilapidated — that is, housing that " . . . in its present condition endangers the health, safety or well-being of the occupants." Among the white households headed by an aged person, only 3 percent

TABLE 3

Sources of Income in 1962 of Population Aged 65 and over: Percentage with Income from Selected Sources for OASDI Beneficiaries and Nonbeneficiaries, by Race, Sex, and Marital Status

White

Source of money income	Married couples			Nonmarried men			Nonmarried women		
	Total[1]	OASDI beneficiaries[2]	Nonbeneficiaries	Total	OASDI beneficiaries[2]	Nonbeneficiaries	Total	OASDI beneficiaries[2]	Nonbeneficiaries
Total population	100	100	100	100	100	100	100	100	100
Earnings	54	49	64	27	24	29	23	26	16
Retirement benefits	85	100	27	75	100	16	66	100	12
OASDI	80	100		68	100		61	100	
Other public programs	12	8	25	8	5	15	8	5	11
Private group pensions	17	21	3	10	13	2	4	5	1
Veterans' benefits	14	14	14	11	11	12	6	7	6
Interest, dividends, rents	66	67	67	48	52	37	53	59	41
Private individual annuities	4	4	5	1	2	1	3	4	2
Unemployment insurance	3	2	2	1	1	(3)	1	1	(3)
Public assistance	6	5	10	16	9	32	15	7	27
Contributions by relatives[4]	2	3	3	2	2	1	6	5	8
Payment under any public program	89	100	45	87	100	57	78	100	42

Nonwhite

Total population								
100	100	100	100	100	100	100	100	100
Earnings	62	60	60	35	28	41	22	26	16

Total population	100	100	100	100	100	100	100	100	100
Earnings	62	60	60	35	28	41	22	26	16
Retirement benefits	73	100	10	61	100	13	50	100	4
OASDI	70	100		55	100		48	100	
Other public programs	10	10	10	8	6	9	2	2	3
Private group pensions	4	5			9	3			1
Veterans' benefits	14	15	14	14	15	13	5	6	3
Interest, dividends, rents	27	30	26	22	22	20	13	15	10
Private individual annuities	(²)	1			2	(³)			
Unemployment insurance	3	2					1	2	
Public assistance	30	26	40	32	19	48	48	35	61
Contributions by relatives[4]	5	4	5	1			8	4	11
Payment under any public program	88	100	60	85	100	68	82	100	66

[1] See table 2, footnote 1.
[2] See table 2, footnote 2.
[3] Less than 0.5 percent.
[4] Relatives or friends not living in households with aged unit.

Source: Social Security Administration, 1963 Survey of the Aged.

87

TABLE 4

INCOME IN 1962 OF POPULATION AGED 65 AND OVER: SHARES OF AGGREGATE INCOME FROM DESIGNATED SOURCES FOR OASDI BENEFICIARIES AND NONBENEFICIARIES, BY RACE, SEX, AND MARITAL STATUS

White

Source of money income	MARRIED COUPLES			NONMARRIED MEN			NONMARRIED WOMEN		
	Total[1]	OASDI bene-ficiaries[2]	Non-bene-ficiaries	Total	OASDI bene-ficiaries[2]	Non-bene-ficiaries	Total	OASDI bene-ficiaries[2]	Non-bene-ficiaries
Total percent	100	100	100	100	100	100	100	100	100
Earnings	39	25	69	27	14	46	19	15	24
Retirement benefits	39	49	13	45	64	16	39	53	11
OASDI	28	39		34	54		33	48	
Other public programs	7	4	13	7	4	14	5	3	10
Private group pensions	4	6	(3)	4	6	2	1	2	1
Veterans' benefits	3	4	3	6	6	7	4	3	5
Interest, dividends, rents	15	17	10	13	13	14	20	18	25
Public assistance	1	1	3	6	2	15	9	3	24
Contributions by relatives[4]	(3)	(3)	(3)	(3)	(3)		2	2	4
Other	3	3	2	2	2	3	6	6	8

88

Nonwhite

Total percent	100	100	100	100	100	100	100	100	100
Earnings	38	29	63	36	12	58	15	18	12
Retirement benefits	41	54	5	37	68	6	36	56	4
OASDI	34	46		30	61		34	55	
Other public programs	6	6	5	4	2	6	2	1	3
Private group pensions	1	2		3	5	(3)	(2)		(1)
Veterans' benefits	5	7	6	3	9	8	4	4	4
Interest, dividends, rents	3	2	3	8	4	1	3	3	3
Public assistance	11	7	23	14	5	24	37	16	70
Contributions by relatives[4]	1	1	(3)	2	1	3	2	1	3
Other	1	1	(3)	2	1	3	3	1	6

[1]See table 2, footnote 1.
[2]See table 2, footnote 2.
[3]Less than 0.5 percent.

[4]See table 3, footnote 4.
Source: Social Security Administration, 1963 Survey of the Aged.

89

of the owned units and 6 percent of those rented were classed as dilapidated.

Because old people in general continue to live on in quarters they have occupied for some time, the inferior housing status of the Negro aged is undoubtedly a continuation of earlier disadvantage rather than solely a reflection of currently inadequate income.

THE INCOME LIFE CYCLE

There appears to be a difference in the ebb and flow of income for Negroes and for white persons, a gap that seems to widen with age as both groups must depend primarily on earned income. Only when, in old age, the weekly pay check is replaced by the monthly benefit from a retirement or income-maintenance program does the gap close somewhat and then only in current income — not in the additional resources that can help stretch the lower income of retirement to a more comfortable level of living.

To compare the cycles of income receipt for Negroes and white persons, it would be desirable to do a cohort analysis — that is, to follow individuals for a period of years from youth to old age. Such data are not generally available. In their absence one can examine cross-sectional patterns — that is, differences by age and race for all persons in the population at a given time. It is not likely that these differences by age accurately represent the fluctuations that the average person experiences as he lives out his allotted span. But it is also not likely that the two paths will be totally unrelated, the more so since the cross-sectional differences between the Negro and the white population are so marked. Sufficient evidence exists to suggest that, just as childhood deprivation often presages proverty in the adult, so the low-income status of the adult during his working years presages his low-income status in old age. The child is the father of the man, even unto age 65 and beyond, and in large measure the inadequate income of our aged Negro is the carry-over from the poverty of his youth.

Because it is the man who is assumed to be the chief family breadwinner and because the married woman depending solely on a husband's earnings must either be reported as having zero income or be assigned some arbitrary proportion of her husband's income — both somewhat unrealistic assumptions — it is the income pattern of white and nonwhite men that is given primary attention.

Generally speaking, nonwhite men are less likely to be in the labor force than white men; they have increasingly less earning power than white men as they grow older; and they suffer higher unemployment rates, particularly at the younger ages. According to the *Decennial Census of 1960* the median income of nonwhite men dropped steadily, from 57 percent that of white men at ages 20-24 to 45 percent for men aged 55-64. But at age 65 and over, when only a minority are in the labor force, the nonwhite median income rises to 51 percent of the white (table 5).

The higher unemployment rate among Negro men — more than twice that among white men — persists even at the older ages, when relatively few are in the labor force (table 6). Inasmuch as most men — and their families — before they reach age 65 rely on earnings as their prime source of income, a comparison of such earnings for white and nonwhite men is of interest. Paralleling the pattern already noted for total income is the ratio of nonwhite to white earnings in a year for the experienced male labor force — that is, all men except those who are seeking work for the first time and who have not yet found it. The young nonwhite male worker's median earnings in 1959 at age 18-24 represented 61 percent of white median earnings, and at age 55-64 only 56 percent of that median (table 7).

For all nonwhite male workers the median earnings in 1962 represented 55 percent that of the white[2] and were only 63 percent even when restricted to persons working the year around in full-time jobs. This is more or less the same degree of income parity, or lack of it, that has prevailed for a number of years.

TABLE 5.

Money Income in 1959 of Men Aged 20 and Over, by Race and Age

Age	Percent with less than $2,000		Median income		Nonwhite as percent of white
	White	Nonwhite	White	Nonwhite	
20-24	41	63	$2,530	$1,435	57
25-34	12	36	4,970	2,740	55
35-44	10	32	5,615	3,050	54
45-54	15	39	5,220	2,635	50
55-64	23	50	4,420	1,985	45
65 and over	58	80	1,725	885	51

Source: *U.S. Census of Population, 1960: Detailed Characteristics,* PC(1)-1D.

The pattern of earnings over a work-life span differs with occupation, and occupations that permit considerable gain in earnings for a worker

---

[2]Bureau of the Census, *Current Population Reports,* Series P-60, No. 41.

as he gains experience — such as the professional, technical, and kindred callings or management of a nonfarm business — are less readily available to the Negro worker than to the white man. In 1962, for example, 13 percent of all employed white men were in professional

TABLE 6.

CIVILIAN LABOR-FORCE PARTICIPATION RATES AND UNEMPLOYMENT RATES IN 1962, BY RACE, AGE, AND SEX

Age	PERCENT IN LABOR FORCE				UNEMPLOYMENT RATE			
	Men		Women		Men		Women	
	White	Non-white	White	Non-white	White	Non-white	White	Non-white
14 and over	79	76	36	46	5	11	6	11
14-19	41	38	30	24	12	21	12	28
20-24	86	89	47	49	8	15	8	18
25-34	97	95	34	52	4	10	5	12
35-44	98	94	42	60	3	9	4	9
45-54	96	92	49	60	4	8	4	7
55-64	87	82	38	46	4	10	4	4
65 and over	31	27	10	12				

Source: "Economic Status of Nonwhite Workers, 1955-62," (Special Labor Force Report No. 33), *Monthly Labor Review,* July 1963.

and technical positions, and 16 percent were classed as nonfarm managers, officials, and proprietors. Among the Negro employed men, by contrast, only 4 percent were in each of these two broad occupational groups.

Indeed, as has been well-documented, even when the Negro achieves such occupational status, he is not likely to get the pay envelope that should go with it.

As reported by Herman Miller of the Bureau of the Census, the Negro has considerably lower occupational status than the white worker, and in most States there has been little improvement in this respect in the past 20 years. Even when compared only with white workers having the same years of schooling, the nonwhite worker can look forward to earning about half as much during his lifetime as his white fellow. What is more, the Negro who has gone to college does relatively worse rather than better, as the following figures show:[3]

[3]Statement before Subcommittee on Employment and Manpower, U.S. Senate Subcommittee on Labor and Public Welfare, July 31, 1963.

Highest grade completed	Nonwhite lifetime earnings as percent of white
Total	51
Elementary school :	
Less than 8 years	61
8 years	64
High school:	
1-3 years	60
4 years	60
College:	
1-3 years	54
4 years	47
5 years or more	53

These figures imply in financial terms a difference ranging from $60,000 over a lifetime for those with the least education to $220,000 for those with 5 years or more of college training.

Of all nonwhite men who were employed during 1962, about 4 out of every 10 were working in jobs as service workers or as nonfarm laborers — jobs that often pay so little, even to a white worker, as to jeopardize the adequate support of a family.

THE ROLE OF OASDI

The Social Security Act of 1935, formulated in the throes of a great depression, was designed to meet certain immediate needs and to help prevent want and dependency. Over the years the programs have become more inclusive in the risks met and the population covered, but protection in old age against loss of income from earnings remains in sheer numbers the most extensive assignment.

Adults in their declining years, particularly those beset with the infirmities of old age, need money to replace the earnings that have stopped because they or those who once supported them no longer work. And the possibility of self-support in old age, once merely a promise, is now looked to by most workers as a cherished right. Currently, 70 percent of the 19 million persons aged 65 or older are receiving monthly benefits, and 9 out of 10 workers are in jobs that make it possible to earn the right to a retirement benefit. Old-age, survivors, and disability insurance has thus become the principal income-support program for the aged.

By definition, social security programs are for all the people, to be administered without reference to race, color, or creed. Hence only a

TABLE 7.

MEDIAN EARNINGS OF EXPERIENCED CIVILIAN MALE LABOR FORCE IN 1959, BY RACE AND AGE, AND NONWHITE EARNINGS AS A PERCENT OF WHITE EARNINGS

| Age | MEDIAN EARNINGS | | | EARNINGS INDEX (MEDIAN FOR WHITE WORKERS AT AGES 35-44 = 100) | |
	White	Nonwhite	Nonwhite as percent of white	White	Nonwhite
18-24	$2,604	$1,584	61	46	28
25-34	5,102	3,004	59	90	53
35-44	5,657	3,332	59	100	59
45-54	5,317	2,966	56	94	52
55-64	4,802	2,678	56	85	47

Source: *U.S. Census of Population, 1960: Occupation by Earnings and Education,* PC(2)-7B.

limited number of program statistics by race are available on a regular basis since they are not normally relevant to program operations.

In the early days of the social security program, the exclusion of farm labor, domestic service, and certain other types of work from the system meant that relatively fewer Negroes than white persons could share in the protection offered. Furthermore, because of his typically lower earnings, the Negro beneficiary generally received lower benefits than the white beneficiary.

The 1950, 1954, and 1956 amendments removed most of the restrictions from coverage. These liberalizations, as well as the accelerated movement of the Negro from farm work into city jobs, mean that more and more Negroes have a stake in the old-age, survivors, and disability insurance program.

By the end of 1962, of the 12½ million persons aged 65 or older who were drawing old-age, survivors, and disability insurance benefits, 6 percent were nonwhite. In the total aged population as of the same date, 8 percent were nonwhite. All told, 3 out of 5 nonwhite aged persons were receiving benefits, compared with 3 out of 4 white persons. Despite this disparity, there has been considerable and steady improvement since the early days of the program, as the following percentages show.

Date	Aged population Receiving OASDI	
	White	Nonwhite
December of—		
1945	8	4
1950	21	13
1955	45	30
1960	67	49
1961	70	53
1962	73	58

For obvious reasons, both white and Negro persons just reaching retirement age are more likely to qualify for a benefit than those already well past age 65. The difference is particularly striking for Negro women: Those women who are aged 65-69 are four and one-half times as likely to receive insurance benefits as those who are aged 85 or over. It is of interest also that Negro men, with their high unemployment rate, have taken advantage of the recent option of retirement at age 62 with a reduced benefit to a greater extent than white men (table 8).

From the 1963 Survey of the Aged made by the Social Security Administration it is possible to compare beneficiary rates by marital status, as well as by race. Among the white population aged 65 or older, those receiving old-age, survivors, and disability insurance benefits represented 80 percent of the married couples, 70 percent of the nonmarried men, and 61 percent of the nonmarried women. Among the nonwhite population, the corresponding beneficiary rates were 70 percent, 55 percent, and 48 percent.

The differences among the women are particularly significant because the nonwhite woman, as we have seen, is more likely to be nonmarried

TABLE 8.

PERCENT OF POPULATION AGED 62 AND OVER WITH OASDI BENEFITS IN CURRENT-PAYMENT STATUS ON DECEMBER 31, 1962, BY AGE, RACE, AND SEX

Age	Total	White			Nonwhite		
		Total	Male	Female	Total	Male	Female
62-64	39	39	25	50	39	35	42
65 and over	72	73	76	70	58	66	51
65-69	72	73	68	76	66	68	63
70-74	80	82	85	79	62	71	54
75-76	74	76	84	69	55	65	46
80-84	62	63	77	54	42	56	31
85 and over	40	41	57	31	25	39	14

— that is, minus a husband — by the time she reaches age 65. Hence if she does not qualify for a benefit in her own right through her own work record, she may well have to look to public assistance. And in fact, as the survey findings reveal, in large measure she does. Thus, despite the program liberalizations and the large-scale movement of the Negro from agriculture to industry, there still remain a substantial number of nonwhite persons (mostly women) whose own work life — or that of the persons on whom they depended for support — did not qualify them for the dignity of old-age, survivors, and disability insurance benefits in old age.

For those aged women who do draw benefits under the Social Security Act, the type of benefit received reflects clearly the difference in marital status and work cycles of the nonwhite and the white woman. With or without children, to supplement the low earnings of her husband or because she herself acts as the head of a family, the Negro woman during her lifetime participates in the labor force to a greater degree than the white woman.

As one example, among Negro women with husband present and with the youngest child between the ages of 3 and 6, every other mother is in the labor force, the same ratio as among Negro wives with no children under age 18. Among white women with husband present, only 1 in 4 mothers with the youngest child over age 3 but under age 6 is in the labor force, and only 35 percent are working, even when there are no children under age 18.[4]

Although among women aged 65 or older the proportion who are widows is a fourth higher for Negroes than for white women, the proportion drawing old-age, survivors, and disability insurance benefits as a worker's widow is a fifth less among Negroes than among the white women, and the proportion drawing a benefit as a worker — that is, on her own wage record — is a fourth greater. Aged women with benefits in current-payment status on December 31, 1962, were distributed by type of beneficiary as follows:

Type of beneficiary	White	Nonwhite
Total	100	100
Retired worker	45	57
Wife of retired worker	30	23
Aged widow	24	19
Other	1	1

[4]See "Marital and Family Characteristics of Workers, March 1962," Special Labor Force Report No. 26, *Monthly Labor Review*, January 1963.

For workers of both sexes, the generally lower earnings of Negroes mean that when they do draw old-age, survivors, and disability insurance benefits, they receive less than white workers. Because the benefit formula is more generous to workers with low earnings, however, the nonwhite beneficiaries receive more both in terms of what they and their employers have paid into the system and as a proportion of the wages replaced.

Thus the average monthly benefits of $69 to the nonwhite retired male worker and $51 to the woman were about four-fifths the average checks ($86 and $65) going to retired white workers. Indeed, for all types of benefit combined, the average payment to an aged nonwhite beneficiary was four-fifths that going to a white beneficiary. By contrast, in 1958 for Negro workers under age 65 average taxable earnings for social security purposes — the amounts on which contributions to the trust fund are based and which help determine the eventual benefit the worker may receive on retirement — where 68 percent of the average amount for white male workers and 63 percent of the average for white female workers (table 9).

In 1958, it will be recalled, earnings over $4,200 a year were not counted for social security purposes. How many of the Negro and white workers for whom earnings were reported had total earnings above the maximum taxable is not known, but there is one clue: For 3 out of 5 white men age 20-64, the reported earnings totaled $3,600 or more, but for only 1 in 4 of the Negro men was this true.

Actually, for all male workers in 1958 — whether or not covered by the social security program — the median wage or salary income for nonwhite workers was 58 percent that of white workers.

The social insurance program, by virtue of its formula, does proportionately better by the aged Negro than by the aged white worker with his higher average earnings. Old-age, survivors, and disability insurance alone, however, cannot atone retroactively for the insufficient earnings of a lifetime. Moreover, low benefits — however high in relation to previous earnings — are not calculated to afford adequate support when there has been no opportunity to accumulate additional resources for retirement.

OLD-AGE ASSISTANCE

The Social Security Act of 1935 also inaugurated a Federal-State program of public assistance for those aged persons whose own resources were insufficient or whose needs were unusually great. All the States have programs of old-age assistance, and most of them also make some payments for medical care received by recipients.

TABLE 9.

MEAN TAXABLE EARNINGS[1] OF WAGE AND SALARY WORKERS REPORTED UNDER
THE OASDI PROGRAM FOR 1958, BY AGE, RACE, AND SEX

Age	MALE			FEMALE		
	Negro	White[2]	Negro as percent of white	Negro	White[2]	Negro as percent of white
All ages[3]	$2,040	$2,970	69	$1,200	$1,845	65
Under 20	595	830	72	495	760	65
20-64	2,170	3,205	68	1,255	1,990	63
20-34	1,905	2,870	66	1,160	1,810	64
35-49	2,390	3,520	68	1,370	2,080	66
50-54	2,365	3,400	70	1,310	2,230	59
55-59	2,310	3,290	70	1,175	2,170	54
60-64	2,320	3,175	73	1,035	1,960	53
65-71	1,630	2,310	71	830	1,520	55
72 and over	1,280	1,845	69	745	1,245	60

[1]Average annual taxable wages. The maximum taxable for a worker during 1958 was $4,200.
[2]Includes nonwhite races other than Negro.
[3]Includes a few workers of unknown age, not shown separately.
Source: Social Security Administration, 1-percent continuous work-history sample data.

With the maturing of old-age, survivors, and disability insurance and its expansion to cover almost everyone who works, the number of persons aged 65 and over receiving benefits has grown from 66,000 in 1940 — when benefits were first payable — to 13 million today. The number receiving old-age assistance, originally the largest and now the second largest income-maintenance program for the aged, reached an all-time high in 1950 and since then has been declining gradually. Recipients now number 2.2 million in contrast to 2.8 million at the peak. More than a third of the aged recipients of assistance also receive old-age, survivors, and disability insurance benefits, but these benefits together with their other resources are insufficient to meet their needs according to the standards of their State.

Although the old-age assistance program is of less importance than formerly, it continues as an important program for many aged persons, particularly those who are nonwhite. A national survey of old-age assistance recipients in the summer of 1960 found that about one-fifth of those receiving such assistance were nonwhite. They represented 38 percent of the total nonwhite aged population, three times the recipient rate among white persons aged 65 or older. For only a fourth of the Negro recipients but for a third of the white recipients was the assistance payment a supplement to old-age, survivors, and disability insurance benefits.

Aged individuals are considered needy if all the income and property they have is less than the amounts set by their own State standards of eligibility for assistance. The assistance paid to a needy person is intended to make up the difference between what he has and what the State's program can support as income maintenance. The States differ, of course, in what they can and will support as a basic standard. States differ in the proportion of the population receiving old-age assistance, but in every State the proportion receiving aid is higher in the nonwhite population.

In any given State, there is practically no difference between white and nonwhite recipients in the amount of unmet need. Like old-age, survivors, and disability insurance, old-age assistance thus serves to reduce income disparity among the needy. Because relatively more of the Negro recipients of old-age assistance live in the low-income South, however, Negro recipients as a group receive somewhat smaller assistance payments, and these payments meet a slightly smaller proportion of budgeted requirements than is true for white recipients as a group — 94 percent compared with 96 percent. Actually, nonwhite persons who require assistance in old age are more fortunate than those who need it earlier in life. As presently constituted, assistance programs for the aged, while by no means overgenerous, nevertheless meet more of the need than do the programs for the younger groups in the population.

OTHER ASSISTANCE PROGRAMS

A number of other assistance programs offer help to some aged persons in need. The newest is medical assistance for the aged, which went into effect in October 1960. Often referred to as the Kerr-Mills program, it provides Federal-State funds for the medically indigent — by definition persons not so needy as to be eligible for cash payments through old-age assistance but nevertheless unable to pay for the medical care that they need. Medical assistance for the aged, now in effect in 32 States, currently is aiding about 150,000 persons, or slightly less than 1 percent of the total aged population. A considerable number of the recipients are old-age, survivors, and disability insurance beneficiaries, but relatively fewer of these recipients than of all old-age assistance recipients are likely to be nonwhite.

Some aged persons receive help in the form of aid to the blind. This program, which has no age restrictions, currently makes payments to only about 100,000 persons, less than 1 percent of the total adult population. Nearly a fifth of the recipients also receive old-age, survivors, and disability insurance, and most of those with income from both programs are aged 65 and over. A sample study of characteristics of persons receiving aid to the blind in late 1962 found that 40 percent of all the recipients were at least 65 years old. Complete statistics by race and age are not yet available, but a preliminary analysis for recipients of all ages shows that 69 percent were white and 29 percent nonwhite and that for 2 percent race was not reported.

A fourth Federal-State assistance program offers aid to persons who are permanently and totally disabled. About 475,500 persons are currently receiving such assistance. A study of the program in late 1962 found only 3 percent of the recipients were aged 65 or older.

PRELUDE TO POVERTY IN OLD AGE

The aged Negro, in common with so many aged white men and women, is likely to find himself with resources that are far from meeting his needs. For many Negroes, however, old age will not be their introduction to poverty but rather the point at which public programs presently are best geared to deal with the situation. Today's aged poor — of whom a disproportionate number are Negro — reflect our past failure to foster self-support in old age by assuring adequate income in middle age and youth. Tomorrow's aged poor may well testify to our continuing failure to do so, unless we can meet the challenge of poverty among younger families.

One conservative estimate places the number of children in families with "very low income" at about three times the number of needy old persons.[5] Yet the number of children receiving aid to families with dependent children today is barely one-third greater than the number of persons receiving old-age assistance. Aggregate assistance expenditures for the fiscal year ended June 1963 were 30 percent less for these children and their families than for the aged. Average payments are not large under either program, but those to the families with children are less nearly adequate in relation to need than payments for aged persons: It is estimated that the payments meet only 57-86

---

[5]Lenore A. Epstein, "Unmet Need In a Land of Abundance," *Social Security Bulletin*, May 1963.

percent of the needs of the recipient children in comparison with 94 percent for aged recipients.[6]

Many young families in the shadow of poverty receive no help at all. As an example, few families with an employable father in the home are eligible for aid even when income is low. Among needy families with the father absent, fewer than half receive any assistance. All told, the 4 percent of our child population currently receiving aid to families with dependent children represents, it is estimated, fewer than a sixth of all children who might be considered poor.[7] Many of these impoverished children are nonwhite. Their present deprivation, unchecked, foreshadows their own place among the aged poor of the future.

For some time to come, many Negroes reaching age 65 will continue to have limited resources and to be more dependent than white persons on public aid. Despite the general upgrading of the labor force, the Negro is still far too well-represented among those who are employed in jobs at which even white workers average low earnings throughout a lifetime — as service workers and nonfarm laborers, for example.

As current efforts result in better employment opportunities for the Negro, the poverty that constantly stalks him and his children solely because of his color should eventually disappear. When the Negro reaches old age, he may still share in the poverty of those, whatever their race, whose energies have been spent at earnings too low to provide for the needs of today, let alone the needs of tomorrow. In our society, however, adequate income cannot be abruptly established at age 65 or age 62. To reduce poverty in old age, we must attack deprivation in early years while at the same time making sure that the protections available to the aged reflect the rising levels of living that our expanding economy makes possible for all.

---

[6]Ellen J. Perkins, "Unmet Need in Public Assistance," *Social Security Bulletin*, April 1960.

[7]Ellen J. Perkins, "Now Much is Enough?," paper presented at the biennial round-table conference of the American Public Welfare Association, Washington, December 6, 1963.

Negro-White Differences in Geographic Mobility

EVA MUELLER AND WILLIAM LADD

INTRODUCTION

THIS REPORT FOCUSES ON DIFFERENCES IN GEOGRAPHIC MOBILITY between the white and the Negro population. It contrasts the rate and geographic pattern of mobility between Negro and white heads of families, distinguishing between Negroes born in the 11 Southern States which formed the Confederacy[1] and those born elsewhere. After highlighting these differences, it attempts to answer the question — Why are Negro families geographically less mobile now than white families?

For purposes of this study mobility has been defined to include all moves across labor market area boundaries. These boundaries are defined by the Department of Labor. In many cases the labor market area is a single county. In other cases a few counties are grouped into one labor market area. For those parts of the country where labor market areas are not designated, county boundaries are used. A person is not regarded as having moved if he changes his place of residence within a labor market area.

The findings presented here are based on 2,669 personal interviews taken between September and December, 1962. These interviews represent a probability sample of all families living in private dwelling units in the conterminous United States. Of the 2,669 respondents, 2,406 were white and 263 non-white. About 86 percent of the non-white

---

[1]For our purposes it seems appropriate to distinguish the eleven States of the Confederacy (Alabama, Arkansas, Florida, Georgia, Louisiana, Mississippi, North Carolina, South Carolina, Tennessee, Texas, and Virginia), from the five border areas (District of Columbia, Kentucky, Maryland, Oklahoma, and West Virginia). As our analysis shows, the pattern of migration is substantially different among the two groups of southern states.

Reprinted by permission of the authors from Economic Development Administration, *Negro-White Differences in Geographic Mobility* (Washington, D.C.: U.S. Government Printing Office, 1964), 19 pages.

respondents in the survey were Negroes. Only the latter are included in this report. In families where the head was married, the head was interviewed in half of the cases, the wife in the other half. In other households the head was always the respondent.[2]

PATTERNS OF MOBILITY

At the present time geographic mobility is considerably lower among Negro than among white families of the U. S. This finding emerges clearly from the Survey Research Center study and is confirmed by Census surveys. The Census data, available annually since 1950, have registered a lower rate of inter-county moves ever since 1950 for the Negro than for the white population. Such data as are available for earlier periods suggest that during World War II, and probably earlier too, the opposite was true: Negro workers seemed to be more mobile than white workers. Therefore, in comparing mobility, the time period under review becomes crucial.

Lifetime mobility

Comparisons of the proportion of Negro and white adults who have moved at some time during their lives are affected both by the high mobility of the Negro population prior to 1950 and its relatively low mobility since then. Looking at the present adult population, we find that nearly equal proportions of Negro and white family heads — about 35 percent — are now living in the same labor market area in which they were born. However, the Negro population does not fit a single pattern of life-time mobility. Of those Negroes who were born in the South of the Confederacy, only slightly more than 1 in 4 are currently living in the area of their birthplace. This group has a decidedly greater lifetime mobility than the white population. By contrast, roughly one-half of the Negroes born outside the South of the Confederacy are still living in the area where they were born. Thus, the northern-born Negro represents a particularly immobile group in the population, and one which is growing in importance.[3]

As is commonly known, migration toward the West and from rural to urban areas has been characteristic of the white population in recent

---

[2]For further detail on the methods of this study, see John B. Lansing, Eva Mueller, William Ladd, and Nancy Barth, "The Geographic Mobility of Labor: A First Report," Survey Research Center, University of Michigan, 1963.

[3]Because of the relatively small number of Negro respondents, figures for Negroes in this report are indicative of orders of magnitude but should not be read too closely. Of the 226 Negro heads of families, three-fourths were born in the eleven States of the Confederacy.

decades; Negro migration has taken place from the South to all other areas of the country and also from farms to urban areas. Life-time mobility patterns reflect these major population movements. . . . Only the West shows a net gain in white population in the sense that a higher proportion of the present white adult population lives there than was born there; all other regions show no significant net change due to migration. All regions except the eleven States of the Confederacy have gained population through Negro migration. Fully three-fourths of present Negro family heads were born in these eleven southern States but only 43 percent of Negro family heads remain there now. Conversely, 6 percent of present Negro family heads were born in the North Central States, but 23 percent live there now.

The differential impact of the farm-urban migration on race groups is illustrated by the following tabulation, which shows the origin of family heads living in metropolitan areas at the time of interview. Slightly over a third of the present white adult population in metropolitan areas was born on a farm or lived for at least a year on a farm.

Race	Percent of heads of families now living in metropolitan areas who once lived on a farm for a year or more
Negro	43
Born in South	56
Born elsewhere	18
White	36

Among Negroes born in the South of the Confederacy and now residing in metropolitan areas, 56 percent have a farm background. Among Negroes born outside the South and now residing in a metro-

Race	Percent of all heads of families having a rural background who are now living in rural areas
Negro	30
Born in the South	31
Born elsewhere	*
White	44

*Too few cases.

politan area, this percentage is much lower: only about 18 percent have a farm background. It is also interesting to note that among white adults who have lived in rural areas, about 44 percent remain rural residents while among adult Negroes with a rural background, only about 30 percent are still in rural areas.

Mobility Since 1950

Data on more recent mobility show that since 1950 the proportion of white family heads who have moved between labor market areas has been nearly twice as high as the proportion of Negroes who have made such moves. Also, since 1950 there has been no significant difference in mobility rates between Negroes born in the South and outside the South. However, since northern-born Negroes are younger and better educated, on the average, than those born in the South, their low geographic mobility remains particularly noteworthy.

For the most recent period, the five years from 1957-62, the contrast between the mobility of the white and that of the Negro population is even greater. Nearly three times as large a proportion of the white as of the Negro population moved from one labor market area into another during that time. Annual Census data for the years since 1950 confirm this declining trend in Negro migration rates. During the three years 1950-1953, the average annual inter-county migration rate for Negroes was 5.6 percent; for 1958-1961, it was down to 4.2 percent. Over the same period the migration rate for the white population declined only from 6.9 to 6.6 percent.

In addition to the proportion of each racial group who moved, the survey measured the number of moves made by each migrant since 1950. Of those who moved since 1950, on the average, white people made multiple moves more often than Negroes. About 17 percent of white family heads have moved four or more times since 1950; for Negroes the corresponding figure is 5 percent.

Besides making more or less permanent moves, people work away from home on a temporary basis. Migratory farm laborers, construction workers, and some types of sales workers are groups for which this kind of mobility is characteristic. Long distance commuting is another sort of recurrent mobility which affects a community's labor supply, but in this case no change of residence is involved. Both temporary moves and long distance commuting have occurred less frequently since 1950 among Negro than among white family heads.

The survey shows that since 1950 about 7 percent of white family heads, as compared with 2 percent of Negroes, have gone away temporarily to work and then returned to their former place of residence.[4] Similarly about 9 percent of white workers, as against 4 percent of Negroes, have commuted 50 or more miles to work for some period since 1950. These figures are another manifestation of the apparently greater mobility of the white than the Negro population, as is shown below:

Race	Went away temporarily to work	Commuted 50 or more miles to work
Negro	2%	5%
Born in the South	2	4
Born elsewhere	3	6
White	7	9

The regional pattern of migration rates since 1950 does not differ greatly from the pattern of lifetime mobility. Among the white population the movement to the West has slowed down since 1950, and inmigration and outmigration are nearly in balance for all regions. For Negroes, all regions but the South continue to be destinations of moves more often than origins of moves; the South shows a substantial net loss of Negro migrants.

Of all moves since 1950, about 20 percent are returns to a place of previous residence. Roughly one-half of the return moves are moves back to place of birth. There is little, if any, difference between Negroes and whites in regard to the proportion of moves that are returns.

Return moves	Race	
	White	Negro
Proportion of all moves	22%	19%
Return to place of birth	9	10
Return to place lived during childhood excluding place of birth	11	8
Return to other place of previous residence	2	1

[4]Migratory workers are not fully covered by the survey since the sample excludes people housed in temporary dwellings and those living in large rooming or boarding houses.

Future mobility

In addition to asking about past mobility, the survey inquired into the likelihood that people might move in the near future. A likelihood of moving might be indicated by dissatisfaction with one's present place of residence or by actual plans to move. A disposition to move in the near future, according to these indicators, was found much less frequently among Negroes than among white people.

People were asked — "If you could do as you please, would you like to stay in . . . or would you like to move?" In their replies, Negroes indicated a greater attachment to the community in which they are now living than did white citizens. The proportion of people reporting a preference for moving away from their present place of residence is nearly twice as high for white adults as it is for Negroes, as is shown in the following:

	Race	
Preference	*White*	*Negro*
Prefers to move	20%	11%
Not sure	3	*
Prefers to stay	73	87
Not ascertained	4	2
	100%	100%

*Too few cases.

Subsequently, respondents were asked whether there was any chance that they might move away from the area of their present residence in the next year. Only a small proportion of Negroes had any moving plans, however uncertain; 97 percent saw no possibility of moving in the 12 months following the 1962 interview. On the other hand, about one in every ten white adults thought they would or might move to another labor market area in the coming year. Negroes who were born outside the eleven States of the Confederacy, the younger and better educated part of the Negro population, expressed moving plans more often than Southern-born Negroes; although since 1950 the two groups have not differed significantly in mobility rates. The data on expressed moving plans below include those who said they would or might move in the following 12 months:

Race	See chance of moving
Negro	3%
Born in the South	1
Born elsewhere	7
White	11

WHY ARE NEGRO FAMILIES GEOGRAPHICALLY LESS MOBILE THAN WHITE FAMILIES?

The lesser geographic mobility of the Negro than of the white population now and in the recent past requires explanation. We shall examine in turn a number of possible reasons for the observed differences in mobility.

Demographic Factors

In the American population as a whole three demographic factors — age, occupation, and education — account for a large part of the difference in mobility between individuals. Young people, college graduates, and those in professional and managerial occupations are much more mobile than people who do not have these characteristics.

With respect to the age distribution, the white and Negro populations resemble each other closely. Negro family heads are slightly younger on the average than white family heads; but the difference is small and should, if anything, lead to higher mobility among Negroes.

Differences in education and occupation between white and Negro family heads are extensive. Data for the population as a whole indicate that a person with a college education is at least three times as likely to have moved in the past five years as a person who has attended only grammar school. Therefore, it is highly relevant that 27 percent of white family heads, but only 12 percent of Negroes, have had some college education. Conversely, only 28 percent of white family heads, as against 59 percent of Negroes, have had 8 years or less of schooling.

Since education and occupation are closely related, it is not surprising that those occupations which require more education are also characterized by a higher level of geographic mobility. Looking at the adult population as a whole we find that the proportion of movers was about twice as high in the last five years among families headed by managerial and professional workers as among those headed by operatives, laborers, and service workers. Negroes are predominantly in the less mobile occupations: 55 percent of them are operatives, laborers, and service workers and only 6 percent are professional workers or salaried managers. The corresponding percentages for white family heads are 19 and 18.

In brief, in a modern economy geographic mobility occurs in part because people with highly specialized knowledge and highly differentiated skills must be matched with job openings which call for specific types of knowledge and training. To use his special qualifications to best advantage, a person may have to move across county or even State lines to the most suitable job opening. This matching of specialized jobs and people affects primarily people in professional, managerial, or skilled technical work. Often it takes place within large companies which "transfer" personnel from one location to another. Since only a small proportion of Negroes are in highly specialized or skilled occupations, this reason for geographic mobility is not applicable to most of them. For example, among recent white movers 15 percent were transferred by their companies, among recent Negro movers only 1-2 percent.

Do educational and occupational differences between the Negro and the white population account fully for the observed differences in recent geographic mobility? The following tabulations show that the answer to this question is clearly — no. Even if we compare Negro and white adults having the same education or occupation, the Negro groups still appear considerably less mobile than the corresponding white groups. It is necessary to search for additional explanations.

Demographic Characteristics	Percentage In Each Group Who Have Moved In The Past 5 Years	
Education	White	Negro
8 grades or less	8%	5%
9-12 grades	14	8
College	28	11
Occupation	White	Negro
Professional, Managerial	30%	8%
Laborers, Service workers, Operatives	15	6
Other	13	6

Financial Factors

A striking difference between the Negro and the white population lies
in the larger proportion of Negroes with very low incomes and no
savings or reserve funds. In 1962, 24 percent of Negro families compared with 9 percent of white families, earned less than $2000. People
in this bottom income bracket are considerably less mobile than others.
However, low income is associated with low levels of education and
occupational skills and with old age, and it seems to reflect primarily
the low mobility associated with those factors.

Regarding financial reserves, there is no evidence, for the population
as a whole or for racial groups, that lack of such funds reduces geographic mobility significantly. Although one might suppose that poverty
would make it more difficult to meet the expenses and the financial
risks involved in moving, the survey data do *not* indicate that the
relatively low income and reserve funds of the Negro population constitute *per se* a barrier to mobility. Low-income Negro movers studied
in the survey usually reported that their moving expenses were small
(the price of a bus ticket) and that they had nothing to take along
but their clothes.

Poverty may lead to dependence on some form of public assistance
or private charity. Among the white population with incomes below
$4000, mobility was significantly lower in recent years if a family re-
ceived public assistance than if it did not receive such support. However, if both private and public assistance are considered, it would
appear that dependence on financial aid on the whole does not have
an important negative effect on mobility. Among low-income Negro
families mobility was, if anything, more frequent among recipients of
financial aid than among non-recipients. Thus, frequent dependence
on private welfare or public assistance among the low-income Negro
population does not help to explain their low geographic mobility.

Community and Family Reasons

Despite the large movements of the Negro population from South to
North and from rural to urban areas within the South during the first
half of the 20th Century, Negroes on the whole seem to have stronger
emotional and family ties to their current place of residence than the
white population. We have noted already that, in reply to the question — "If you could do as you please, would you like to stay here
in . . . or would you like to move?" — 87 percent of Negroes compared
with 73 percent of white adults indicated a decided preference for
staying in their present community. When asked further whether there

might be any disadvantages in staying "here" only 29 percent of Negroes, but 44 percent of whites, mentioned some disadvantages. Interestingly, economic or job disadvantages were cited with equal frequency by both groups; but criticisms of the community — its size, climate, schools, traffic congestion, and the like — were voiced much less frequently by Negroes than by white respondents.

The ties of the Negro to the community seem to be to an important extent family and friendship ties. Apparently the Negro migrant from the rural South, like the immigrant from Europe before him, often sent for or was followed by other members of his family. As a result we find that, even though only one-third of Negro adults are still living in the county where they were born 59 percent have all or most of their relatives living near them now in the same community. Most of the remaining Negro families reported that "some" relatives are living in the same community where they are. The survey shows that only 6 percent of Negro families, in contrast to 21 percent of white families, have no relatives in the community where they are now residing. It should be added that 48 percent of Negro families, but only 37 percent of white families, reported that *all* their close friends are living in their current place of residence. These contracts between the Negro and the white populations are important since the survey shows that both past geographic mobility and moving plans are particularly low among families who have all or most of their relatives living near them.

When a family does decide to move, relatives may play a further role in facilitating and guiding the move. In discussing their most recent move across county lines, most Negro as well as most white families mentioned job or economic factors as the primary reason for moving. However, among Negroes who were born in the South and have moved North or West, family reasons were mentioned with considerable frequency. A third of this group said that they moved in order to be closer to a relative who had moved earlier. A closer look at cases of recent Negro migrants in the survey suggests that job and family considerations tend to be inseparable in many instances, since relatives are the major source of job information and often help the migrant to find work. For example:

• A 51 year-old Negro and his wife moved from Arkansas to California where their daughter and her family lived. The son-in-law told him he could get work there as a common laborer and in fact helped him to locate his first job as a janitor.

• A young Negro moved from Louisiana to the West Coast to join a brother who urged him to come. The brother then helped him to find a job in a shipyard by sending him to the appropriate union.

- A 30 year-old single Negro had moved from Kansas to California and had made several moves in California in an attempt to find suitable work. Then he heard that his father was in San Francisco and he joined him there. The father had an apartment and took him in until he had work; the father also took him around in his car to look for a job. He is now a waiter.

Similarly, in the case of return migrants to the South:

- A young Negro woman, domestic worker, who had been living in New York with her mother, returned to North Carolina when her mother died. All her other relatives were living in North Carolina.
- A middle-aged Negro born in the South had migrated to New York City in the early 1950's. In 1959 his boss died, and he became unemployed. He and his family returned to his wife's home town in the South. A friend there gave him a job as a farm laborer.

It seems then that family ties and emotional ties to a place and to friends are a greater barrier to mobility among Negro than among white families. Furthermore, such geographic moves that do occur, particularly among unskilled workers, in many instances seem to be guided by the location of relatives as much as by job opportunities. The role which relatives play in determining Negro moves may help to solve the difficult problems of adjustment to a new environment which the Negro migrant faces. But this system hardly provides an effective mechanism for guiding Negroes into areas of new opportunities or expanding employment.

Economic Incentives

The history of Negro migration during recent decades demonstrates clearly that the Negro population *does* move in response to strong economic incentives. According to Census data, the growing inadequacy of employment opportunities in Southern agriculture induced a net migration from the South of over 700,000 Negroes between 1920 and 1930. During the 1930's, when few job openings were beckoning, net Negro migration out of the South fell below 350,000. During the decade of World War II large numbers of job openings for unskilled workers at rising rates of pay led an unprecedented 1,200,000 Negroes to leave the South. The migration rate during World War II was higher for Negro than for white men; it was particularly high among unskilled Negro workers. We have noted already that since 1950 inter-county migration rates have been consistently lower for Negro than for white heads of families and that the Negro migration rate has declined while the rate for the white population has remained fairly constant. It is likely that the recent decline in the Negro migration rate reflects the growing deficiency of employment opportunities for unskilled workers.

For many Negroes the economic incentive which persuades them to move need not be a higher wage somewhere else; it might simply be the prospect of steady work. At least at present, when unemployment among unskilled Negro workers is high, the economic advantage of moving is stated most often in terms of available jobs.

The relation of unemployment to mobility is best studied by classifying people according to their unemployment experience over a long period rather than their current employment status. Accordingly the question was asked — "Some people are out of work for a time every year, others are unemployed every few years, and still others are almost never unemployed. What has been (head of family's) experience?" In the white population, both recent mobility and moving plans were only slightly higher for those who reported that they were often unemployed than for those who had never or rarely been unemployed. Among Negro families, on the other hand, mobility seems to be much higher if the head suffered repeated unemployment than if he experienced steady employment. In fact, it appears that the contrast in past mobility between Negroes and white people is pronounced only for that part of the population which has not suffered unemployment. That is, Negroes with steady jobs are considerably less likely to move than white workers who are continuously employed. But Negro families subject to repeated unemployment do not have an appreciably lower mobility rate than white families in a similar unemployment situation.

Thus it appears that emotional or family ties to a place, or uneasiness about unfamiliar surroundings, are barriers to mobility among the Negro population primarily when economic incentives to move are weak. Unemployment creates an economic incentive to move, yet most of the unemployed — Negro or white — remain in the same labor market area. Having relatives elsewhere may bring better job opportunities to the Negro worker's attention; and at the same time it may lower his reluctance to leave a familiar place of residence.

Policy Implications

The policy implications of this study may be considered with the assumption that greater geographic mobility on the part of the Negro population would enhance its economic welfare and would make for a more efficient utilization of the labor force generally. We have seen that the relatively low rate of geographic mobility of nonwhite workers is related to their low level of education and occupational skills. An improvement in education, vocational training, and employment opportunities for Negroes in skilled occupations of itself should lead to greater mobility. Secondly, racial discrimination may be responsible for the disinclination of Negroes to leave family, friends, and a familiar place of residence. Most likely, the elimination of discrimination (together with better education) would lessen the Negro's uneasiness about finding a job and suitable housing in a new community.

Besides these longer range objectives of national policy, direct steps might be taken to overcome the dependence of potential Negro migrants on relatives and friends in connection with the migration and job seeking process. Such efforts would grow out of the recognition that, until racial discrimination has been wholly overcome, it is more difficult for Negroes than for other workers to find jobs and settle down successfully in a strange community. This assistance could take the form of providing, preferably in a single office, information about job openings, aid in filling out job applications, housing information, and information about community and religious organizations which would welcome the new-comer. One could go even further in aid to newly arrived Negro job seekers by providing transportation and temporary housing while they look for work. For such an effort close cooperation between public agencies and Negro community organizations would be essential. Negro community organizations could be particularly useful in transmitting information about possible job openings. Such personal help might well be more effective than financial subsidies, in the form of moving or resettlement allowances.

Finally, the recognition that unskilled Negro workers are a particularly immobile group underlines the importance of efforts to create new employment opportunities for unskilled workers in depressed areas.

Portrait of the Self-Integrator

HELEN MacGILL HUGHES AND LEWIS G. WATTS

DE TOCQUEVILLE FOUND THAT THE EUROPEAN, TRANSPLANTED TO North American shores, became a new man. Historians ever since have been busy distinguishing various regional Americans, defining each by peculiarities which are the mark of the geographical and social frontiers to which he had repaired. And it might be said that the Negro American is the latest in the succession of new men, evolving like those before him in response to new conditions of life. Among Negroes today the Northern, city-bred proletarian — urban in greater proportions than his white fellow-citizen — is a dominant type. The newest of all the new men, however, is a different Negro, one who is achieving recognizable shape before our eyes as a consequence of a generation or two of education and experience with city life and the modern organization of society.

It must be said at the outset that the everlasting special truth of the Negro bourgeoisie in the United States is not Negro history but white history. The early Negro middle-class, the minuscule elite of educated mulattoes and freedmen in the Southern towns, was devout, puritanical and devoted to the advancement of the race in a white society. In *Black Bourgeoisie,* Frazier describes another much later type of middle-class Negro as he saw it, with undisguised scorn.[1] He speaks of its members as seeking in conspicuous expenditure in a make-believe world of glamorous play some compensation for the recognition the white world withholds; as having money, but not enough of it, and no mission. Their news is personal gossip; their heroes are white playboys and the stars of the entertainment world; their cause is not the struggle against poverty

---

[1] E. Franklin Frazier, *Black Bourgeoisie* (Glencoe, Ill.: The Free Press, 1957), pp. 235-238.

Reprinted by permission of the publisher and authors from *Social Issues,* XX (April 1964), 103-15.

and ignorance but for white acceptance; and their lives, he says, lack content and significance.

Still another reaction to white pressure was already apparent when Frazier wrote, but its exemplars are now much grown in numbers and importance. Briefly put: in social type and style of life it is nearly impossible to distinguish them from their white counterparts. With them, the self-integrators, we are here concerned.

There have always been Negroes who "pass" by concealing their identity, who bury a Negro past and live a white present. They play a dangerous game and they play it solo. And there are some who "pass" on the job by day and return to the local Harlem after hours. But here we are discussing the *self-integrators,* the Negro family which takes the plunge, moves out of the Negro ghetto and establishes itself in the midst of white neighbors *as a Negro family*. This is the very opposite of passing; they conceal nothing but live a white present while remaining exactly what they are — or what they look.

This phenomenon is not "block-busting," which occurs when a real estate agent instigates a Negro family to move into a white street which is then rapidly filled up by more Negro families and eventually — things being what they are — is converted into a slum: an unhappy and all too familiar aspect of segregated housing. This new thing is quite different: the settling in a stable, middle-class and wholly white suburb of a single family of "respectable" Negroes whose presence seems to have no more effect upon property values or the social composition and population density of the neighborhood than would that of a white family of like standing. New and rare, the phenomenon of self-integration merits scrutiny and discussion, even though, the number being small and their experience brief, any generalizations must be tentative.

THE SETTING AND THE STUDY

Washington Park, a small section of Roxbury, which is Boston's Negro section, is in part to be rehabilitated, in part to be demolished and rebuilt as a project of urban renewal. Relics of long-departed comfort and decorum remain here and there in roomy New England mansions, curving driveways and tree-arched streets. Most of them are abused and neglected, but on certain streets well-to-do Negro property-owners carry on the prideful modes of the neighborhood's past; they have landscaped the grounds, air-conditioned the big houses, and their sports cars stand in the portes-cochères. But, cheek by jowl with them — this being a ghetto and a slum and cursed with the twin blights of segregation and over-crowding — are ramshackle buildings, their broken windows stuffed with paper and rags, their porches sagging, their paint blistered and peeling. There has been constant movement of Negro families from Washington Park,[2] but for the most part it does not remove them from the Negro world. Here we will describe nine self-integrating families who formerly lived in certain school districts of Washington Park and are now established in white suburbs. As far as we know, they are all who have done so in the past five years. The wives were our informants.

If it is hard to draw a composite picture of the self-integrators, it is perhaps because they range fairly widely through middle-class occupations and experiences. In all cases but one, the bread-winners are professional men: a $25,000-a-year physicist, a $15,000-a-year general medical practitioner, a $10,000-a-year dye designer, a $9,000-a-year computer programmer. The teacher whose salary is $9,000 is the only one with an employed wife, a teacher also, with a salary of $7,000; a third teacher earns $7,300, the mechanical engineer makes $8,000, the personnel officer, $7,000. The lowest earnings are those reported by the lone non-professional, a $6,000-a-year skycap at the airport, but he enjoys a handsome unspecified supplement in the form of tips. The families are small and young. In skin color the suburban couples are concentrated at the light end of a scale of six shades,[3] but the wives are the lighter. Four of the latter are rated as light, of whom two are light enough to "pass"; two are dark. Four husbands are also at the light end of the range, but none is very light; three are dark.

The self-integrators are city people. Half the spouses were born in Boston and the rest in northern cities, but for a wife from Ashville,

---

[2]Time will tell if this is the "unslumming" Jane Jacobs speaks of in her controversial book, *The Death and Life of Great American Cities* (New York: Random House, 1961), pp. 279, 284. She notes that "unslumming" in a racial ghetto comes hand-in-hand with relaxed discrimination: ". . . inner cities will go on losing too much of the Negro middle-class almost as fast as it forms until, in actual fact, the choice of remaining there no longer means for a colored person an implied acceptance of ghetto citizenship and status" (p. 285).

[3]As a device for rating skin color, interviewers were given a card depicting six hands in a row, colored in six shades, from nearly white to very deep brown. Repeated tests of the judgments of a number of the interviewers confirmed their ratings and justified confidence in the instrument.
This is to consider skin color in relation to "whiteness." But there is a more intriguing aspect of skin color: as a variable between husband and wife. It belongs in the sociology of color, a subject first broached in 1941 in *Color and Human Nature: Negro Personality Development in a Northern City* by W. Lloyd Warner, Buford H. Junker and Walter A. Adams (Washington, D.C.: The American Council on Education). In three of the self-integrating couples, the wife was the darker. Would she shrink from the image of herself, conspicuous and marooned among white neighbors, while her lighter husband, accepted by his white colleagues in the office, is ready, perhaps even eager, to hazard residential integration?

North Carolina, one from Warrington, Georgia, and a husband from Dallas, Texas. Of the two women, the first was taken to Boston at the age of seven and has lived there for 45 years; the second came at eight and remained in Roxbury for 37 years. Two wives were life-long residents of Roxbury, and two more came from other parts of Boston.

The most striking attribute of the self-integrating couples is their prolonged schooling. Of the suburban husbands, all but one finished high school, and six had graduated from college. They named Lincoln, Fisk, Howard, Virginia State and Texas College, and the integrated schools, Boston University, Northeastern, Michigan, Illinois, M.I.T., and Harvard. Four had Master's Degrees and one is a Ph.D. Of their wives, seven had gone to college. Not only are they educated themselves, but several grew up in educated families.

Thus education among most of the suburbanites has meant not only a lengthy period of preparation for highly respected careers but for most of them association with white classmates and instructors in an atmosphere where equality is more nearly a fact than anywhere else in the United States.

Our interviews with the wives in 250 families of middle income still living in Washington Park[4] establish the fact that in many of their social characteristics[5] they, like the self-integrators, are middle-class. Thus, leaving the ghetto cannot be explained as simply a matter of social economics. Yet it is safe to say that qualities of middle-classness are prerequisites of moving into a suburb — just as with white people.

WHY AND HOW THEY MOVED

The self-integrators' stated reasons for moving are in no sense racial — at first glance. They are the reasons that Rossi found actuate white families to move.[6] The Washington Park schools with their double shifts,

---

[4]To reduce housing problems to race, the criteria set up for the sample were selected so as to eliminate attributes which would make financing the purchase of a house difficult. Thus, the households were headed by couples (none widowed or divorced); none was over the age of 52; incomes were over $5,000; and none was in a disqualifying occupation. In short, all were, on the face of it, acceptable credit risks.

[5]Which are primary properties and which are their consequences is a moot question tackled by Hortense Powdermaker, for one, as long ago as 1939. (*After Freedom*, New York: Viking Press, p. 70.) Historically, a light skin was primary; a well-regarded occupation, income and prestige followed. *Cf.* Glenn's recent discussion of this point: "Negro Prestige Criteria: A Case Study in the Bases of Prestige," *American Journal of Sociology*, LXVIII, no. 5 (May, 1963), p. 645.

[6]Peter H. Rossi, *Why Families Move: A Study in the Social Psychology of Urban Residential Mobility* (Glencoe, Ill.: The Free Press, 1955).

their broken windows, their hordes of children from lower-class families lately arrived fom the South, would supply a reason for moving in the mind of any middle-class parent.[7] Nor are the next-commonest reasons, the need for more space and to be closer to the husband's work, related to race; nor the determination to escape disorder, vice and crime, the filthy, unsafe streets and the ignorant, roistering neighbors; nor the shrewd calculation arrived at by two of the wives that money goes further for rent, food and clothing, elsewhere.

To attribute moving to ambitions for their children's education is a generally acceptable and praiseworthy version of the mobile Negro family's aspirations, whereas — as Horace Cayton pointed out in a recent conversation — to admit to a longing to join the white man in the white man's world is doubly dangerous. On the one hand, the whites may slap down invaders; on the other, the Negroes will cry "Traitor!" There is, no doubt, honest and urgent conviction behind the plea of education, but at the same time, may there not be a readiness to claim it, before others and themselves, that is not extended to their more complicated and ambivalent motives which, things being what they are, are racial reasons? Be that as it may, urban renewal, it seems, is just the final spur to an action long contemplated and desired, and typically precipitated by the school situation.

The wife of the doctor, now established in one of the "good" suburbs, related:

> You somehow just put off moving. . . . We may have looked at half-a-dozen places before we bought. With the eldest in a good private school and the two younger children doing well for the time being in the Roxbury school, we could take our time. It will be several years before the two little ones will be ready for junior high school. But then we heard about this house. The owner was a Veterans' Administration doctor who was being transferred. He told my former boss, who is the head of the psychiatric department of the medical center; I was his secretary. But he found this house was not big enough for him and he told me about it. I phoned the owner and I told him we were colored — so there would be no trouble — but he said he did not care. And I loved this house at first sight. It cost us $23,000. We paid $8,000 in cash and we had no trouble in getting an FHA loan for improvements. Most of our friends who are professional people are ready to leave Roxbury now. They have the

---

[7]James A. Davis established the fact that the strongest correlate of advanced education is a mother who had it herself. *Cf. Great Aspirations: Volume I: Career Decisions and Educational Plans During College.* National Opinion Research Center Report 90, March, 1963. (Chicago, Ill.: The National Opinion Research Center, University of Chicago.)

money. Maybe a few don't but they'll be tickled pink when they get the money for their houses from the Redevelopment Authority and can buy a new house with it. The push is what they need — and that's what urban redevelopment is: a push.

Race was not an immediate issue with her story. But not all transitions were so happy. To begin with the bitterest:

The personnel man's wife made 1,000 phone calls between 1958 and 1961 (but that may mean an average of just one a day). She believes the address and telephone exchange betrayed them on the occasions when she did not specify they were colored buyers, and she is sure they were treated prejudicially. The Chinese owner of an apartment refused to sell to them, and they resorted to the Fair Housing Committee and the Massachusetts Commission Against Discrimination, which induced the owner to change his mind. The apartment is in a white suburb formerly of very high standing but now going downhill. Here they pay $150 a month, but the difference between that and the $70 they had been paying in Washington Park is much reduced by the fact that the larger rental includes utilities and heat and the new quarters are twice as large.

In all these trials they were encouraged by a white friend of the husband's in the office, who lives in the same section. Their neighbors, all white, have been cordial and helpful. The couple hopes eventually to buy a house there — which makes it appear they are reassured after their initial rebuff.

Of the other families, some were denied chances to buy; others thought they were; for example:

The suburban science teacher wanted better schools for his children, a shorter journey to work and more commodious quarters for himself, his wife and two small boys than they had when living in a $55-a-month apartment with relatives in Washington Park. They were sold a house by a family whose children had been his pupils. His wife had been rebuffed twice by agents and suspected more incidents of discrimination when agents made excuses. But when they bought their $19,000 house it was through a realty firm in their suburb and with a mortgage insured by a local bank.

To summarize: six dealt directly with owners and four of the seven who bought (two rented) got money for the purchase or for improvements from local suburban institutions. One family bought through a white broker in a neighboring suburb and one raised money in a Boston bank. At least three had the active help of white colleagues in finding new quarters. In the experience of these buyers, discrimination is most likely to be met with at the hands of owner or agent and may be encountered again at the bank. Thereafter the way is smooth. In nearly every case the new neighbors have proved helpful and congenial.

This is not to say that the self-integrators are completely at ease. The physician's wife, recounting amiable gestures made in her direction on the street and at a PTA meeting, more than once interjected, "Do they go out of their way to be nice because I'm colored, I wonder?"

How They Live

With astonishing rapidity, the self-integrators' lives take on the character and tempo of the white suburbanites', all about them. Said the doctor's wife:

> When we decided to move out to this suburb, my husband and I thought it all out and we vowed we would not change churches or Sally's Brownie Troop or neglect our old friends in Roxbury, or change the children's music teacher. I kept the two younger ones in school until the end of the term and for two months I drove them every day back to Roxbury and then called to bring them home. The elder boy goes to a private school in another suburb and is driven there by an M.D. (white) with a son in the school; and I drive the boys home.
>
> And now we've been here six months and we find it just can't be done. The days aren't long enough for all that running around. Sally has a new lot of friends here in school, and she wants to be in *their* Brownie troop. And I just can't run back and forth to Roxbury for her music lessons, though she had a fine teacher there. Besides that, she's in the community music center now, and it's just wonderful. The community has the money to try out new methods and keep up first-class equipment. It's a wonderful opportunity for her, and how can I keep her away from it?
>
> The children go back to Roxbury to their friends' birthday parties, and our friends there come here to ours. But it's true, too, that when we go back to see our friends we keep finding they are moving away, too. I don't know any professional family in Roxbury that would not move now; they can afford it.
>
> We do keep some ties, though. We are still going back to Roxbury to church. But the new bishop (he is a Negro) and his wife have both called on us and remarked that they hope to see us in church in the locality — they live here, too. But so far we have not changed.
>
> I still do voluntary work at the hospital in Roxbury on certain mornings, and I try to get to the board meetings of the neighborhood house there, but it is hard for me to get away from here in the evenings the way I used to when I lived just a few blocks away from it. And I still work on the Cancer Drive and the March of Dimes, and I'm still in Am Vets. But now I'm a room-mother in the school

here where our children are. My husband belongs to a lot of organizations, as well: The Elks, Am Vets, The Boston Professional Credit Union and others. But he never goes. Our pediatrician is white, a woman. She has her office on the outskirts of Boston, but she's on the staff of the Roxbury hospital where my husband is.

We have five dentists, between us! You know, professional courtesy prevents them from charging a doctor's family. So we spread it out. And all five are Negro dentists in Roxbury—all friends of ours.

Our lawyer is a Roxbury man. In fact, we have two, both Negroes. We go out of our way to get colored professional help whenever we can. There are so many good Negro lawyers. My husband's medical practice is ninety percent colored.

This is a picture of a family which has had to make deliberate choices in almost every area of its life and has ended, so far, with what seems to it to be the best of the alternatives, sometimes drawing upon Roxbury, sometimes turning to resources convenient to their new home and perhaps better. Of course, none of the self-integrators has lived for long in the suburbs and with the passing of time they may commit themselves more deeply to suburban life. But some measure of living with one foot in the city, the other in the outskirts, may be common to all suburbanites. Thus two Negro and eight white medical doctors are consulted by the self-integrators. Of the latter, one, a woman pediatrician, has an office in Roxbury, but four are in the same suburbs as the patients, and two more are in nearby communities, for the mother needing a pediatrician or family doctor evidently does not hesitate to drop the Roxbury connection for help nearer at hand. They have thirteen dentists, of whom ten are Negro, Roxbury-based. The only dentist consulted in the patient's own suburb was white. Needing lawyers when buying their houses, the self-integrators turned to two who are white, eight Negro: of the latter, six are in Roxbury.

Where the sense of racial identity is strong, the uprooted family may regularly return to the Negro church, that particular and almost symbolic institution. But several families in the suburbs have not yet made up their minds about church. "Our church in Roxbury," observed the science teacher's wife, "is friendly and church is a social occasion as much as religious. Everyone makes a point of greeting everyone else. But here people are more reverent (formal?) and not so friendly and they don't all speak to each other when they come out." Nevertheless, two Roman Catholic, one Congregational and one Episcopalian family have joined suburban churches. Three maintain their membership in Roxbury congregations (including the physician, 90% of whose patients are in Roxbury), and two compromise by joining an interdenominational university chapel whose chaplain is a well-known Negro minister.

The special art of pressing hair is a wholly racial practice; indeed, at the handling of their hair, many Negroes say the untrained hair-dresser is inept and it is not surprising that four of the suburban housewives go to Roxbury and three go to one of the big Boston department stores with specially trained operators. Children are attended to at home or taken to suburban establishments.

The suburban husbands go back to Roxbury barbers. One wonders if, as much as anything, they are drawn back by the convivial atmosphere of the accustomed Roxbury barbershop, that haven "where the women cease from troubling and the wicked are at rest!" It is not irrelevant that the suburban school teacher complains that he never sees any Negro men any more and that when he wants a game of golf he has to go all the way to Roxbury for partners. For it may be that the suburbs offer the adult Negro male little by way of relaxed fun. In his new middle-class orbit he — she, too — must, or thinks he must, watch every gesture made in his direction and judge whether it is calculated or sincere. To exchange the knowns of the ghetto for the perhaps perilous unknowns of the white world in some induces a nervous watchfulness — "Lately I've been going with my husband to the agency's parties," confessed the personnel man's wife, "and I felt peculiar and a bit uncomfortable when the boss asked me to dance. This is the first time I have ever danced with a white person." — "Did the school principal remember my name, among all those people at the PTA meeting," asks the doctor's wife, "because of what we are?"

Yet, even within the race, the self-integrators are not to any notable degree joiners. They lean toward social, fraternal and professional clubs and are not quick to ally themselves with specifically racial organizations. Only three families among them contain members of the NAACP, and one husband is on the board of the Urban League. None belong to CORE. All in all, their attitude to the racial organizations appears to be one of passive approval. But the Black Muslims they logically repudiate as separatist — though the doctor's wife observes that they imbue their members — ("the ones I know are poor and not well-educated") — with racial pride and morale.

Several of the suburban spouses who belong to social clubs or college fraternities or sororities report that they find it too far to go to the meetings; or, as the science teacher's wife admitted, it costs too much. The wife who teaches, the doctor's and the engineer's wives return to Roxbury to give their services to a settlement house, but each complains of the long trip. Yet the engineer's wife appreciates the institution as a bridge between the families "brave enough to move out" and their friends back in the slums.

Little by little the suburban families are for the most part disengaging themselves from their ties to the city and becoming enmeshed in school, church and neighborhood where they now find themselves. But if they end by abandoning their churches and clubs and their share in Washington Park's communal life, most of them were not, in any case, leaders there. The race leaders remain in Roxbury. A few politicians, ministers and other civic leaders in Roxbury tried to dissuade one or two of the self-integrators from moving: for one thing, they deplore the attrition of Roxbury's elite and, for another, they have high hopes that urban renewal is about to usher in a revitalized, well-balanced Negro life there.[8] But for these and an occasional ambivalent or disapproving individual, the families and friends of the suburbanites have acclaimed their moving with enthusiasm. — "My sisters just love to come here," exclaims the personnel assistant's wife. — At their children's birthday parties, the self-integrators' conscientious hospitality includes guests from the old and the new localities and cuts across race lines. Several of the suburban couples have already begun to play a part in their new communities. Four parents go to PTA meetings; two are leaders in children's groups: the Boy Scouts, Brownies and Little League baseball. The teacher's wife has already entertained the nominating committee of the "young marrieds" of the Congregational Church — but she admits wryly that several Southerners among the members have not yet spoken to her. The physicist's wife remarks that fifty members of the suburban Congregational Church have invited her to join them. At the same time, her Roxbury social club has met in her new home and she herself goes thrice weekly to engagements in town. The dye designer's neighbors have asked him to be a candidate for selectman. Thus the web of life of the Negro suburbanite changes decisively at critical points.

Meanwhile, it must be said that the child integrators have played their social roles well and apparently at no great emotional cost to themselves. But as an educational experience, suburban life may here and there prove traumatizing at first. A second-grader transplanted from the ghetto may find himself demoted to the first grade in the new school. For, as the doctor's wife was warned by her seven-year-old son's teacher

---

[8]Whereas in Chicago and New York and certain sections of Boston, urban renewal is denounced as "Negro clearance," in Roxbury it is supported by local Negro leaders. A local congregation is organizing to draw up its own plans for rebuilding a tract and to apply for federal aid. Of the 250 Washington Park wives, 64% think urban renewal will promote integration in housing and 72% said, "Yes" when asked: "Do you think urban renewal will improve housing opportunities for you?"

and as the boy himself is learning by hard experience, it is one thing to mark time with slum children in a Negro school and another to compete with ambitious Jewish children in the suburbs!

How Much Integration Do They Want?

The children for whose sake the drastic step was taken have, on the whole, become happy and successful suburbanites, even when they are the only ones of their race in their classrooms. The dye designer's 13-year-old boy had to fight his way to acceptance on the school ground and finally succeeded, but his four little sisters, too young for school, have taken longer to find friends. Their experience suggests the hypothesis that the self-integrating child's sex may enter into his adjustment.

The mothers are all looking ahead to the time when their sons will want teen-aged girl friends. (Of 23 children in the self-integrating families, the only three of high school age are boys; all the others are very young.) The doctor's wife is "not offended" by mixed marriages but "would not wish it" for her own children. But the teacher's wife thinks that when the time comes she will let the child decide, though she knows her husband would never consent even to mixed dating — "and the white girl's parents would not want it, either." Although the 17-year-old son of the school-teaching couple, a popular high school football captain, is already having dates with white girls, his mother, unequivocally opposed to intermarriage, speaks of "cultural differences." On the other hand, the program director's wife, who had dates with white boys when in high school, says she has no objections to interracial social life at all; nor does the dye designer's wife, mother of a 13-year-old and four small girls; and she adds that her husband agrees. Briefly, their opinions cover the range of conventional stands on *ethnic* mixture, as though the situation paralleled the Cohens-and-Kelleys dilemma. But the realities are yet to be faced.

Conclusions

This is a portrait of the new Negro. A few outstanding men of the race have become personages in the bigger world of white people, hitherto, but always because of some signalizing talent. But the self-integrators of Boston are not touched by genius. The frontiers on which they press are those of personality and class: self-confidence — or desperation — and bourgeois aspirations.

Such people hold dear good schools, the regard of congenial neighbors and a clean, orderly community — values of the middle class to gain which they will plan and save, deferring immediate gratification.[9] Socially mobile, they move their place of residence, as middle-class Americans do, to match their rising socio-economic status.

But this status cannot be matched in the ghetto-slum. Nor can they remain there if they are to rescue their children from the negligible challenge of the slum school and slum classmates and give them the education suited to their class in appropriate settings. And over and above the indictment of the racial ghetto is the longing to be part of the better world of white people — to enter the mainstream of American life, as two of the wives put it — that is not always acknowledged, perhaps not always admitted to full consciousness, and is not inconsistent with their determined efforts not to lose touch with members of their own race. Their personal experience has imparted to the nine self-integrating families not enough of the too-often well-grounded fear and dread of whites which, as Cayton so tellingly describes it, has in many Negroes become an almost crippling phobia,[10] to keep them from moving out.

Given his education and his professional mentality, the new middle-class suburban Negro is, properly speaking, a function, too, of something else: the expanding housing market. In Boston there are houses which Negroes can buy in large enough supply to permit reasonable choice[11] and the self-integrators are precisely the individuals with the

---

[9]*Cf.* comparison of the key values of the middle and the working class in *Status of the Working Class in Changing American Society*, by Lee Rainwater and Gerald Handel (Chicago, Ill.: Social Research Inc., 145 E. Ohio St., no. 173/1, February, 1961), pp. 47, 78-86. The authors show the middle-class spends to achieve status, the working-class comfort; the middle-class plans for their children's education, and 33% of their sample families were already saving toward it, but the working-class talk of it yet only 14% were putting money by. These findings are also reported in the authors' *Working Man's Wife* (New York: Oceana Publications, 1959).

[10]Horace R. Cayton, "Psychology of the Negro Under Discrimination," in Arnold M. Rose (ed.), *Race Prejudice and Discrimination: Readings in Intergroup Relations in the United States* (New York: Alfred A. Knopf, 1951), pp. 276-290. Also James Baldwin, "Down at the Cross," in *The Fire Next Time* (New York: The Dial Press, 1963), pp. 67-70, 82-83. Of the 250 wives interrogated in Washington Park, 9% thought it "unsafe" for Negroes to buy or rent in white neighborhoods; 10% said "Yes" to the question: "Do you think homes purchased by Negroes in white neighborhoods in Boston are ever destroyed by bombs or fire?"

[11]The Federation of Fair Housing Committees between March and November, 1962, had listed 400 houses and apartments in the center and suburbs of Boston whose owners agreed to put them on the market without restrictions as to race or creed. They range in price from $10,000 to over $40,000. This supply far exceeds the demand.
An analysis of the housing market as it extends to Negroes in Boston appears in Lewis G. Watts, *The Mobility Inclinations of Middle-Income Negro Families Residing in a Neighborhood Undergoing Urban Renewal*, esp. Chapter VI: "Can Negro Middle-Income Families Integrate?" (On file at The Florence Heller Graduate School for Advanced Studies in Social Welfare, Brandeis University.)

class-bound qualities and ambitions, the money and the urge to seek suburban life for what it offers. And if the transplanting calls for courage and encouragement, they have enough of both. As the physicist's wife put it: "The real problem in race relations is the lower-class Negro. In Boston the upper- and middle-class family has no great handicap — but many of them don't know it."

In the suburbs the self-integrator's style of life matches that of the other residents, different in color but alike in social class. While most of them belong in the Negro elite,[12] in white suburban Boston they fit into the human surroundings as middle-class, of middle-class

---

[12]The disparity between class position in society including both races and in society of Negroes only is shown in the following data from the sample of Washington Park wives:

"Compared with most people — white and Negro — what class do you consider yourself in? Lower, working, middle, or upper class?"

	Lower	Working	Middle	Upper	Don't Know
no.	2	98	133	13	4
%	0.8	39.8	54.1	5.3	1.6

"How about comparison with Negroes only? Lower, working, middle, or upper?"

	Lower	Working	Middle	Upper	Don't Know
no.	0	64	140	36	10
%	0.0	26.7	58.3	15.0	4.0

The social distribution of these families, as rated by Warner's Index of Social Characteristics, in the middle categories is:

	Upper Lower	Lower Middle	Upper Middle
no.	69	94	24
%	27.6	37.6	9.6

Judith R. Kramer and Seymour Leventman report the upper class among third-generation Jews as more acculturated than the middle and lower classes. *Cf. Children of the Gilded Ghetto: Conflict Resolutions of Three Generations of American Jews* (New Haven, Conn.: Yale University Press, 1961). If, for the moment, integration may be equated with acculturation, then the suburban Negroes, like the country-club Jews of the "gilded ghetto," lead the way.

income, though several will certainly have had an education superior to their neighbors'.

But to the self-integrators it is not at all necessary to be assimilationists.[13] They think of themselves as Americans who differ from their white neighbors in certain biological ways which they expect to see perpetuated in their children. The suburban Negro family — if this small sample is any test — looks like just that: a Negro family living in the suburbs.

---

[13]Parenthetically, the road traveled by the immigrant from Europe is, of course, far from fully comparable to that of the Negro. The latter, for one thing, had no competing culture to repudiate. For another, he entered at the bottom, not of urban society, as did the Irish and the immigrant Jews, but of agrarian, which has long been a shrinking fraction of the national economy, and so has had additional adaptations to make, apart from the encumbrance of color and high visibility.

Part 2

Stability
and Instability
in Family Life

Marital Stability as a Social Indicator

PAUL C. GLICK

In view of the counteracting effects of a rising marriage rate and a rising divorce rate during the 1960's,[1] answers to several questions are sought in this paper: What has been the net change in the proportion of adults currently living in the married state?[2] Has the change been the same for young persons as for persons of more mature age? Has the change occurred uniformly among men and women and among white and nonwhite persons? What kind of "indicators" can be devised to summarize the "favorableness" of the observed changes in terms of increasing (or decreasing) marital stability?[3]

The data in the accompanying tables show the directions and magnitudes of recent changes in marital status, including substantial increases in the proportion married for some population groups which have been partly offset by decreases in the proportion married for other groups and by an upturn in the proportion divorced among most population groups.

As the findings are presented, the reader may wish to consider the probable reasons for the recent changes in marital status. Thus, the proportion married among those below old age has risen partly because couples are surviving jointly for an increasing number of years. But, in addition, the proportion living as bachelors and spinsters has been falling steadily as a larger proportion of the people are becoming financially able and socially free to marry or to remarry according to their personal choice while they are in the preferred age range to be married. Likewise, more people are now divorced, but the basic data do not reveal whether this means that more of them have serious marital discord or whether more of those who have serious marital troubles are becoming financially able and socially free to settle those

Published by permission of the author. Revision of a paper presented at annual meeting of the Population Association of America in 1968. The opinions expressed in this paper are not necessarily those of the Bureau of the Census.

troubles by shifting out of the status of an intolerable marriage into that of divorce and perhaps tolerable remarriage.

The findings in this study consist of a summary evaluation of recent changes in marital status (by age, color, and sex) in terms of net movement of social groups in "favorable" or "unfavorable" directions. The changes are divided into 40 components, based on sample data from the Census Bureau's Current Population Survey, and a judgment is expressed about each component as to whether it represents a favorable or an unfavorable change. Discussion of the judgment factor is given in a later section. The components are identified as the 20 detailed cells in the third and sixth columns of Table 1 labeled "change" (excluding the cells for total men and total women) and the 20 corresponding cells in Table 2. Attention is directed first to the steps taken in developing these 40 components.

DEVELOPMENT OF COMPONENTS OF CHANGE

Table 1 shows changes in marital status between "1960" and "1965" for persons 18 to 24 years old, and Table 2 shows similar data for persons 25 to 64 years old. These groups were selected for presenta-

TABLE 1.

PERCENT DISTRIBUTION BY MARITAL STATUS, FOR PERSONS 18 TO 24 YEARS OLD, BY COLOR AND SEX, STANDARDIZED FOR AGE: UNITED STATES, 1960 AND 1965

Marital status and sex	WHITE			NONWHITE		
	1960[1]	1965[1]	Change	1960	1965	Change
Men 18-24	100.0	100.0	0	100.0	100.0	0
Single	64.5	65.6	1.1	71.6	70.0	−1.6
Marriage intact[2]	33.2	33.2	0	25.7	28.2	2.5
Marriage disrupted:						
Separated	1.8	0.5	−1.3	1.9	1.5	−0.4
Divorced	0.4	0.6	0.2	0.7	0.2	−0.5
Widowed	0.1	0.1	0	0.1	0.1	0
Women 18-24	100.0	100.0	0	100.0	100.0	0
Single	40.9	44.4	3.5	45.7	47.9	2.2
Marriage intact	55.1	52.3	−2.8	44.4	44.8	0.4
Marriage disrupted:						
Separated	2.5	1.6	−0.9	7.8	5.9	−1.9
Divorced	1.3	1.5	0.2	1.4	1.1	−0.3
Widowed	0.2	0.2	0	0.7	0.3	−0.4

[1]Average for 5 years, centered on the stated year.
[2]Married, except separated.
Source: U.S. Bureau of the Census, *Current Population Reports*, Series P-20, Nos. 87, 96, 105, 114, 122, 135, 144, 159, and 170.

tion because recent changes in the percent married have been generally in opposite directions for the younger and older of these two groups. Persons under 18 were omitted from this study because the proportions married are small. The general pattern in this very young group, however, was favorable in the sense that it was toward a decline in marriage. Persons 65 and over were omitted because of the small proportion of persons at that age who marry, and the present study is oriented toward those of the main ages for marriage.

The first step in assembling the data was to combine the published figures from *Current Population Reports* for 5-year periods in order to stabilize the results. As the footnotes on the tables state, in effect, the columns labeled 1960 contain data averaged for the 5 years 1958 to 1962 and those labeled 1965 contain data averaged for the 5 years 1963 to 1967. A secondary consideration in making these combinations is that none of the children born soon after World War II had reached 18 years of age by 1962 but several million had done so by 1967. A tertiary consideration is the timing of the recent upturn in divorce in the United States; between 1962 and 1967 the number of divorces went up 20 percent (413,000 to 534,000). After the basic data were combined for the two 5-year periods the distributions for 1960 were

TABLE 2.

PERCENT DISTRIBUTION BY MARITAL STATUS, FOR PERSONS 25 TO 64 YEARS OLD, BY COLOR AND SEX, STANDARDIZED FOR AGE: UNITED STATES, 1960 AND 1965

Marital status and sex	WHITE			NONWHITE		
	1960[1]	1965[1]	Change	1960	1965	Change
Men 25-64	100.0	100.0	0	100.0	100.0	0
Single	10.5	9.0	−1.5	14.0	12.8	−1.2
Marriage intact[2]	84.1	85.7	1.6	71.4	72.7	1.3
Marriage disrupted:						
Separated	1.4	1.3	−0.1	7.9	7.7	−0.2
Divorced	2.4	2.7	0.3	3.2	4.1	0.9
Widowed	1.6	1.3	−0.3	3.5	2.7	−0.8
Women 25-64	100.0	100.0	0	100.0	100.0	0
Single	7.2	6.2	−1.0	6.6	6.3	−0.3
Marriage intact	79.9	81.1	1.2	63.1	64.9	1.8
Marriage disrupted:						
Separated	1.9	1.8	−0.1	11.7	12.0	0.3
Divorced	3.2	3.9	0.7	4.9	5.8	0.9
Widowed	7.8	7.0	−0.8	13.7	11.0	−2.7

[1]Average for 5 years, centered on the stated year.
[2]Married, except separated.
Source: Same as Table 1.

standardized for age within each cell of Tables 1, 2, and 5, using 1965 data as the base. The full age detail available was used in this process (18-19, 20-24, 25-29, 30-34, 35-44, 45-54, and 55-64).

Table 3 shows a number and a direction (up or down) for each of the 40 components of change in marital status. The direction stated for each component is the favorable one, and the sign of the number "1" in front of it indicates whether the observed change between 1960 and 1965 was or was not in the favorable direction. To illustrate, "1 up" for single white men 18 to 24 years of age means that an upward movement in percent single for this group (signifying a tendency to delay marriage) was judged to be a favorable change, and the fact that the "1" is positive means that the actually observed change between 1960 and 1965 was in the favorable direction. The "0 down" for white men 18 to 24 with marriage intact means that a

TABLE 3.

CHANGES IN MARITAL STATUS AS SOCIAL INDICATORS, FOR PERSONS 18 TO 24 AND 25 TO 64 YEARS OLD, BY COLOR AND SEX, STANDARDIZED FOR AGE: UNITED STATES, 1960 TO 1965

Marital status and sex	Changes in Marital Status Between 1960 and 1965[1]						
	Total 18-64	White			Nonwhite		
		Total	18-24	25-64	Total	18-24	25-64
Both sexes (net)	16[2]	9	3	6	7	3	4
Men (net)	7	4			3		
Single			1 up	1 down		−1 up	1 down
Marriage intact[3]			0 down	1 up		−1 down	1 up
Marriage disrupted:							
Separated			1 down	1 down		1 down	1 down
Divorced			−1 down	−1 down		1 down	−1 down
Widowed			0 down	1 down		0 down	1 down
Women (net)	9	5			4		
Single			1 up	1 down		1 up	1 down
Marriage intact			1 down	1 up		−1 down	1 up
Marriage disrupted:							
Separated			1 down	1 down		1 down	−1 down
Divorced			−1 down	−1 down		1 down	−1 down
Widowed			0 down	1 down		1 down	1 down

[1]Average for 5 years, centered on the stated year.

[2]This figure means that 16 more "changes" in Tables 1 and 2 were in a favorable direction (denoted by a positive 1) than in an unfavorable direction (denoted by a minus 1) between 1960 and 1965. Zeros indicate no change. This figure could have ranged from positive 40 to negative 40.

[3]Married, except separated.

Source: Tables 1 and 2.

downward movement for this group was judged to be favorable, but the "0" means that no change took place in the 5-year period among these persons (who were married but not separated). And, the "−1 down" for divorced white men 18 to 24 means that a downward movement was judged favorable for them, but the "−1" means that the actual change was in the unfavorable direction.

In the first two rows of components, for single persons and persons with marriage intact, the determination of favorableness was contingent upon age. Thus, an upward change in the percent single was judged to be favorable for those under 25, but a downward change was considered favorable for those 25 to 64. Consistent with these norms, changes in the opposite directions for persons with marriage intact were considered favorable. As stated above, comments about the propriety of the norms adopted will be made in a later section of the

TABLE 4.

MAJOR CHANGES IN MARITAL STATUS AS SOCIAL INDICATORS, FOR PERSONS 18 TO 24 AND 25 TO 64 YEARS OLD, BY COLOR AND SEX, STANDARDIZED FOR AGE: UNITED STATES, 1960 TO 1965

Marital status and sex	Total 18-64	MAJOR CHANGES IN MARITAL STATUS BETWEEN 1960 AND 1965[1]					
		WHITE			NONWHITE		
		Total	18-24	25-64	Total	18-24	25-64
Both sexes (net)	14[2]	9	5	4	5	2	3
Men (net)	6	4			2		
Single			1	1		−1	1
Marriage intact[3]				1		−1	1
Marriage disrupted:							
Separated			1			1	
Divorced						1	−1
Widowed							1
Women (net)	8	5			3		
Single			1	1		1	
Marriage intact			1	1		−1	1
Marriage disrupted:							
Separated			1			1	
Divorced				−1			−1
Widowed				1		1	1

[1]Average for 5 years, centered on the stated year.
[2]This figure means that 14 more "changes" in Tables 1 and 2 were "major changes" (0.4 percent or more) in a favorable than an unfavorable direction between 1960 and 1965, as indicated by the norms in Table 4. This figure could have ranged from positive 40 to negative 40.
[3]Married, except separated.
Source: Tables 1, 2, and 3.

paper. The remaining three marital status categories relate to marriages which are "not intact," and for each the favorable direction for change was judged to be downward.

In the total rows and columns of Table 3 the summary numbers shown are net counts of favorable changes in marital status. They were obtained by subtracting the number of negative "1's" from the number of positive "1's" and disregarding "0's." For example, as footnote 2 on Table 4 implies, the figure 16 in the upper left corner means that 26 favorable changes were counterbalanced by 10 unfavorable changes, with the result that 16 more changes among the 40 components were favorable than were unfavorable. Instead of positive 16, this figure could have been as high as positive 40 or as low as negative 40.

Table 4 shows numbers with the same meaning as those in Table 3, except that, as footnote 2 indicates, only the "major" changes are shown, where major is defined as a change of four-tenths of one percent or more. (All changes of 0.4 percent or more were statistically significant at the two sigma level.) For example, in Table 1 the percent single for young white men rose by 1.1 percent between 1960 and 1965; since that increase was more than 0.4 percent and in a favorable direction, it is shown as a positive "1" in Table 4.

ANALYSIS OF COMPONENTS OF CHANGE

Fully 20 of the 40 components of change in marital status over the last decade, as defined for this study, were interpreted as major changes in a favorable direction, and only 6 of the 40 as major changes in an unfavorable direction. (The other 14 components of change were not classified as major.) Within this generally favorable picture, however, some similarities and some very wide differences between findings for white and nonwhite groups are apparent.

Both color groups were alike in that they scored 10 favorable major changes. Among whites, 7 of these 10 changes were consequences of an increasing tendency for white persons to be married; that is, to marry rather than become bachelors or spinsters, to remain married, or to remarry rather than remain widowed or divorced. The other favorable changes for whites consisted of very sharp declines in the percent separated among young persons (with no compensating major rise in percent divorced) and a decline of about one-tenth in the percent widowed among white women 25 to 64. Among nonwhites, 4 of the 10 favorable major changes reflected shifts toward mature adult age at marriage, 2 were for declines in percent separated among young persons (the same as for whites), 1 for a substantial decline in percent divorced for nonwhite men 18 to 24, and 3 for sharp declines in percent widowed.

Five of ‹the 6 components denoting unfavorable major changes were found among the nonwhites. The only white component in this category was an increase in percent divorced for white women 25 to 64 years old. Among nonwhites, 3 of the 5 changes identified as unfavorable — but to be challenged below — were associated with increasing entrance of nonwhite young people into marriage. The other 2 identified as unfavorable — but also to be challenged below — represented substantial increases in the percent divorced among nonwhite men and women 25 to 64 years old.

The net scores on components of major change varied from a high of 5 favorable for white women to a low of 2 favorable for nonwhite men:

Group	Favorable	Unfavorable	Net favorable
White women	6	1	5
White men	4	0	4
Nonwhite women	5	2	3
Nonwhite men	5	3	2

Moreover, the net scores varied from 5 favorable for young white persons to 2 favorable for young nonwhite persons, though all four groups by color and age scored 5 favorable major changes:

Group	Favorable	Unfavorable	Net favorable
Young whites	5	0	5
Older whites	5	1	4
Older nonwhites	5	2	3
Young nonwhites	5	3	2

When the eight groups by age, color, and sex were compared, young white women ranked highest with 3 favorable and no unfavorable major changes, whereas young nonwhite men ranked lowest with 2 favorable and 2 unfavorable major changes:

Group	Favorable	Unfavorable	Net favorable
Young white women	3	0	3
Young white men	2	0	2
Older white men	2	0	2
Older white women	3	1	2
Young nonwhite women	3	1	2
Older nonwhite men	3	1	2
Older nonwhite women	2	1	1
Young nonwhite men	2	2	0
Total	20	6	14

The results in Tables 3 and 4 provide a basis for concluding that more major as well as minor changes in marital status between 1960 and 1965 were favorable than unfavorable. They also provide a basis for judging the respects in which improvements and reverses have occurred, as long as the criteria for determining improvement and reverses are accepted. The next section raises questions about several of the assumptions made in developing the components of change and show how alternative assumptions would alter the conclusions.

ALTERNATIVES IN THE MEASUREMENT OF CHANGE

Use other age detail

If the analysis in Table 4 had been carried out for the combined age group 18 to 64 on the basis of the data in Table 5, the general pattern of the results would have been very similar to the pattern for the group 25 to 64 years old in Table 4. This finding is a consequence in part of the use of the same norms of favorableness for persons 18 to 64 as for those 25 to 64. But using a single complete age range (instead of using the younger and older groups separately in a disaggregated analysis) obscures the internal "mix" and therefore provides less basis for pinpointing the groups which are changing their marital status in one direction or another.

If the basic data had been available in finer age detail, somewhat different age groupings of younger and older persons might have been selected. Thus, for women, relatively young marriage might have been defined as something like 16 to 20 years of age, and for men young marriage might have been defined as something like 18 to 22. Beginning with Current Population Survey tabulations made in 1968, age detail

TABLE 5.

Percent Distribution by Marital Status, for Persons 18 to 64 Years Old, by Color and Sex, Standardized for Age: United States, 1960 and 1965

Marital Status and sex	White			Nonwhite		
	1960[1]	1965[1]	Change	1960	1965	Change
Men 18-64	100.0	100.0	0	100.0	100.0	0
Single	19.7	18.7	−1.0	25.6	24.4	−1.2
Marriage intact[2]	75.4	76.8	1.4	62.1	63.7	1.6
Marriage disrupted:						
Separated	1.5	1.1	−0.4	6.7	6.4	−0.3
Divorced	2.0	2.3	0.3	2.7	3.3	0.6
Widowed	1.4	1.1	−0.3	2.9	2.2	−0.7
Women 18-64	100.0	100.0	0	100.0	100.0	0
Single	13.3	13.1	−0.2	14.5	14.7	0.2
Marriage intact	75.3	75.9	0.6	59.3	60.8	1.5
Marriage disrupted:						
Separated	2.0	1.7	−0.3	10.9	10.8	−0.1
Divorced	2.9	3.5	0.6	4.2	4.9	0.7
Widowed	6.5	5.8	−0.7	11.1	8.8	−2.3

[1]Average for 5 years, centered on the stated year.
[2]Married, except separated.
Source: Same as Table 1.

by single years from 16 to 25 will become available annually for single and ever-married persons by sex and race.

Reverse norms for certain components of change

In the preceding section, some doubts were expressed about the appropriateness of some of the norms used in preparing Tables 3 and 4. Specifically, alternative norms were seriously considered as follows:

(a) For young nonwhites count a decrease in percent single as favorable, and for consistency count an increase in percent with marriage intact as favorable; these new norms for young nonwhites would then be opposite those used for young whites. The rationale behind this proposal is the fact that in 1960 the percent with marriage intact was much lower for young nonwhites than for young whites and the assumption that an increase in this percentage would largely reflect improved circumstances among young nonwhites which offered them a greater measure of free choice about age at marriage. This rationale was not considered sufficiently plausible, however, to justify the use of opposing norms for young whites and young nonwhites.

(b) For all groups (by age, color, and sex) count an increase in divorce as favorable. The rationale behind this proposal rests on the observation that some segments of the population have decreased their percent separated at the same time that they have increased their percent divorced; the inference suggested by this simultaneous shift was that improved financial ability and social freedom were permitting more people to end marriages that were no longer viable by obtaining a divorce rather than lingering in a state of separation. Important factors in rejecting this alternative were the speculative nature of the inference just cited and the irregularity with which increases in divorce have been counterbalanced by decreases in separation.

Despite the rejection of these two alternative sets of norms, the effects of accepting them were tested by modifying the entries in Table 4. The modified results are shown in the following exhibit, which reveals the impressive fact that when these alternatives are used the number of *unfavorable* components of major change in marital status is *reduced* from six to only two. These two "unfavorable" components, as newly defined, are a decrease in divorce for young nonwhite men and an increase in percent single for young nonwhite women — neither of which seems particularly unfavorable, in the context of substantial declines in percent separated for young nonwhite men and women.

Group	*Favorable*	*Unfavorable*	*Net favorable*
Older nonwhite women	4	0	4
Older nonwhite men	4	0	4
Young white women	3	0	3
Older white women	3	0	3
Young white men	2	0	2
Older white men	2	0	2
Young nonwhite women	3	1	2
Young nonwhite men	3	1	2
Total	24	2	22

The alternative norms place older nonwhite persons at the top of the list in regard to net major favorable changes and leave young nonwhite persons in the lower division.

Attach weights to components

Another variation in summarizing the marital changes would be to attach weights to the components, such as the algebraical amount of the changes recorded in Tables 1 and 2, with the signs modified as necessary to agree with the norms given in Table 3. This procedure would show young white women clearly as having made the largest volume of favorable change and young white men as having made relatively little change, according to the norms in Table 3.

Show rates of change

An alternative to the simple arithmetic changes in Tables 1 and 2 would be to replace them with *rates* of change over the 5-year period. Among the considerations for rejecting this alternative was the smallness of several of the marital status categories; not only the amounts of change but also the bases of the rates of change would be subject to considerable variation because of sampling error. At the same time, this alternative might dismiss as minor some substantial changes in the larger marital categories (amounting to 1.0 percent or more).

Change the number of marital status categories

The number of components of change could be reduced by combining percent separated and percent divorced into a single category for "percent with marriage disrupted." The following exhibit shows that the "net favorable" count would not be very different whether marriage disrupted is counted as one or two components. However, showing only the combined category would obscure the considerable differences in the internal "mix" of the component changes by age, color, and sex.

Color	*Favorable*	*Unfavorable*	*Net favorable*
Marriage disrupted as one item:			
Total	4	3	1
White	2	1	1
Nonwhite	2	2	0
Marriage disrupted as two items (Table 4):			
Total	6	5	1
White	3	3	0
Nonwhite	3	2	1

SUMMARY

This study of recent major changes in marital status justifies the conclusion that a clear majority of the changes were favorable, where "favorable" reflects an increase in the proportion single among young adults and an increase in proportion married among adults of more mature age. According to the criteria used, nonwhites recorded 10 *favorable* major changes out of a possible 20, 5 *unfavorable* major changes, and 5 which were not classified as major. Whites likewise recorded 10 *favorable* major changes, but only 1 *unfavorable* major change and 9 changes not classified as major. Thus, despite the evidence of gains in marital stability among nonwhites, the evidence of such gains among whites was even stronger. By various ways of measuring and evaluating changes in marital status between 1960 and 1965, young white women scored relatively high, and young nonwhite men scored relatively low, on net favorable change.

Advantages and disadvantages of several alternative measures of change in marital status were presented, together with the effects that some of the alternatives would have had on the evaluation of changes if they had been adopted. In general, if the alternative procedures had been adopted, similar overall conclusions, but somewhat unlike detailed conclusions, would have been drawn about changes in marital status for subgroups by age, color, and sex.

NOTES

[1]The marriage rate for the 12 months ending November 1968 was 10.3 per 1,000 population; the corresponding rate for 1960 was 8.5. The divorce rate per 1,000 population was 2.7 in 1967 as compared with 2.2 in 1960. See National Center for Health Statistics, *Monthly Vital Statistics Report*, Vol. 17, Nos. 10, 11, 10 supplement, and 11 supplement; also *Marriage Statistics Analysis: United States, 1963*, and *Divorce Statistics Analysis, 1963*.

[2]Changes in marital status by age and race for the period 1930 to 1960 are featured in Hugh Carter and Paul C. Glick, "Trends and Current Patterns of Marital Status Among Nonwhite Persons," *Demography*, Vol. 3, No. 1, 1966, pp. 276-288.

[3]This paper is an extension of the analysis presented in a background paper on marriage trends which was prepared at the request of staff members of the Department of Health, Education, and Welfare who were in charge of exploring the possibility of assembling "social statistics and indicators" for the Nation. Information on "these yardsticks" was issued in January 1969 as a report from Secretary Wilbur J. Cohen to the President entitled *Toward a Social Report*. The letter of transmittal states that the report "deals with such aspects of the quality of American life as: health and illness; social mobility; the physical environment; income and poverty; public order and safety; learning, science, and art; and participation and alienation."

Marital Instability by Race, Sex, Education, Occupation and Income

J. RICHARD UDRY

UNTIL ABOUT TWENTY-FIVE YEARS AGO, IT SEEMS TO HAVE BEEN generally believed that divorce was more prevalent in the well-to-do groups. In 1938 Terman wrote: "it is well known that more divorces occur in the higher classes."[1] The lower-status groups, it was believed, tended either to separate informally or suffer together. As Goode indicates, this may well have been true at some previous period when the general standard of living and level of development was lower.[2] After 1940, as better data became available, sociological studies in the United States showed the inadequacy of this generalization.[3] These studies, based usually on small populations, consistently have demonstrated that the higher the socioeconomic status of a group, the lower their divorce and separation rates.

With the 1950 Census came the first opportunity to measure the relationship between status-related variables and certain aspects of marital stability, using the entire population. Glick, using 1950 Census data to calculate separation and divorce rates by race and education, found a curvilinear relationship of divorce to educational level for each race, with divorce rates highest in the middle levels of education. His

---

[1]Lewis M. Terman, *Psychological Factors in Marital Happiness* (New York: McGraw-Hill Book Co., 1938), p. 167.

[2]William J. Goode, *World Revolution and Family Patterns* (New York: Free Press of Glencoe, 1963).

[3]H. Ashley Weeks, "Differential Divorce Rates by Occupation," *Social Forces*, XXI (1943), 334-37; August B. Hollingshead, "Class Differences in Family Stability," *Annals of the American Academy of Political and Social Science*, CLXXII (1950), 39-46; William A. Kephart, "Occupational Level and Marital Disruption," *American Sociological Review*, XX (1955), 456-65; William J. Goode, *After Divorce* (Glencoe, Ill.: Free Press, 1956).

Reprinted by permission of the publisher and author from *The American Journal of Sociology*, LXXII (September 1966), 203-9, and LXXII (May 1967), 673-74.

data show a consistent inverse relationship between separation rates and educational level for each race.[4]

Hillman used 1950 Census data to calculate separation and divorce rates by sex for each race by status-related variables.[5] The breakdown of the data by sex showed the relationships between various status indexes to be quite complex. According to her method of calculation, the inverse relationship between marital instability (divorce and separation) and status held only for white males, with varying patterns occurring for non-white males and for females of both races. Figure 1 is prepared from her data, based on 1950 Census tabulations for race, sex, and educational level. Other tables in her original article present similar data for occupational and income groups by race and sex.

These conclusions fly in the face of conclusions from small studies, and also contain patterns which are difficult to reconcile. For example, Hillman's tables show an inverse relationship between marital instability for white men, but a direct relationship for white women. In a population in which educational homogamy is the rule the result is improbable.[6] The problem is in the method of calculation of instability rates used by Glick and Hillman, necessitated by the limitations of their data. They had available only figures from which to calculate the proportion of those ever married who were *at the time of the Census* either divorced or separated. It is possible that differences in the rate of remarriage and time lag in remarriage explain the differences in rates shown in their analyses, or at least the discrepancies between the Census data and previous studies. For example, if two groups have the same over-all percentage of couples who divorce each year, but one group has a

---

[4]Paul C. Glick, *American Families* (New York: John Wiley & Sons, 1957), p. 154, Table 102. Glick's rates are calculated as rate of divorce or separation among those "subject to" divorce or separation. "Subject to" divorce is defined as married plus one half of those divorced at the time of the census who divorced in the two years previous to the census. His rates are adjusted for age.

[5]Karen G. Hillman, "Marital Instability and Its Relation to Education, Income, and Occupation: An Analysis Based on Census Data," in Robert F. Winch, Robert McGinnis, and Herbert R. Barringer (eds.), *Selected Studies in Marriage and the Family* (rev. ed.; New York: Holt, Rinehart & Winston, 1962), pp. 602-8.

[6]In 1960 the probability of a married college-graduate female being married to a no-college male was about 0.25, while the probability of a no-college male being married to a female college graduate was about 0.07 (calculated from *U.S. Census of Population, 1960: Families.* PC (2) 4A, Tables 25 and 26). This does not exclude the possibility that many short heterogamous marriages occur which then collapse to swell the ranks of the broken-marriage group. However, marriage license studies make this seem unlikely (see, e.g., Lee G. Burchinal and Loren E. Chancellor, "Survival Rates among Religiously Homogamous and Interreligious Marriages" [Agricultural and Home Economics Experiment Station, Iowa State University, Research Bulletin No. 512, December, 1962], for some pertinent data).

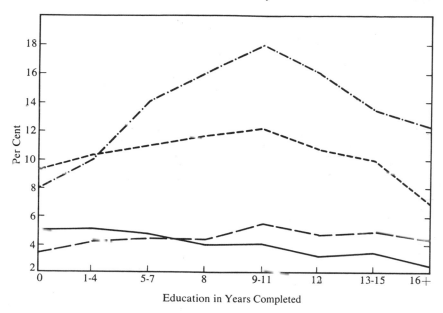

FIGURE 1.   Percentage of those ever married who were divorced and
separated at the 1950 Census. *Solid line*, white males; *long-dash line*, white females;
short-dash line, non-white males; *dash-dot line*, non-white females.
(Source: Hillman, *op. cit.*)

remarriage rate of 90 per cent in five years and the second has a
remarriage rate of 45 per cent in five years, then at any one time many
more people in the second group will be in a divorced status. Likewise,
if the remarriage rate for the first group is 50 per cent in two years, and
in the second is 50 per cent in four years, then at any one time the
second group will have many more persons in a divorced status, even
though the ultimate divorce and even remarriage rates for the two groups
are identical.[7]

The data presented below are calculated from unpublished tables from
the 1960 Census, based on a 5 per cent sample of the U.S. population,
and provided the author by the Bureau of the Census. For most of the
categories calculated by Hillman for 1950, the 1960 data offer the same

[7]Exactly the same problems are inherent in Glick's analysis of marital disruption
using the 1960 Census data (Paul C. Glick, "Marriage Instability: Variations by
Size of Place and Region," *Milbank Memorial Fund Quarterly*, XLI [January,
1963], 43-55). Neither Glick nor Hillman had available the category "persons married more than once" to add to the numerators of their ratios, and hence they were
unable to discuss the extent of marital instability at all but were required to limit
themselves to marriages currently disrupted.

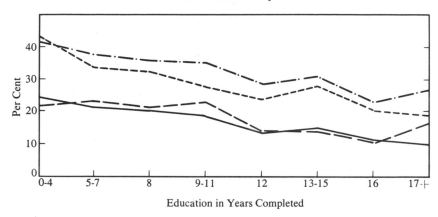

FIGURE 2.   Percentage of those ever married who were divorced,
separated, or had been married more than once at the 1960 Census, by
education (age 14 and over). Legend same as in Fig. 1.
(Source: Unpublished data furnished by the Bureau of the Census.)

relationships. For some categories data are not available for one census
or the other. The 1960 analysis contains no rates by income. The 1950
data provide no rates for females by occupational status of the woman.
Differences in educational categories between 1950 and 1960 should
also be noted.

In order to take into account the fact that most persons who divorce
remarry, disruption rates were calculated in the present analysis by
adding together the number divorced, the number separated, and the
number married more than once, and dividing by the number ever
married.[8] In the total population, of course, this calculation is con-
taminated by the number of widowed persons who have remarried,
which might conceivably vary by socioeconomic status. Death rates also
vary by race, marital status, and socioeconomic status, and serve as
another contaminant, removing from enumeration more Negroes, low-
status persons, and divorced persons than their proportion in the population. Therefore all calculations were also made on the age group 25-34.
In this group most persons who will ever marry are married,[9] most have

---

[8]This calculation cannot catch the instability which takes the form of separation
and reunion with the same spouse, since there is no category "ever separated."

[9]Of all females who eventually marry, about nine in ten do so before age 25, and
of all males who eventually marry, about nine in ten do so before age 30 (calculated from Paul H. Jacobson, *American Marriage and Divorce* [New York: Holt,
Rinehart & Winston, 1959], pp. 78, 80).

been married long enough to have a chance for disruption,[10] and few have had time to be widowed and remarried.[11] However, the data for the age group 25-34 so calculated show relationships identical to those calculated on all persons over 14 years old (see Figs. 2 and 3).

There are still weaknesses in the Census data from which the tables are calculated, as shown in the data. Men of each race, for example, show substantially lower disruption rates than women. Several factors could contribute to this picture: higher mortality for men with disrupted marriages than for similar women, underreporting of broken marriages by men (it is known that men who are separated or divorced are more likely to report themselves single than are separated or divorced women), reporting of a previous marital state by unmarried women with children, and other factors. Studies of the effect of race of the interviewer on responses of Negro respondents have shown that white interviewers find

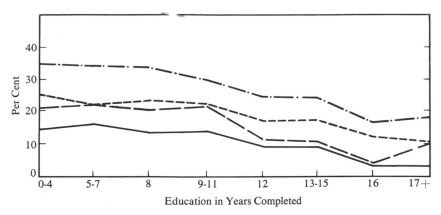

FIGURE 3. Percentage of those ever married who were divorced, separated, or had been married more than once at the 1960 Census, by education (ages 25-34). Legend same as in Fig. 1. (Source: Unpublished data furnished by the Bureau of the Census.)

[10]For all couples who divorce, the median number of years of marriage before divorce in 1957 was 6.7 years (National Office of Vital Statistics, *Special Reports*, L, No. 18 [1959], lviii). But most of these were separated earlier. Kephart reported that in Philadelphia more than half of those divorcing were separated by the fifth year of marriage (William M. Kephart, "The Duration of Marriage," *American Sociological Review*, XIX [June, 1954], 287-95). The modal length of marriage at separation in Kephart's figures was less than one year, and Jacobson (*op. cit.*, p. 94) reported that post-World War II marriages which end in divorce had a modal length less than two years.

[11]Of course using a young age group introduces other biases. Negroes, low-status persons, and females marry earlier and are therefore exposed to the risk of disruption more years by a given age than whites, high-status persons, and males, respectively.

higher proportions of separated women while Negro interviewers find higher proportions of single women. Whether inaccurate reporting of marital status varies by socioeconomic or educational status is not known, but the data available encourage this hypothesis. Yet another factor is the fact that women marry at earlier ages than men, and therefore are exposed to the risk of marital disruption longer by a given age. Table 1 suggests that, if education is controlled, the sex difference in age at marriage is not so great And of course at every age mortality is higher for men than women.

There remains one serious problem which these data cannot resolve. The average age at first marriage is directly related to number of years of education. Therefore, at least in the group age 25-34, the most educated have been exposed to the risk of marital disruption for a shorter period of time. Table 1 shows that more than one-third of those with less than eight years of education are married before age 22, while only about one-sixth of those with 16 or more years of education are married before age 22. On the other hand, one-fourth of those with under eight years of education, but one-third of those with sixteen or more years of education, are married at or after age 28. These figures, however, do not vary much by race and sex, and therefore probably bias the race and sex differences in approximately the same way. (Unfortunately, those not in husband-wife family status in 1960 do not form part of the proportions shown in Table 1.) Other studies indicate

TABLE 1

PROPORTION OF HUSBANDS AND WIVES WHO WERE MARRIED BY CERTAIN AGES, BY EDUCATIONAL ATTAINMENT, BY RACE, FOR HUSBAND-WIFE FAMILIES IN THE UNITED STATES, 1960

AGE AT TIME AT MARRIAGE	YEARS OF SCHOOL COMPLETED			
	HUSBAND		WIFE	
	Less than 8	16 or More	Less than 8	16 or More
White:				
Under 22	0.34	0.15	0.35	0.12
28 and over	.25	.27	.25	.32
Non-white:				
Under 22	.39	.15	.39	.17
28 and over	0.28	0.35	0.28	0.35

Source: Computed from *U.S. Census of Population, 1960:* Families (PC (2) 4A), Table 45, p. 358.

that the rate of divorce in those who marry very early is greater than those who marry very late. If, of all marriages which are broken by divorce, half are broken by the fifth year of marriage, then by age 27, at least twice as great a proportion of those in the lowest educational category will have been exposed to the maximum risk of divorce as will those in the highest educational category.[12] If early marriage contributes to high disruption rates independently of education (and this is not certain), then these two factors of greater exposure to risk could account for most of the difference in the disruption rates by education shown in Figure 3. The fact that the pattern for all persons over 14 years of age (Fig. 2) is very similar to the pattern for those 25-34, which is in turn very similar to the pattern for those age 35-44 (not shown), weakens the likelihood that the greater exposure to risk explanation is the entire explanation, although it does not eliminate the possibility.

Hillman reviews other weaknesses of Census data on divorce, which also apply to the present data. The number of divorced persons is underestimated in the Census, but it is not known how the underestimation of divorced persons varies by the characteristics of this analysis. Within the limitations inherent in the data, the following observations can be made.

EDUCATION AND MARITAL STABILITY

When looking at total disruption rates, it is obvious that there is a clear inverse relationship between disruption rate and educational status for both sexes and both races. The elevated rate for women with graduate training compared with the low rate for men with graduate training (most of whom are married to women without graduate training) is an interesting but minor exception (see Figs. 2 and 3). When we compare non-whites and whites of the same sex, non-white rates of disruption are from one and a half to more than two times the rates for whites of the same educational level. The higher the educational level, the more different are white and non-white rates of divorced status at the time of the 1960 Census (Fig. 4), but a comparison with Figure 3 suggests that this is largely due to differences in rates and lags in remarriage, since it does not hold when the "married more than once" group is added to the numerator. The ratio between white and non-white disruption rates

---

[12]Furthermore, of all women who divorce, those who dropped out of high school tend to divorce after fewer years of marriage than those who graduated from college. This increases the exposure to risk of the least educated group, since the period of greatest risk occurs earlier in marriage and earlier in life (Glick, *American Families*, pp. 149-50).

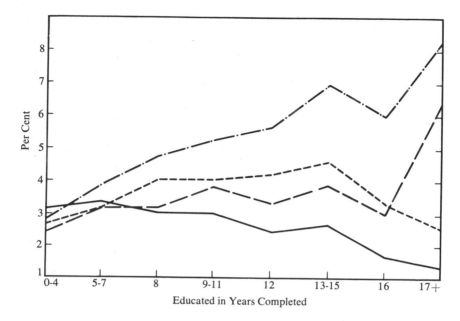

Per Cent

Educated in Years Completed

FIGURE 4.   Percentage of those ever married who were divorced but not remarried at the 1960 Census, by education (age 14 and over). Legend same as in Fig. 1. (Source: Unpublished data furnished by the Bureau of the Census.)

in 1960 is fairly constant over different educational levels (Fig. 3). These observations do not give unqualified support to the frequent suggestion that increasing non-white status will obliterate racial differences in marital patterns, although they indicate that it should reduce these differences.

Being separated is still a characteristic reported primarily by the uneducated and the non-white (Fig. 5). Since these data only show those separated at one point in time, the pattern of Figure 5 cannot be taken to represent the relative frequency of the occurrence of separation in each category. In this sense it has the weakness inherent in the data Hillman and Glick worked with.

The percentage divorced may be viewed as a way of estimating differentials in the rate and time lag in remarriage among divorced groups. Comparison among the figures presented invites (but does not establish) the following interpretations as hypotheses for further exploration. Among whites without college, the men remarry more rapidly than the women, while among whites with college, the women remarry more rapidly than the men. Younger white females with graduate educa-

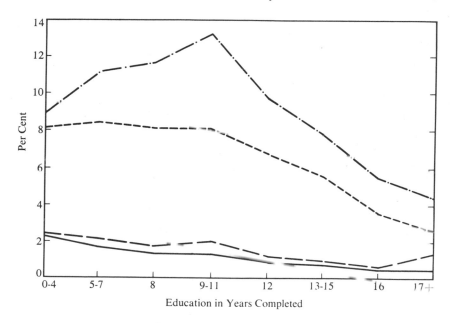

FIGURE 5. Percentage of those ever married who were separated at the 1960 Census, by education (age 14 and over). Legend same as in Fig. 1. (Source: Unpublished data furnished by the Bureau of the Census.)

tion remarry more rapidly than older white women with similar education. The divorced per cent for these educated women age 25-34 is only 0.5 per cent, while among all white women with graduate education it is 6.3 per cent. There is virtually no difference for white men of this educational level between percentage divorced among the young and percentage divorced among all ages. Among non-whites, more-educated women remarry more slowly than less-educated women, while the relationship for men is curvilinear. There are, of course, other interpretations of these differences in rates. Many of the differences are no doubt due to differential accuracy of reporting in different groups, and to other limitations in the data discussed above.

OCCUPATIONAL AND MARITAL STABILITY

Occupational status and its relationship to marital stability must be considered a different phenomenon for each sex (Fig. 6), since marital disruption may lead some women into certain occupational categories, while it is more difficult to conceive of men being led into certain

Marital Instability

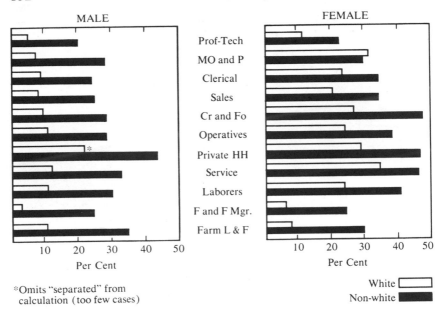

FIGURE 6.   Percentage of those ever married who were divorced, separated, or had been married more than once at the 1960 Census, by occupation (ages 25-34). (Source: Unpublished data furnished by the Bureau of the Census.)

occupations as a result of marital disruption. Generally speaking, there is lowest marital stability in the lowest-status occupation for men, and highest stability in the high-status occupations, with highest instability in men in personal service and domestic service. Occupational status has the same relationship to marital stability in non-white and white males, except that non-white rates are more than double the white rates. The relationship between occupational status and marital stability for men is direct and unequivocal.

Peculiar disruption rates are associated with each occupational category among women who are employed, and these rates cannot be said to be associated with the status level of the occupational group. Since occupational status of employed women cannot be said to be a primary socioeconomic status attribute of women, and since less than half of women are included, this finding does not vitiate the fundamental inverse relationship between socioeconomic status and marital disruption. The female rates by occupation are unexplained, and the pattern invites research into the functional relationship between marriage and various occupations for women.

SUMMARY AND DISCUSSION

Analysis of 1960 Census data shows the relationship between status and marital disruption to be inverse for both sexes and for both whites and non-whites, when status is measured by educational level. When measured by occupational status, the relationship of status to marital disruption is still inverse and clear for men. The far greater instability of non-white marriages is shown not to be attributable solely to the general low educational and occupational status of this group, but a characteristic of non-white groups of all educational and occupational levels. By occupational status there is practically no overlap in rates between white and non-whites of any status level, and the overlap between the two groups on disruption rates by education is slight. Of course occupational and educational differences within the non-white group are related to marital instability in the same way as among whites.

The analysis presented here does not explain white-non-white differences but simply delineates them more clearly. Socioeconomic status differences not tapped by education and occupation may still explain much of the difference. For example, non-whites and whites matched on occupation or education are still grossly unequal in income, which may be related to divorce rates independently of occupational status. Perhaps the "caste" position of Negroes has a relationship to marital instability. Perhaps a historical-cultural explanation, tracing the Negro family pattern to roots in the slavery system, is made more tenable in the light of the above data.[13] Census data cannot lead to a definitive choice among the possible explanations.

EPILOGUE: MARITAL INSTABILITY BY RACE AND INCOME

In my recent article, "Marital Instability by Race, Sex, Education, and Occupation Using 1960 Census Data" (*American Journal of Sociology,* LXXII [September, 1966], 203-9), I omitted consideration of income, because when the original manuscript was prepared these data were not available to me. The data on which the original article was based were published during 1966 (U.S. Bureau of the Census, *U.S. Census of Population: 1960. Subject Reports. Marital Status,* Final Report PC(2)-4E [Washington: U.S. Government Printing Office, 1966], Tables 4 and 5). The reader who has this publication will immediately see that the same calculations I performed on Tables 4 and 5 can be applied to the income

---

[13]E. Franklin Frazier, *The Negro in the United States* (New York: Macmillan Co., 1957) and *The Negro Family in the United States* (Chicago: University of Chicago Press, 1939).

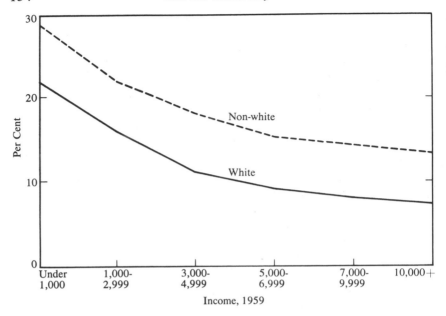

FIGURE 7.   Percentage of ever-married males 25-34 years of age who were
separated, divorced, or had been married more than once at the time of the 1960
Census, by income and race; based on a 5 per cent sample. (Source:
U.S. Bureau of the Census, *U.S. Census of Population: 1940. Subject Reports:
Marital Status,* Final Report PE(2)-4E [Washington: U.S. Government
Printing Office, 1966], Table 6.)

data of Table 6. Figure 7 above presents marital instability by personal
income by race for males ages 25-34 in the same form as the other data
in the original article. The female data are confusing, and I am not
presenting them here. It is too easy to see how marital status of women
can influence their personal income to try to explain from these data
how women's income might affect their marital status. This problem
seems much less important in the case of men. In Figure 7, the inverse
relationship of income to marital instability is quite unmistakable. It is

TABLE 2

RATIO OF NON-WHITE TO WHITE MARITAL INSTABILITY
BY INCOME FOR MALES AGES 25-34
(FROM FIG. 7)

Under 1,000 . . .	1.24	5,000-6,999	1.74
1,000-2,999	1.38	7,000-9,999	1.81
3,000-4,999	1.59	10,000+	1.95

also quite clear that the ratio of non-white to white marital instability grows consistently with increasing income (see Table 2). These income data serve only to reinforce the arguments given in the original paper that the white-non-white difference in marital instability cannot be explained solely by differences in present socioeconomic status. For further analysis of 1960 Census data on this topic, the reader is referred to an article by Jessie Bernard, and comments thereon by others, in the November, 1966, *Journal of Marriage and Family*.

Family Stability and Occupational Success

BEVERLY DUNCAN AND OTIS DUDLEY DUNCAN

THE INSTABILITY OF FAMILY LIFE FOR NEGRO MEN, AS MANIFEST IN the absence of a father in the childhood home and the absence of a wife during adulthood, may bear a causal relation to their lack of occupational success or so it has been argued. That Negro boys are more likely to be living in a broken home than are their non-Negro age-mates is well documented. Equally well documented is the relatively high proportion of Negro men who are not married or, if married, are not living with their wives. Less well documented are the effects of family instability in the parental generation on family instability among their sons, and largely unmeasured are differentials in occupational success which might be attributed to family instability in any direct sense.

The analyses reported here bear on only a few strands of the web of relations among economic conditions and family structure pointed up by the so-called Moynihan report and the commentaries engendered by that report (Rainwater and Yancey, 1967). Both the form and substance of the report have been controversial issues; for clarity a brief quotation seems in order.

> In essence, the Negro community has been forced into a matriarchal structure which, because it is so out of line with the rest of the American society, seriously retards the progress of the group as a whole, and imposes a crushing burden on the Negro male and, in consequence, on a great many Negro women as well.
>
> There is, presumably, no special reason why a society in which males are dominant in family relationships is to be preferred to a matriarchal arrangement. However, it is clearly a disadvantage for a minority group to be operating on one principle, while the great majority of the population, and the one with the most advantages

Reprinted by permission of the publisher and authors from, *Social Problems*, XVI (Winter 1969), 273-85.

to begin with, is operating on another. [Rainwater and Yancey, 1967, p. 75.]

Not all commentators on the report have accepted as clearly established the fact of disadvantage stemming from the matriarchal arrangement as such. Gans is among these commentators.

> ... the matriarchal family structure and the absence of a father has not yet been proven pathological, even for the boys who grow up in it. Sociological studies of the Negro family have demonstrated the existence of an extended kinship system of mothers, grand-mothers, aunts, and other female relatives that is surprisingly stable, at least on the female side. Moreover, many matriarchal families raise boys who do adapt successfully and themselves make stable marriages. The immediate cause of pathology may be the absence of a set of emotional strengths and cultural skills in the mothers, rather than the instability or departure of the fathers. A family headed by a capable if unmarried mother may thus be healthier than a two-parent family in which the father is a marginal appendage. If this is true, one could argue that at present, the broken and matriarchal family is a viable solution for the Negro lower-class population, for given the economic and other handicaps of the men, the family can best survive by rejecting its men, albeit at great emotional cost to them. [Rainwater and Yancey, 1967, p. 451.]

Measures on the current marital and occupational statuses of men in the Negro minority and the non-Negro majority who report growing up in a family headed by a female cannot purport to measure fully the hypothesized liabilities of matriarchy, even when compared with the corresponding measures for men of the same race reared in intact families. As Gans has pointed out, the mere presence of the father in the home does not ensure a stable family life and an effective male role model. Moreover, the presence of the father may take on a different meaning in a group unambiguously organized along patriarchal lines than in the group where matriarchal arrangements are common. Nonetheless, it seems worthwhile to assess the differences in current marital and occupational statuses between adult American males reared in broken families and their counterparts whose youth was spent in an intact family.

INTER-GENERATIONAL TRANSMISSION
OF FAMILY INSTABILITY

That, in America, the Negro man is more likely to be reared in a broken family and to be living apart from his wife than is the non-Negro man is a widely known fact. Less adequately measured, though subject to widespread speculation, is the influence of a broken-family background on marital status in adulthood. Data recently have become available from a nationwide survey of American men which permit a new reading on the influence of family background on marital status.

Among the items of information collected for civilian noninstitutional males included in the March, 1962, Current Population Survey conducted by the United States Bureau of the Census was current marital status. Information about the structure of the family in which the man had lived in his youth was obtained through a supplementary questionnaire, "Occupational Changes in a Generation." Descriptions of the survey procedures and evaluations of data quality are available in published sources (Blau and Duncan, 1967). The population under study here is represented by respondents between the ages of 25 and 64 in 1962 who had been living in a family headed by someone other than a farmer or farm worker when they were 16 years old.

Men who had grown up in an intact family, that is, who had lived with both parents "most of the time" until they reached age 16, are substantially under-represented among the Negroes. Only three-fifths of

TABLE 1.

DISTRIBUTIONS BY CURRENT MARITAL STATUS FOR NATIVE CIVILIAN
NONINSTITUTIONAL MALES OF NONFARM BACKGROUND, AGED 25
TO 64, CLASSIFIED BY RACE AND FAMILY BACKGROUND:
UNITED STATES, 1962

Race and family background	Per cent never married	PER CENT OF EVER MARRIED					
		Spouse present	Spouse absent	Separated	Divorced	Widowed	Number (000's)[a]
NEGRO							
All	11.7	82.3	1.9	9.6	3.6	2.6	1,870[b]
Both parents	13.2	81.6	1.3	11.6	3.0	2.6	1,124
Female head	11.5	82.8	2.3	7.7	4.0	3.2	531
Male head	...	...	...	...	...	...	171
NON-NEGRO							
All	9.5	94.7	0.6	1.0	2.5	1.2	22,638[c]
Both parents	9.7	94.5	0.6	1.0	2.6	1.2	18,785
Female head	9.6	95.9	0.5	1.1	1.4	1.1	2,393
Male head	7.4	94.6	0.2	1.4	2.8	1.1	1,324

... Percentage not calculated; base fewer than 150 sample cases.

[a] Approximate sample frequencies may be obtained by dividing population frequencies, in thousands, by 2.17.

[b] Includes 44,000 not reporting on family background.

[c] Includes 136,000 not reporting on family background.

Source: Unpublished tabulations from March, 1962, Current Population Survey and supplement thereto, Occupational Changes in a Generation, conducted by the United States Bureau of the Census.

the Negro men, in contrast to four-fifths of the non-Negroes, report that both parents were present in their childhood home. This difference is compensated by a sharp over-representation among Negroes of men who grew up in a family headed by a female. Nearly three-tenths of the Negroes, as compared with a tenth of the non-Negroes, report that a woman, typically the respondent's mother, headed the family in which they spent most of their youth.

The Negro respondents were a little less likely than the non-Negroes to report ever contracting a marriage; and relatively few of the Negroes who had contracted a marriage were living with their wives at the time of the survey. Disproportionate numbers of Negro men appear in each "broken" marital status, but the over-representation is far sharper for the separated status than for any other "broken" status. The tabulations by current marital status do not permit the calculation of rates of marital disruption, which would require information on the outcome of each marriage contracted.

The data presented in Table 1 have been arranged to bear on the question: Does the experience of growing up in a broken family increase the probability that a man will be found unmarried or living apart from his wife in adulthood? The answer, insofar as it can be revealed by the results of this survey, is no. For neither the Negro nor the non-Negro men does an inter-generational transmission of family instability appear to be operating, insofar as instability is indexed by the absence of a parent or spouse from the home.

There is, then, no sound basis for postulating a cycle of broken family relations, such that failure of the parents to share a home with one another and their offspring predisposes their sons to life without a spouse.

DIFFERENTIAL OCCUPATIONAL SUCCESS

A socio-economic status score was assigned to the current, or most recent, occupation and to the occupation of the first full-time job held by each respondent (Reiss and others, 1961, Ch. 7). In the total population under study here, the mean value of the current-occupation scores is 42, with a standard deviation of 24; the mean value of the first-occupation scores is 29, with a standard deviation of 22. The difference in mean occupation score between the Negro and non-Negro men approximates in magnitude a standard-deviation unit, for the groups as a whole and for subgroups defined by family background and current marital status.

Of primary interest here, however, are the differences to be observed among groups defined by family background and current marital status for men of the same race. Inspection of the mean scores reported in Table 2 reveals that within-race differences by family background and current marital status are modest in magnitude *vis-à-vis* the between-race differences. The maximum within-race difference amounts to no more than a fourth of a standard-deviation unit, in contrast to the between-race difference of a full standard-deviation unit. Insofar as differential occupational success can be detected, the advantage typically lies with the man raised in intact families and the men currently living with their wives, however.

For only a few subgroups defined by family background and current marital status are the numbers of sample cases sufficiently large to yield reliable measures of occupational success; and for only two subgroups can such measurements be made for both Negroes and non-Negroes. Two-thirds of the Negro respondents and four-fifths of the non-Negro respondents fall into one or the other of these categories, however. The modal combination of family background and current marital status is

TABLE 2.

MEAN SOCIO-ECONOMIC STATUS SCORE OF OCCUPATIONS HELD BY NATIVE CIVILIAN NONINSTITUTIONAL MALES OF NONFARM BACKGROUND, AGED 25 TO 64, CLASSIFIED BY RACE, FAMILY BACKGROUND, AND CURRENT MARITAL STATUS: UNITED STATES, 1962

Family background	NEGRO				NON-NEGRO			
	All	Married, spouse present	Other marital status	Never married	All	Married, spouse present	Other marital status	Never married
			CURRENT OCCUPATION					
All	19.75	20.00	. . .	. . .	43.47	44.20	37.48	39.91
Both parents	20.67	21.80	. . .	. . .	44.40	45.12	37.79	41.40
Female head	18.09	17.93	. . .	. . .	39.25	40.28	. . .	. . .
Male head	. . .	. . .	. . .	. . .	39.45	40.05	. . .	. . .
			FIRST OCCUPATION					
All	16.70	16.95	. . .	. . .	30.36	30.20	28.50	32.76
Both parents	16.86	16.91	. . .	. . .	31.11	30.95	28.98	33.67
Female head	16.54	17.07	. . .	. . .	27.60	27.51	. . .	. . .
Male head	. . .	. . .	. . .	. . .	25.39	25.15	. . .	. . .

. . . Mean not calculated; base fewer than 150 sample cases.
Source: See source note, Table 1.

TABLE 3.

MEAN SCORES AND STANDARD DEVIATIONS ON SELECTED SOCIO-ECONOMIC CHARACTERISTICS FOR NATIVE CIVILIAN NONINSTITUTIONAL MALES OF NONFARM BACKGROUND, AGED 25 TO 64, MARRIED AND LIVING WITH THEIR WIVES, BY RACE AND FAMILY BACKGROUND: UNITED STATES, 1962

Characteristic	MEAN-SCORE				STANDARD DEVIATION			
	NEGRO		NON-NEGRO		NEGRO		NON-NEGRO	
	Both parents	Female head	Both parents	Female head	Both parents	Female head	Both parents	Female head
Current occupation	21.80	17.93	45.12	40.28	18.95	14.77	24.46	24.34
Age at first—								
Marriage	23.96	24.61	24.20	24.24	5.26	6.43	4.73	5.16
Job	18.49	17.25	18.59	17.79	4.64	3.36	2.97	3.31
First occupation	16.91	17.07	30.95	27.51	15.00	13.14	22.43	20.22
Education	10.10	8.51	11.87	10.97	3.39	3.31	3.22	3.42
Siblings, number	5.30	3.87	3.89	3.63	3.61	3.34	2.92	2.87
Father's occupation	20.49	...	34.58	...	19.17	...	22.87	...
Head's work status[a]	...	0.25	...	0.55	...	...	...	0.50
Head's occupation[b]	...	20.28	...	32.21	...	13.68	...	21.26
Father's education	7.36	...	8.61	...	3.47	...	3.66	...
Head's education	...	6.89	...	8.97	...	3.41	...	3.44

... Item does not apply.

[a] No reported occupation scored zero; any reported occupation scored unity. See text.

[b] Excludes cases not reporting head's occupation.

Source: See source note, Table 1.

161

"both parents — married, spouse present." A substantial minority of Negro respondents (44 per cent) and a substantial majority of non-Negro respondents (71 per cent) fall in the modal category. The other sizable category is made up of men, currently married and living with their wives, who had grown up in a family headed by a female.

Since both groups of men were "married, spouse present" on the survey date, any difference in occupational success must be attributed to family background and its correlates rather than to current marital status. The socio-economic status of the occupations currently pursued by the group of men with intact-family backgrounds is slightly higher than that of the occupations pursued by men who grew up in families headed by a female. The absolute difference in current occupational status is of about the same magnitude for Negroes and non-Negroes, four and five scale points, respectively.

Moreover, promotion in the work force, as indexed by the difference between the scores for first and current occupations, has been slightly more rapid for men with intact-family backgrounds than for men of the same race reared in families headed by a female. The differential promotion is especially pronounced among Negroes: the status score of the current occupation was five scale points higher than the status score of the entry occupation for the men with intact-family backgrounds; the corresponding difference for men with broken-family backgrounds was only one scale point.

Inspection of the mean scores on antecedent socio-economic characteristics reported in Table 3 suggests that the somewhat greater occupational success of men with intact-family backgrounds may simply reflect their superior job qualifications. They had entered the work force at a later age than men of the same race reared in families headed by a female (1.2 years for Negroes and 0.8 years for non-Negroes) and were better prepared for work-force participation in terms of formal schooling completed (1.6 grades for Negroes and 0.9 grades for non-Negroes). This possibility is explored more systematically in the regression analyses which follow.

OCCUPATIONAL SUCCESS AND JOB QUALIFICATIONS

When the socio-economic status score of the occupation currently held by the respondent is regressed on his age at first marriage, the age at which he took his first full-time job, the socio-economic status score of that job, and the grades of school completed, the amount of formal schooling is found to be the most important determinant of occupational success. Schooling has, of course, a consistent positive effect on occupational success; but men reared in intact families have translated their formal schooling into occupational achievement more effectively than have men of the same race with a broken-family background. Whether the socio-economic status score of the current occupation is regressed on education alone or in combination with first occupation and the age variables, the increase in occupational status associated with an additional year of schooling is greater for the group of men with intact-family backgrounds. Relevant raw-score regression coefficients are reported in the upper panel of Table 4.

The match of men and jobs in terms of educational qualifications and status in the occupation structure probably is closer for men with intact-family backgrounds at the point of work-force entry as well as at a later stage in working life. When the socio-economic status score of the first occupation is regressed on school years completed, the regression coefficients in raw-score form are found to be: 1.24 for Negroes with intact-family backgrounds; 0.78 for Negroes reared in families headed by a female; 3.85 for non-Negroes with intact-family backgrounds; and 3.19 for non-Negroes reared in families headed by a female. The qualification "probably" is needed, however, because tabulations of survey respondents by grades completed and age at first job imply that a substantial minority of men attended school at some time subsequent to work-force entry, that is, the number of grades completed exceeds the number that could reasonably have been completed by that age. The occupations of the first jobs held by men in this "inconsistent" minority appear more appropriate for men of the given age than for men with the given level of educational attainment (Duncan, 1965, Ch. 5).

To the advantage of men with intact-family backgrounds, then, is not only a higher mean level of educational attainment, but also a more efficient translation of educational attainment into occupational achievement.

A somewhat different impression of the influence of education on current occupation for men of intact- and broken-family backgrounds, respectively, might be formed from the magnitudes of the regression coefficients expressed in standard-deviation, rather than raw-score, units. Because the ratio of the standard deviation of the occupation scores to the standard deviation of the education scores is of greater magnitude for the men of intact-family backgrounds within each racial group, the pattern of differentials does not remain constant. The shifts can be detected by comparison of entries in the upper panel of Table 4 with corresponding entries in the lower panel.

There is a detectable positive influence of the occupation of the first job held on current occupational status, net of the effects of education and the age variables on occupational success. Uncertainty about whether

TABLE 4.

SUMMARY OF MULTIPLE REGRESSION ANALYSES OF CURRENT OCCUPATION ON SELECTED INDICATORS OF JOB QUALIFICATIONS FOR NATIVE CIVILIAN NONINSTITUTIONAL MALES OF NONFARM BACKGROUND, MARRIED AND LIVING WITH THEIR WIVES, BY RACE, AND FAMILY BACKGROUND: UNITED STATES, 1962

Characteristic	NEGRO		NON-NEGRO		NEGRO		NON-NEGRO	
	Both parents	Female head	Both parents	Female head	Both parents	Female head	Both parents	Female head
	(1)	(2)	(3)	(4)	(5)	(6)	(7)	(8)
				Coefficients, raw-score form				
Age at first—								
Marriage	0.39	0.12	0.07	0.35	...	...	...	...
Job	0.16	−0.12	−0.32	0.06	...	...	...	...
First occupation	0.30	0.20	0.29	0.33	...	...	...	...
Education	2.33	2.10	3.63	3.05	2.75	2.21	4.61	4.15
			Coefficients, standard form					
Age at first—								
Marriage	0.11	0.05	0.01	0.07	...	...	...	...
Job	0.04	−0.03	−0.04	0.01	...	...	...	...
First occupation	0.24	0.18	0.27	0.27	...	...	...	...
Education	0.42	0.47	0.48	0.43	0.49	0.50	0.61	0.58
Coefficient of determination	.306	.276	.416	.401	.241	.246	.368	.340

. . . Item excluded from regression analysis.
Source: See source note, Table 1.

some schooling occurred subsequent to work-force entry is unimportant here, for both the most recent period of school attendance and the time of work-force entry are antecedent to the reading on current occupation. The effect of entry occupation on current occupational status is somewhat stronger for Negro men with intact-family backgrounds than for Negroes reared in families headed by a female, but no corresponding difference by family background is observed among the non-Negroes. In evaluating differential promotion by entry level between the Negro groups, it should be recalled that entry level in the work force had been the same for Negro men in the intact-family and broken-family groups. Differential promotion serves to differentiate the groups in terms of occupational status, rather than to accentuate a difference in status established at the point of work-force entry.

The net effects of age at first marriage and age at first job on occupational achievement are of quite modest magnitude for all groups, and the strength of their influence is not consistently patterned by race or by family background. If the timing of these events does have an appreciable influence on occupational success, this influence is not apparent in the analysis reported here. Linear additive models may fail to capture the impact of timing variables; this does not seem implausible, supposing that it may be modal timing that is most favorable to success. Moreover, insofar as the influence of timing operates by way of education, separate measures on schooling completed prior to work-force entry or marriage and schooling acquired subsequent to the event would be required for an adequate modeling of the process. No substantive interpretation of the differentials revealed by this part of the analysis appears justified.

By way of summary, an intact-family background seems to confer a long-run advantage with respect to occupational success, not accounted for simply by the superior job qualifications of men who grew up in a home in which both parents were present. Whether it is the role model provided by the father maintaining an intact family or whether it is some other element in the intact-family setting that is conducive to the son's ultimate occupational success cannot be determined with the data at hand. The analyses reported below suggest that the intact-family advantage is not simply one of more favorable socio-economic circumstances.

Occupational Success and Socio-economic Origins

The education and occupation of his father and the number of his siblings offer a somewhat crude, but nonetheless fairly comprehensive description of the socio-economic status of a man's family of origin.

For the man who grew up in a family headed by a female, head's education, occupation, and the number of his siblings conveys less information about the socio-economic circumstances of the family. There is, then, no real hope of equating intact and broken families with respect to social standing or economic resources given only these items of information.

Particularly difficult to handle analytically is the occupation of the female family head. An occupation was reported for only a quarter of the Negro female heads and half the non-Negro female heads. No report on occupation was taken to mean that the woman was not a regular member of the work force. (Data of the 1960 Census, published in Report PC(2), 4B, Tables 8b and 9b, lend some credibility to the assumption: Among females who headed a nonfarm family which included a child between the ages of six and 17, the proportions employed were 45 per cent for nonwhites and 54 per cent for whites.) A work-status variable for the female heads was constructed by assigning the score of zero to heads for whom no occupation was reported and the score of unity to heads for which a report on occupation was made. The variable identified as head's occupation pertains only to female heads assumed to be regular members of the work force by virtue of a reported occupation; the score assigned a working female head is identical to the score assigned a father pursuing the same occupation. When both variables are entered in the regression analyses, two net coefficients are obtained: one measures the effect of work-force participation *per se;* the other measures the effect of occupation given the fact of work-force participation.

When current occupational status is regressed on these indicators of the socio-economic circumstances of the family in which the respondent grew up as well as the indicators of his job qualifications, there remains some evidence of: (a) more efficient translation of educational attainment into occupational achievement on the part of men reared in intact families within both the Negro and non-Negro populations; and (b) within the Negro population, differential promotion by entry level favorable to men reared in intact families. Introducing measures of socio-economic origins into the regression analysis along with the measures of job qualifications results in only minor changes in the magnitudes of the net effects of the job-qualifications measures and a very slight increase in the "explained" variance in occupational achievement. The relevant comparison is between entries in Columns (1) through (8) of Table 5 and the corresponding entries in Columns (1) through (8) of Table 4. Socio-economic origins have little bearing on occupational success given a man's job qualifications.

TABLE 5.

SUMMARY OF MULTIPLE REGRESSION ANALYSES OF CURRENT OCCUPATION ON SELECTED INDICATORS OF JOB QUALIFICATIONS AND SOCIAL ORIGINS FOR NATIVE CIVILIAN NONINSTITUTIONAL MALES OF NONFARM BACKGROUND, MARRIED AND LIVING WITH THEIR WIVES, BY RACE AND FAMILY BACKGROUND: UNITED STATES, 1962

	Negro		Non-Negro		Negro		Non-Negro		Negro		Non-Negro	
Characteristic	Both parents	Female head	Both parents	Female head	Both parents	Female head	Both parents	Female head	Both parents	Female head	Both parents	Female head
	(1)	(2)	(3)	(4)	(5)	(6)	(7)	(8)	(9)	(10)	(11)	(12)
					Coefficients, raw-score form							
Age at first—												
Marriage	0.41	0.11	0.07	0.40	...	...	...	...	...	...	...	...
Job	0.09	−0.06	−0.37	0.03	...	...	...	...	...	...	...	...
First occupation	0.30	0.21	0.27	0.33	...	...	...	...	...	...	...	...
Education	2.18	2.12	3.36	2.99	2.56	2.13	4.05	3.93	...	...	...	...
Siblings, number	−0.11	−0.14	−0.14	−0.21	−0.08	−0.13	−0.24	−0.35	−0.31	−0.47	−1.30	−0.55
Father's occupation	0.02	...	0.11	...	0.01	...	0.15	...	0.03	...	0.30	...
Head's work status[a]	...	2.52	...	3.62	...	3.58	...	2.09	...	5.81	...	1.09
Head's occupation[b]	...	−0.09	...	−0.01	...	−0.12	...	0.02	...	−0.12	...	0.16
Father's education	0.41	...	0.02	...	0.48	...	0.09	...	1.23	...	0.79	...
Head's education	...	−0.18	...	−0.05	...	0.08	...	0.11	...	0.99	...	1.57
Coefficient of determination	.313	.280	.425	.406	.250	.251	.387	.346	.065	.080	.180	.120

... Item excluded from regression analysis.

[a] Net effect of regular work-force participation. See text.

[b] Net effect of occupation given regular work-force participation. See text.

Source: See source note, Table 1.

This is not to say that socio-economic origins have little bearing on occupational success, but rather that their effect occurs primarily by way of relations between job qualifications and socio-economic origins and between occupational achievement and job qualifications. In Columns (9) through (12) of Table 5 are summarized analyses in which current occupation is regressed only on the measures of socio-economic origins. Reservations about the adequacy with which the socio-economic origins measures reflect the status and resources of the female-headed family preclude systematic inter-group comparisons. It is worth noting, however, that the occupational success of the non-Negro is more closely tied to the socio-economic circumstances of the family in which he grew up and that the differential *vis-à-vis* the Negro is sharper for the man with an intact-family background. The transmission of status between generations, in either a gross sense or net of job qualifications, is strongest for non-Negro intact families.

The factors favorable to occupational success among both Negro and non-Negro men reared in intact families are a well-educated father, a father who himself has been successful in the occupational sphere, and a father whose offspring are few in number. The strength of the respective effects is not constant in the two racial groups, however. Although occupational achievement is influenced as strongly by father's educational attainment for Negro men as for non-Negroes, parental occupational achievement and the size of the family of origin have relatively slight influence on the occupational success of the Negro male.

Among both Negro and non-Negro men raised in families headed by a female, occupational success is influenced positively by the education of the head and negatively by the number of siblings. Most interesting, however, are the effects of work status and occupation level, respectively. The non-Negro female family head contributes to her son's occupational success both by maintaining a regular work-force attachment and by securing a job which ranks relatively high in the occupational structure. The contribution of the Negro female family head to her son's occupational success comes not through the kind of work that she does, but rather through her regular work-force attachment. If the figures can be believed, the magnitude of this effect in Negro families headed by females (5.8 points on the occupation scale) is fully as large as the effect of broken-family status itself (for Negroes, 21.8-17.9 = 3.9 points). The size of the sample from which these relations are inferred is exceedingly small, however, and the findings are best thought of as leads for further investigation. Possibly, however, a regular work-force attachment on the part of the female head can substitute, at least in part, for the absent father in providing the son with orientation to the world of work.

SPECULATION ON SUCCESS AND MATRIARCHY

The analyses reported above lend some support to the notion that the son raised in a family headed by a female is handicapped with respect to occupational success, even when allowance has been made for such salient job qualifications as his education and point of entry into the occupation structure. The handicap to success associated with a broken-family background and the disproportionate numbers of Negro men reared in broken families contribute to, but by no means account for the racial difference in occupational success. If Negro men reared in broken families were able to translate their educational attainment into occupational achievement as effectively as do Negro men reared in intact families, for example, the socio-economic status scores of their current occupations would average nearly five scale points higher. If Negro men reared in intact families were able to translate their educational attainment into occupational achievement as effectively as do non-Negro men reared in intact families, the socio-economic status scores of their current occupations would average nearly 19 scale points higher. (These calculations involve regression coefficients reported in Columns (5) through (7) of Table 4 and means reported in Table 3.)

The foregoing comparison serves to illustrate another point as well: what, for want of a better term, can be called the powerlessness of the Negro man with respect to attaining success. He can acquire more schooling, but an incremental year completed is worth less to him than to the non-Negro. Moreover, the average increase in the socio-economic status score of his occupation over the score of his entry occupation will amount to something under five scale points, in contrast to an average increase of nearly 14 scale points for the non-Negro. His occupation score will average only one scale point higher than his father's occupation score although he will have had three more years of formal schooling than his father; the non-Negro's score will average some ten scale points higher although he too will have had only three additional years of formal schooling. Judging from the experience of his father, the Negro man cannot expect to transmit to his son such occupational status as he has been able to achieve with an effectiveness approaching the non-Negro standard. When son's current occupation is regressed on father's occupation, the increase in son's socio-economic status score accompanying an increase of one score point in father's score amounts to only 0.14 points for the Negro as compared with 0.40 for the non-Negro.

The evidence in this paper obviously does not constitute "proof" that the matriarchal family structure and the absence of a father are "pathological." For Negroes as for non-Negroes, however, the indication that an intact-family background facilitates occupational success is quite compelling. This is not to say that it is necessarily the intactness of the family unit *per se* that facilitates success. Gans may be correct in identifying "a set of emotional strengths and cultural skills in the mothers" as the relevant factor, a factor which facilitates maintenance of the family unit as well as occupational success of the offspring. It may be this same set of "strengths and skills" that are indexed by a regular work-force attachment. At least until additional evidence on the point is available, efforts directed to maintenance of family units which include a man and his wife cannot be dismissed as misguided, however.

A close reading of the so-called Moynihan report can make clear that the powerlessness of the Negro male with respect to occupational achievement is conceived to be at the heart of "the problem" and that this powerlessness, or matriarchy by default, traces back to a social system which kept the Negro male "in his place." It has been the misfortune of the report that it seems to offer a different formulation of "the problem" to each reader, depending upon his own predilections (Rainwater and Yancey, 1967). That this particular formulation is not wholly irresponsible is suggested by the substance of a paragraph in the Presidential Address "To Fulfill These Rights," the tenor of which was influenced by the Moynihan report.

> Perhaps most important—its influence radiating to every part of life—is the breakdown of the Negro family structure. For this, most of all, white America must accept responsibility. It flows from centuries of oppression and persecution of the Negro man. It flows from long years of degradation and discrimination, which have attacked his dignity and assaulted his ability to provide for his family. [Rainwater and Yancey, 1967, p. 130.]

There is, indeed, a tangled web of relations among economic conditions and family structure; and the analyses reported here do not go far toward identifying causal relations. They do provide some additional documentation of an association between family stability and occupational success.

REFERENCES

Blau, Peter M., and Otis Dudley Duncan. *The American Occupational Structure.* New York: John Wiley and Sons, 1967.

Duncan, Beverly. *Family Factors and School Dropout: 1920-1960,* Final report on Cooperative Research Project No. 2258, Office of Education. Ann Arbor: The University of Michigan, 1965.

Rainwater, Lee, and William L. Yancey. *The Moynihan Report and the Politics of Controversy.* Cambridge, Mass.: The M. I. T. Press, 1967.

Reiss, Albert J., Jr. *Occupations and Social Status.* New York: Free Press of Glencoe, 1961.

Trends in Marital Status Among Negroes

REYNOLDS FARLEY

INTRODUCTION

DANIEL MOYNIHAN AUTHORED A REPORT WHICH POINTED OUT THAT while some young Negroes were moving ahead in socio-economic status, many more were falling behind. The breakdown of the Negro family was, in Moynihan's view, the major reason for the lack of progress. Negro wives were commonly deserted by their husbands and this, combined with a high illegitimacy rate, meant that many black children grew up in disrupted homes without the helpful influence of a father and mother. Moynihan believed there was a trend toward greater disruption of Negro families. Two causes of this were noted. First was the continuing shift of blacks from rural to urban residence and second was the persistence, even in times of prosperity, of high rates of unemployment and poverty among blacks.[1]

Thirty years earlier Frazier observed identical trends. He believed that many Negro men migrated from the rural South to northern cities during and after World War I to seek better jobs. Some men brought their families with them and others attempted to establish families after they got to the cities. However, they faced immense difficulties. Housing was costly and very crowded. Jobs were not secure and often black men found themselves unemployed, without marketable skills and unable to support their families.[2] In Frazier's view desertion and illegitimacy were inevitable consequences of urbanization and as more Negroes left the South he expected family disruption to become more common.[3]

Forty years prior to Frazier's writing, DuBois studied Negroes in Philadelphia and reached a similar conclusion. He found that few Negro men could afford to marry. Many of those who did were unable to establish households so frequently wives and children were sent to relatives in the South. DuBois argued two factors exacerbated the problems of blacks in the city. First were the low wages they received

Published by permission of the author.

and second, were the premium rents property owners demanded from Negroes.[4]

Despite the lengthly period of time during which such comments have been made, few studies have investigated trends in the marital or family status of blacks. This paper first examines trends in marital status, particularly changes in the frequency of desertion. Second, the consequences of urbanization upon Negro marital status are explored. Finally the effects of socio-economic variables are studied.

TRENDS IN MARITAL STATUS

Since 1890 decennial censuses have asked adults about their marital status and more recently the Census Bureau asked this question annually of a sample of the population. Table 1 shows the marital status distribution of Negroes 15 and over for the period 1890 to 1967. To eliminate any confounding influences of changes in the age distribution, the data have been standardized for age.

Between 1890 and 1967 there was a geographic redistribution of blacks and a change in their economic and social status. Despite these changes, the marital status distribution of Negroes changed very little. There has been some fluctuation but it is difficult to detect long run shifts in the proportion who were single or who were married. Examination of data used to construct Table 1 reveals two periods during which marriage patterns changed. During the Depression decade the marriage rate was low, many blacks postponed marriage and the Census of 1940 found that an unusually large proportion of young Negroes were single. During the prosperous post-World War II years, age at marriage fell sharply and the Census of 1950 discovered that an unusually large proportion of Negroes were married. In the recent period— since 1960 — age at marriage has gone up, for an increasing proportion of young blacks are delaying marriage. This pattern is not solely a consequence of the marriage squeeze for age at marriage has increased among males as well as among females.[5]

There have been changes in the causes of marital disruption. The change in proportion widowed has been greater than changes in either the proportion single or married. Negro mortality rates did not fall significantly until public health programs were initiated in the 1930's but after 1938 they fell rapidly.[6] One result was a reduction in the frequency with which death terminated marriages. The proportion of Negro women who were widows fell from 22 per cent in 1930 to about 13 per cent at present and among men the decline was from 8 to 4 per cent.

Divorce, on the other hand, has become more common as a cause of marital disruption, although at present no more than 4 per cent of the adult Negroes report divorce as their marital status. The rise in divorce has occurred since 1940. Among Negro women increases in divorce have been more than offset by decreases in widowhood but among men the rise in divorce has matched the decrease in widowers.

TRENDS IN DESERTION

Data shown in Table 1 do not pertain to desertion. Even if a woman's husband left her years previously she should report herself as married unless she obtained a divorce or had her husband declared dead.

TABLE 1

MARITAL STATUS OF NEGROES 15 AND OVER; 1890-1967[a]

DATE	NEGRO FEMALES					NEGRO MALES				
	Total	Single	Married	Widowed	Divorced	Total	Single	Married	Widowed	Divorced
1890	100%	20%	57%	22%	1%	100%	29%	65%	6%	...
1900	100	21	56	22	1	100	30	62	8	...
1910	100	19	58	22	1	100	29	62	8	1%
1920	100	19	59	21	1	100	28	63	8	1
1930	100	19	57	22	2	100	28	63	8	1
1940*	100	20	58	20	2	100	31	61	7	1
1950*	100	18	62	17	3	100	27	65	6	2
1957*	100	21	60	16	3	100	31	63	4	2
1958*	100	21	60	16	3	100	31	62	5	2
1959*	100	20	61	16	3	100	31	61	5	3
1960*	100	20	62	14	4	100	28	64	5	3
1961*	100	20	61	15	4	100	30	63	5	2
1962*	100	22	60	14	4	100	31	61	5	3
1963*	100	22	60	14	4	100	31	62	4	3
1964	100	20	63	13	4	100	30	64	4	2
1965	100	21	62	13	4	100	29	64	4	3
1966	100	21	61	14	4	100	30	62	4	4
1967*	100	21	61	14	4	100	29	63	5	3

a. These data have been standardized for age. The age distribution of the Negro population age 15 and over in 1960 was used as the standard. Data for dates marked with an asterisk refer to non-whites.

Sources: U. S., Census Office, *Eleventh Census of the United States: 1890*, Part III, p. 18. U. S., Bureau of the Census, *Twelfth Census of the United States: 1900*, Vol. II, Table XLIX; *Thirteenth Census of the United States: 1910*, Vol. I. Marital Condition, Table 14; *Fourteenth Census of the United States: 1920*, Vol. II, Marital Condition, Table 2; *Fifteenth Census of the United States: 1930*, Vol. II, Marital Condition, Table 5, *Census of Population: 1960*, PC(1)-1D. Table 177 *Current Population Reports*, Series P-20, nos. 81, 87, 96, 114, 122, 135, 142, 155, 168, and 170.

To eliminate this difficulty the Census Bureau introduced the categories "married-spouse-present" and "married-spouse-absent." If a woman reported she was married, the enumeration schedule for her household was scanned to see if her husband was living with her. Thus, information about the presence of a spouse was obtained not by asking a question but rather by observing household composition.[7] Table 2 shows the distribution of Negroes who had ever married by their current marital status for dates between 1910 and 1967. Again the data have been standardized for age.

The frequency with which desertion is discussed sometimes suggests that very many married blacks live apart from their spouse. Such is not the case. Table 2 indicates that at each date about four-fifths of the married men and three-fifths of the women lived with their mates and that until recently, widowhood was more common than desertion as a cause of marital disruption.

TABLE 2

DISTRIBUTION OF EVER-MARRIED NEGROES BY CURRENT MARITAL STATUS; 1910-1967[a]

DATE	NEGRO FEMALES					NEGRO MALES				
	Total	Married Spouse Present	Married Spouse Absent	Widowed	Divorced	Total	Married Spouse Present	Married Spouse Absent	Widowed	Divorced
1910	100%	67%	5%	27%	1%	(not available)				
1940	100	62	11	25	2	100%	78%	11%	9%	2%
1950*	100	62	14	21	3	100	76	13	8	3
1957*	100	63	13	20	4	100	79	10	6	4
1958*	100	61	15	21	3	100	77	12	7	4
1959*	100	59	18	20	3	100	75	13	8	4
1960*	100	62	15	18	5	100	76	14	6	4
1961*	100	61	15	19	5	100	79	11	7	3
1962*	100	61	16	18	5	100	77	12	7	4
1963*	100	60	16	18	6	100	76	13	6	5
1964	100	61	17	17	5	100	80	11	5	4
1965	100	60	18	17	5	100	77	13	6	4
1966	100	60	17	17	6	100	77	11	6	6
1967*	100	61	17	17	5	100	78	12	6	4

a. These data have been standardized for age. The age distribution of the Negro population age 15 and over in 1960 was used as the standard. Data for dates marked with an asterisk refer to non-whites.

Sources: U. S., Bureau of the Census, *Sixteenth Census of the United States: 1940*, Vol. IV, Part 1, Table 8; Differential Fertility: 1940 and 1910, Women by Number of Children Ever Born, Tables 12 and 16; *Census of Population: 1950*, PC-I, Table 104; *Census of Population: 1960*, PC(1)-1D, Table 176; *Current Population Reports*, Series P-20, Nos. 81, 87, 96, 114, 122, 135, 142, 155, 168 and 170.

Between 1910 and 1940 the proportion of Negro women who were deserted increased. There was little change in the proportion widowed or divorced so the rise in desertion had the net effect of reducing the proportion of married Negro women who lived with husbands.

Since 1940, desertion has become more common among Negro women and there has also been an increase in divorce. However, these changes have not lessened the proportion of women who live with a husband because there has been a decrease in widowhood. Examination of the trends for specific age groups of women reveals much the same pattern. In particular, among women in the child rearing ages decreases in widowhood have offset the recent increases in desertion.

Figures showing the presence of wives for Negro husbands are available only for the post-Depression period. During this time there has been no change in the proportion of men who live apart from their wives and only modest changes in the proportion widowed or divorced.

Moynihan and Frazier were correct in describing increases in desertion but this observation needs elaboration. Improvements in health conditions and living standards have engendered greater marital stability by reducing the proportion widowed. As a result, there has been little change since 1940 in the proportion of married Negroes who live with their mates. This period differs from the earlier span during which marital instability apparently increased.

THE EFFECTS OF URBANIZATION

It is difficult to assess the effects of urbanization upon marital status. There have been changes from census to census in the types of tabulation which are provided; and, in addition, census information indicates a person's marital status at one point and does not provide either a marital or migration history.

We can infer, however, that city living has an effect for there have always been rural-urban differences in marital status. In the past, urban areas contained unusually large proportions of single and widowed blacks while rural areas had an unusually large proportion married. Over time rural-urban differences have diminished and almost disappeared. The proportion of urban Negroes who are married has increased while in rural areas the proportion single has gone up. City living is now not as incompatible with marriage as it apparently once was.

Additional information about marital status and desertion in rural and urban areas is provided by Table 3 which shows the marital status of ever-married blacks for four geographic areas; the North and West,

TABLE 3

DISTRIBUTION OF EVER-MARRIED NEGROES BY PLACE OF RESIDENCE AND
CURRENT MARITAL STATUS, 1910-1960[a]

DATE	NEGRO WOMEN					NEGRO MEN				
	Total	Married Spouse Present	Married Spouse Absent	Widowed	Divorced	Total	Married Spouse Present	Married Spouse Absent	Widowed	Divorced
			North and West							
1910	100%	62%	8%	27%	3%	...				
1940	100	58	15	25	2	100%	72%	18%	8%	2%
1950*	100	61	15	19	5	100	72	16	8	4
1960*	100	63	16	15	6	100	75	15	5	5
			Entire South							
1910	100	68	5	26	1	...				
1940	100	65	10	23	2	100	81	11	7	1
1950*	100	65	13	19	3	100	80	12	6	2
1960*	100	65	15	16	4	100	79	13	5	3
			Urban South							
1910	100	54	8	36	2	...				
1940	100	54	13	32%		...				
1960*	100	60	17	18	5	100	77	14	6	3
			Rural South							
1910	100	74	4	21	1	...				
1940	100	73	7	20%		...				
1960*	100	72	12	14	2	100	81	12	5	2

a. These data have been standardized for age. The age distribution of the Negro population age 15 and over in 1960 was used as the standard. Data for dates marked with an asterisk refer to non-whites.

Sources: U. S., Bureau of the Census, *Negro Population in the United States: 1790 to 1915* (Washington: Government Printing Office, 1918), p. 259; *Sixteenth Census of the United States: 1940*, Population, Vol. IV, Part 1, Tables 30 and 32; Differential Fertility: 1940 and 1910, Women by Number of Children Ever Born, Tables 71 and 74; *Census of Population: 1950*, P-C1, Table 147; *Census of Population: 1960*, PC(1)-1D, Table 242.

the entire South, the urban South and the rural South. Almost all Negroes in the North and West have resided in cities.[8]

Urban living is related to desertion for at each date the proportion of married blacks who lived apart from their spouses was higher in the North than in the South and higher in the urban South than in the rural South. Over time widowhood has decreased and divorce increased in each area. Changes in desertion are quite different. Between 1910 and 1940 the proportion of Negro women deserted went up in all areas but since 1940 the proportion deserted has remained the same in the North while increasing in the South.

In the fifty year period between 1910 and 1960 the proportion of married women who lived apart from their husbands went up from 6 to 16 per cent.[9] This was a result of both urbanization and changing rates of desertion within different areas. Table 4 presents results of an investigation to ascertain the relative influences of these factors for two periods; 1910 to 1940 and 1940 to 1960. The components of difference between two rates methodology was used.[10]

In both spans the regional redistribution and urbanization of Negroes contributed to a rise in desertion. However, even if there had been no shifts in areal distribution, desertion would have increased. This is because there was a substantial increase in the rates of desertion within the urban and rural South.

TABLE 4

COMPONENTS OF CHANGE IN THE PROPORTION OF NEGRO WOMEN WHO WERE
MARRIED–SPOUSE–ABSENT, 1910 TO 1940 AND 1940 TO 1960

	1910 to 1940	1940 to 1960
Percentage of Married Women with Spouse Absent—Original Year	6.0%	11.9%
Percentage of Married Women with Spouse Absent—Later Year	11.9%	15.9%
Total Change	+5.9%	+4.0%
Change attributed to:		
Change in Age Distribution of Women	−0.3%	−0.8%
Change in Areal Distribution	+1.3%	+2.0%
Changes in Rates in North and West	+0.9%	+0.1%
Change in Rates in Urban South	+1.4%	+1.3%
Change in Rates in Rural South	+2.2%	+2.6%
Interaction of Factors	+0.4%	−1.2%

Source: U. S., Bureau of the Census, *Sixteenth Census of the United States: 1940*, Population, Differential Fertility: 1940 and 1910, Women by Number of Children Ever Born, Tables 80 and 82; *Census of Population: 1960*, PC(1)-1D, Table 242; PC(2)-1C, Table 19.

Table 4 indicates that some of the increase in desertion can appropriately be attributed to urbanization. A fuller explanation of changes in the Negro family system, however, must account for the finding that since 1940 desertion has not increased in northern cities but gone up in the South.

SOCIO-ECONOMIC VARIABLES AND THEIR RELATIONSHIP TO
MARITAL STATUS

Descriptions of the Negro family system claim that poverty is one of the major reasons why marriages are unstable. The relationship of economic factors to marital status is another complex area for it is not easy to determine the influence of economic variables apart from the effects of age at marriage, rural background or remarriage rates. Table 5 (on p. 180), however, presents some pertinent information. It shows the marital status of Negroes by socio-economic characteristics in 1960.

This table indicates that there are important socio-economic differences in marital status. Negro men and women with the characteristics of higher social standing are more likely to be living with their spouses than Negroes with the characteristics of lower status. There is little variation in the prevalence of divorce but socio-economic factors are related to widowhood and desertion. These two causes of marital disruption are both inversely related to socio-economic status. Not only is a poorly educated woman more likely to be deserted than a well educated woman, she is also more likely to lose her husband by death. Similarly men with low status jobs are more likely to be widowers than men with prestigeous occupations. Of the three socio-economic variables described in Table 5, income is most strongly linked to marital stability. The lower the income level, the higher the proportion of men living apart from their wives.

Comparison of Table 5 with similar information for whites shows that at each socio-economic level desertion and widowhood were more common among Negroes than among whites but racial differences in divorce were very small.

Changes over time in the relationship in socio-economic status to marital status were studied by examining trends in the marital status of different educational attainment categories. Between 1940 and 1960 widowhood decreased and divorce increased among Negro men and women at all educational levels. Among those with only a few years of schooling desertion increased while among those at the upper educational attainment levels desertion remained at about the same level or even decreased by a small amount.

OVERVIEW OF FINDINGS

This analysis of demographic data has shown, first, that for a long time span there has been relatively little change in the marital status of Negroes, the age at which Negroes marry or the proportion who ever marry. Second, causes for marital disruption have changed. Desertion has increased at least since 1910 while widowhood has decreased since the late 1930's. Third, socio-economic and place of residence variables are linked to marital status and marital disruption. Finally the data suggest that since 1940 desertion has become more common among blacks of lower status and among those within the South but desertion

TABLE 5

Distribution of Ever-Married Non-whites 25 to 64 by Socio-economic Characteristic and Current Marital Status, 1960[a]

	Non-White Men					Non-White Women				
Characteristic	Total	Married Spouse Present	Married Spouse Absent	Widowed	Divorced	Total	Married Spouse Present	Married Spouse Absent	Widowed	Divorced
Educational Attainment										
College 4	100%	85%	9%	3%	3%	100%	73%	11%	9%	7%
College 1–3	100	80	12	3	5	100	71	12	9	8
High School 4	100	79	13	3	5	100	70	14	10	6
High School 1–3	100	78	14	4	4	100	66	17	11	6
Elementary 5–8	100	74	14	4	4	100	65	17	14	5
Elementary 0–4	100	77	15	5	3	100	62	17	18	3
Occupation in 1960						not computed				
Professionals	100	88	7	2	3					
Managers	100	87	7	2	4					
Clerical Workers	100	87	8	2	3					
Sales Workers	100	85	9	3	3					
Craftsmen	100	86	8	3	3					
Operatives	100	85	9	3	3					
Priv. Household	100	55	25	13	7					
Service Workers	100	79	13	4	4					
Laborers	100	79	13	5	3					
Farmers	100	92	4	2	2					
Farm Laborers	100	79	13	5	3					

Personal Income in 1959

					not computed
$10,000 and over	100	89	6	2	3
$ 7,000 to 9,999	100	88	7	2	3
$ 5,000 to 6,999	100	87	7	2	4
$ 3,000 to 4,999	100	83	11	3	3
$ 1,000 to 2,999	100	77	15	4	4
Less than $1,000	100	69	20	7	4
No Income	100	46	37	9	8

a. These data have been standardized for age. The age distribution of non-whites 25 to 64 in 1960 was used as the standard.

Source: U. S., Bureau of the Census, *Census of Population: 1960*, PC(2)-4E, Tables 4, 5 and 6.

has remained about the same or even decreased in northern cities and among blacks with the characteristics of higher status.

These findings seem consistent with the views of Moynihan, Frazier and DuBois that Negro family status reflects the social and economic position of Negroes. Between the time of Emancipation and early this century the economic status of blacks may have improved. By 1890 about 20 per cent of the blacks owned their farms or homes and by 1910 this increased to about 25 per cent.[11] Negroes remained in rural areas and this, combined with economic progress, may have resulted in a growing number of stable marriages.

From early this century until World War II, the economic position of blacks may have deteriorated. To be sure, urban Negroes made gains during World War I but the economic slowdown of the 1920's and then the Depression wiped out these improvements.[12] In rural areas black farmers were adversely affected by falling crop prices during the 1920's and by federal agricultural programs during the 1930's.[13] During this period increases in marital dissolution resulted from urbanization and the unfortunate economic changes.

Since 1940 the incomes of blacks have risen more rapidly than prices[14] and this improvement in living standards has helped to reduce widowhood which used to be the most common cause of marital disruption. We know little about which Negroes have benefited most from economic gains in recent years. We can speculate that the economic status of blacks in northern cities and those with extensive educations improved most rapidly and among these blacks desertion has not increased. The economic status of Negroes who have little education or those in the rural South may have deteriorated, rather than improved, and among these Negroes desertion has increased.

Further investigation using both demographic data and descriptions of Negro life styles is needed to verify these explanations for changes in Negro marital status.

NOTES

[1]U. S., Department of Labor, *The Negro Family, The Case for National Action* (Washington: Department of Labor, 1965).

[2]E. Franklin Frazier, *The Negro Family in the United States* (Chicago: University of Chicago Press, 1939), Part 4.

[3]*Ibid.*, p. 255.

[4]W. E. B. DuBois, *The Philadelphia Negro* (Reprint ed., New York: Benjamin Blom, 1967), Chap. VI and pp. 192-196.

[5]Men typically marry women who are two or three years younger than themselves. The baby boom after World War II produced a disparity between the num-

ber of prospective brides and grooms. For instance, for every 100 black men born in 1945, there were 130 black women born in 1948. Thus, there was a "surplus" of women born in the post war years. Women born 1946 through 1949 will likely forego marriage or wait to marry men who are no older than themselves. For further information see: Donald S. Akers, "On Measuring the Marriage Squeeze," *Demography*, IV (1967), 907-924.

[6]Iwao M. Moriyama, *The Change in Mortality Trend in the United States*, U.S., National Center for Health Statistics, Vital and Health Statistics, Series 3, No. 1 (March, 1964).

[7]While the married-spouse-absent category includes women who have been deserted, other women are also in this group.

"This group includes married women whose families have been broken by separation (often preceeding divorce), immigrants whose husbands were left abroad, wives of persons enumerated as inmates of institutions and other married women whose usual place of residence was not the same as that of their husbands, including wives of soldiers, sailors, men in labor camps, etc." U. S., Bureau of the Census, *Sixteenth Census of the United States: 1940*, Population, Differential Fertility: 1940 and 1910, Women by Number of Children Ever Born, p. 3.

[8]In 1910, 77 per cent of the Negroes in the North and West lived in urban areas and by 1960 this increased to 95 per cent. U.S., Bureau of the Census, *Negro Population In the United States 1790-1915* (Washington: Government Printing Office, 1918), p. 92; *Census of Population: 1950*, PC(2)-1C, Table 1

[9]These figures refer to Negro women aged 15 to 74.

[10]For an example of this methodology see: Wilson H. Grabill, Clyde V. Kiser and Pascal K. Whelpton, *The Fertility of American Women* (New York: John Wiley & Sons, 1958), pp. 365-371.

[11]U. S., Bureau of the Census, *Negro Population in the United States: 1790-1910*, pp. 467-470.

[12]Sterling D. Spero and Abram L. Harris, *The Black Worker* (Reprint ed., New York: Atheneum, 1968); Gunnar Myrdal, *An American Dilemma*, I (Reprint ed., New York: McGraw-Hill, 1964), Chap. XIII.

[13]Myrdal, *op. cit.*, Chap. XII.

[14]Between 1939 and 1959 the income in male non-white workers increased by a factor of six while the index of consumer prices doubled. U. S., Bureau of the Census, *Historical Statistics of the United States: Colonial Times to 1957* (Washington: Government Printing Office, 1961), Series G 147-148 and G 169-190; *Historical Statistics of the United States: Continuation to 1962 and Revisions* (Washington: Government Printing Office, 1965), Series G 75-149.

Part 3

**Family Structure
and Interaction
Among the Poor:
Variations and
Adaptations**

The Structure and Composition of "Problem" and "Stable" Families in a Low-Income Population

CHARLES V. WILLIE AND JANET WEINANDY

THE PAST DECADES HAVE SEEN A GROWING INTEREST IN MULTI-PROBLEM families on the part of social researchers, social workers, and community planners for health and welfare services. Contributing to our knowledge of these families have been the extensively published St. Paul studies.[1] Other communities have followed suit in developing rehabilitation projects or in studying the conditions and characteristics of problem families.[2] Baltimore, for example, has developed very good statistics on multi-problem families living in public housing.[3]

Most of the studies, however, are not definitive in that they do not compare multi-problem families of low-income status with other families of similar status. It is therefore difficult to determine if the characteristics of multi-problem families differ significantly from other families when social status is held constant.

This study is designed to compare the similarities and differences, if any, between "problem" families and "stable" families living in the same low-rent public housing project. This analysis is limited to a comparison of the structure and composition of problem and stable families. Thus, housing, neighborhood, and other environmental circumstances of life are similar for all families.

---

[1]Bradley Buell, "Planning Community-wide Attack on Behavior Disorders," *The Annals,* CCLXXXVI (March, 1953), pp. 150-157.

[2]Roland Warren, *Multiproblem Familes,* New York: State Charities Aid Association, 1960; "Trouble and Troublesome Families," *Journal of Housing,* XIV (April, 1957), pp. 111-147; Elizabeth Wood, *The Small Hard Core,* New York: Citizens' Housing and Planning Council of New York, Inc., 1957.

[3]Research and Statistics Division, *Problem Families in Public Housing,* Baltimore: Housing Authority of Baltimore City, 1956.

Reprinted by permission of the publisher and authors from *Marriage and Family Living,* XXV (November 1963), 439-46.

DATA AND METHOD

The study was conducted in Syracuse, New York, in one of the city's four low-rent public housing projects. The Syracuse University Youth Development Center, in cooperation with the Syracuse Housing Authority, established a family consultant research-demonstration program in this housing project in September, 1960. The family consultant is a social worker who gives intensive help to problem families. She seeks out those in need of immediate help instead of waiting to be sought.

At the beginning of the study, the housing project manager listed 54 of the 678 households, or about eight per cent of all family units, as being in need of immediate help. Because some elderly persons live in the project, the manager was asked to include only those households in which there are dependent children under 21 years of age. One problem family moved out of the project before this investigation began and another did not complete the interview, so the study population among problem families consists of 52 households.

After the manager had identified the problem families, he was asked to provide the names of his most stable families in the housing project. He listed 40 stable families.

A 13-page schedule was administered by trained interviewers in the homes of the 92 problem and stable families in the Spring of 1961. Households were informed that they were selected at random to participate in a city-wide study of social and recreational opportunities available in the community. A large section of the schedule dealt with family participation in voluntary associations.

In addition to background data on the members of each household, the interviewers obtained information on the sex category of the head of household, his or her marital status, history of multi-marriages if any, age at marriage for male and female parents, and total number of children in the family.

Thus, the 52 problem and 40 stable low-income families were identified by a common source, the housing project manager. Without knowledge of his classification of a family and his criteria, the interviewers — social workers and social science graduate students — made their own evaluation of the problem or stable status of each family on the schedule after each interview was completed. There was agreement between their classification of a family and the classification of the housing project manager for 72 per cent of the households.

FINDINGS

In addition to housing, neighborhood, and environmental circumstances of life held constant because of their residence in the same public housing project, the problem and stable families are similar in education, occupation, and religion. Approximately 80 per cent of the problem and nearly 75 per cent of the stable parents have not graduated from high school; median school year completed is 10.2 and 10.7, respectively, for problem and stable parents.

The rate of unemployment is very high; approximately 30 per cent of the men in all families are unemployed. About 35 per cent of the problem and slightly less than 25 per cent of the stable two-parent families have unemployed fathers. Most of the employed are "blue-collar" workers — nearly 90 per cent of the problem and almost 80 per cent of the stable fathers. Three-fourths of both problem and stable families earned less than $4,000 per year.

There are few Jewish and Catholic families in the housing project; slightly more than 85 per cent of the problem and 80 per cent of the stable families are Protestant.

One minor difference between problem and stable families in demographic characteristics is racial. A majority of both problem and stable households have Negro heads; but approximately five out of every six problem families are Negro while about four out of every six stable families are of this race. Excepting race, none of the demographic characteristics that differentiate problem and stable families are statistically significant at the five per cent level of confidence, according to Chi square tests. Because the total number of families is 92, Chi squares are computed for four-fold tables only. Each variable is dichotomized to increase the reliability of statistical computations. Nevertheless, the small N is a limitation of this study, indicating that caution should be exercised in generalizing these findings.

Although similar in many respects, the stable and problem families are significantly different in family structure. As seen in Table 1, 78

TABLE 1

SEX OF HEAD OF HOUSEHOLD OF STABLE AND PROBLEM FAMILIES IN A LOWER-RENT PUBLIC HOUSING PROJECT, SYRACUSE, NEW YORK, 1961

Sex of Head of Household	STABLE FAMILY		PROBLEM FAMILY		TOTAL	
	Number	Per Cent	Number	Per Cent	Number	Per Cent
Male	31	77.5	25	48.1	56	60.9
Female	9	22.5	27	51.9	36	39.1
Total	40	100.0	52	100.0	92	100.0

$X^2 = 5.25$ (using Yates' correction); $p < .05$.
$Q = .576$.

per cent of the stable and 48 per cent of the problem families have male heads of household; all families with male heads are two-parent families. Consequently, a majority of the problem families are broken, having only one parent — the mother — present in the home.

Much of the disintegration in family structure occurs after moving into public housing. The Syracuse Housing Authority, by policy, favors two-parent over one-parent families for admission into its low-rent public housing developments. Inspection of applications for admission revealed approximately 85 per cent of the stable and about 75 per cent of the problem households consisted of married adults with spouse present in the household. When this study was conducted after their admission to the housing project, three out of every four stable families were still intact, as compared with only two out of every four problem families, as seen in Table 2. Though not statistically significant, there also is a greater tendency for the head of household in problem families to have been party to two or more marriages. About 20 per cent of problem-family heads have had multiple marriages. Slightly less than ten per cent of the stable-family heads have married two or more times.

Disintegration occurs most frequently during the first ten years of marriage.[4] Thus, the stable families have an advantage in that half have been together 13 or more years while two-thirds of the problem families have been married less than eight years, according to Table 3.

TABLE 2

MARITAL STATUS OF HEAD OF HOUSEHOLD OF STABLE AND PROBLEM FAMILIES IN A LOWER-RENT PUBLIC HOUSING PROJECT, SYRACUSE, NEW YORK, 1961

Marital Status of Head of Household	STABLE FAMILY		PROBLEM FAMILY		TOTAL	
	Number	Per Cent	Number	Per Cent	Number	Per Cent
Married	31	77.5	25	48.1	56	60.9
Separated	4	10.0	22	42.3	26	28.3
Widowed	4	10.0	1	1.9	5	5.4
Divorced	1	2.5	3	5.8	4	4.3
Single	—	—	1	1.9	1	1.1
Total	40	100.0	52	100.0	92	100.0

$X^2 = 5.25$; $P < .05$ (Based on four-fold table of married—non-married by problem-stable status, and using Yates' correction.)
$Q = .576$.

[4] William F. Ogburn, "Marital Separations," in Marvin B. Sussman (ed.), *Sourcebook in Marriage and the Family*, Cambridge: Houghton Mifflin Co., 1955, p. 350.

TABLE 3

NUMBER OF YEARS OF MARRIAGE OF PARENTS IN TWO-PARENT STABLE AND PROBLEM
FAMILIES IN A LOWER-RENT HOUSING PROJECT, SYRACUSE, NEW YORK, 1961

Years of Marriage	STABLE FAMILY		PROBLEM FAMILY		TOTAL	
	Number	Per Cent	Number	Per Cent	Number	Per Cent
0- 2 years	—	—	2	7.7	2	3.5
3- 5 years	2	6.5	10	38.6	12	21.0
6- 8 years	7	22.7	6	23.1	13	22.7
9-11 years	5	16.1	3	11.5	8	14.0
12-14 years	4	12.9	1	3.8	5	8.8
15-17 years	5	16.1	3	11.5	8	14.0
18-20 years	4	12.9	1	3.8	5	8.8
21-23 years	1	3.2	—	—	1	1.8
24-26 years	1	3.2	—	—	1	1.8
27-29 years	1	3.2	—	—	1	1.8
30 or more	1	3.2	—	—	1	1.8
Total	31	100.0	26	100.0	57	100.0
Median	13.1		6.5		9.5	

$X^2 = 7.62$; $p < .01$ (Based on four-fold table of under 9—over 9 years of age by stable-problem status; using Yates' correction.)
$Q = .692$.

In general, the problem parents are very young. A majority of the fathers in problem families are under 35 years of age, as compared with one-third of the fathers in stable families. Mothers in problem families tend to be younger, too. These facts might lead one to conclude that, given sufficient time, the younger problem families will emerge as stable family units.

Further analysis of the data reveals this to be a premature and possibly invalid conclusion. In their young adult years, the behavior of many problem families is quite different from the way most stable families behaved when they were at that age level. Moreover, the consequences of some of the behavior of young problem families are irreversible. For example, 39 per cent of the mothers in problem families, as compared with 14 per cent of the mothers in stable families, were brides before their 19th birthday; actually, two-thirds of the mothers in problem families were married before they came of age at 21. Although problem families are younger than stable households and have been married fewer years, they nevertheless have produced more children; the average number of children in problem households is 3.9 as compared with 2.7 for stable families. Probably a more important difference is that only one stable household has as many as seven chil-

TABLE 4

AGE AT MARRIAGE OF MALE AND FEMALE PARENTS IN TWO-PARENT STABLE AND
PROBLEM FAMILIES IN A LOWER-RENT PUBLIC HOUSING PROJECT,
SYRACUSE, NEW YORK, 1961

Age at Marriage	STABLE FAMILY			PROBLEM FAMILY			GRAND TOTAL		
	Male	Female	Total	Male	Female	Total	Male	Female	Total
18 or less	—	4	4	2	9	11	2	13	15
19-20 years	5	7	12	4	6	10	9	13	22
21-22 years	8	5	13	7	5	12	15	10	25
23-24 years	6	3	9	2	1	3	8	4	12
25-26 years	3	1	4	2	—	2	5	1	6
27-28 years	—	1	1	—	—	—	—	1	1
29-30 years	1	3	4	2	1	3	3	4	7
31-32 years	1	—	1	1	—	1	2	—	2
33-34 years	1	3	4	—	—	—	1	3	4
35 and over	3	1	4	3	1	4	6	2	8
Total	28*	28*	56*	23*	23*	46*	51	51	102
Median	23.3	22.2	22.8	22.6	19.8	21.3	22.9	20.9	22.1

*Ns vary because age at marriage unknown.

$X^2 = .48$; $p < .50$ (Based on four-fold table under 21—above 21 years by problem-stable status for males.)

$X^2 = 3.45$; $p < .10$ (Based on four-fold table under 21—above 21 years by problem-stable status for females.)

dren while six, or ten per cent of the problem households, have eight or more children — the largest family consisting of 11, as shown in Table 5. Though the median length of marriage is about six years less than the median for stable households, problem families tend to average one child more.

There is evidence obtained from official records and interviews, and suggested in the data of Table 5, that several women (ten to 15 per cent of the mothers) in problem families identified by the housing project manager had out-of-wedlock children.

In summary, their early betrothal and fertile parenthood are irreversible phenomena that problem families cannot outgrow. Although younger than stable parents, it would appear that these two family types are developing along separate career lines and that increasing age will not necessarily bring one family type to the stability experienced by the other.

On the basis of this analysis one might infer that the difference between problem and stable families is one of kind rather than one of degree. It is further indicated that the study of factors surrounding their early marriage, their rapid reproduction rate, their frequent sep-

TABLE 5

NUMBER OF CHILDREN PER HOUSEHOLD BY MARITAL STATUS OF HEAD OF
HOUSEHOLD IN STABLE AND PROBLEM FAMILIES IN A LOWER-RENT
PUBLIC HOUSING PROJECT, SYRACUSE, NEW YORK, 1961

Number of Children	STABLE FAMILY					PROBLEM FAMILY					Grand Total
	Married Male Head	Separated Female Head	Divorced Female Head	Widowed Female Head	Total	Married Male Head	Separated Female Head	Divorced Female Head	Widowed Female Head	Total	
One	3	1	1	2	7	3	1	—	—	4	11
Two	10	2	—	—	12	9	4	1	—	14	26
Three	5	1	—	1	7	4	5	1	—	10	17
Four	9	—	—	1	10	3	5	1	—	9	19
Five	2	—	—	—	2	1	4	—	—	5	7
Six	—	—	—	—	—	3	—	—	—	3	3
Seven	1	—	—	—	1	—	1	—	—	1	1
Eight	—	—	—	—	—	1	1	—	—	2	2
Nine	—	—	—	—	—	1	1	—	—	2	2
Ten or more	—	—	—	—	—	1	1	—	—	2	2
Total	30[a]	4	1	4	39	26	23[b]	3	—	52	91

[a]Excludes 1 for whom number of children is unknown.

[b]One "Single female head" reported 1 child; the child is included with number of children of separated female head.

aration from spouse, and their tendency to continue to bear children with no male spouse legally present might yield valuable information on how, when, and why these families began career lines of development deviant from those of stable families and how these career lines might be changed.

DISCUSSION

. . .

Hypotheses of two of the possible causes of instability among low-income problem families — the absence of control and lack of commitment — contradict the proposition that the high rate of separations between husband and wife and the tendency for some persons to reproduce children out-of-wedlock are culturally sanctioned behavior of low-income families consistent with the values of their community, neighborhood, or ethnic group. While such behavior may be normative statistically, it is not the product of a community value system. Such statistically normative behavior may or may not be value oriented. We are not alone in rejecting the theory of a lower-class cultural system that generates deviant behavior among some low-income families. Hylan Lewis, studying child rearing among low-income families in Washington, D.C., concludes that "neither the quality of life in most low-income neighborhoods nor the child rearing behaviors of low-income families is to be interpreted as generated by, or guided by, what one student calls 'a cultural system in its own right — with an integrity of its own.' " Lewis further states that "the behavior observed in . . . varying low-income families does not represent the kind of organization or cohesion suggested by these phrases."[5] Moreover, this study, comparing the structure and composition of two kinds of households, clearly demonstrates that some low-income families do not engage in deviant behavior associated with family instability. One-fifth of the stable families have been married more than 18 years.

We hypothesize that much of the behavior of persons in low-income problem families is without reference to any structure or viable social system. Instead of conforming to the values of a sub-cultural system, it would appear that the activities of persons in some problem families are deviant from and in opposition to the kinds of commitments and cooperation necessary for the continued existence of any social organization. In short, they pledge little, if any, allegiance to any reference group; they lead un-regulated lives.

Thus, their problem may be one of inadequate socialization for life in human social organization. Any purposeful association of human beings must place limits and controls upon its members; they in turn must commit themselves to support the association. In no other way can a society of human beings continue to function. Yet human beings, unlike other animals, have the freedom and privilege to ignore controls or withhold support. The exercise of this privilege may be blatant and brash but not always deliberate. This is why problem families are described possibly as inadequately socialized; their orientation toward others may be arrested and underdeveloped.

The anthropological studies of Malinowski present information which underscores the hypothesis that the behavior of problem families represents inadequate socialization for participation in human social organization. He states in an article entitled "Parenthood — the Basis of Social Structure" that the typical family among the vast majority of tribes "seem[s] hardly to differ at all from its civilized counterpart."

---

[5]Hylan Lewis, "Child Rearing Among Low Income Families," Washington D.C.: Washington Center for Metropolitan Studies, June 8, 1961, pp. 10-11.

In all societies, for example, "mother, father, and children share the camp, the home, and the life." He further states that members of the family in both European and non-European society are closely bound and attached to each other, "sharing life and most of its interests, exchanging counsel and help, company and cheer, and reciprocating in economic cooperation." Malinowski asserts that his observations have been confirmed by other ethnographers. They, too, have seen "parental love, the kindly treatment of children, their obedience and affection in return, the enduring of family bonds throughout life. . . ."[6] Although polygamous family structures have been observed in some societies, Ralph Linton points out that "polyandry — that is plurality of husbands — is . . . comparatively rare" and that "most families are monogamous through force of circumstances" even in societies which consider polygyny — that is plurality of wives — the ideal form of marriage.[7]

Malinowski finds "in all human societies the father is regarded by tradition as indispensable. The woman has to be married before she is allowed legitimately to conceive." He indicates that "this is by no means only a European or Christian prejudice; it is the attitude found amongst barbarous and savage people as well." Though societies may vary in many of their characteristics, Malinowski states that a common rule is that "the father is indispensable for the full sociological status of the child as well as of its mother, [and] that the group consisting of a woman and her offspring is sociologically incomplete and illegitimate." Although sex and parenthood are obviously linked biologically, he points out that "[motherhood] is never allowed to remain a mere biological fact. Social and cultural influences always indorse . . . the biological fact." According to Malinowski, sexuality is controlled by parenthood. "To satisfy the fundamental function of sex, we have the institution [of the family] which makes full sex, that is, parenthood, exclusive and individual," concludes Malinowski.

In the light of Malinowski's theory, one may surmise that the sharing of a common domicile by husband, wife, and children is an essential condition of human social organization, a condition present in most if not all societies. Yet, a majority of problem households are one-parent families. According to Malinowski, family members help each

---

[6]Bronislaw Malinowski, "Parenthood—The Basic of Social Structure," in Marvin Sussman (ed.), *op. cit.*, p. 22.

[7]Ralph Linton, "The Natural History of the Family," in Ruth Nanda Anshen (ed.) *The Family: Its Function and Destiny*, New York: Harper and Brothers, 1949, pp. 26-27.

other and reciprocate in economic cooperation. Yet, fathers in half of the problem households have abandoned them physically and economically; more than 80 per cent of the one-parent problem families receive public welfare as a means of economic support. Malinowski finds that fatherhood is essential for the full social status of the child and the full status of the mother. Yet, half of the problem families have female heads of household. One female head had such antipathy for the impregnating male that she insisted our interviewers record her marital status as single rather than as married, separated, or divorced — not withstanding her seven children — and she proudly used her maiden name. Malinowski finds that the institution of the family is designed to satisfy full sex. Yet, sexual experience resulting in extra-marital parenthood occurs in more than one out of every ten problem families, with the impregnating male not legally present in the household as father.

Malinowski points out that the institution of the family makes parenthood exclusive and individual. Yet, several problem households have one mother but many fathers. To illustrate, one mother had children by so many different fathers that she listed her surname as the last name for all of the children to avoid confusion. When asked what were some of her outstanding problems, another mother said she wished that she could get a divorce from the father of her first three children so that she could marry the father of her last three children. In these illustrations, full sex resulting in parenthood is not restricted to the institution of the family; parenthood is neither individual nor exclusive.

These characteristics of family structure and composition Malinowski and other anthropologists have observed in different societies with different cultural systems.[8] These characteristics of family structure and composition must, therefore, transcend any specific cultural system. Apparently, they are necessary and essential in human social organization which accounts for their presence in societies that subscribe to a wide variety of moral and ethical values. Thus, the violation of these structures would appear to be the activities of those in opposition to or unaffected by the requirements of a basic structure essential for the continued existence of human society. Of course, human beings may will *not* to exist. The activities of the problem families in violation of this basic and universal structure are possibly not so much an expression of the will to disintegrate as an expression of lack of knowledge, understanding, and orientation as to what members of a society must do, individually and collectively, to survive. For this reason, it is suggested that low-income problem families are inadequately socialized.

---

[8]Malinowski, *op. cit.*, pp. 24-26.

Family Life Among the Poor in the Cardozo Area of Washington, D.C.

CHARLES V. WILLIE AND
THE RESEARCH STAFF OF WASHINGTON ACTION FOR YOUTH

FAMILIES WHO LIVE IN A LOW-INCOME COMMUNITY ARE EXAMINED IN depth as a basis for planning programs of intervention that might prevent juvenile delinquency.

The Cardozo Area is below the city average on most measures of socio-economic status. It has a population of a few more than 104,000 people: 13 percent of the city's population. Blacks represent 72 percent of the population. Whites account for 28 percent of the population.

The median number of school years completed by the adult Cardozo population is 10.3, while 11.7 years of school completed is the median for the city's adult population. In addition, almost 11 percent of the adults in Cardozo are functional illiterates who have had less than five years of school. Functional illiterates in the city as a whole account for seven percent of the adult population. More than half of its employed population are blue collar workers employed as craftsmen, operatives, service workers and laborers, and its average of median family incomes is $4,464 as contrasted with $5,993, the city's median in 1960. Between 13 and 20 thousand people in the area are living in overcrowded and substandard dwelling units.

Nearly three out of every 10 families in the Cardozo Area have incomes of $4,000 a year or less, and are living at what is regarded to be a subsistence level. Welfare recipients account for almost seven percent of the Cardozo population while welfare recipients in the city represent only four percent of the city's population.

. . .

Published by permission of the author. The original manuscript was prepared in 1964. Washington Action for Youth was a delinquency prevention planning project sponsored by the President's Committee on Juvenile Delinquency and Youth Crime. Members of the research staff were: Norma Metzner, Walter Riddick, Anita Gershenovitz, and Myrna Levine.

Youth under 18 are one-fourth of the area's population. Of the youth under 18 years of age in the Cardozo Area, 61 percent live with both parents while 71 percent of the total city's youth live in two-parent households. In addition, the area's juvenile delinquency rate of 60.6 (youth referred to Juvenile Court) per 1,000 youth is twice as high as the city's rate of 29.2.

• • •

A CASE OF A MARGINAL LEVEL FAMILY

What are the actual problems facing a family living on a marginal income in the Cardozo area? How do the family members deal with the stresses and strains they experience? How do they perceive the community in which they live? What are their goals?

In order to gain some insight into these questions, let us consider one such family who fell into the sample of approximately 1,000 households interviewed in a diagnostic survey conducted during the summer of 1963.

The family consists of husband, wife, and four children, ranging in age from three to seven. The man is a cement finisher with a con-struction firm; he is 29 and his wife is 27. Both husband and wife were born in Georgia, they married young; he was 19 and she was 17.

Two years after their marriage, they moved to the District where they have now lived for eight years. They have experienced many ups and downs and the neighborhood in which they are presently residing was described as "not as nice" as some in which they have lived. On the other hand, the rental for the three-room apartment in which this six-person household lives is only $50 a month, which is all they can afford. Although their income varies, it is never more than $65 per week. They have occupied this apartment for more than two years even though they consider the neighborhood dangerous and the streets and buildings unclean. They simply haven't been able to find a larger dwell-ing in a different section.

Both husband and wife share joint responsibility in disciplining their children but the husband is not home very much due to his long working hours. He doesn't eat breakfast, lunch, or dinner with his family and because of this, the mother and children have no specific mealtimes. In spite of this, the wife feels the family is "real close." The children appear to be well behaved, but she has no advice on child rearing methods that may help them to grow up without getting into trouble.

From time to time, they have had to turn to the Salvation Army for clothes and to the Welfare Department for surplus food. They have also used free facilities at D. C. General Hospital and Children's Hospital; but other than these particular sources, they have depended little on the community for support.

Although the husband completed only nine years of school and the wife has less than a fifth grade education, both have high hopes for their children. She would like a profession like nursing for the girls and the practice of law for the boys. She says that she thinks her youngsters will need an "average" education to achieve these goals. Thus, there is inadequate information about requirements for these vocations and there are insufficient financial resources, since money is a major problem for the family. There isn't enough now for the school needs of the children according to the mother. The seven year old child has never attended school and is, therefore, already one year behind.

The wife, who is home all day, knows 20 to 30 persons in the neighborhood well enough to stop and chat. One is her best friend, a housewife living next door toward whom she would turn if she had a serious problem requiring outside help.

This family has few connections with the community organizations, except for the church, which the family attends regularly on Sunday. They attend Sunday school, morning and evening services, and the mother sings in the choir. Going to church is a family affair. This family has heard about two civic action groups, but does not participate in any. No one in the family is a member of any union, business, political, recreational, social, fraternal, or school organization. They have no contact with case work or social services in the community and no connections with character building agencies or group work recreational programs. With the community at large, this family has contact only through the job, the church, the daily newspaper, and television. The family has a telephone, but no radio.

This, then, is a family struggling valiantly to make it on their own. One is convinced immediately of their terrific push to make a go of it. But as one absorbs the details of their lives, it becomes immediately apparent that the community also has a responsibility to help pull them along. This is a hard-working stable family, but highly vulnerable to even a slight change in the circumstances of life.

A CASE OF A SUBSISTENCE LEVEL FAMILY

Another family interviewed in the diagnostic survey was merely subsisting.

This is a family consisting of one 38 year old woman, (separated from her husband) and her four children, who range in age from one to 11 years. This mother has completed the second grade of elementary school, is unemployed, and has lived in Washington for 15 years. These five persons live in a two-room apartment, share a bath and pay a rental of $70 per month. Their monthly income is between $140 and $180. The only two public agencies which have served this family in the last year have been D. C. Welfare, including surplus food, and Children's Hospital. The family all go to church, but that represents the limit of their connection with society. She described her family as "real close." The children have never been in trouble with the police and were described as performing at about an average level in school. She wants one of them to be a doctor and the others, nurses, and feels it will take "a long time" for them to achieve these goals. She described the other children in the neighborhood as "rough" and would like to move to another section and have more room but she has been unable to find anything. She tries to keep her children away from other children, feeling that the neighborhood is a dangerous area with more delinquents than most. She doesn't know anyone in the neighborhood and if she had a serious problem, she said she would go to the police. The family has no clock, no telephone, no television. They read no newspapers. They have a radio in working condition, their only connection with the larger community.

. . .

POVERTY AND CHILD-REARING METHODS

The kind of living conditions and the daily stresses which low and fluctuating income impose might well produce certain common problems in children in these families. The methods of dealing with them and the general ways of coping with the responsibilities of child raising were investigated in another study conducted in the District of Columbia among poor families by Hylan Lewis.[1] In many such families, it was found that parents relinquish control over their children at a fairly young age so that external groups become an important early influencing force. Despite this lack of communication, these mothers often have high goals for the education and welfare of their children — like the two cases cited from the Cardozo survey — but, again, with little idea of what is involved in attaining them. Under these conditions, coupled with their very limited resources, they frequently lose confidence and become negligent parents.

---

[1] Hylan Lewis, "Child Rearing Practices Among Low Income Families in the District of Columbia," Washington, D.C.: Washington Center for Metropolitan Studies, 1961.

• • •

Lewis points out the dangers involved in assuming that low income families represent a homogeneous culture. It should be remembered that in many instances more money will improve the conditions, but, in others, extensive additional rehabilitation is needed as well.

RESPONSE OF YOUTH TO CIRCUMSTANCES OF LIFE

So far we have been considering family patterns of living under different socio-economic conditions and the methods adopted by low income families in reaction to crisis situations. Let us turn now to the youth themselves and try to understand their perception of the world, their neighborhood, home and school. Paul A. Fine conducted a study of youth living in the southeast corner of the Cardozo Area, some delinquent, some not.[2] They described their neighborhood as dilapidated, neglected, full of adult criminal behavior, uninteresting with no place to play, hostile, and generally discouraging. There is little in the way of reward for socially desirable behavior, much in the way of punishment for negative acts. They resent sharing their mothers' affection with anyone and are shifted around very often from one confused household to another. Even when maintained within one family, however, the pattern of treatment is often erratic and provides little in the way of a consistent style of life. In addition to this, there is the usual absence of a strong male figure with which to identify. They generally perceive most homes as happy ones, but not their own. The changes they would make, however, would be in living conditions rather than in their parents or removing themselves from the home.

CONNECTIONS AND DISCONNECTIONS WITH THE COMMUNITY

The case histories and other studies already described furnished some information, but the Cardozo interview survey provides more systematic data on the following questions.

What are the aspirations that parents in the Cardozo Area have for their children? What are the major problems facing these families? What kinds of connections have they made with existing services that might serve in some way to bridge the gap between their hopes and the realities of their world? One of the questions asked in the diagnostic survey had to do with what they thought the future holds for their

---

[2]Paul A. Fine, "Neighbors of the President: A Study of the Patterns of Youth Life in the Second Precinct," Washington, D.C. Prepared for the President's Committee on Juvenile Delinquency and Youth Crime, October 25, 1963.

children, with what they hope their children will be when they grow up. Of those for whom the question was appropriate (those with children) two-fifths wanted their children to be professionals, such as doctors, lawyers, engineers; almost half felt that it was up to the child to decide. Together these two categories account for almost all of the responses.

What are the major problems of these families? Of those reporting problems, approximately half stated they were financial and another 15 percent reported family relationship difficulties, such as child-rearing problems, marital troubles, lack of discipline in the home, and family member's drinking. The rest of the responses were scattered.

Are these families utilizing agencies and services that can reasonably be expected to assist them in meeting their problems and implementing their hopes for the future? No agency has contact with more than 18 percent of these families. The few associations that have contact with a modest number (10 percent or more of the families) are (1) playgrounds and parks, (2) religious and church groups, and (3) hospitals.

A picture emerges then of low-income families with aspirations undistinguishable from anyone else's, perceiving that they have financial and family instability problems and yet not being served by the community organizations that have presumably been established to deal with at least some of these difficulties. Certainly a more active role must be played by these agencies. They must be willing and able to reach out.

Tracktown Children

MARY ELLEN GOODMAN AND ALMA BEMAN[1]

TRACKTOWN BEGINS ABOUT A MILE FROM DOWNTOWN. IT IS A JUMBLE
of small businesses, small churches, rows of unkempt wooden shotgun
houses separated by five-foot walkways, a very few larger houses,
parked cars and abandoned wrecks, a set of railroad tracks, and an
occasional debris-strewn and weed-choked empty lot. Its population
is almost entirely Negro and it is largely lower-class with respect to
education, occupation, and income.

The people of Houston, Texas, know something about Tracktown
(but they do not know the area by the pseudonym we are using here).
They know enough about Tracktown to avoid it, at night particularly.
Ryan Avenue, which cuts across the Tracktown area from east to
west, is studded with joints and hangouts which not infrequently figure
in the city's news. "Outside the _____ Lounge last night at 12:05
there was an exchange of gunfire which left one man dead, another
in critical condition at Ben Taub Hospital. The shooting is said to
have resulted from an argument over payment for a drink." Fights
that terminate short of murder are too numerous to be newsworthy.

The average Houstonian, if he thinks about it at all, may wonder
what goes on in Tracktown between fights. Do these people work?
Do they have a home life? Do they love and look after their children?
Is theirs a world wholly alien to the world of the middle-class?

We can provide some insights relevant to these questions. Our data
come mainly from Tracktown children. We set out, in the spring and
summer of 1967, to get acquainted with school-age children (grades
one through six) and then to interview them systematically and in-
tensively. In a Tracktown neighborhood we interviewed thirty-three
children (seventeen boys, sixteen girls), and supplemented the interviews with observation over several months.

Published by permission of the authors.

While the Tracktown study was going on we were observing and interviewing school-age children in two other carefully selected low-income areas — an inner city Mexican-American "Barrio" (where we interviewed thirty-four children evenly divided between boys and girls[2]) and a city-perimeter Anglo neighborhood (where we interviewed forty-three children, twenty-three boys and twenty girls). In each of the three ethnic neighborhoods our primary objective was a child's-eye-view of life in the homes, the schools, and in the neighborhoods, along with information from the children about their aspirations and values. In this paper we focus on the Tracktown children; we take note of the other two groups only for purposes of comparison and contrast.

For this study we devised and pre-tested a rather lengthy interview schedule. It contains 123 questions, largely open-ended. It was our intention to interview all school-age children in each of the three small ethnic neighborhoods we had selected for socio-economic comparability. We succeeded in interviewing 75% of the Barrio children, approximately the same proportion in the Tracktown neighborhood, and about 95% in Northboro — the Anglo neighborhood.

We approached tabulation of the open-ended interview material with the intent of preserving as much detail as possible. There are few precedents on which to pre-code such a children's interview, and pre-coding could have lost the nuances of the children's statements. Two persons worked on the coding independently, and then tabulated each other's work as a check on agreement. Multiple responses were recorded, except where clearly illogical, for example, in answer to such a question as "What is *the* best . . . .?" We make statements about differences between groups using a rough gauge of statistical significance as a guide.[3]

HOMES

In the Tracktown neighborhood the thirty-three children we interviewed live in twenty different households. Only eight of these households are headed by fathers; six are headed by "stepfathers," two by grandfathers, and four by mothers. All but two of the Tracktown mothers work. In the Mexican-American Barrio fathers head thirteen of sixteen households, and only three mothers work away from home. In Northboro, the Anglo neighborhood, twenty-one households (out of twenty-three) have paternal heads, and six mothers work outside the home.

These differences are in accord with reasonable expectations, in view of Houston census data, social agency reports, and studies of ethnic subcultures. Such sources of data agree that, in low-income areas, Negro households are less likely than Mexican-American or Anglo to have a male head, or a marital relationship of long standing. Negro children are less likely than Mexican-American or Anglo to be living with both parents.

Tracktown children express strong loyalty and affection for their mothers. Their comments suggest that mother is for them the center and the anchor. She sets the atmosphere in most of the homes. She assigns chores, sees homework, metes out punishment, and warns against hazards (Ryan Avenue, for example, is off-limits except for essential trips to school or to the store). Children credit their mothers with many virtues ("she's nice"; "she don't be yelling at us all the time"; "she gives me money and food"; "I love my mother"). About half the children report that, although their mothers work, they still manage to supervise the early morning activities — getting children up, fed, clothed, and sent off to school with a lunch. The percentage of Tracktown mothers who tend to early morning chores equals, and sometimes exceeds, that of Northboro mothers, where few go out to work. Mother may be still at work when the children return from school in the afternoon, but her authority is felt. They change their clothes, sweep, clean, run errands to the store or to the laundromat, and look after the babies and toddlers — all in accord with mother's instructions. Whether this picture of dutifulness is somewhat overdrawn is of no great moment; the important thing is that the children think of their mothers, and of maternal standards and expectations, as authoritative and prevailing.

Fathers, "stepfathers," or other adult males in Tracktown households ordinarily figure much less importantly. Attitudes towards them range from appreciation to dislike. Fewer than half the children mention a father figure as one of the sources of authority in the household, and an older brother or sister is quite as likely to be mentioned in connection with the exercise of authority.

In spite of much that has been said about the grandmothers and their importance in Negro society, our children displayed either disinterest or ambivalence. This was true even when grandmother had stepped in to raise the young.

No matter who the authority may be in a given instance, the form of discipline applied is varied in accord with the misbehavior. In Tracktown, children who don't come home at the time they've been told to be at home expect to be whipped (so half the children tell us). This is serious misbehavior. About half the Barrio children would expect to be spanked. More than half the Anglo children would expect a spanking or a whipping, usually the latter. In general, Tracktown child discipline, and child play too, are heavy on "whuppings" and on fights.

Among Mexican-American children the domestic scene is in certain respects viewed quite differently. Mother is again a prime focus of affection and appreciation ("she's good and looks pretty"; "she is always helping us and is a lot of fun"). To a lesser extent all members of the household, and indeed all relatives, are declared by the children to be objects of their affection. No Barrio child included any but relatives in his roster of persons he loves, not even a peer or close neighbor. Negro children — boys particularly — and Anglos often included friends in their lists when we asked "who do you love?"

In the Barrio fewer mothers work outside the home, yet the children's reports on what they do are not greatly unlike the reports of the Negro children whose mothers work. The Barrio mothers apparently call rather less on their children for household help, however. Mothers prepare breakfast, lunch to be taken to school, after-school snacks, and supper. They wash dishes, make beds, "make everything clean for us," sweep, and mop. The girls help, and occasionally the boys too. Barrio mothers make and enforce household rules about hours for getting up, for coming in from play, and for going to bed. It is primarily mothers who enforce the rules by scolding, by slapping, or by spanking. In households where there are grandmothers their roles are much like those of the mothers, but grandmothers are viewed more as companions.

The responsibility held by Tracktown mothers is highlighted when contrasted with the Barrio child-view of other family members. In the Barrio father is the ultimate domestic authority. The child may not feel particularly close to him, he may go seldom to his father for information, he may know little of his father's work, and he may have no thought of following in his father's footsteps. Barrio girls are in fact rather closer to their fathers than are the boys. But boys and girls alike agree that father is the head of the household, and that he has two principal roles: to earn money for the family, and to act as the high court in case of major indiscretions or in family crises. Grandfathers too may fill these roles.

Barrio grandparents command respect, affection, and appreciation. They exercise a considerable influence. The children report that grandparents teach them "what is right and not right," and that they are "fun."

The Barrio child regards older siblings, and other relatives only a little older than himself, with mixtures of respect and affection. Many of the children hope that when they grow older they will be like these relatives. Tracktown mothers do not have this network of family members to support and augment their authority.

The Anglo children of Northboro, like the Negro and Mexican-American children, are especially aware of and affectionate toward their mothers, whom they see as regulators of domestic routines. However, the Anglo children are more inclined to speak of "my parents" as a unit, whether with respect to discipline, work, or recreation. The Anglo boys, more than Negro or Mexican-American, admire their fathers. More than half want to be like their fathers when they grow up. Girls, in about the same proportion, admire and want to emulate their mothers.

Anglo children report having relatively few chores, and often being paid for those they do. They report also a clear-cut division of labor by sex; boys seldom do any but outdoor chores such as yard work and carrying out the trash. Girls do the indoor chores usual to their sex. Neither sex looks with joy on the care of very young children, who are regarded as rather disagreeable little creatures. Negro and Mexican-American children, by contrast, often express pride in their small siblings and find pleasure in playing with them.

Anglo children, like Negro boys and unlike Negro girls and Mexican-American children of both sexes, include friends as well as relatives in their rosters of people they love. The Anglos exhibit significantly less attachment to relatives than do the children in the other ethnic groups. In reciting lists of "loved" persons, the Anglos begin with nuclear family, include extended family, and then a myriad of peer and adult friends. Barrio's young citizens mention no one beyond extended family. In Tracktown the major emphases are on mother, siblings, and neighborhood peers.

SCHOOLS AND NEIGHBORHOODS

The worlds of school and of home are bridged for the children by trips between the two, by overlapping rules laid down by adults in both places, and by such interest as adults at home show in what the children do at school.

In Tracktown only six children ride to school. The rest walk, and much of the walk is along notorious Ryan Avenue. Because of the Avenue's reputation, the children are warned not to stop along the way. Many of them do, however. They stop mainly at a corner grocery where they sometimes buy something extra for their lunch boxes. For about half the children "the store" is also a stop on the way home. The pattern for Mexican-American children is much the same. They too walk to school, and sometimes stop at a small store for a small purchase. But they are not warned against doing so. We judge that the walk poses more threat for the Negro children, both from their stories and from the strong injunctions they receive against loitering on the way. The Anglo children, whose school is farther from their homes, ride a school bus.

What goes on at school, as the Tracktown children report it, is just short of bedlam, and it is precisely this that is to them most interesting and memorable. The children told us, with a mixture of annoyance, admiration, and resigned amusement, many stories about small and large crises — hair pullings; "when people be running around"; "somebody stole my teacher's purse, they had to call the police. . . ." Half the children report that the teacher or the principal whips ("whups") for serious misbehavior. The "good" children are the obedient, quiet, non-fighters, but of them we hear very little. And we hear little about "school work," except in answer to our question: "what is your best subject in school?" About half the children, both boys and girls, claim arithmetic as their "best," with spelling (girls only) and reading (boys and girls) second and third in frequency.

We did not ask the children about their school marks nor about whether they are in the grades appropriate to their age. We have, however, a few small clues to their levels of factual knowledge. We asked: "who is President of the United States?" "what town do you live in?" "what state do you live in?" and "the United States is a big country; what are some other big countries?" A sizable majority (almost three-fourths) of Tracktown children gave correct answers when asked about the President and the name of their state. An even larger majority (nine-tenths) know the name of their city. Very few (three) were able to answer the "other big countries" question. The responses of Mexican-American and Anglo children do not differ significantly, but the latter are somewhat less accurate with respect to the names of their town and state.

The "most fun at school" is almost unanimously identified with "recess" and with "play." In this the children of the three ethnic groups are essentially agreed. However, the Anglo children show somewhat more enthusiasm for that part of school which has to do with "work."

Although the Tracktown children report so much disturbance in the schoolroom and so much disciplinary action by the teacher, they report favorable impressions of their teachers. A few describe the teacher as "mean" or "bad"; but with some redeeming feature or features. Only one child had nothing good to say. More than a third of the children describe their teachers as "good," "very good," or even "great." Many are delighted when the teacher plays with them "sometimes," and when "she let us play cards and games and talk a little bit" or "tell stories to us." However, the incidence of enthusiastic comments about teachers runs significantly higher among both Anglo and Mexican-American children, and the incidence of gossip about whippings runs lower, especially among the Anglo children. The Anglos compain mainly about teachers who "yell" at them and about other forms of non-physical disciplinary action.

Tracktown children show their schoolwork mainly to their mothers and grandmothers, rarely to their fathers (two children), and seldom to both parents (six children in five families) Responses from the adults are for the most part perfunctory, but nearly half the children report more than that; for example, the adult "helps me" or "tells me to learn more." Mexican-American children — three-fourths of them — know that their parents and siblings care about their work and progress at school. It is the mother especially who expresses interest, but only a third of the children report comment as specific as "you ought to learn more." Educational levels of adults in the Barrio, and in Tracktown as well, are low. Few children in either place can get help at home with school work. As one Tracktown fourth grader told us, "Don' nobody know my work." His parents do see his younger siblings' papers. Anglo children report a relatively high frequency of help, encouragement, and strong positive and negative reactions when they show their schoolwork at home.

Homework is seldom mentioned by Tracktown children. Only three report doing homework after supper; none does homework or reads when he comes home from school. Few Barrio children (two) mention homework as an after-school activity, and but one Anglo boy does so. Six Anglo girls tell us they read or do homework when they return from school.

Afternoon and evening activities in Tracktown are fairly evenly divided between play and chores. When we asked about after-school activities only three children report that they watch TV on school days. But later when we asked, in another context, "when do you watch TV?" eleven children reply "every day." There is somewhat more viewing on weekends, but an even greater frequency of movie-going. As compared with Mexican-Americans and Anglos, the Tracktown children seem somewhat light on TV and heavy on movies. This may be merely the result of accessibility; we do not know the comparative frequencies of TV ownership, but we do know that a movie house is a feature of our Tracktown neighborhood, but not of either the Barrio or of Northboro.

Tracktown child society appears to be highly solidary. More than four-fifths of the children have "best friends" living within a five block radius. After-school play takes place nearby (playground, school yard, vacant lot, street, backyard, friend's house) but seldom within the child's own house. "Best friends" of Anglo children are a little more geographicaly disbursed, and those of Barrio children (girls especially) even more so. Tracktown children, more than those of the Barrio or of Northboro, admire individuals among their peers. Conversely, children in the latter two groups more often respond by identifying an adult friend — someone over eighteen — when we ask: "who's a great person that you know — somebody that lives around here?" and, a little later, "who else that you know is a great person?" In response to the second of these questions Tracktown children confirm their early emphasis, both relative and absolute, on peers, and Mexican-Americans and Anglos confirm their previous emphasis on older persons.

ASPIRATIONS

Tracktown children tend to state their educational and vocational aspirations in rather extreme terms. More than a third declare they want or expect to go to college. Some of our young informants declare "I'm goin' all the way, 's far 's I can go." "How far is that?" "To high school," or "to the eight grade," was often the answer. A somewhat larger proportion plan college than in the Barrio, and about the same as among the Anglo children. But the Negro children considerably exceed the other two groups in the proportion (about one-fifth) who state flatly their intention to take as "little [school] as possible," or "less than six [grades]," or no more than "grammar school." Vocational aspirations of Tracktown children are heavy on the side of heroic, dramatic, and starring roles. Among the Anglo and Mexican-American children there are no parallels to these statements by Negro children (more than one-fourth of those responding): "I want to be a space scientist, like on TV"; a star of movies or TV; an athletic hero. Prominent among more mundane ambitions (usually stated by girls) are those for nursing (especially), teaching, and secretarial work. The boys, except for three who would be policemen, two "in the army," and one cowboy, express no other ambitions. The vocational aspirations stated by Mexican-American and Anglo Children seem to be more realizable. The boys would be policemen or firemen (especially among the Mexican-Americans), skilled or semi-skilled manual workers (especially among the Anglos). Girls in these groups would be mainly teachers and nurses.

VALUES

What do Tracktown children regard as "good" and "bad?" We asked a variety of questions designed to provide some insight on these basics of a values system.

We asked what are good things for a child to do. One third of the Tracktown children tell us that it is good to work, both at school and at home. They emphasize the latter, and among home chores "cleaning" takes precedence, making things "nice and neat and clean." The Anglo children, almost a third of them, comment about work in similar terms, stressing the nature of the specific jobs. Personal pleasures, especially through play or TV viewing, are "good" for one-fourth of both the Negro and the Anglo children. More than a third of the Mexican-American children emphasize personal pleasures. Obeying rules, and being considerate of others — each is a "good" mentioned by a fifth of the Negro children, and by about the same proportion of Mexican-Americans. Anglo children put somewhat more emphasis on the importance of observing the rules (for example: obey; behave; "don't cuss"; don't steal). For all the children "bad" things to do are largely the reverse of the good.

We get other values insights as a result of our questions about "best" and "worst" of "things that ever happened to you." The Tracktown children who responded to these questions are almost evenly divided between those for whom "best" has to do with material things (getting a bike, receiving presents or money) and those for whom it is rather a matter of an outstanding experience (a trip, a party, seeing friends, going to the movies, and — for three boys — a fight). Mexican-American children somewhat emphasize events over things, and Anglo children make this emphasis strongly. No child in either group mentions a fight as a "best thing," but three in each group recall it as a "worst thing." So too, however, do more than a third of the Negro children who responded to the question. Punishments (mainly spanking and whipping) are worst things for almost a third of the Tracktown children, and for more than that proportion of Mexican-Americans. Few Anglos (only two) mention punishment in this context. Personal accidents or sickness stand out as "worst" in the minds of about a third of the Negroes, more than a third of the Mexican-Americans, and for most (four-fifths) of the Anglos.

The children tell us that they get money by working for it ("shine shoes," "run errands," "sell stuff," etc.) or — predominantly — someone in the family gives it to them. We asked: "What do you do with money?" A large majority of the Tracktown children (almost four-fifths) spend it on treats, candy, clothes, pencils and paper for school. But five of the Tracktown children tell us they spend their money for food or milk. No child in either of the other groups mentions these items. Very few Negro children speak of saving money; Mexican-Americans are a little more inclined toward saving, and Anglos still more. No Tracktown child mentions turning over his money to his parents. Very few Anglos do so, but almost two-fifths of the Mexican-Americans claim they give money to their parents.

We have clues to values also in the reasons the children gave us for wanting to be like particular people when they grow up. Tracktown children, and Anglo children too, admire their heroes especially for what they do or are (athletes or TV stars for example) and secondarily for their fame, money, power, or looks. Some (about one-fourth) of the Negro children want to be like people who are "good" or to whom they are related. For Mexican-American children these personal considerations take precedence. In all three groups, but among the Barrio children especially, significant numbers have no answer at all when asked why they want to be like the person they have identified as a model.

As our final question to the children we asked: "if you could make three wishes and get what you wished for, what would you wish?" Among Tracktown children one-third of the wishes are for things, ranging from small toys through bikes, autos, better homes, and clothes. Money is next most frequently wished for (one-fourth of the wishes). Others are for self-gratifications, some of rather extravagant sorts (for example: "I want to be a king"; "to have a racing track") or — somewhat more frequently — for a gratification for someone else. Things loom even more importantly and money far less importantly in the views of Anglo and Barrio children. Their wishes for others (for example: "for Mother to be a teacher"; "for this to be a happy country") are a little more numerous or, in the case of the Anglos, significantly more numerous, than those of the Tracktown children.

LIFE IN TRACKTOWN: AN OVERVIEW

What goes on in Tracktown, beside the violent encounters the media like to feature? A great deal that is quite normal and unremarkable in big city living; so, at any rate, the children tell us. Do its people work? Yes; but we hear little about what they do, quite probably because the children hear little about it. The types of work done by Tracktown people are not likely to lend themselves to sparkling conversation, nor are their rewards dependent on communication skills.

Do Tracktown people love and look after their children? Those about whom we hear from the children do, most emphatically.

Is the Tracktown neighborhood a world wholly alien to the world of the middle-class? It is by no means so different as that question suggests, but it is different and distinctive in important ways.

According to Tracktown children and to what they are willing and able to tell us, life in their neighborhood is not so strange or alien as writers about "the Negro ghetto" would have us believe. There are in this ghetto rules and standards for behavior, children are well aware of them, and they are punished for failing to keep the rules and meet the standards. Cleanliness is an important standard, and a great amount of effort goes into keeping things clean, or trying to. Obedience and "behaving" are important standards, and clearly many parents — mothers especially — work hard at the task of holding children to these standards. There are deep bonds of respect and affection between household members, between mothers and their children and between siblings particularly. There are also strong ties between peers; Tracktown society is distinctly less family- and kin-centered than Barrio society. It has a mother-child-peer orientation.

Some of the ghetto stereotypes are supported by what we know of Tracktown and its children. Relatively few fathers live with and support their children. Most mothers work and either support or help to support their children. Mothers are the most important, the most influential and authoritative, of the household members. Household discipline is heavy on "whuppings." Peer group fights, though the children incline to deplore them, are not uncommon.

The atmosphere of Tracktown life, as we infer it from the comments of the children, is relatively hectic. This is strikingly true of school, of Ryan Avenue, and of some neighbors. School routines are punctuated with disorders and misbehaviors, and the children are excited and stimulated by them. We get from Tracktown children surprisingly little in the way of reports on fights and arguments in the home and neighborhood; perhaps the children preferred not to talk about them.

Tracktown children are not enjoying the amenities — the educational and "cultural" advantages — of middle-class life. Not surprisingly, they do not exhibit the intellectual interests and sophistication which are likely to characterize middle-class children. There is no talk among Tracktown children about the vocational or intellectual interests of their parents or of other adults; they do not mention organizations to which their parents belong (not even PTA). There is no mention of such events as music lessons, dancing lessons, swimming lessons. Trips and parties are seldom mentioned. If we judge by what they say (and by what they do not say, as well) Tracktown children and their parents do not read for pleasure. Their occupational goals are either modest or extravagant; a good many of them deal only in dreams of glory when asked to look ahead toward education and occupation.[4] They probably have given such questions little thought or none, and their parents are unlikely to have done so either.

Material possessions, even food, and money loom very large on the horizons of their interests. Fame and power are also among the good things, but clearly these children have little or no idea how people in our society go about achieving such goals. The goals themselves are by no means unusual in American society; the lack of realism or information about steps and requirements toward achievement is prevalent among Tracktown children. The boys especially are given to self-glorifying fantasies without foundation. This is perhaps the distinctive feature of Tracktown as compared with the Barrio and with Northboro, as well as with middle-class neighborhoods — the wild fantasies which flourish among its children, and no doubt among its adults as well. An eleven-year-old boy responded to our "three wishes" question with a statement quite in the spirit of this world of utter unrealism. He said: "I wish for all the money in the world, for no one to be selfish, and I hope to be a doctor." There is a chance, in the case of this particular boy, that he might achieve his hope. It is a rare case. There is, unfortunately, little sign that Tracktown children are any more likely to become doctors than they are to command "all the money in the world."

NOTES

[1]We join in thanking the Texas Department of Mental Health and Mental Retardation for a grant in support of the early phases of this research, and the Center for Research in Social Change and Economic Development, Rice University, for principal support. This Center-sponsored research was funded by the Advanced Research Projects Agency under ARPA Order No. 738 and monitored by the Office of Naval Research, Group Psychology Branch, under Contract number N00014-67-A-0145-0001, NR 177-909.

[2]A full report on the Barrio children is available (see Beman and Goodman, 1968).

[3]Our references to differences between groups (Tracktown, Barrio and Northboro) are based on statistical significances. Were Chi square feasible, a rough approximation of differences required (translated to percentages) was arrived at using Zubin's monograph, as it appears in Oppenheim. Note also that a given difference (say fifteen percentage points) may be significant at the extremes, where one of the percentages approaches zero or one hundred, but not in the middle ranges (Oppenheim 1966:288). We present sample values in the mid-range, the largest differences required should two groups only be compared.

Significance Level	N₁=34, N₂=43	N₁=17, N₂=17	N₁=20, N₂=23
10%	58% and 42%	64% and 37%	63% and 38%
5%	62% and 40%	67% and 34%	65% and 36%
1%	65% and 35%	72% and 29%	69% and 31%

[4]This inclination to "dreams of glory" was conspicuous also among Negro teen-agers interviewed in connection with a Rice University study of a low-income census tract (see Goodman and Price-Williams, 1965).

REFERENCES

1. Alma Beman and Mary Ellen Goodman, "Child's-Eye-Views of Life in an Urban Barrio," *Spanish-Speaking People in the United States*. Proceedings of the 1968 Annual Spring Meeting of the American Ethnological Association.

2. Mary Ellen Goodman and Douglass Price-Williams, *The People of Census Tract 16,* Project Houston Report Number One, Rice University, 1965.

3. A. N. Oppenheim, Questionnaire Design and Attitude Measurement, New York, Basic Books Inc., 1966.

Mothers and Children in Public Housing

CAMILLE JEFFERS

. . .

FOUR CHILDREN* WERE MORE THAN MRS. TODD HAD WANTED. SHE would have preferred only three. There were many indications, sometimes from Mrs. Todd, that even three would have been too many. One outstanding characteristic of her child-rearing behavior was the contrast between what she said and what she did.

. . .

Mrs. Todd's facility in expressing her thoughts about child rearing was tied in with her own sense of past and present deprivations. She wanted "something different" for her children, yet her background experiences and present resources did not prepare her to offer them that something different. She knew how she thought family life and child rearing should be, but she did not think she could bring it about.

It was probably this awareness of the gap between what she said and what she did that made her say she did not consider herself such a good mother.

EMOTIONAL CARE: "NOT TOO CUDDLESOME"

Mrs. Todd's relationship with her children was marked by a seeming diffidence and reluctance to respond to them emotionally. She was undemonstrative most of the time. When nine-month-old Shirley would tug at her skirt to be picked up or would try to sit on her lap, Mrs. Todd would usually push her away roughly, saying, "Get away from me, I'm not your mother," or, "Don't always be calling me Mama."

---

*They were Elsie, age five; Philip, age four; Nicholas, age three; Shirley, age nine months.

Reprinted by permission of the publisher and author from *Living Poor* (Ann Arbor, Michigan: Ann Arbor Publishers, Copyright 1967), pp. 52-96.

On one occasion Mrs. Todd told about one of her visits to an acquaintance in the building. As she entered the apartment, she overheard the mother criticizing her to a neighbor for not being affectionate to children.

"I didn't get angry," said Mrs. Todd. "I just said, 'You're right!'"

Mrs. Todd explained that her friend talked about her because she never picked children up; another acquaintance claimed that Mrs. Todd was the only one who came into her home who did not pick up the baby. Mrs. Todd asked:

> Why should I pick up her child when I don't even pick up my own? But when I do go there, I always give some attention to the one she leaves in bed all day, as I don't think it's right to give all the attention to one child.

On another occasion when Mrs. Todd was asked to pick up her neighbor's crying baby, she refused and explained to me: "Maybe I'm funny, but I just don't believe in it."

Among the mothers, Mrs. Todd was not alone in her negative attitude about picking up children. I observed a similar reaction in my neighbor, Mrs. Norris, whose two-year-old son I sometimes picked up. One consequence was that, whenever he saw me, he came toward me expectantly and held out his arms to be picked up. If I did pick him up, he would sit contentedly clutching me around the neck. Often, in order to put him down, I had to pry his hands apart, so tight was his hold. When I told Mrs. Norris that her son seemed to like me, she said, "That's because you pick him up. You're spoiling him, and I'm not going to pick him up." Some mothers seemed to equate overt demonstrations of warmth and affection with spoiling.

A suggestion that this parental attitude got transferred to children came from Mrs. Todd's five-year-old daughter, Elsie. She had been playing with my son two days in succession. The second day, she asked me if my son was sick. Since my son was actively playing with her, I was puzzled and asked why she wanted to know this. "Well," she replied, "you were carrying him last night!" I then recalled that I had automatically picked my son up when he had fallen, hit his head and begun to cry. Elsie made no association between his fall and my picking him up. Apparently, in her experience, only a child's illness called for this behavior.

During my early association with Mrs. Todd, I was strongly tempted to apply the familiar psychological label of rejection to her refusal to pick up her children unless they were ill or incapacitated beyond any doubt. As time went on, this early temptation to apply a hackneyed label was weakened and eventually eliminated. I became much more uncertain about my diagnostic abilities in this and other matters.

I frequently found myself wondering why I could be so fond of a person who treated her children the way Mrs. Todd did. By the time I left the project, I wondered how she did so well. This change in my thinking about her child-rearing behavior was not due merely to the understanding that is likely to come with friendship.

My speculations about Mrs. Todd's behavior continued after I left the housing project. When I viewed her in the context of all the other mothers that we had observed and interviewed in the Child Rearing Study, a possible explanation of a real puzzle began to emerge. I think that there may be a basic difference between the mother who defines a good mother as loving and the mother who defines a good mother as "not too cuddlesome."

I think that the failure of the first type of mother to be loving is due to reasons that are different from those usually given for the failure of the second type of mother to be loving. The behavior of the first type of mother suggests the classical picture of rejection. But, if we attempt to describe the behavior of the second type of mother in the same way, we might be somewhat wide of the mark because we are judging her in the light of child-rearing values to which she gives different priority and weight. Other family values might take precedence.

In Mrs. Todd's case, I think the child-rearing values which take precedence are those related to independence training. Some mothers seem to withhold affection not because they reject their children, but because they want to train their children away from depending on them. They are under pressure to get each child "out of the way" as soon as possible in order to go on to the next child. But, in these terms, as well as in the mothers' views, the response to these pressures is not rejection. This is, perhaps, why Mrs. Todd could point to the paradox of her friend criticizing her for not picking up her children but complimenting her on how nice a child Mrs. Todd's nine-month-old daughter was.

INDEPENDENCE TRAINING: BEING ON YOUR OWN EARLY

One evening, Mrs. Todd was seated at our kitchen table with Helen, drinking hot tea. When her youngest daughter, Shirley, tugged at her skirts for a drink of the tea, Mrs. Todd held the cup to her daughter's lips, but the heat of the cup made the child flinch. The following interchange occurred:

Helen: Don't give her that hot tea! She'll burn herself.
Mrs. T: That's the only way for her to learn what it means. When she sees it's hot, she'll leave it alone.

Annoyed by what she had seen and by the exchange with Mrs. Todd, Helen got up and drew a glass of water from the kitchen faucet for Shirley. She held the glass as the child drank thirstily.

Mrs. T: (*pretending to address her daughter*) I'm going to leave you with Helen, because she's making it hard for me.
Helen: What do you mean? She's thirsty! I only gave her some water.
Mrs. T: But you didn't have to hold the glass! She knows how to hold a cup.

Mrs. Todd believed in early training in everything. Her last child, Shirley, was toilet trained in less time than any of the others. She stressed having her children learn to feed and dress themselves early. At less than a year, Shirley was seated at the table with her brothers and sister, perched on a pile of books, with a plate of food before her just like the rest. It was also true that at the ages of two and three, Mrs. Todd's children had made considerable progress in dressing themselves. Her three-year-old son, Nicholas, could tie his shoe laces, and my four-year-old son could not. It did not matter to Mrs. Todd that a child's shirt was on backwards; the point was that the child had put it on.

Mrs. Todd thought it scandalous that the parent who criticized her for not picking up her children did not permit her own children to dress themselves, especially since the oldest child would soon be going to kindergarten. Once when Mrs. Todd was in this parent's home and was asked to help dress the children, Mrs. Todd tested them out by handing them each an article of clothing to put on. She found out, to her satisfaction, that the children could dress themselves, if need be, and this made her friend's behavior inexcusable.

On more than one occasion, I saw Mrs. Todd demonstrate skill and patience in teaching a child how to do something. One of her demonstrations, which I shall not soon forget, involved me.

My son and Phillip, her four-year-old, had been wrestling on the floor on a blanket. When they finished wrestling and started on some other activity, I arose to pick the blanket up.

"Sit down!" Mrs. Todd said firmly, and I obeyed instantly. "Let me show you how to do it," she said, as she called the boys and had them spread the blanket out smoothly on the floor. Without moving from her chair and never changing her tone of voice, she gave clear, concise, step-by-step instructions to each of the children. This one was to take this corner and bring it to that corner, and that one was to take the other corner and bring it to this corner. The children followed her instructions with ease, and my son's pride in his accomplishment made me chagrined at my hastiness in assuming the responsibility.

Baby sitting was another child-rearing role which Mrs. Todd began teaching her children early. She taught her three-, four-, and five-year-olds how to dress and feed the baby.

In spite of the fact that Mrs. Todd complained of the child-rearing responsibility for her own brothers and sisters that she had had as a child, she appeared to be giving her children the same kind of responsibility. Her five-year-old daughter, Elsie, was given a major baby-sitting responsibility. Mrs. Todd would sometimes leave all the children in Elsie's charge for two and three hours at a time. She gave Elsie authority to hit the other children with a ruler if they misbehaved; the other children seemed to recognize that to go against their sister was tantamount to going against their mother. Elsie, sometimes tyrannical in her rule, handled easily the discipline of her younger brothers and sisters; yet, she was just a year or two older than the others.

Possibly as a result of Elsie's "Little Mother" role, a very close relationship developed between her and three-year-old brother Nicholas. He went to her with his injuries and problems, often even if his mother was at home. The ties between the two became so strong that they caused Mrs. Todd to refer to the trouble she was having trying to "get Nicholas away from [five-year-old] Elsie" because the latter "had him so tight."

CONTROL: MAKING THEM MIND

According to Mrs. Todd her husband had been the disciplinarian in the family. She could mimic the way he would bark "Attention!" to call the children to order as though he were giving a military command. But she was aware that there were other aspects of her husband's relationships with the children:

> I don't say anything; they are his children, but his mother and father say that he is mean. That's all right, they love him. In fact, they like him better than they like me.

· · ·

Mrs. Todd's characteristic demand was for instant compliance, and she generally got it. Some times she would line the children up on the sofa and dare them to move. There they sat like frozen little statues; fear, anxiety and consternation were written all over their faces.

Mrs. Todd showed some awareness of the questionable nature of her behavior in controlling the children. One day she knew that I was aware of her beating one of the children since he had screamed so loud. Later in the day, she said that she guessed I thought she was beating him half to death. When I told her that was the way it sounded, she mentioned that four-year-old Phillip had poured a cupful of dirt in the baby's crib. She said reflectively that she just did not know what to make of him; she was looking forward to her husband's return at which time she would turn Phillip over to him.

From time to time, Mrs. Todd made remarks which indicated her opinion that Phillip was a child "born to be bad." The "born to be bad" theme was not unique to Mrs. Todd. Certainly the black sheep is not a new idea* and I encountered variations on the concept in field interviews. According to Mrs. Todd, Phillip was more aggressive than her other children and could not be trusted. He was constantly getting into difficulty because of his bizarre (disturbed?) behavior. On one occasion he set fire to a bedspread. Another time, when I was baby sitting with him in the court, he picked up an empty Clorox bottle and suddenly smashed it on the sidewalk.

Sometimes Mrs. Todd referred to him as being "not all there." She cited the following incident: one day Phillip had come to her complaining that he had nothing to do. Exasperated that he would say this when she had just gotten him toys for Christmas, she told him to go bump his head against the wall in his room. He not only did this but returned to her saying he was tired of doing it and asking for something else to do. Still annoyed, Mrs. Todd told him to go and bump his head against the other wall.

Mrs. Todd ended her story with an amazed, "And do you know that he did it!"

PROVIDING THE BASIC NECESSITIES: PRIORITIES AND PROBLEMS

My experience at the housing project taught me that it is no small accomplishment for low-income families to provide "decent food, clothing and shelter." I came to realize why so many mothers in and outside

---

*The black-sheep idea is a part of our American heritage. I think that we may not realize the extent to which this idea is still held. There are still those who believe that there is such a thing as an intrinsically bad child and that his badness was not of the parents' making. It may well be that some of the children who get written off early in life, as Mrs. Todd appears to have written off this son, are the ones thought "born to be bad."

the project considered the provision of adequate physical care a major, if not the major, aspect of good motherhood. Adequate physical care could not be taken for granted, and seeing that the children got food, clothing and shelter was sometimes quite a feat. Different mothers had different physical-care problems, and these differences usually affected priorities.

With Mrs. Todd, rent had first priority among physical-care categories. She was determined to keep the roof over their heads until her husband got back. The rent bill was the first thing she paid when she got her allotment, even though she did not always have enough money left to meet other needs.

Clothing was one of these needs. Trying to keep her four children clothed was a critical problem. One way of easing it was to develop different styles of dress to fit varied situations. For example, Mrs. Todd had four clothing levels for her children, ranging from complete undress to Sunday best.

One day I knocked on Mrs. Todd's door and found her five-year-old daughter in charge of what looked like a small nudist colony. Since it was somewhat chilly, I asked Elsie if she didn't think it was too cold for the baby and, without hesitation, she replied, "That's the way my mother wants her."

Mrs. Todd, like other mothers, frequently let her children run naked around the house. Sometimes the reason they were stripped was that it was wash day and there was nothing extra to put on while their clothes were being washed. At other times, the nakedness of a small child could be due to the heat or to efforts to save clean clothes for more public occasions.

Now and then I found the children, particularly baby Shirley, in semi-dress, wearing an undershirt but no panties. This was a pervasive pattern of dress for small children. At first I did not know how to interpret this semi-dress; I found mothers, who exhibited high standards for their children's welfare, dressing (or not dressing) their children in the same way. The more I saw of Mrs. Todd and other families, the more a relatively simple explanation for the practice began to take shape in my mind. Families just did not have the quantity of diapers and training pants needed for children who were not yet completely toilet trained. When funds were limited, priority had to be given to the purchase of outer clothing rather than underwear.

One result of this semi-dress was frequent urine puddles on the floor and I heard one exasperated mother cry, "I'm sick of wiping up this pissy floor." One mother had an alternative to floor wiping; she passed this job on to her children. Once when this mother's four-year-old son reported in an alarming voice that the baby had "made doo-doo" on the floor, the mother said, "Well, you know what to do; get a rag and clean it up."

Sometimes Mrs. Todd's children were dirty and disheveled. I never knew whether their appearance on these occasions was due to a lack of money to buy soap powder or to Mrs. Todd's low spirits. Either explanation could have been right. I observed, however, that when the children were dirty, Mrs. Todd was careful to see that they stayed in the building and played only in the house or in the hall. Going outside was a different matter; she always made them more presentable then. As she put it, she wanted them to look decent enough so people wouldn't talk about the way she kept her children.

This concern about what other people had to say about their children was pervasive among the mothers. In general, children who came into the court to play looked presentable. I noticed, for example, that raggedy and unkempt children were much more in evidence within a block or two of the project, in areas that were still physically deteriorated.

Proximate living in the project appeared to have been a factor in many efforts to conform to better standards of public dress for their children and, to a lesser degree, for themselves.

When Mrs. Todd's children left the grounds of the housing project, she made a special effort to dress them as well as she could. Once Mrs. Todd refused an invitation to take Phillip on an automobile trip to the airport because he had "nothing to wear." When she was pressed for an explanation, she said that the clothing he had was not suitable enough for him to go. It was only after a neighbor lent him some pants and socks that she let him go. When she took her children to visit relatives, they would be clean and neat. She took special pains to see that they looked their best whenever they went to her mother's house in a middle class residential neighborhood. For their out-of-town vacation trip to visit relatives in a nearby state, she bought each child a completely new outfit.

Mrs. Todd managed the problem of clothing the children as well as she did only because of help from family and friends. She received hand-me-downs for her daughters from a sister who had several girls. When Phillip, her older son, outgrew clothes he had, they were passed down to Nicholas. Keeping Phillip adequately clothed was Mrs. Todd's biggest clothing problem; she had no ready-made or easy source of hand-me-downs for him. Occasionally her mother-in-law furnished items of clothing for the various children, particularly for Elsie, who seemed to be her favorite. From time to time, Mrs. Todd's mother gave her dresses for the girls. Friends in the project would also give her clothing that their children had outgrown. Despite her children's clothing needs, Mrs. Todd thought about helping others. She asked if I might know some family among those in CRS's study group that could use her youngest daughter's hand-me-downs.

Ranking second among the basic things Mrs. Todd wanted for her children was "decent food." This was a chronic need and made for continuing frustration. She tried to stay abreast of things by juggling the regular expected income and the hoped-for extra money from her husband. One month she would pay all the bills with her allotment and buy food with any extra money that her husband sent. The next month she would use her allotment to store up on food and rely on the extra money expected from her husband to pay bills. However, this juggling act failed when no extra money came from Mr. Todd.

Mrs. Todd's food standards and tastes were relatively high as measured by the cheaper and inferior fare offered in some neighborhood stores. She scorned the neighborhood stores that regularly slipped handbills under the apartment doors advertising their weekly specials.

• • •

Mrs. Todd said that she would not buy any old thing to feed her children as neither they nor she were used to cheap foods. Describing a breakfast that the Todds had one day when a visiting friend purchased the food, she said, "We had bacon, eggs, grits and biscuits," and added, "One day my children eat like kings, and the next day they have nothing."

Her children liked to have two eggs apiece, and, with her income and its ups and downs, it took too many eggs for one such breakfast. She said that, occasionally, she gave them each one egg, but it took her a day or two to make up the expense for this kind of breakfast. The children were much more apt to get a dish of cereal or grits.

Mrs. Todd preferred to do her shopping at a commissary for service men and their families where food was cheaper. Unless she had someone to drive her there she could not save enough to make a trip to the commissary worthwhile because the round trip taxi fare wiped out any savings. Several times when she was offered a ride, she refused, saying that she had so little money to spend that it was not worth going so far.

Their diet was generally starchy, with emphasis on beans, spaghetti, noodles and potatoes. The children were particularly fond of canned meat balls and spaghetti; she gave this to them quite frequently. Another frequent meal was frozen fish sticks and frozen French fries. It was not that Mrs. Todd did not know how to prepare a balanced meal; it rather was that she chronically lacked the money and, frequently, the incentive to do it.

Often, Mrs. Todd went without meals herself because she did not like the food that she gave the children. Now and then, long after the children had gone to sleep, she would treat herself to a small, treasured piece of steak.

Numerous, undramatic little events taught me the meaning of hunger. Some lessons in hunger were provided unwittingly by the Todd children. For example, a bowl of fruit usually stood on my dinette table. When Mrs. Todd's children came over to play, they would eye it longingly and sometimes ask for an apple or a banana. As we became more friendly, their requests increased with the frequency of their visits. First, I tried to regulate demand and supply by keeping the fruit elsewhere. I began to notice that when the children came over, they would eventually make their way to the kitchen; and there, their eyes would roam around the room as though looking for something. It began to dawn on me that the fruit was less a snack or treat than a supplement to, or even a substitute for, a meal. It was an important means of appeasing the hunger that was such a constant part of the lives of many children in the project.

One day I found Mrs. Todd's nine-month-old Shirley picking dirt off the wheels of a child's tricycle and eating it. I was so startled that I shouted at her to stop. Mrs. Todd came to see what the trouble was. Her daughter did not stop for me nor did she stop the first time her mother spoke to her. Finally, Mrs. Todd had to pick the dirt out of the girl's mouth. When I asked if Mrs. Todd had ever seen her daughter eat dirt before, she said that she had seen her pick the dirt off her brother Phillip's tricycle and eat it. She was at a loss to explain Shirley's behavior.*

On one occasion Mrs. Todd described a food fantasy she often had, one involving her teen-age brothers and sisters: she imagined she had taken them on a beach picnic and had so much hot food cooked up that they were able to eat all they wanted.

She followed this image with: "Can you imagine a loaf of bread lasting two days with six children?" When I showed some doubt, she said, "Well it did in my house because my mother wouldn't permit us to touch it unless she gave it to us. We would get a beating if we did."

Such expressions of Mrs. Todd's feelings, thoughts, and memories involving food helped me understand better what seemed to be a contradiction in her behavior toward her children. Relying on what I

---

*This particular instance of "hunger" is probably best classified as an example of what is medically called *pica*.

thought I knew about Mrs. Todd, I had fully expected her to get angry when I saw her children go into the groceries she had brought home one day and eat a loaf of bread before she got a chance to put the rest of the purchases away. Instead of anger or annoyance, she showed the opposite, pleasure and permissiveness. It appeared that hunger was one of her children's experiences with which she readily identified. This same permissiveness and lack of anger, in matters where food for her children was involved, showed in her amusement when a three-layer cake she had baked disappeared in two hours.

One of her often repeated wishes was to be able to set one loaf in front of each of her children and let them eat until they had had their fill of bread — at least once.

Despite the trouble she had providing adequate food, Mrs. Todd was reluctant to acknowledge how bad at times the situation was for her. Some of the facts and many of the dimensions of her family's food story came out only gradually. Some were revealed in situations like the following:

One day she interrupted a conversation to ask if I had ever heard of anybody filling up on ice cream when hungry. When I asked why anybody would make such an odd choice, she replied, "Well, when that's all you can get on your Central Charge Account, ice cream is better than nothing, and with a few cup cakes you can make a meal."

When I pressed to find out whether she was saying obliquely that she had no food, she insisted that she had food. The next day she mentioned that she was thinking about asking to be referred to Surplus Foods by the agency from which she was asking help with the beds. I told her that she could make an application to Surplus Foods without an agency referral and offered to take her there. She said she could do this the following week since she had to remain at home for a few days, waiting for a visit from a social worker with information about the beds.

The following day when I came home from work, Mrs. Todd was waiting for me. Hearing my key in the latch, she poked her head out of her door and asked if I was too tired to do her a favor: she wanted to go to a Peoples Drug Store. Recalling her comment about filling up on ice cream, I immediately offered my services and took her to the drug store. The bulky bag she came out with looked like it might contain ice cream, and I also caught a whiff of tomato soup. Mrs. Todd offered no explanations.

On our return home, I mentioned that I was going to the A&P grocery and asked if she wanted anything. "I don't have any money," she said. "I'm expecting some tomorrow. If I don't get it, I will probably have to go over to my mother's." I asked what she needed but she replied,

"Nothing. I have things at home. It's just that I never have everything at one time to make something."

I asked her what she needed in order to make something. She again refused to acknowledge any need at first, but after a pause she blurted, "You can bring me a loaf of day-old bread." I said that I didn't know what she planned to make out of the bread but there must be something else she needed. She delayed answering and then said, "Well if you just want to be real nice, bring me anything!"

As we separated, she asked if my son could come over and have some ice cream.

Mrs. Todd did receive some money from her husband the next day. The following week she asked me to take her to apply for surplus food. Perhaps some of the significance this trip had for her — and for me — came through in her wry but warm remark when we returned home: "Thank you, Mother, for taking me there."

When she eventually got her first supplies from Surplus Foods, she immediately offered some to me. The following week, however, she was in the doldrums again. I did not see her or the children for two successive days. The second evening of her two days of being incommunicado, she telephoned to say that she had decided that she had better call her mother (meaning me) and tell me where she was as she knew that I would be worried. She had no food in the house so she had taken all the children and gone to her mother-in-law's home.

These incidents and exchanges give some idea of the inconsistent way things went for Mrs. Todd — a good meal, a slim meal, no meals. But, somehow, she made it; and, despite circumstances, bursts of enthusiastic creativity would occasionally flare up.

One Easter, I shared some Easter egg dye with her. She later came over to borrow "any kind of flavoring" I had and invited me to see the cake she was making. When I went to Mrs. Todd's apartment, the children were gathered around the table, intently watching as she put finishing touches on the cake. She had tinted some coconut brown and formed it into a basket which nested in grass of green-tinted coconut on white icing. In the basket were several jelly beans representing Easter eggs. In addition to the cake, there was an impressive roasted turkey. The children were looking on excitedly and anticipating their out-of-the-ordinary meal. Everything was pleasant and harmonious.*

In general, Mrs. Todd was very interested in food and its preparation. She could watch someone prepare a dish she had never cooked before

---

*It was this kind of experience that led me to be leery of the easy and sometimes automatic label, "maternal rejection," for a mother like Mrs. Todd.

and then duplicate it with no difficulty. She used to joke that her husband would not know what had happened when he returned home, and she would prepare new dishes like chili and chop suey she had learned to prepare as a result of watching and listening to me.

Mrs. Todd was also interested in the proper service of food. One day she was present when I was setting the table for guests and began helping me. When she asked me where the salad plates were, I told her that I did not feel like dirtying so many dishes and was not going to use them. With a disdainful grunt, she overruled me, got out the salad plates and, as if to silence any protest I might have had, told me that she would come back and do the dishes.*

GETTING AN EDUCATION: TO BENEFIT THE WORLD

Mrs. Todd left school when she was in the twelfth grade to get married. She said that going to school had not been a particularly pleasant experience; frequently, she had to go without food and adequate clothing. She received fifty cents a week for lunch money. When her clothes were burned in a fire in her home and not replaced, she had to wear what she could of her sisters' clothing. When she took courses like interpretive dancing and drama, she never had money to buy costumes and other necessary equipment. She finally became disgusted because such lacks prevented her from taking part in many activities.

Mrs. Todd had liked school and wished she had been able to finish high school. The fact that her brother was now in college and doing well gave her some vicarious pleasure.

History had been her favorite subject; she had taken it every semester. She had had three years of typing and some courses in operating office machines. Frequently she would assist a neighbor in her lessons by dictating to her for speed-writing practice. Occasionally, Mrs. Todd would borrow my typewriter; she would always show me what she had typed when she returned it.

In speaking about the education of her own children, Mrs. Todd gave the cautiously hopeful answer:

> As long as they are interested in it, they should go on and do whatever they want to. College, if you have the money, or a part-time job to help work their way through college. I don't think I would force my children to go to college, or anywhere else, because it would be useless spending your money to force them to go. I just

---

*I have often wondered whether Mrs. Todd was really saying to me, "I might have to use jelly glasses to drink out of in my house, but if you have salad plates in your house, then there is no reason to act as if you do not have any. I use what I've got, why don't you do the same thing?"

wouldn't force them to do anything that they wouldn't want to do after they finish high school. If they wanted to go to college I would try to help them if I could. If they didn't, I would guide them into what they wanted to do, but they should finish high school.

Mrs. Todd showed active interest in providing support and some enrichment for her children's present education:

I've joined the book club, those read-by-myself books, so that I can read them to Elsie and she'll know more about them. I guess that if I read them to her and she knew about them, it would make her more alert when she got in school and the teacher was reading them to the kids. The only other thing is that we bought her a set of encyclopedias, but that isn't too beneficial to her now. By the time she gets ready to use them she will probably have a need for more because I guess they would be too old.

In terms of careers, she repeated the high aspirations for at least one of her children that are recurrent [statements for many parents]:

I think they should become what they want to become. But I would like to see one become a biochemist, because that's what I had on my mind at one time — or something that would be beneficial to the world today — some sort of field where there aren't many people working but they need more in that field.

In encouraging her children's development (and independence) Mrs. Todd seemed to be at her best and most consistent.

She acted upon her belief that every child should have some preschool training by putting her children in the half-day nursery school that was operated by the Recreation Department. She said she wanted much more than the school could give. She expressed her disappointment in the Mothers' Club, composed of mothers of children in the nursery school. As she saw it, instead of talking about what to do about the children, the mothers who attended the meetings of the Mothers' Club spent their time gossiping. She said they were interested in only two things, "trying to outdo the others and trying to keep the women away from their husbands."

She said that she used to play with her children a lot, teaching them various things, and she would always read to them at night before they went to bed. The result of her instruction showed. Her oldest daughter, Elsie, could read at a third-grade level when she completed first grade. Elsie was interested in books; whenever she visited, the first thing she did was to go to the bookshelf and then sit and read one book after another. She was very alert. So was her younger brother, Nicholas, who was so closely attached to her. He showed that he had picked up quite a bit from her. At the age of three, he knew the alphabet and could count; and he was better than his four-year-old brother at recognizing colors.

A part of the problem Mrs. Todd had in preparing her children for starting school was getting enough clothing for them. She sent her children to relatives in the South for the summer as part of her plan to free herself for summer work in order to earn money to buy their clothes.

Mr. Todd was also aware of the continuing pressure and threat exerted by the need to get clothing for children. In a letter to his wife, he expressed understanding that she might not be able to feed them properly, but that she should concentrate on getting them clothing for school even if they had to eat beans every day.*

On an occasion when we were making a tape recording of the children to send to her husband, Mrs. Todd skillfully guided and encouraged responses from the small children. She worked patiently with them to overcome their fear of the machine. She was very proud when they finally came through with their recitations: nursery rhymes, The Lord's Prayer, and the Pledge of Allegiance to the flag.

Mrs. Todd's displays of marked potential for being a better than ordinary mother, wife and human being sparked occasionally but, seemingly, never had the opportunity to develop fully and to be sustained. That they did not develop fully and were not sustained in Mrs. Todd's case — as in that of many of the mothers — was clearly one of the consequences of not enough money and of the uneven flow of available money.

·   ·   ·

---

*My observation of this struggle to get adequate clothing for school made me wonder whether, in much of the speculation and theory about the failure of low-income parents to motivate their children, we may be overlooking an important factor. Many of these parents remember from their own experience that their motivation was dulled by the lack of adequate clothing and sufficient food. Therefore, they see these needs as essential and much of their energy is absorbed in trying to meet these elementary needs. Perhaps they remember, too, that without some minimum sense of physical well-being, it is useless to worry about academic motivation.

The Role of the Boyfriend in Lower-class Negro Life

DAVID A. SCHULZ

IN THIS STUDY I WILL EXAMINE THE NON-MARITAL RELATIONSHIPS
that exist between a small number of lower-class Negro men and women
in a large urban public housing project. My data, drawn from observations and open ended interviews collected over a three and one half
year period, suggest that, contrary to the popular image of the lower-
class Negro male, he exhibits a concern for and support of his woman
that is not commonly acknowledged. I see this evidence of "stability"
as an important, if possibly subordinate, theme in the life of this
community. The amount and degree of support varies considerably
and suggests a four-fold typology which may for some men be seen
as sequential phases in a trajectory that may or may not culminate in
marriage. For others one type may remain a dominant motif throughout
life. Finally such evidence of support in non-marital liaisons reinforces
the argument that improved income and job opportunities for the
Negro male will indeed result in more stable families.

Just as slavery and discrimination have, for the most part, been
harder on the Negro male than on the female, so also has the image
of the Negro man in the eyes of the white middle-class suffered greater
reproach. In the common stereotype the lower-class Negro man is
lazy, shiftless, undependable and a veritable bastion of raw sexuality,
preferring to live off his woman than earn his own way in life. John
Dollard summarizes a part of this white image of Negro male sexuality
in his *Caste and Class in a Southern Town.*

> The idea seems to be that they are more like savages nearer to
> animals, and that their sexual appetites are vigorous and ungov-
> erned. There is a widespread belief that the genitals of Negro males
> are larger than those of whites; this was repeatedly stated by white
> informants . . . one thing seems certain — that the actual differ-

---

*Reprinted by permission of the author.

ences between Negro and white genitalia cannot be as great as they seem to the whites; it is a question of the psychological size being greater than any actual differences could be.[1]

While such an idea may well be held with greater conviction in the South, it is a part of the common stereotype in the North as well.[2]

When we turn to the sociological literature we find that it is common to stress the economically dependent and sexually exploitive role of the lower-class Negro male. Thus we read in the now classic study *The Negro Family in the United States* by E. Franklin Frazier

> . . . at the present time his sexual life is entirely of a casual nature. When he arrives in a city, he approaches women on the street or gets information on accessable women from men of his type. Usually he goes up to lonely women in domestic service and wins their sympathy by telling them 'hard luck' stories of his life on the road. They take him to their lodgings where he remains until his hunger as well as his sexual desires are satisfied, and then takes to the road again.[3]

A similar image can be found in such studies as Drake and Cayton's *Black Metropolis,*[4] Kenneth Clark's *Dark Ghetto,*[5] Hylan Lewis' *Blackways of Kent,*[6] and Kardiner and Ovesey's *Mark of Oppression.*[7]

In the more recent documentation of what, from the point of view of the middle-class, would be called the "disorganization" or "tangle of pathology" of ghetto life that centers around the report by Daniel Patrick Moynihan, *The Negro Family: The Case for National Action,*[8] the same general image prevails. The lower-class Negro man, unable to find status by means of employment, exploits his sexual relationships with women leaving behind illegitimate children and deserted women. Indeed, some who read this literature argue that it can be used to support the white stereotype and is evidence of a new, if subtle, "white racism." Thus comments Joseph Alsop on Lee Rainwater's *Crucible of Identity*[9] in the *Washington Post.*[10]

---

[1]John Dollard, *Caste and Class in a Southern Town*, 2nd ed., p. 160-161.

[2]Kenneth Clark, *Dark Ghetto*, pp. 67-80.

[3]E. Franklin Frazier, *The Negro Family in the United States*, p. 214.

[4]Sinclair Drake and Horace Cayton, *Black Metropolis*, p. 570ff.

[5]Kenneth Clark, *loc. cit.*, particularly p. 71.

[6]Hylan Lewis, *Blackways of Kent*, p. 83ff.

[7]Abraham Kardiner & Lionel Ovesey, *Mark of Oppression*, pp. 69-70.

[8]Dept. of Labor, *The Negro Family: The Case for National Action*, 1965.

[9]Lee Rainwater, "Crucible of Identity." *Daedalus,* Winter, 1966. See also Boone Hammond, *The Contest System: A Survival Technique*, Memo. for a documentation of the street system in our study community.

[10]Joseph Alsop, January 27, 1967.

However, there is also in the literature some evidence that these non-marital liaisons between men and women of the Negro lower-class are more stable than commonly depicted. In *Blackways of Kent* Lewis mentions in passing that "Gifts and some degree of support from the male are a constant in non-marital liaisons; they are taken for granted and freely discussed. There is some informal ranking of men on a basis of the regularity and amount of gifts or support."[11] Frazier also speaks of "those rare cases in which these roving men and homeless women in the city settle down to a quasi-family life and rear their children."[12] Finally Drake and Cayton speak hesitantly of a norm against "living sweet" stating that "a woman who 'pimps a man' is considered something of a sucker by other women. Although such 'lucky men' may be looked upon with some envy by their fellows, it is generally considered unfair to 'live on a woman'."[13] All of these represent tendencies running counter to the dominant motif stressing the necessity to "cash in" on a relationship with others and exploit them for one's own benefit.

In this paper I want to attempt to provide a fuller documentation of this support in non-marital relationships than is suggested in the literature. I will argue that in the role of the boyfriend, Negro men are able to express much more concern for their women, and do in fact care for them and their children to a much greater extent than is commonly acknowledged. The kind of quasi-familial relationship thus entered into can be seen as a mode of adaptation to the oppression and deprivation of their environment. Because of the smallness of the sample from which I draw my conclusions and its non-randomness I cannot state with certainty how extensive my generalizations about this role are.

The setting for my study is a large high rise public housing project in the city of St. Louis comprising 33, 11-story buildings and about 11,500 persons when fully occupied. An unusually high vacancy rate — in the last five years over 20% — brings the project population closer to 10,000. Since 1963 when the last white family of a Mennonite missionary moved out, the community has been totally Negro. It has a bad press image and means "vertical slum" to all who read about it. As verified by a random questionnaire administered in the summer of 1964, its inhabitants see it as a "world of trouble."[14] These troubles derive both from its social life and its still inadequate physical environ-

---

[11] Hylan Lewis, *op. cit.*, p. 84.

[12] E. Franklin Frazier, *op. cit.*, p. 215.

[13] Drake and Cayton, *op. cit.*

[14] *Perspectives on Pathology, Socialization, Religion and World View of Pruitt Igoe Residents*. Occasional Internal Working Paper #V.

ment. It tends to concentrate large, female headed families who are on welfare.

This report is based mainly on observations and interviews of 38 subjects (23 women, 15 men; 15 adults, 23 teenagers) living in ten families, six of which still reside in the project. These data were collected over the past three and one half years as a part of a larger study on the internal dynamics of these family worlds. In addition I have talked with and observed eight boyfriends of women who live with five of these ten families in the project. Only three of these, however, have been interviewed to any extent. Finally this study draws from a much larger body of data containing now well over 20,000 pages on this community.

The importance of the boyfriend's role became apparent when I first realized that four of the five women in female headed households that were part of my larger study were receiving support from boyfriends. The amount of support and the type of relationship that exists varies considerably and has led me to develop a typology consisting of four different roles which a boyfriend may play and for which there is some support from segments of this population. These types I call: the quasi-father, the supportive biological father, the supportive companion, and the pimp. The image of the pimp has dominated the literature thus far.

The Quasi-Father

The distinguishing marks of the quasi-father in my mind are that 1) He supports the family regularly over long periods of time (11 years is the longest I know of though this was interrupted by a short marriage; five years is the longest consecutive time known at present). Often he will go with his woman to the store and buy her week's food. 2) His concern extends to her children more directly as well. He will give them allowances or spending money, attempt more or less successfully to discipline them, and will take them out to the park or the movies or other places for entertainment. 3) He frequently visits the family during the week and may, or may not reside with them. 4) Usually the relationship is conducted not clandestinely, but in the full knowledge of kin on both sides particularly the parents if they reside in the same city with the couple. In return for this he receives 1) his meals (some or all if residing with the family); 2) washing and ironing; 3) sexual satisfaction; and 4) *familial companionship*. In short he seems to be bargaining for more than just a woman in seeking intimacy in the context of a family. To illustrate let us take the example of Ray and Laura.

Laura 33, went with Ray, 24, for over five years. During that time he took her out, bought her the majority of her furniture, and supplied her with $15 to $20 per week usually by means of buying her week's food. In addition his family contributed several additional pieces of furniture and invited Laura over for meals on occasion. None of her six children are his. Laura describes Ray as a "nice person . . . kind hearted" and by this she means that ". . . he believes in survival for me and my family, me and my kids. He don't mind sharing with my youngsters. If I ask him for a helping hand, he don't seem to mind that. The only part of it is that I dislike his drinking." It's not the drinking as much that Laura dislikes, but the man Ray becomes when he drinks. He becomes angry and quick tempered, but has yet to beat Laura when in such a state.

Ray's concern for Laura's children is expressed in various ways. As Ann, Laura's 15 year old daughter, sees Ray he tends to be bossy. "He be alright sometimes but he drinks and that's the reason I don't like him, . . . He tries to boss people. Like if my boyfriends come over here he be saying I can't have no company." But Jean, her 18 year old daughter, tells us that Ray gave her a small washing machine for her babies' diapers. She said, "My mother's boyfriend bought it. . . . It was about three days after my baby was born."

Ray's concern is expressed in other ways as well. He took them to the movies, to the park, gave them a small allowance as spending money each week when he bought the groceries and once, when Laura was sick, he took care of the youngest two for nearly a month while she was in the hospital. During the years that they were going together Ray visited the family several times a week most frequently spending the weekend with them. He continually asked Laura to marry him though Laura felt he was only half serious. I asked Ray why he bothered to take care of Laura and he replied, "That's a personal question. . . . Well, first of all I help her because I love her and we're going to get married sometime, but not just now because we can't afford it."

A second example is that of Adrian, 33 and Ernest 34 — looks 25. Adrian has been going with Ernest for over 11 years even while married to her second husband whom she finally left for Ernest. He helps the budget regularly out of his pay as a dock worker in a river barge yard. Adrian says, "Ernest gives me $30.00 a week." He has also bought several small pieces of furniture and takes her out almost every weekend. He lives just around the corner with his cousin, visits the family almost every night, and sometimes spends the night though he usually sleeps with his cousin.

Adrian feels that Ernest "treats her kids better than their daddy do. He buys them certain things (such as) clothes. He spanks them. . . . He takes them different places." She further feels that it is very important that a man treat her kids right. "If they don't care for the kids or anything then that's a bad man. . . . first he's got to love your kids before he loves you."

Her sons Ronald (10) and Winifred (17) confirm the fact that Ernest is concerned about the kids. Ronald says, "He takes up for us when we get a whipping. . . . He tells her not to whip us this time." When I asked, "Does he have pretty good control over the kids?" Winifred replied, "They do what he says most of the time. Kenneth (18) don't but the rest of them will."

They are still going together and Ernest proposes marriage with some regularity but Adrian shies away, "I think I'm better off just not having a husband . . . I wouldn't definitely say I would get a good one. I might get a bad one. I don't want to take a chance." Even though she has known Ernest since childhood she is not certain about him. He drinks a lot but is not to her knowledge the violent type — at least he is not as a single man. Her fear is that when he "has papers on her" he might change. Adrian's second husband beat her up on her wedding night when drunk and the next week sent her to the hospital as a result of his beating on her.

And so Laura broke up with Ray and never seriously considered marriage while going with him and Adrian says that *maybe* in three or four years she will be ready for a marriage to Ernest. Marriage has not yet resulted because in both instances the family is doing better under the combined resources of welfare and the boyfriend's assistance than they could do under his wages alone and in both instances the woman is afraid of the man's drinking behavior. In both instances the boyfriends are well known by the women's family and visit frequently with them.

Since breaking with Ray, Laura has been living with a new boyfriend, Kenneth, 29, and says that she is seriously considering marriage to him, enough so that she has decided to get a divorce. Thus marriage may or may not be in the cards as a result of a quasi-father relationship, but it does provide the context in which a woman with children is likely to make up her mind one way or another about a man.

THE SUPPORTIVE BIOLOGICAL FATHER

A second type of boyfriend is the supportive biological father. Here the concern of the man — and largely that of the woman also — is to support the children that they have brought into the world without seriously considering marriage to one another. In some instances the man or woman may well be married to someone else. The man's support may be voluntary as in the case of Mr. A., 45, or it may be as the result of a voluntarily signed acknowledgement that the children are his.

In the case of Dorothy, 50, and Leonard, 49, Dorothy was married once and had four children by her first husband, Lewis. His cutting out and drinking lead to a separation and Dorothy took up with Leonard who gave her three children, in ages now from 18 to 13, before he married another woman a couple of years ago. He played the role of supportive biological father before he married. They had been going together for nearly 16 years though only Dorothy was true to the relationship. She has never remarried and claims that even now she has no boyfriend because they are too much trouble at her age although she admits that she would enjoy a companion in her declining years.

Leonard has taken the kids on long trips like the one to Arizona in 1963, he has bought them clothes especially at Christmas time and has paid regularly the amount of $15 to $20 per week for their support since 1954. At that time he acknowledged that the kids were his and the court fixed the amount of their support.

Dorothy's being true to Leonard is a part of her rearing as she sees it. Her mother died in 1927 and "daddy went haywire" so she went to live with her maternal auntie and her husband, uncle Saul — "gentle Saul" — who was a Baptist minister. Her auntie was a very strict woman and quite respectable. Consequently Dorothy had but one boyfriend prior to meeting her husband and was proud to have married as a virgin.

> I had a wedding when I married him and I believe in it right today. When I married I was in white satin . . . Any time I look in the paper and see a girl with a gown cut off, short sleeves and marrying, she's no virgin. A virgin marries when you see nothing but a very little bit of her neck.

This marriage lasted 14 years and at the end she left him because he had been cutting out and was undependable in his support of her and the children. While separated she met Leonard, her boyfriend.

> At the time I met Leonard, Lewis and I wasn't together. I met Leonard through the (same) church. He asked me (to marry) and I told him not until my husband's children got off my hands and out of the way. I never wanted a stepfather over my children . . . it

was something that Lewis and I have always said. We said we never would have a stepfather over our children.

Her main departure from her rearing was having children out of wedlock, and while she loves the children, she regrets the departure.

That's the only thing in life I didn't want — to have children without being married. I just wasn't reared like that. But they are all by one man. They're not by this one, that one, nor the other one. They're all by one man.

Dorothy is proud to be able to say, "I have been by Leonard as if he and I were married."

While it is true that Leonard is legally obligated to care for his kids, it is noteworthy that he claimed the kids as his in the first place and that he supports them in gifts over and above his legal obligations. His inability to believe that Dorothy was true to him, plus her reluctance to have a stepfather over her husband's children, at least one of whom has not yet left the home, contributed to the factors otherwise economic that mitigated against their marriage — but did not prevent them from courting for 16 years.

Most of the care that fathers give to their outside kids seems to be much less regular than Leonard's, but is, nevertheless, largely voluntary. Mr. A., for example, has three outside kids by two different women. He is married and has 11 children by his wife. His outside kids live with their mothers and when he gets fed up with his wife he moves out and lives with Jessie B. by whom he has had two kids. His legitimate children complain that when he goes to visit one of the outsiders, he gives her and her siblings more money for spending than he gives his legitimate kids. His wife protests that he stole their t.v. set and gave it to the mother of one of these children, and his son claims that when he returned to his home in the country recently, he bought several dresses for his outside child living there. Mr. A. will not speak of these outsiders to me and he keeps his money matters to himself. His wife has opened letters from the mothers of these children requesting regular support, but does not know if he is giving any to them. She believes that he spends most of the $406 a month take home pay he earns from his job on these women and their children.

SUPPORTIVE COMPANION

A less durable relationship exists in the case of the "supportive companion" who keeps a woman. Here the concern of the male is mainly to have a good time with a clean woman. The concern of the woman is for support and companionship. Such a relationship is not here to be confused with prostitution for it is not a mere matter of a business transaction but a search for intimacy on both parts, a search conducted in the context of severe economic and emotional handicaps. In this community such a relationship is likely to occur between an older man (late twenties, early thirties) and a younger woman (early twenties, teens) who has had children "outside of wedlock."

He rarely keeps her in her own apartment as would be the case in more solvent circumstances where the woman is usually single and without kids. Rather he provides a regular "weekend away" at his apartment or other suitable place where they can be together away from the kids. He takes her out, provides her with spending money and a good time. Should she conceive a child, he is least likely of all types to want to assume support of the child. Responsibility is what he is avoiding if at all possible.

As an example Henretta, 16, knew Joe, 23, for about a year during 1959-60. Henretta had already had two children by two other men. Joe came by for dinner occasionally, but usually he made the weekend scene at a motel apartment he rented for the occasion. When Friday came round, he would give Henretta money which she often turned into dresses, or other items to enhance her appearance. Henretta says, "Joe's not like a lot of men that you find. A lot of men, if they do something for you they feel they own you." Joe gave her "fifteen or twenty dollars sometimes more" each week and had keys to a two room kitchenette for the weekend. Henretta says, "We were always together (on the weekend). Where I went he usually went, where he went I went. We'd go to the apartment and everything. But lots of time we would go and just watch t.v. or sit and talk or have a drink or something. Then we would go — especially in the summer time — we'd go there because they had air conditioning."

Joe was very jealous and very cautious. He broke with Henretta when he suspected that she might be pregnant and she has not heard from him since. Three of the five women heading households in our study have been "kept" in such a manner for a brief period of time.

THE PIMP

In this type of relationship the woman supports the man. In the classic understanding of the term, a pimp may live off the labors of several prostitutes getting a stylish living in return for services such as protection, banking for jail bond and saving purposes, and fix procurement in the case of legal action. This type is still prevalent. Thus

Ernest tells of his friend who has diamond rings and Cadillacs derived from the income of five prostitutes who live with him and his wife and children, but conduct their business elsewhere. Mr. T., 55, confides that for about three years he enjoyed the life of a pimp as a young man and remembers that he always had several hundred dollars in his pocket and always dressed in the best style.

But the term also covers the more general situation where a man lives off a woman who is not a prostitute and who earns her living legitimately as a professional, a well paid clerk or domestic, or a welfare recipient.[15] Hence the excitement of "Mother's Day," the tenth of the month when welfare checks come in the mail. Pimping seems to be the younger man's approach to the dilemma of poverty, low status in the larger culture, and unemployment. In the language of the street a "cat" is usually a pimp. Thus Jean, 18, says that a "cat" can

> be a girl or a boy and they wants to be cool, wants to be hip, jive, you know. If it's a boy, he try to pimp off a woman. He going to lovey dovy up on her . . . if she got some money . . . they gonna use their power to get the money from you. . . . you know like telling the girl that she got "Cleopatra eyes" and that she be "sweeter than a cherry" . . . she probably buy him clothes and he ain't giving her nothing but a little love and stuff like that. . . . for instance a lot of these cats gets a woman about 39 or something and she not married and got a good job.

The role of the pimp, then, is most characteristically that of a young man seeking an older woman who may have a comfortable income and feels that her powers of persuasion are fading. Ernest explains the willingness of a woman to "pimp a man" under the rubric of "she loves him." Love, for Ernest, implies a willingness to do anything for a person who is loved including "bringing them their slippers, lighting their cigarettes . . . man if a woman loves you, you got it made, there ain't nothing you have to do . . . you don't have to lift your little finger." This is in keeping with a general tendency to demand evidence of concern even to the point here of exploitation in the small as well as the large matters of everyday life. In fact Kenneth, 17, explains the problems of the city life in terms of a declining emphasis upon concrete and traditional expression of love. He believes that kids are so bad these days because they are raised on cow's milk rather than their mother's milk, they have been placed more often in the hands of baby

---

[15]The more general term covering the situation where a woman supports a man is not acceptable usage to a professional pimp who calls these persons "studs" and claims they have no expertise or professional skills.

sitters, and no longer as infants receive their food premasticated from their mother's mouth. The pimp takes advantage of this need to concretize relationships.

Jean maintains that she knows a "boy who is 19 years old and he got a woman 39, 'up tight' . . . She's a nurse and she gets paid every month . . . and he gets just about half of her check and he comes and spends it on us." The final insult of the pimp and the fear of any woman keeping one is that he will take her money and spend it on other women demonstrating that, despite her care for him, he cares not a whit for her.

It must be noted that the pimp is, in some sense, the urban counterpart of relationships between rural women and the wandering men who moved from lumber camp to lumber camp living off the women they could find in each. Here the exchange, however, was rarely money, but rather more an exchange of intimacies. Mr. T. recalls the days of his youth when he lived off women like this. One such relationship lasted for over a year.

> You go along, single men, single women, families, all kinds of people live there (in lumber camps). Some people live there that don't work at all. So you get in a place like this, get you something to eat, get your clothes washed and take a bath, look for a woman then. You try to find a single one and this is what you do . . . and usually you have a pretty good chance, because you feel like you going to get a job in a day or two, and she'll have somebody to give her some money. And they take you in, talk pretty nice, they'll clean you up, give you some of the last old man's clothes, and let you sleep with 'em.

Finally it should be noted that I have not covered all of the nonmarital relationships that might exist between a man and a woman in this community, but have rather attempted to define four types which on the basis of our small sample have some persistence in time and hopefully some extensiveness in the current life of the community as well. A purely exploitative relationship may exist as in the case of Laverne and Tommy where he rapes — she claims she does not consent — her from time to time but receives nothing else from her. This is, however, a relationship in only the broadest possible definition.

SPECULATION ON EXTENSIVENESS AND RELATIONSHIP IN TIME

While I do not have any measure of the extensiveness of these four types of boyfriends, I do have some impressions based on our data. The pimp is the most talked about male-female non-marital relationship in the literature. Our data, however, suggests that it is not as prevalent in the project as commonly assumed. It is possible that pimping may be more or less restricted to the younger men and may phase out into less exploitative relationships with females as the men grow older. Therefore the frequency of the pimping relationship may well be exaggerated since the younger men tend to be more vocal about their exploits and the older men who now view such activity with a certain resentment may bewail the fact that "things used to be much better." The next most frequent type, we would estimate, would be the supportive biological father. Here, in all probability, the most characteristic support is gifts, trips and other items on an occasional basis with fewer men assuming as much responsibility as Leonard. The quasi-father may be more extensive than the supportive biological father, but we guess not. What does seem important in the quasi-father case, however, is the extent of the support and its regularity. Finally the supportive companion is, I suspect, least frequent if for no other reason than that the women tend to place such importance on the norm "love my children before you love me" and by this encourage their boyfriends to at least seek acceptance from their children.

A man may play one or more such roles in his life. We can thus see these types as phases in a developmental sequence. The pimp is an early role of the young man of the street who would rather "live sweet" than work, or who has found that his value on the love market is greater than it is on the labor market. My data suggest that such a relationship is quite likely to terminate when the man reaches his mid-thirties. He may then decide to marry the woman he has pimped off, because by then he has had one or more children by her, or because he is, after having sown his wild oats, seeking now a more intimate and lasting relationship. If he does marry her then he comes under the norm that it is "unfair" to pimp off a woman you are married to.

We knew of one, however, who has gone from a pimping relationship directly to marriage with the same woman. In the case of Mr. T., who pimped off several woman for several years before marriage, a quasi-father relationship was entered into with another woman for four or five years before he married her as the result of an unwanted pregnancy. This marriage has lasted 19 years.

The quasi-fathers we know are in their late twenties, early thirties and in one of the three instances, marriage is sought by the woman, in the other two the males are still being tested. This opportunity to get to know a man under near familial situations is a boon to these women who have been disappointed in marriage one or more times.

He can prove that he is a good provider and a gentle "good" man. Not all quasi-father relationships terminate in marriage.

The supportive companion is, if our inferences are correct, more likely to be the relationship that exists between an older man (late 20's, early 30's) and a younger woman (late teens, early 20's). It may be the alternative of a rejected quasi-father who sought but could not obtain marriage, and whose income is stable enough to permit such indulgence. Finally, most men can play, if they so desire, the role of supportive biological father throughout most of their lives since almost every male has had at least one child outside of wedlock. For some who never marry, this may be the extent to which their craving for familial companionship is expressed — the occasional gift to an illegitimate child.

CONCLUSIONS

1) My data suggest that some men, perhaps most at some time in their lives, assume a very responsible "quasi-father" role *vis à vis* their women and her children. They seem to spend a considerable portion of their lives bargaining for a familial relationship, the major obstacle to which seems to be a limited income that cannot equal the combined resources of their present jobs plus their woman's welfare check.

2) The quasi-father role provides the women, who have been hurt in previous marriages, an opportunity to test their men by the adage, "love my children before you love me" before entering again into marriage.

3) Aside from this relationship there are other situations in which the men play a more supportive role than is generally acknowledged. Such is the case of the supportive biological father, and the supportive companion. In such roles the man also provides a male role model for her kids, the value of which has not been discussed in the literature.

4) Such male support in the lower-class life — in situations where it is extremely difficult to render such assistance — argues for the view that improved income and job opportunities for the lower-class Negro male will indeed result in more of these relationships terminating in marriages and, in general, more stability in family life.

Our impression of the supportive role played by the lower-class Negro male as a boyfriend contrasts with the exploitative one commonly held. More research is needed to determine the extent of the types proposed and their more precise relationship over time.

Part 4

Family Circumstances and Social Consequences: Is the Black Family Crumbling?

Class Structure, Mobility, and Change in Child Rearing

ZENA SMITH BLAU

CHILD REARING IS ONE OF THE MANY AREAS OF CONTEMPORARY SOCIAL life where the authority of tradition has diminished and the continuities that formerly prevailed from one generation to the next have given way to intergenerational change. Studies that deal with the problem of innovation in child-rearing practices have been largely limited to investigations of the changes that have taken place in the writings of child-rearing *experts* since the turn of the century.[1] Ample evidence exists, however, that outside the white middle class significant proportions of women have little or no direct exposure to this body of literature.[2] It could therefore be expected that changes in child-rearing practices either are less prevalent in these groups or are due to other influences than the writings of experts. There is no empirical basis for choosing between these alternatives since virtually no research exists that deals directly with the incidence of intergenerational change in child rearing among different subgroups in the society or with the

---

[1] Martha Wolfenstein, "Trends in Infant Care," *American Journal of Orthopsychiatry*, 28 (1953), pp. 120-130; and Celia B. Stendler, "Sixty Years of Child Training Practices," *Journal of Pediatrics*, 26 (1950), pp. 122-134.

[2] See, for example, Martha Sturm White, "Social Class, Child Rearing Practices, and Child Behavior," *American Sociological Review*, 22 (December, 1957), pp. 704-712; Melvin L. Kohn, "Social Class and Parent-Child Relationships: An Interpretation," *American Journal of Sociology*, 68 (January, 1963), pp. 471-480; and Zena Smith Blau, "Exposure to Child Rearing Experts: A Structural Interpretation of Class-Color Differences," *American Journal of Sociology*, 69 (May, 1964), pp. 596-608.

Reprinted by permission of the publisher and the author from *Sociometry*, XXVIII (June 1965), 210-19.

conditions and social processes that predispose women to adopt innovation in this realm.[3]

Intergenerational occupational mobility into a new stratum constitutes
one social process through which people may become exposed to new
social influences and ideas that differ from those which prevailed in
their class of origin.[4] The occupational achievements of the male make
status mobility possible but it is the woman, in her roles of wife, mother,
and homemaker, who actually effects many of the changes in style of
life that are necessary to raise the social status of the family.[5] One would
expect patterns of child rearing to be one of the important areas of
behavior affected by mobility. There is probably no other aspect of their
daily existence that mothers converse more about than their child-rearing
experiences and problems, and such discussions constitute an important
opportunity for the exercise of interpersonal influence. To the extent
that mobile women form social ties with others in their class of destination, they are likely to become exposed to patterns of child-rearing
behavior which differ from those prevalent in their original stratum,
and thereby to become subject to a strain toward change.

The foregoing hypothesis assumes that occupational mobility enhances
an individual's opportunities for exposure to a social milieu different
from the one that prevailed in her class of origin. But would mobility
also create a pressure toward change in the case of individuals whose
class of destination is largely composed of other mobiles? The fact that
American society contains two largely separate stratification systems —
white and Negro — constitutes an opportunity to compare how differences in the proportion of mobile and stationary individuals in a social
system condition the effects of occupational mobility on orientations
toward change in the realm of child rearing.

The present paper compares the attitudes toward change of Negro
and white mobile and non-mobile mothers, and relates differences

---

[3]Only two sources could be located in the empirical literature that deal with the
question of change in child-rearing practices as distinct from changes in expert
opinion. See Urie Bronfenbrenner, "Socialization and Social Class through Time
and Space," in Eleanor E. Maccoby, Theodore M. Newcomb, and Eugene Hartley
(eds.), *Readings in Social Psychology* (New York: Henry Holt and Company,
1958), pp. 400-425, and Daniel R. Miller and Guy E. Swanson, *The Changing
American Parent* (New York: Wiley and Sons, 1958). The approach of the present
paper toward the study of change is quite different from each of these studies.

[4]This does not imply, of course, that occupational mobility constitutes the only
source of intergenerational change in child-rearing practices. We might note, however, that preliminary analysis of our data on geographic mobility indicates no direct
effect on orientations toward change among either white or Negro mothers.

[5]For the classic distinction between class and status, see Max Weber, "Class,
Status and Party," in Hans Gerth and C. Wright Mills (eds.), *Max Weber: Essays
in Sociology* (New York: Oxford University Press, 1946), pp. 180-195.

between them to differences in the homogeneity of the social systems of the two color groups.

THE DATA

The analysis is based on interviews of a quota sample of 250 mothers of one or more children selected on the basis of race and class position. The interviews were obtained during their confinement on the maternity floors of four hospitals located in different parts of Chicago.[6]

The interviews dealt with various aspects of child rearing, and included the question, "Looking back to your own childhood — how would you compare the way your mother raised you with the way you want to raise your children?"[7] Thirty-eight per cent of the respondents did not mention any changes; 20 per cent showed an inclination toward more restrictive practices, e.g., more discipline, less freedom, more chores, etc.; 33 per cent tended toward less restrictive practices, e.g., less arbitrary or harsh methods of control, the use of more love-oriented techniques, fewer chores, etc.; and 9 per cent mentioned diverse other changes that could not be properly classified as either more or less restrictive.[8] Greater strictness is most frequent in the white middle class; and a change toward less strictness is most frequent in the Negro middle class.

---

[6]Respondents with husbands in non-manual occupations are classified as middle class, and those with husbands in manual occupations are defined as working class. This index of class position is the one most commonly employed in child-rearing studies.

The field work was carried out in two stages. In 1961-2 we obtained the interviews with all the white respondents, and a majority of Negro respondents, but were unable to fill our quota of Negro middle-class respondents. Analysis of these data revealed a number of unanticipated differences between white and Negro middle-class women, but there were too few cases of the latter to place much confidence in the results. In 1964 an opportunity arose to return to the field and double the number of middle-class Negroes in our sample. These additional cases not only confirmed the results of the original analysis but also made possible other comparisons for which we had earlier lacked data. The total sample, however, is still not large, and our conclusions, admittedly tentative, are intended solely as hypotheses to stimulate more systematic research in an area that hitherto has gone unexplored.

[7]This question is virtually identical to one in the interview schedule of Robert Sears, Eleanor Maccoby and Harry Levin, *Patterns of Child Rearing* (Evanston: Row, Peterson and Company, 1957), p. 501.

[8]A possible criticism of this question might be that its "openness" invites a change-oriented response. An indication that this is not the case is the fact that it predicts rather well responses to related types of questions. For example, a considerably smaller proportion of change-oriented women mentioned their mother as a source from whom they would seek advice on child-rearing matters (39 per cent) than of those not so oriented (63 per cent), and the magnitude of this difference remains approximately the same in all four color-class groups.

The present paper is confined to an analysis of the differences between women who are oriented toward change, regardless of direction, and those who are not. The related but analytically distinct problem of identifying the variables that predispose women to change in one direction rather than another is reserved for a future paper.

ORIENTATIONS OF WHITES AND NEGROES

The proportion of mothers oriented toward change is 72 per cent in the white middle class, 61 per cent in the white working class, 62 per cent in the Negro middle class and 51 per cent in the Negro working class. These variations are not due simply to differences between the four class-color groups in education or exposure to child-rearing literature.[9] Negro mothers, as might be expected, are less disposed toward change if they are less educated and do not read the experts (31 per cent) than if they are either better educated or read the experts (59 per cent

TABLE 1

PER CENT CHANGERS, BY EDUCATION AND CHILD-REARING MEDIA EXPOSURE,
AMONG NEGROES AND WHITES

Media Exposure	WHITE		NEGRO	
	8-12 Grades	High School Graduate or Higher	8-12 Grades	High School Graduate or Higher
None	63 (19)	62 (13)	31* (29)	65 (20)
Some	63 (19)	73 (88)	72 (18)	59 (41)

*Differences between this proportion and all other proportions for Negroes significant at .05 level.

or more), as Table 1 shows. The orientations toward change of white mothers, however, seem little affected by education or exposure to experts' writings. Thus, nearly two-thirds are oriented toward change even among those white women who have little education and no exposure to experts' writings. These findings suggest the presence of other influences in white society that create a pressure toward intergenerational change.

[9]The measure of exposure to child-rearing literature is based on three items. "No exposure" indicates that a respondent has not read any books, such as Spock, and does not read child-rearing articles in newspapers or magazines. Respondents with exposure to at least one of these sources are designated as having "some" exposure.

CLASS HOMOGENEITY, MOBILITY, AND CHANGE

An earlier paper revealed that large differences in the proportion of mobile individuals in the Negro and white class systems helped explain why the pattern of reading experts was more prevalent among white mothers, regardless of educational level and class position.[10] Analysis of orientations to change helps to clarify further how these variations in class structure condition the orientation of women toward change.

Table 2 (Columns 1 and 2) presents the proportions of stationary and mobile individuals that compose the four class-color groups in our

TABLE 2

PER CENT CHANGERS BY HOMOGENEITY IN FOUR CLASS-COLOR GROUPS

Color	Class Position	Per Cent of Stationary and Mobile in Class Sample:	National	Ours	Per Cent Changers in Class	Total N*
White	Middle class	Stationary Upward mobile	44 56	65 35	72	81
	Working class	Stationary Downward mobile	87 13	79 21	61	53
Negro	Middle class	Stationary Upward mobile	19 81	24 76	62	42
	Working class	Stationary Downward mobile	94 6	96 4	51	69

*The class origin of 5 respondents could not be ascertained, and these cases are excluded from the analysis. Figures for national sample also exclude such cases and those not in the labor force.

sample and also, as a validity check on our data, the corresponding proportions based on a representative national sample. Stationary individuals are those who presently occupy the same class position as that of their family of origin.[11] Upwardly mobile respondents are those presently in the middle class who have working class origins, and downward mobiles are those presently in the working class who have middle class origins. It can readily be seen that the four class-color

---

[10]Zena S. Blau, *loc. cit.*

[11]The index of class origin is father's occupation when the respondent was sixteen years old. Respondents with non-manual fathers are considered to be of middle-class origin, and those with manual fathers, of working class origin.

groups differ in the degree of homogeneity of the social origins of their members, that is, in the difference in the proportion of individuals of similar social origin that they contain. Evidence that these variations in homogeneity[12] of the four strata are not simply artifacts of our sample is provided by the figures (shown in Column 1) derived from a national sample of nearly 17,000 cases interviewed in 1962.[13] Although the proportions of stationary and mobile individuals in each stratum in the two samples are not identical, the rank order of the degree of homogeneity of the four strata is the same. Thus, in both samples the white middle class is least homogeneous, having the smallest majority of members with the same social origins (less than two-thirds); the Negro middle class and the white working class rank second and third, respectively (in the one about four-fifths are upward mobiles, and in the other over four-fifths are stationary); and the Negro working class is most homogeneous, with over 90 per cent stationary members.

Variations in the homogeneity of strata seem to condition the orientations of its members toward change. It can be seen in Table 3 (Column 3) that the proportion of women oriented toward change varies *inversely* with the homogeneity of the stratum in which they are located. Thus, the white middle class, which is least homogeneous, contains the highest proportion of change-oriented individuals (72 per cent); the Negro middle class and the white working class, which are intermediate in homogeneity, contain fewer changers (62 per cent and 61 per cent, respectively), and the Negro working class, which is most homogeneous, contains the fewest changers (51 per cent).

The degree of homogeneity may simply constitute a crude manifestation of the chances that exist within a stratum for associations between individuals of diverse social origins.[14] The greater the heterogeneity in social origins in a stratum, the greater are the opportunities for social

---

[12]The term "homogeneity" refers, of course, only to the single structural variable under discussion and does *not* imply that if other criteria were used the rank order of the strata would necessarily be the same. Within the present context, a stratum in which half of its members were stationary and half were mobile would rank lowest, and one in which all members were of the same social origin would rank highest in homogeneity.

[13]These data are from a study currently in progress, "Occupational Changes in a Generation," by Otis Dudley Duncan and Peter M. Blau, based on a representative sample of 20,000 American men between twenty and sixty-four years old. Figures shown are for the married men with wives in the twenty-two to forty-one year age cohort in their sample, which corresponds to the age range of our respondents. I am grateful to Otis Dudley Duncan for making these tables available.

[14]The degree of homogeneity of a stratum, as defined here, is, of course, only one of many possible variables that may condition the extent of association between its mobile and non-mobile members.

contacts in which women encounter others with *different* ideas and hence are influenced to adopt new practices. We would expect, therefore, both mobile *and* non-mobile women in the white middle class, the most heterogeneous stratum, to be more prone to change than those in the less heterogeneous strata.

TABLE 3

PER CENT CHANGERS BY CLASS ORIGIN IN FOUR CLASS-COLOR GROUPS

Color	Class Position	Class Origin	Per Cent Changers	Total N
White	Middle class	Stationary	68	53
		Upward mobile	82	28
	Working class	Stationary	62	42
		Downward mobile	82	11
Negro	Middle class	Stationary	90	10
		Upward mobile	53	32
	Working class	Stationary	48	66
		Downward mobile	*	3

*The three downward mobiles in our sample are all change-oriented.

However, Table 3 reveals a pattern different from the expected one. Among whites, the upward and downward mobiles are more inclined toward change than the non-mobiles in their class of destination.[15] Indeed, the higher frequency of changers in the middle class, originally noted, is due mostly to the fact that it contains a larger proportion of mobiles than the working class. In other words, in white society, mobility in either direction appears to foster an orientation toward change whether the stratum of destination is more or less homogeneous.[16]

---

[15]There is some variation in the age composition of these groups. Thus, the proportion over twenty-five years old in the white middle class is 58 per cent among stationary respondents and 45 per cent among the upward mobiles; in the white working class this proportion is 30 per cent among the stationary respondents and 27 per cent among the downward mobiles; and among Negro respondents it is 40 per cent among the upward mobiles, 80 per cent among the stationary middle class, and 44 per cent among the stationary working class. However, the pattern of difference in change orientation shown in Table 3 persists, in every instance, even when age is controlled.

[16]The greater proneness toward change of white mobiles, compared to non-mobiles, helps to account for the finding (see Table 1) that, unlike Negroes, better educated white mothers are *not* more prone to change than the less educated. The proportion of high school graduates is lower among upward mobiles (84 per cent) than among white middle-class non-mobiles (98 per cent), but higher among downward mobiles (64 per cent) than among non-mobiles in the white working class (40 per cent).

Among white women, then, both the upwardly and downwardly mobile are more prone to change their child-rearing practices than either the middle-class or working-class stationaries, but the pressures that prompt them to favor innovations may well be of different kinds. The forms of behavior that have become associated with middle-class status command greater respect than those of the working class. In social encounters, therefore, the upwardly mobile individual probably is more likely to be influenced by than to influence the more established and prestigeful stationary members of the middle class. In this case, the direction of influence is probably governed by differences in prestige rather than by preponderance of numbers, but the reverse is probably true in the case of the working class. Differences in prestige between the downward mobile who has experienced failure and the stationary member of the working class who lacks middle-class origins are not clear cut. However, the stationaries outnumber the downward mobiles in the working class four to one, and this preponderance in numbers appears to enable the stationaries to exert the dominant influence on the mobiles in their stratum, as reflected by the finding that the latter are more disposed toward change than the stationary members.

Among Negroes, in sharp contrast, social mobility does not increase the proclivity toward change. Among upwardly mobile Negro women, as Table 3 shows, the proportion of change-oriented mothers is hardly higher (53 per cent) than in the Negro working class (48 per cent). Mobile Negroes are considerably less often oriented toward change than mobile whites. Moreover, they are less inclined toward change than stationary middle class Negroes (90 per cent), a reversal of the relationship between mobility and change orientation found among whites.

The different implications that mobility has for change in the case of white and Negro women may well be due not so much to any basic differences in their individual attributes as to differences in the homogeneity of their social milieu. The long history of economic discrimination against Negroes, particularly in non-manual occupations, has prevented the development of an established middle class in Negro society that is anywhere near the proportionate size of that in white society. In recent years opportunities for Negroes in non-manual occupations have increased but the Negro middle class, at the present time, is still composed predominantly of people with working-class origins, and contains only a small proportion of individuals with middle-class origins. Thus, the opportunities for the formation of social ties with other Negroes whose patterns of behavior *differ* from those in their class of origin are far more limited for upwardly mobile Negroes than for upwardly mobile whites. Moreover, the pervasive pattern of residential and social segregation greatly restricts opportunities for contact with the white middle class, thereby further insulating the Negro upward mobile from pressures toward change.

It is interesting, although hardly a conclusive test of the hypothesis, that among the nine Negro respondents in our sample who live in

TABLE 4

PER CENT NEGRO MIDDLE CLASS CHANGERS, BY CLASS ORIGIN AND NEIGHBORHOOD

	NEIGHBORHOOD	
Class Origin	Integrated	Segregated
Stationary	75 (4)	100 (6)
Upward mobile	80 (5)	48 (27)

integrated neighborhoods upward mobiles are as often change-oriented as non-mobiles in their own stratum, and as mobiles in the white strata (see Table 4).[17] It is only the upward mobiles in segregated neighbor hoods who show relatively little inclination toward change. Stationary members of the Negro middle class, however, show at least as much proneness toward change in segregated as in integrated areas. This suggests that interpersonal influences may hasten the rate of diffusion of middle-class culture in Negro society but that other forces such as formal education and exposure to experts bring about similar effects, albeit at a slower pace.

CONCLUSION

In closing, some implications of the foregoing analysis for the study of change in patterns of child rearing and in other realms of behavior might be mentioned. A small beginning has been made here in the analysis of the significance of attributes of social structure as well as those of individuals for the circulation of new ideas in a complex society, and for the patterns of change from one generation to the next that have become a characteristic feature of contemporary societies. The particular structural variables that are relevant to the study of change need to be further specified through empirical research in various realms of behavior

---

[17]Proneness toward change may not be simply an effect of living in an integrated neighborhood but also a predisposing factor in the choice to live there rather than in a segregated neighborhood.

and in various kinds of social structures. An understanding of the processes that promote change or the diffusion of innovation in a given social system requires the use of comparative materials from other social systems. For example, if our analysis had been confined to a sample of white women, as most studies of child rearing have been, we might have discovered that occupational mobility of husbands is a relevant variable for the study of intergenerational change in child-rearing patterns. But we could not have become aware of the conditions under which mobility does not lead to change had Negro women not been included in our sample. The existence of a dual stratification system in American society, although it represents a grave social liability, also represents, while it survives, an unmined opportunity for the comparative study of social structures and social processes within a common cultural framework. As the current struggle against economic discrimination and social segregation begins to achieve its objectives such comparative analyses could serve as a baseline for the study of the impact of these changes on Negro and white social structures, and on the behavior and attitudes of the individuals within them.

The Relative Contribution of Family Status and Economic Status to Juvenile Delinquency

CHARLES V. WILLIE

A REVIEW OF THE LITERATURE INDICATES TWO BASIC CONDITIONS associated with juvenile delinquency that have been confirmed in several studies. They are (1) poverty and poor living conditions and (2) broken homes and inadequate family life.[1] It is sometimes assumed that poverty and family instability are so closely intertwined that one is but a reflection of the other. Probably the best summary on the association between family instability and economic insecurity is provided by Abram Kardiner and Lionel Ovesey. They state that "the broken home in the lower-class family is very commonly attributed to the precarious economic conditions under which these families live. This statement is not untrue; it is merely incomplete."[2]

The general hypothesis of this study is that economic status and family status make both joint and independent contributions to deviant behavior. Family instability is aggravated by economic insecurity but is not limited to poor households. Also, inadequate family finances do not always result in broken marriages. It is of particular importance to study this hypothesis (1) since doubt has been cast upon the assumption that family instability and economic insecurity are but different reflections of the same phenomenon, and (2) because of the recent debate surrounding the Moynihan Report on *The Negro Family*,[3,4] which discusses

---

[1]Leslie T. Wilkins, "Juvenile Delinquency: A Critical Review of Research and Theory," *Educational Research*, 5 (February, 1963), pp. 104-119.

[2]Abram Kardiner and Lionel Ovesey, *The Mark of Oppression*, Cleveland: The World Publishing Co., 1962, p. 344.

[3]United States Department of Labor, *The Negro Family—The Case for National Action*, Washington, D.C.: U.S. Government Printing Office, 1965.

[4]Lee Rainwater and William L. Yancy, "Black Families and the White House," *Transaction*, 3 (July-August, 1966), pp. 6-11, 48-53.

Reprinted by permission of the publisher and author from *Social Problems*, XIV (Winter 1967), 326-35.

the relationship between family instability, economic insecurity, and deviant behavior.

Daniel Patrick Moynihan concluded that federal government programs should be designed to enhance the stability and resources of the Negro family. What is unclear in this conclusion is the relationship between stability and resources. Belton Fleisher in a recent study of the economics of delinquency stated that "when family income increases . . . the number of women over 14 who are separated or divorced will decline. . . ."[5] It was suggested by Fleisher that family stability is a function of economic security. But Moynihan implied that upward mobility and economic security would continue to elude Negroes "unless the viability of the Negro family is restored."[6] Moynihan, of course, does not rule out increasing the economic resources of the Negro family as a way of contributing to its viability; but it is clear that his focus is upon the social integration of family members.

So a study is needed not only of the independent contributions of family status and economic status to deviant behavior such as juvenile delinquency but also of their interaction effect. Which comes first — family stability or economic security? Does one give rise to the other? With reference to juvenile delinquency, this question might be asked: Is the rate higher among children of poor stable families than among children of affluent unstable families?

Because the findings to date about the correlation between delinquency rates and race are ambiguous, as pointed out by Roland Chilton in his study of Baltimore, Detroit, and Indianapolis,[7] a study of the relative contribution of economic and family status to juvenile delinquency should attempt to study whites and nonwhites separately to determine if the association (if there is any between race and delinquency) is similar or different in these two populations. Unequivocally, Fleisher has stated that "in areas of high tendency toward crime, a 10 per cent rise in income might well result in a 20 per cent decline in delinquency."[8] It should be determined, if possible, whether this phenomenon would be true both of white and nonwhite populations.

Chilton has wisely pointed out that "questions concerning the relationship of delinquency to the degree of organization of an area or to the

---

[5] Belton M. Fleisher, *The Economics of Delinquency*, Chicago: Quadrangle Books, 1966, p. 117.

[6] U. S. Department of Labor, *op. cit.*, p. 30.

[7] Roland J. Chilton, "Continuity in Delinquency Area Research: A Comparison of Studies for Baltimore, Detroit and Indianapolis," *American Sociological Review*, 29 (February, 1964), pp. 75-78.

[8] Belton M. Fleisher, *op. cit.*

degree of agreement on norms cannot be adequately answered with delinquency area data and procedures."[9] Social area data and ecological correlations are basic to the analysis in this study and therefore limit the kinds of inferences that may be drawn. No attempt is made to correlate delinquent behavior with certain sociological conditions such as anomie. This investigation has two goals which are quite modest: (1) to determine whether or not earlier findings regarding the association between economic status and juvenile delinquency and family status and juvenile delinquency hold when populations of whites and nonwhites are analyzed separately, and (2) to determine the joint effect, if any, of these two variables.

DATA AND METHOD

The study area was Washington, D.C. The basic unit of analysis was the census tract. Analysis of the association, if any, between juvenile delinquency and economic status and juvenile delinquency and family status was determined by computing Pearsonian correlation coefficients for 115 of the 125 census tracts in the city (the 10 tracts eliminated were sparsely settled or consisted of institutional populations).

There are, of course, dangers in using ecological correlations, which W. S. Robinson has discussed.[10] The dependent variable, juvenile delinquency, accounted for only three per cent of the youth population 10 to 17 years of age in the total city and varied from census tracts in which less than one per cent of the youth had been referred to court during the course of a year to a high-rate tract in which 11 per cent of the youth had been referred to court. The small proportion of the population in each census tract that was delinquent means that caution should be exercised in interpreting the findings. However, some of the problems of ecological correlations were guarded against by relating the dependent variable to independent variables such as socio-economic status (which was a composite value that characterized most of the people in a census tract) and the proportion of children in broken families (which varied from a small minority to a large majority of the families in many census tracts). Because the number of census tracts in the predominantly white area and in the predominantly nonwhite area of Washington was relatively small (41 predominantly white and 51 predominantly nonwhite tracts), this would further complicate a correlational analysis. And so patterns of variations within racial populations by socio-economic and

[9]Roland J. Chilton, *op. cit.*, p. 83.

[10]W. S. Robinson, "Ecological Correlations and the Behavior of Individuals," *American Sociological Review*, 15 (June, 1950), pp. 351-357.

family status were determined by using the methods of social area analysis.[11]

Data for the study are records of 6,269 youth referred to the District of Columbia Juvenile Court for reasons other than traffic offenses and dependency during a 33-month period from 1959 to 1962. Another study conducted by this author in Washington and using the data of a single fiscal year, 1963, revealed a high correlation between the rates for youth who came in contact with police only and youth who were referred to court; the Pearsonian correlation coefficient for 113 census tracts included in that study was .90. This means that a strong socio-economic bias, which could result in a much higher proportion of police contacts being referred to court in the poorer than in the more affluent neighborhoods, does not appear to contaminate these data. For the city as a whole, 37 per cent of the youth contacted by police were referred to court; the percentage in a more affluent socio-economic area was 32 and in a low-income area, 40. This was not a large difference in per cent of court referrals between populations of high and low socio-economic status. While the bias was not completely eliminated, it was controlled. This may be because Washington has a separate youth aid division in the police department staffed by officers who give full-time attention to youth and who must be consulted on all police contacts that are referred to court.

The 1960 census population 10 through 17 years of age was used as the base for computing rates. The base was limited to these particular age levels because less than five per cent of court-referred youth were under 10 years. Because these youth are not as vulnerable as those over 10 years, their inclusion in the population base would have distorted the actual incidence of delinquency by depressing the rate. Data for three years (33 months) were used to increase the reliability of rates since only a small proportion (about three per cent) were referred to court each year. The population base was multiplied by 2.75 to make it comparable to the 33-month study period so that annual rates could be computed for each census tract. The total city population in 1960 was approximately 764,000, about 45 per cent white and 55 per cent nonwhite.

The economic status and family status of the population, the former of which is more appropriately called socio-economic status in this

---

[11]Eshref Shevky and Marilyn Williams, *The Social Areas in Los Angeles*, Berkeley: University of California Press, 1949. Wendel Bell, "Economic Family and Ethnic Status: An Empirical Test," *American Sociological Review*, 20 (February, 1955), pp. 45-51. Eshref Shevky and Wendel Bell, *Social Area Analysis*, Stanford: Stanford University Press, 1955.

study, was measured by a composite index score for each census tract and the per cent of broken homes. Five highly correlated variables were used in the index:[12] (1) percentage of the employed in the combined categories of operatives, service workers, and laborers; (2) median number of years of school completed by the population over 25 years of age; (3) estimated market value of owned homes; (4) the gross monthly rental for tenant-occupied dwellings; and (5) percentage of sound dwelling units. (The first factor was inverted so that it varied directly with the other four.) Distributions of each of the five variables were converted into standard scores with assigned means of 50 and assigned standard deviations of 10. The five standard scores for each census tract were simply averaged into a socio-economic status composite score. The per cent of children under 18 years of age not living with both parents was computed as an indicator of the family status of a census tract. Studies of indices of social status, such as one conducted by John Haer, indicate that a composite index of several variables is a better predictor of differentiation within a population than a single variable.[13] In delineating family status, a gross indicator like the number of children in one-parent families was believed to be sufficient. While one parent may be absent from the household due to death, divorce, or desertion, the functional consequence for the child — particularly if the absent parent is the father which is usually the case — is more or less the same. No one is present who has a primary responsibility, as Malinowski has described it, of orienting the child to the community at large.[14]

Census tracts were classified as white and nonwhite for the social area analysis; tracts in which two out of every three persons were white were classified as part of the white area. A similar procedure was followed in delineating the nonwhite area. In spite of the criterion used, 95 per cent of the total population in the white area was of Caucasian racial stock and 90 per cent of the total population in the nonwhite area was of that color category. Most of the census tracts in Washington are racially homogeneous; only about one-fifth of the population lives in racially mixed residential areas.

---

[12]Charles V. Willie, and Morton O. Wagenfeld, *Socio-Economic and Ethnic Areas, Syracuse and Onondaga County, New York, 1960*, Syracuse: Syracuse University, Youth Development Center, 1962.

[13]John L. Haer, "Predictive Utility of Five Indices of Social Stratification," *American Sociological Review*, 22 (October, 1957), pp. 541-546.

[14]Bronislaw Malinowski, "Parenthood—The Basis of Social Structure," in Marvin B. Sussman (ed.), *Source Book in Marriage and the Family*, Cambridge: Houghton Mifflin Co., 1955, p. 25.

White census tracts were grouped into poor and affluent areas and into areas of few and many broken homes. Those census tracts above the city-wide socio-economic composite standard score of 50 (that is, those tracts in which the median family income was above $4,500) were included in the affluent area. The median family incomes for some census tracts in the affluent area were well above $10,000. Those census tracts below the city-wide average composite score (that is, those tracts with median family incomes below $4,500) were classified as part of the poor area. Several of the tracts in this area had medians that were below the $3,000 level of extreme poverty. The area of few broken homes consisted of those tracts in the affluent and poor areas in which the per cent of children not living with both parents was above the city-wide percentage. There were four area types into which census tracts with predominantly white populations were grouped: Area A, the affluent area characterized by few broken homes; Area B, the affluent area characterized by many broken homes; Area C, the poor area characterized by few broken homes; and Area D, the poor area characterized by many broken homes. The number of delinquents and the population 10 through 17 for all census tracts in an area were totaled. With these summations, delinquency rates per 1,000 youth were computed for each. Area A had 32 census tracts, Area B, 4 census tracts, Area C, 4 census tracts, and Area D, 1 census tract classified as white.

The same procedure was followed in delineating areas for the non-white population and in computing area delinquency rates. Area A had 6 census tracts, Area B, 2 tracts, Area C, 5 tracts, and Area D, 38 census tracts.

Classifying white and nonwhite populations into these four types of social areas made possible a comparative analysis controlled for variations in socio-economic and family status that tend to differentiate these two populations. The conditions of the populations in each of the areas were, of course, not identical because of the crude technique of dichotomizing the economic and family status variables above and below the city-wide average.

About 18 per cent of the total population of juvenile delinquents was eliminated from that part of the study which compared white and nonwhite areas. These were the youthful offenders who lived in racially mixed areas. The remaining population of 5,148 delinquents was divided this way: 737 or 14 per cent in the white areas and 4,411 or 86 per cent in the nonwhite areas. The large imbalance of delinquency within the different racial areas is further indication that any meaningful comparison of whites and nonwhites must control for socio-economic and family status. Although the number of census tracts was few in one or two of the four areas among white and non-white populations, no area had a base population of less than 300. Thus, the rates that were computed for comparative analysis were reasonably reliable.

FINDINGS

As reported in a previous study, the correlation coefficient for juvenile delinquency rates and socio-economic status scores was significantly different from zero and so was the correlation coefficient for delinquency rates and the per cent of children with one or both parents absent from home.[15] In this city-wide analysis, the correlation coefficient for juvenile delinquency and socio-economic status was −.65. And the correlation coefficient for juvenile delinquency and family instability was .64. This means that juvenile delinquency rates tended to increase as the socio-economic status level of census tracts decreased, and that juvenile delinquency rates tended to increase as the per cent of broken homes in the census tracts increased. These findings are in accord with those of other investigators mentioned at the beginning of the paper.

Although socio-economic and family status variables both correlated highly with juvenile delinquency rates (having coefficients of a similar magnitude), this did not mean that the two variables were identical. To determine the degree of association between these variables, socio-economic status scores were correlated with the per cent of children in broken homes; the correlation coefficient was −.65. This coefficient indicated that slightly more than 40 per cent of the variance in the ecological distribution of the family instability factor could be attributed to variation in levels of socio-economic status. While this was a high degree of association, the correlation coefficient also indicated that nearly 60 per cent of the variance must be attributed to factors other than socio-economic status. Clearly, the two variables did not duplicate each other. Although there was some overlap, they were not simply different ways of measuring the same phenomenon.

A multiple correlation coefficient was computed to determine the independent and joint contribution of economic and family status to the pattern of variation in juvenile delinquency on a city-wide basis. These two variables correlated with the dependent variable — juvenile-delinquency — at .71. The multiple correlation coefficient accounted for a larger proportion of the variance in the ecological distribution

---

[15]Charles V. Willie, Anita Gershenovitz, Myrna Levine, Sulochana Glazer, and Roy J. Jones, "Race and Delinquency," *Phylon*, 26 (Fall, 1965), pp. 240-246.

of juvenile delinquency than either family status or economic status separately correlated with the dependent variable.

Beta weights were obtained to continue the analysis of the independent and joint effects of these two factors upon the dependent variable. They indicate that about 16 per cent of the variance in the ecological distribution of juvenile delinquency rates could be attributed to variation in levels of socio-economic status; approximately 14 per cent could be attributed to variation in the distribution of the per cent of youth who lived in broken families; and about 20 per cent of the variance was due to the joint effect of these two factors. The finding that socio-economic and family status make a joint contribution to the pattern of variation of juvenile delinquency within an urban community is important. It may help explain why the debate over whether economic status should be upgraded or family stability secured initially, as a way of dealing with deviant behavior, has not been resolved satisfactorily for advocates of either form of action.

This finding suggests that some juvenile delinquency is associated with unstable family life which is unstable because of impoverished economic circumstances; and some juvenile delinquency is associated with families which are economically impoverished and that these families are impoverished because they are unstable. Nevertheless, family status and economic status are independently associated with juvenile delinquency too. This fact should be remembered when assessing the joint effects of these variables. Obviously, the relationship between delinquency, family life, and economic circumstances is complex. A major error in many discussions about the relative importance of different independent variables in preventing deviant behavior has been the tendency to oversimplify.

The contribution of socio-economic and family status to variations in the pattern of juvenile delinquency in separate white and nonwhite populations is presented now. Fourfold tables were constructed for this analysis.

The data in Tables 1 and 2 indicated both similar and different ecological patterns of distribution for juvenile delinquency in white and nonwhite populations. The white and nonwhite areas are similar in that circumstances contributing to the lowest and highest delinquency rates were the same for both races. The area of affluent socio-economic status in which there were few broken homes (as seen in cell A of Tables 1 and 2) tended to have the lowest delinquency rate in the city, while the highest rate was found in that area characterized by low socio-economic status and many broken homes (as seen in cell D of Tables 1 and 2) for white and nonwhite populations. These areas

TABLE 1

JUVENILE DELINQUENCY RATE PER 1,000 YOUTH 10 THROUGH 17 YEARS OF AGE IN
NONWHITE AREA, BY FAMILY STATUS AND SOCIO-ECONOMIC STATUS,
WASHINGTON, D.C., JULY, 1959-MARCH, 1962

| | JUVENILE DELINQUENCY RATE AMONG NONWHITES | |
	Area of Few Broken Homes	Area of Many Broken Homes
Affluent Area	a 19.7	b 20.9
Poor Area	c 26.5	d 42.4

TABLE 2

JUVENILE DELINQUENCY RATE PER 1,000 YOUTH 10 THROUGH 17 YEARS OF AGE IN
WHITE AREA, BY FAMILY STATUS AND SOCIO-ECONOMIC STATUS,
WASHINGTON, D.C., JULY, 1959-MARCH, 1962

| | JUVENILE DELINQUENCY RATE AMONG WHITES | |
	Area of Few Broken Homes	Area of Many Broken Homes
Affluent Area	a 10.6	b 30.4
Poor Area	c 19.6	b 44.3

provided the least favorable and most favorable circumstances for the development of delinquent behavior. Apparently, these circumstances affect whites and nonwhites in similar ways.

White and nonwhite populations differed in the way in which delinquency rates were distributed between affluent areas characterized by many broken households and poor areas consisting of many stable or intact families. Data for this analysis are found in cells B and C of Tables 1 and 2. Among the affluent, the absence of one or both parents from the home tended to be associated with a higher delinquency rate for whites than nonwhites. And among the poor, the presence of both parents in the household tended to be associated with a lower delinquency rate among whites than nonwhites. It would appear that family status had a greater affect upon the white than nonwhite population in contributing to a lower delinquency rate.

TABLE 3

A COMPARISON OF THE JUVENILE DELINQUENCY RATE IN THE HIGH-RATE AREA WITH
THE RATES IN THREE OTHER SOCIAL AREAS, FOR WHITE AND NONWHITE
POPULATIONS, WASHINGTON, D.C. 1959-62

	PER CENT OF CHANGE IN DELINQUENCY RATE FOR THREE SOCIAL AREAS COMPARED WITH THE HIGH-RATE AREA[1]			
	White Areas		Nonwhite Areas	
	Per cent of change from High-Rate Area	Rank	Per cent of change from High-Rate Area	Rank
High family stability and high economic status[2]	76	1	54	1
High family stability and low economic status[3]	56	2	36	3
High economic status and low family stability[4]	31	3	51	2

[1]The high-rate area is Cell D in Tables 1 and 2
[2]Cell A in Tables 1 and 2
[3]Cell C in Tables 1 and 2
[4]Cell B in Tables 1 and 2

Differences between rates for comparable white and nonwhite areas are not great, never exceeding 11 points. This means that one should exercise caution in drawing inferences from these data. A persistent pattern, however, does merit attention. Further analysis of the data is pursued to confirm or cast doubt on tentative conclusions based on analysis of patterns discussed above.

The goal of this analysis was to examine further the differential white and nonwhite populations alluded to, especially the possibility that family status may be more specifically and immediately associated with delinquency among whites than nonwhites. Since the most favorable circumstances for the development of juvenile delinquency was similar for both racial categories — that is, a low-income area characterized by many broken families — cell D in Tables 1 and 2 was identified as the high-rate area, having a similar juvenile delinquency rate for both races, i.e., 44 and 42 for whites and nonwhites respectively.

The analysis was designed to determine which area type exhibited the greatest difference in delinquency rate between it and the high-rate area. Rates for Areas A, B, and C, therefore, were substracted from the rate in Area D for both white and nonwhite populations. For the white population, the greatest difference was between Areas D and A;

this was also the case for the nonwhite population. The delinquency rate in this low-rate area was 76 per cent lower in the white population and 54 per cent lower in the nonwhite population than the delinquency rate in the high-rate area. In this respect, the two racial populations were similar as mentioned above. They differed, however, in the kinds of areas that resulted in the second and third greatest difference. For the white population, Areas D and C exhibited a 56 per cent difference in rates while Areas D and B revealed a 51 per cent difference in rates among nonwhites. The second greatest difference for whites occurred in an area characterized by high family stability and low economic status, while among nonwhites the second greatest difference occurred in an area characterized by high economic status and low family stability. Although the economic circumstances were relatively favorable, the white population had a delinquency rate that was only 31 per cent lower than the high-rate area, when there was a considerable amount of family instability in the area. But nonwhite households that lived under similar affluent economic circumstances tended to exhibit a 51 per cent difference in delinquency rate below that of the high-rate area even though the area consisted of many unstable households. The area among nonwhites which registered the smallest difference in delinquency rate between it and the high-rate area was the one characterized by high family stability and low economic status.

Thus, it would appear that the extremes — those circumstances that were the most and least favorable for the development of delinquent behavior — had similar consequences for white and nonwhite populations. But in between these most and least favorable circumstances, whites were more affected by family composition while nonwhites were more affected by economic circumstances. Because of the kinds of data and methods used in this analysis, these differential effects cannot be stated with certainty. But the findings do suggest that different approaches may be needed for white and nonwhite populations in the United States to solve some problems of deviancy, like juvenile delinquency.

There are, of course, no innate differences between these two races that would cause one to be more affected by economic or family circumstances than the other. One possible explanation of the differential affects of family and economic status in white and nonwhite populations is their different positions in the opportunity system as described by Cloward and Ohlin.[16] In Washington, D. C., 80 per cent of the white

---

[16]Richard A. Cloward and Lloyd E. Ohlin, *Delinquency and Opportunity*, New York: The Free Press of Glencoe, 1960.

population lives in economically affluent areas while 67 per cent of the nonwhite population lives in neighborhoods of poverty or marginal economic condition. Since poverty was no longer an overwhelming problem for most white people, family instability was a major remaining and outstanding problem contributing to the incidence of juvenile delinquency.

Although the per cent of nonwhite children growing up in one-parent families was greater than the per cent of white children who had this kind of experience, the impoverished economic circumstances of non-whites was overwhelming. In the light of the data and analysis of this study, it is hypothesized that nonwhites may be able to deal with the family instability factor which is associated with juvenile delinquency only after notable improvements have been experienced in their economic circumstances. The hypothesis is advanced on the basis of the findings in this study, particularly the findings pertaining to the white population which is largely beyond the pale of poverty.

Out of this analysis, then, has come the sociological principle that the solutions of some social problems occur in a serial pattern, that the solution of one problem makes possible the solution of another. There is an ordering of social events into a sequential pattern. Obviously, white and nonwhite populations are in different stages of the series. Most whites have passed beyond the stage of economic insecurity.

This means that efforts to strengthen family ties and increase family stability in the nonwhite population probably will not be very successful until opportunities for economic upgrading are provided. This society may have the possibility of helping a population achieve greater family stability to prevent delinquency only after it has assisted a population to achieve greater economic security. The longitudinal unfolding of life in the social system needs to be studied in a much more refined way. This study has suggested the significance of this kind of investigation and called attention to the inadequacy of explanation that does not take into consideration a serial or developmental view of social conditions.

CONCLUSIONS

A general conclusion emerging from this study is that juvenile delinquency will not be greatly reduced in Washington, or in cities like Washington with a large nonwhite population, until there is a substantial increase in the nonwhite population's economic status. The low rate of delinquency among white youth who are members of a population that has achieved economic affluence is further evidence supporting this conclusion. Other conclusions of the study are these:

Socio-economic and family status are phenomena that have overlapping but different ecological patterns of distribution in an urban community.

Socio-economic and family status make independent as well as joint contributions to variations in the ecology of juvenile delinquency.

The preventive potential of two-parent households against juvenile delinquency tends to be impaired by circumstances of poverty.

The preventive potential of affluent economic status against juvenile delinquency tends to be impaired by family instability.

Delinquency rates are similar for members of white and nonwhite populations who live in the most disadvantaged environment characterized by many broken homes and low income.

Community programs designed to prevent juvenile delinquency associated both with family instability and economic insecurity will probably have greater success if they focus first upon increasing the economic status of a population.

The full answer, however, to the question of whether community programs should attempt first to create more economic security or develop greater family stability depends upon the target population and the stage through which it is passing. More than four out of every five youth referred to juvenile court in Washington, D.C. are Negro. If a community is really interested in reducing delinquency in this kind of a city, it would appear, according to the findings of this study, that much assistance must be rendered to the nonwhite population, in the form of increased economic opportunities.

Rearing Children for Educational Achievement in Fatherless Families

LOUIS KRIESBERG

IT IS NOT ONLY THE PSYCHOLOGICAL SIGNIFICANCE OF NOT HAVING A father that may create difficulties for the educational achievement of children in fatherless families. His absence is likely to mean that his former wife is poor, lives in generally poor neighborhoods, and lacks social, emotional, and physical assistance in child-rearing. Furthermore, how husbandless mothers accommodate themselves to these circumstances can have important consequences for their children.

A consequence of particular social concern is the educational handicap which children from fatherless families seem to suffer. There is evidence that such children have lower I.Q.'s, are retarded in school, and complete fewer years of study than do children of complete families.[1] The evidence, however, is not unequivocal: some studies report no differences.[2] Furthermore, even where differences are reported and are statistically significant, there is a very large overlap between the two

---

[1]For example, see Martin Deutsch and Bert Brown, "Social Influences in Negro-White Intelligence Differences," *The Journal of Social Issues*, 20 (April, 1964), pp. 24-35; and M. Elaine Burgess and Daniel O. Price, *An American Dependency Challenge*, Chicago: American Public Welfare Association, 1963. For studies of broken families and dropouts from high school, see John Roberts, "Let's Keep Them in School," *California Journal of Secondary Education*, 33 (January, 1958), pp. 115-118; J. Armand Lanier, "A Guidance-Faculty Study of Student Withdrawals," *Journal of Educational Research*, 43 (November, 1949), pp. 205-212; William Evariff, "How 'Different' Are Our Drop-Outs?" *The Bulletin of the National Association of Secondary Schools*, 41 (February, 1957), pp. 212-218; other studies cited in S. M. Miller, Betty L. Saleem, and Herrington Bryce, *School Dropouts: A Commentary and Annotated Bibliography*, Syracuse, N.Y.: Syracuse University Youth Development Center, 1964.

[2]Lee N. Robins, Robin S. Jones, and George E. Murphy, "School Milieu and School Problems of Negro Boys," *Social Problems*, 13 (Spring, 1966), pp. 428-436; F. Ivan Nye, "Child Adjustment in Broken and in Unhappy Unbroken Homes," *Marriage and Family Living*, 19 (1957), pp. 356-361.

Reprinted by permission of the publisher and author from *Journal of Marriage and the Family*, XXIX (May 1967), 288-301.

categories of children. Many fatherless children do as well as children from complete families, and many children from complete families do less well than fatherless children.

It is necessary to specify the conditions and processes associated with family structure that affect children's educational achievement. As Miller, Saleem, and Bryce point out in reviewing studies of high school dropouts and family structure:

> Since broken families occur with much greater frequency in the lower socio-economic levels, general social class factors rather than specific dropout-producing factors may be involved in high rates of broken families among dropouts.[3]

Numerous studies have documented that children of parents with low education, income, or occupational status generally have lower academic achievement than do children of higher socioeconomic levels.[4] To some extent this is attributable to many conditions in the home, such as low aspirations or expectations by the parents, lack of financial support for incidental needs in public schools and for the ability to forego earnings, crowded living quarters, lack of parental knowledge for educational guidance and modeling, and numerous siblings sharing finite adult social and other resources. In addition, class-segregated housing means that neighborhoods and schools can exist which are largely utilized by persons with such characteristics. The consequences are then compounded. Several recent studies have documented the influence of the socioeconomic composition of high schools upon children's academic achievement and aspirations for continued education.[5] Thus, children of working-class parents in schools with predominantly middle-class students tend to score better on achievement tests and are more likely to aspire to college education than are working-class children in

---

[3]Miller, Saleem, and Bryce, *op. cit.*, p. 14.

[4]For example, see Joseph A. Kahl, *The American Class Structure*, New York: Rinehart & Co., 1953; W. H. Sewell, A. O. Haller, and M. A. Straus, "Social Status and Educational and Occupational Aspiration," *American Sociological Review*, (February, 1957), pp. 67-73; S. M. Lipset and R. Bendix, *Social Mobility in Industrial Society*, Berkeley: University of California Press, 1960, pp. 227-259; and Louis Kriesberg, "The Relationship Between Socio-Economic Rank and Behavior," *Social Problems* (Spring, 1963), pp. 334-353.

[5]See, for example, Alan B. Wilson, "Residential Segregation of Social Classes and Aspirations of High School Boys," *American Sociological Review*, 24 (December, 1959), pp. 836-845; John A. Michael, "High School Climates and Plans for Entering College," *Public Opinion Quarterly*, 25 (Winter, 1961), pp. 585-595; and Robert H. Hardt, "The Impact of School Milieu on Pupils' Educational Plans," paper read at the annual meetings of the Eastern Sociological Society, New York City, April, 1961.

predominantly working-class schools. The evidence does not make it possible to be certain of the processes. Do working-class families who live in middle-class school districts differ from those working-class families who live in other areas? Do the middle-class schools provide better physical facilities and more skilled and concerned teachers? Do the children themselves establish a normative climate which influences each child, or do the parents influence each other and then influence the children?

The educationally handicapping conditions associated with low socio-economic levels may, however, be particularly severe for fatherless families. Thus, if a fatherless family is living in a low-income neighborhood in which educational achievement is generally low and the expectations of the children's peers are low, a husbandless mother may be less able to compete effectively with her children's peers than would the married parents in a complete family. Or consider employment by the mother. A husbandless mother without a good income from pensions, insurance, or alimony must choose between (1) dependence upon public assistance and poverty or (2) somewhat more money and employment which makes extra claims upon her time and energy. Although employment may not adversely affect the educational achievement of married mothers' children,[6] among husbandless mothers the extra demands of employment may be deleterious.

Finally, there is the possibility that not having a father is in itself educationally handicapping for children. Even aside from the absence of a male model, the lack of his support and aid in child-rearing may reduce the effectiveness of the mother's efforts. It is even possible that the husbandless mother may withdraw and reject her children or push them toward independence at too young an age. On the other hand, she may be overly indulgent or overly interfering.

An assessment of the educational consequences of growing up in a fatherless family should include a differentiation of these many possible conditions and processes. In this paper the author will examine educationally relevant attitudes and conduct of husbandless mothers, under certain conditions related to not having a husband.[7] The analysis

---

[6]F. Ivan Nye and Lois W. Hoffman (eds.), *The Employed Mother in America*, Chicago: Rand McNally and Company, 1963; also see D. H. Stott, "Do Working Mothers' Children Suffer?" *New Society*, August 19, 1965, pp. 8-9.

[7]Among the many studies relating home conditions and academic achievement of children, see Robert E. Herriott, "Some Social Determinants of Educational Aspiration," *Harvard Educational Review*, 33:2 (1963), pp. 157-177; Alvin L. Bertran, "School Attendance and Attainment: Function and Dysfunction of School and Family Social Systems," *Social Forces*, 40 (March, 1962), pp. 228-253; Parlett L. Moore, "Factors Involved in Student Elimination from High School," *Journal of*

will attempt to answer questions such as: Do husbandless mothers have lower educational aspirations for their children than do married mothers? Do husbandless and married mothers differ in the implementation of their attitudes? Are such differences attributable to or conditioned by circumstances related to being husbandless: poverty, employment, or residence in low-income neighborhoods? Given the evidence regarding neighborhood effects and given the research design of the study from which data for this paper are drawn, particular attention will be given to an examination of possible consequences of living in different neighborhoods.

Sources of Data

This paper is based upon data from a study of families in four Syracuse, New York public housing projects and the neighborhoods surrounding each.[8] The housing projects range in size from 200 to 675 units. More significantly, two of the projects, called Evans and Stern here, are in middle-income neighborhoods. The neighborhood around Stern is somewhat higher and more varied in occupational and income status compared with the neighborhood around Evans. The two other projects, Grant and Park, are in low-income neighborhoods; the latter in a Negro ghetto at the time of the study.

This kind of sample facilitates the comparison of husbandless and married mothers, since one can compare them in the same neighborhoods and income levels. As in the nation as a whole, about half of the fatherless families live in poverty. Almost half of the husbandless mothers interviewed are separated; most of the rest are divorced or

---

Negro Education, 23 (1954), pp. 117-122; Ravindrakumar H. Dave, *The Identification and Measurement of Environmental Process Variables that are Related to Educational Achievement,* unpublished Ph.D. dissertation, Department of Education, University of Chicago, 1963, cited in Benjamin S. Bloom, *Stability and Change in Human Characteristics,* New York: John Wiley & Sons, Inc., 1963, pp. 68-80, 124-125, and in Robin H. Farquhar, "Home Influences on Achievement and Intelligence: An Essay Review," *Administrator's Notebook,* 12 (January, 1965), pp. 1-4; and Esther Milner, "A Study of the Relationship Between Reading Readiness in Grade One School Children and Patterns of Parent-Child Interaction," *Child Development,* 22 (June, 1951), pp. 95-112.

[8]Separate samples were drawn of families in each project and the area within four or five blocks surrounding each project. Varying sampling ratios were used to yield approximately an equal number of cases in each project and neighborhood.

In all, 1,274 respondents were interviewed; husbands and wives in the same families were interviewed. The personal interviews averaged about an hour and a half for the women. The survey was conducted in the spring of 1963. For additional information regarding the sample and data collection procedures, see Louis Kriesberg and Seymour S. Bellin, *op. cit.,* Appendix A. In this paper, only the mothers or maternal surrogates of minor children are reported upon.

widowed; and only a few were never married. Many of the husbandless mothers have been husbandless for only a short time, and some will remarry. The distinction between husbandless and married should not be considered a sharp and permanent division.

PARENTAL ATTITUDES RELEVANT TO CHILDREN'S EDUCATIONAL ACHIEVEMENT

Given the handicaps generally associated with raising children without a husband, husbandless mothers might be expected to accommodate by devaluing education for their children. However, from their responses to interview questions, it is clear that, in the abstract and without considering alternative values, obtaining a lot of education and working hard in school are universally valued by both husbandless and married mothers. Each mother was also asked whether she preferred (1) that her children receive much more education than she had even if this meant estrangement from her or (2) that her children remain close to her rather than get much more education. Most mothers prefer more education, and this is slightly more likely among the husbandless than among the married mothers. The mothers were also asked whether or not they believed estrangement would actually occur if their children obtained much more education than they had. Most mothers thought this unlikely. Mothers who wish a child of theirs would obtain much more education and do not believe that this would lead to estrangement probably most consistently support the child's educational efforts. Three-fourths of the husbandless mothers fall in this category, a somewhat larger percentage than among the married mothers.

Greater differences might be expected when specific aspirations are examined. These are more likely to be affected by current circumstances than general values about the desirability of education. This paper will examine educational aspirations as indicated by the number of years of schooling which a child would have to complete not to disappoint his mother and the school marks he would have to obtain not to disappoint her.

The standards about marks do not seem to differ between husbandless and married mothers. Husbandless mothers are as likely to be disappointed if their children do not obtain A's and B's as are married mothers. There is other evidence, however, that the husbandless mothers are actually more likely than married mothers to make high demands upon their children. The mothers were asked what marks a particular child usually attained in school and, next, how satisfied the mother was with the study child's school work. The reports of the husbandless mothers and married mothers yield about the same distribution of marks for their children. Yet, among mothers who report that a particular child usually earns high marks, husbandless mothers are more likely than married mothers to say they are dissatisfied or the child has sometimes received too low marks. Even among the mothers with children receiving low marks, husbandless mothers are more likely than married mothers to say they are dissatisfied or the child has sometimes received too low a mark.

Aspirations involve consideration of what is attainable as well as what is valued. Children's grades in school are not as subject to the external constraints associated with being husbandless as is the children's completing more than 12 years of education. To enter college requires not only the expenditure of money but the loss of earnings which might otherwise be gained. The quality of high school education, the influence of the children's age-mates, and the awareness that entering college is uncommon in low-income neighborhoods all would combine to make husbandless mothers willing to accept completion of

TABLE 1

INDEX OF WISH FOR EDUCATION AND BELIEF THAT CHILD WILL BECOME ESTRANGED, BY WORK STATUS* AMONG HUSBANDLESS AND MARRIED MOTHERS

Index	HUSBANDLESS MOTHERS			MARRIED MOTHERS		
	Work Full-Time	Work Part-Time	Not Work-ing	Work Full-Time	Work Part-Time	Not Work-ing
(1) Wish for more education and believe unlikely child become estranged	90.2	78.8	67.8	66.7	58.2	66.8
(2) Wish for more education and believe not unlikely child become estranged	4.9	6.1	13.6	14.0	11.8	9.5
(3) Do not wish for more education and believe unlikely child become estranged	4.9	15.2	8.5	14.0	24.6	17.2
(4) Do not wish for more education and believe likely child become estranged	0.0	0.0	10.2	5.3	5.5	6.5
Total %	100.0	100.1	100.1	100.0	100.1	100.0
(N)	(41)	(33)	(59)	(57)	(110)	(232)

*Work full time means being employed full time when interviewed; work part time refers to part-time employment or any employment in the previous 12 months but not currently employed full time; and not working means not currently employed and not employed during the preceding 12 months.

high school as a successful achievement and not be disappointed if the child does not go further. As a matter of fact, the husbandless mothers are less likely to aspire for more than a high school education for their sons than are married mothers. The difference is small but statistically significant.[9]

On the basis of other evidence from his study, husbandless mothers generally do not reject or withdraw from their children; indeed, this relationship takes on relatively greater importance than among married mothers. Husbandless mothers therefore would be expected to be more likely than married mothers to have high educational aspirations. But husbandless mothers often have low income and live in poor neighbor-

TABLE 2

PERCENT OF MOTHERS WHO WOULD BE DISAPPOINTED IF THEIR CHILDREN EARNED
LESS THAN B, BY PER CAPITA DISPOSABLE HOUSEHOLD INCOME*
AMONG HUSBANDLESS AND MARRIED MOTHERS

Mother	PER CAPITA DISPOSABLE HOUSEHOLD INCOME	
	Less than $500	$500 or more
Husbandless	61.8	81.7
	(68)	(60)
Married	46.4	66.1
	(69)	(295)

*Per capita household refers to income from all sources in the household minus the annual rent and divided by the number of persons in the household.

TABLE 3

PERCENT OF MOTHERS WHO WOULD BE DISAPPOINTED IF A SON DID NOT ATTAIN
MORE THAN A HIGH SCHOOL EDUCATION, BY PER CAPITA DISPOSABLE HOUSE-
HOLD INCOME AMONG HUSBANDLESS AND MARRIED MOTHERS

Mother	PER CAPITA DISPOSABLE HOUSEHOLD INCOME	
	Less than $500	$500 or more
Husbandless	2.9	40.0
	(69)	(60)
Married	10.3	34.1
	(68)	(296)

[9] Chi-square is 6.66, 2 df, $p = .05$; Kendall Tau C is $+.06$, $p = .05$, based upon 544 cases.

TABLE 4

PERCENT OF MOTHERS WHO WOULD BE DISAPPOINTED IF THEIR CHILDREN EARNED
LESS THAN B'S, BY WORK STATUS AMONG HUSBANDLESS AND MARRIED MOTHERS

Mother	WORK STATUS		
	Work Full Time	Work Part Time	Not Working
Husbandless	82.9	78.8	60.7
	(41)	(33)	(61)
Married	61.4	71.2	60.4
	(57)	(111)	(235)

hoods; and such circumstances may restrain, and even depress, valuing education and educational achievements. These possibilities will now he considered.

Employment and Income

Employed husbandless mothers or those who are not poor are particularly likely to desire more education for their children and believe they will not become estranged as a result. (See Table 1.) Among married mothers, neither working nor income is related to this belief and value regarding education. These findings suggest that husbandless mothers are especially likely to value education but that some of them may be held back to the same level as married mothers if the circumstances are not supportive of their values. This idea is consistent with the findings in regard to educational aspirations.

Among the poor mothers, as among those who are not poor, husbandless mothers are *more* likely to be disappointed than are married mothers if their children receive less than B's. (See Table 2.) Furthermore, among the mothers who are poor, as among those who are not, husbandless mothers are equally likely to be disappointed if their children do not attain more than a high school education. (See Table 3.) Employment, especially for husbandless mothers, means more income; it also means greater involvement in the community beyond family and neighborhood and greater control over one's fate. As one would expect, then, employment has some of the same effects as income. Working husbandless mothers tend to have high aspirations in regard to grades, compared to married mothers; nonworking mothers do not differ. (See Table 4.) Among employed mothers, the husbandless are as likely as the married to aspire for more than high school attainment by their children. But, among the non-working mothers, the hus-

TABLE 5

PERCENT OF MOTHERS WHO WOULD BE DISAPPOINTED IF A SON DID NOT ATTAIN
MORE THAN A HIGH SCHOOL EDUCATION, BY WORK STATUS AMONG
HUSBANDLESS AND MARRIED MOTHERS

Mother	WORK STATUS		
	Work Full Time	Work Part Time	Not Working
Husbandless	34.2	30.3	4.8
	(41)	(33)	(62)
Married	38.6	33.9	26.0
	(57)	(112)	(235)

bandless are still less likely than the married to be disappointed if
their children do not go beyond high school. (See Table 5.) Non-
working husbandless mothers are obviously worse off economically
and in ways associated with low income than are nonworking married
mothers. These handicaps affect aspirations about years of schooling
to be attained more than aspirations about grades.[10]

Neighborhood

The other objective circumstance to be considered is the neighborhood
in which the mothers live. Residential areas can affect mothers' aspirations by providing opportunities or handicaps for their children's realization of the aspirations. In addition, other persons in the neighborhood
may directly influence the mothers. The study includes information
about the normative climate in the areas and the mothers' perceptions
of the educational efforts of the children, parental valuation of education, and the quality of the schools. This is based upon the respondents' answers to a series of questions. The respondents were asked
if they thought better or worse of people if their children "don't do

---

[10]Since low income and nonemployment are each independently associated with
low aspirations, and since income and work status are associated with each other,
it is necessary to examine the way they simultaneously affect aspirations. Among
husbandless mothers, income and work status each continue to be associated with
aspirations when the other is held constant. Among married mothers, an examination of both income and work status in relationship to aspirations about marks
reveals that it is the married mothers with low incomes and who are not employed
who are relatively unlikely to aspire for high marks (only 37 percent do so). Therefore, among those with high income, work status is not related to aspirations about
marks; among those with low income, work status is related. Among those employed
full or part time, income is no longer associated with aspirations. Among those who
are not employed, low income is associated with low aspirations.

TABLE 6

PERCENT OF MOTHERS WITH SELECTED EDUCATIONAL BELIEFS AND NORMS BY AREA*

| | AREAS | | | | | | | |
| | Projects | | | | Neighborhoods | | | |
Beliefs and Norm	Evans	Grant	Park	Stern	Evans	Grant	Park	Stern
False that parents rather children work than go to to school	86.2 (80)	94.1 (84)	86.2 (80)	81.2 (69)	98.1 (53)	87.5 (24)	80.2 (41)	97.9 (47)
Nearly all children try to do well in school	49.3 (69)	58.5 (82)	30.9 (68)	46.9 (64)	73.9 (46)	69.9 (23)	31.3 (32)	79.1 (43)
Think worse of people if their children do not do well in school	20.5 (88)	18.8 (96)	31.7 (82)	17.1 (88)	12.5 (56)	25.0 (32)	32.7 (52)	14.6 (48)
Think teachers more interested†	42.9 (28)	30.0 (40)	21.1 (19)	32.1 (28)				
Think schools are better†	41.2 (34)	29.8 (57)	9.1 (22)	61.0 (41)				

*Those with no opinions are omitted. Mothers whose children are too young to be in school are included.

†In addition, respondents who are in same school districts as they were in their previous residence are omitted; in Park, naturally, this reduces the base markedly.

well in school." They were asked how many children in their area "try to do well in school." The respondents were also asked whether they thought it was true or false that, in their residential areas, "parents would rather have their children go to work than stay in school." In addition, public housing tenants were asked whether the schools were better or worse in their present neighborhoods compared to where they lived before.

The summary results of these questions for each area provide a profile of the social environment relating to education for each project and the neighborhood surrounding each. (See Table 6.) Thus, the mothers in Park housing project do not think the schools are good, and the children in the project and in the surrounding neighborhood are not viewed as trying to do well in school. Although nearly all mothers thought it false that parents would rather that their children go to work than to school, in Park neighborhood the proportion who believed this to be false is relatively low. On the other hand, there is relatively — but not absolutely — high normative pressure upon the parents to make sure that their children do well in school; that is, a relatively high percentage of mothers in the project and the surrounding

TABLE 7

PERCENT WHO WANT A SON OF THEIRS TO ATTAIN MORE THAN HIGH SCHOOL
EDUCATION, BY AREA AMONG HUSBANDLESS AND MARRIED MOTHERS

Mother	AREA				
	Evans	Grant	Park	Stern	Neighborhood*
Husbandless	33.3	31.0	2.9	24.1	13.0
	(21)	(29)	(35)	(29)	(23)
Married	21.7	16.4	22.5	18.3	45.4
	(69)	(67)	(49)	(60)	(163)

*In this table and in succeeding tables, "neighborhood" refers to the four neighborhoods surrounding each project; there are too few husbandless mothers in each neighborhood to permit separate calculation of percentages.

neighborhood report that they would think worse of someone if his children did not do well in school.[11]

The profile for Grant, the project in the other low-income neighborhood, is somewhat different. The schools are more often thought to be good. Children are generally viewed as trying to do well in school, and parents in the project are particularly likely to be seen as valuing education. Normative pressure upon the parents in regard to their children's education is less widespread than in Park and more like the other projects.

Evans and Stern projects have similar profiles. The neighborhoods are ones in which the parents are universally seen as valuing education. Nearly all the children are generally viewed as trying to do well in school. The schools are considered good or excellent. Within the projects, however, the parents are less commonly believed to value education and the children thought to be trying to do well in school, compared to the respondents in the surrounding neighborhoods. Nor-

[11]It is possible that the proportion saying they think worse of someone if their children do not do well in school is not a valid indicator of normative pressure. Two considerations should be noted. There may be a greater sense of privacy in middle-class neighborhoods, making normative judgments of others less likely; but that would not nullify the interpretation of the question. There may also be a tendency for persons of low socioeconomic status to be more readily coerced into choosing one of the forced alternatives posed in the question. Other persons might feel freer to volunteer responses such as "it depends" or "it does not make any difference." Let one combine the responses of "think worse" and "it depends," which imply normative judgment under certain conditions. Park neighborhood still has the highest proportion indicating normative pressure: 56 percent of the mothers say they would think worse or it depends. Stern and Grant neighborhoods, however, now have higher normative pressure than Evans neighborhood. Among the projects, normative pressure is relatively high in Stern as well as Park.

TABLE 8

PERCENT WHO WOULD BE DISAPPOINTED IF THEIR CHILDREN EARNED LESS THAN B,
BY AREA AMONG HUSBANDLESS AND UNMARRIED MOTHERS

Mother	AREA				
	Evans	Grant	Park	Stern	Neighborhood
Husbandless	85.0	65.5	68.6	69.0	73.9
	(20)	(29)	(35)	(29)	(23)
Married	65.2	68.7	55.1	44.8	69.5
	(69)	(67)	(49)	(58)	(164)

mative pressure in the projects and in the surrounding neighborhoods is relatively low. For different reasons, then, the mothers in Evans, Stern, and even Grant are likely to see greater educational opportunities for their children than the mothers in Park.

Now one can look at the effects of these differences in residential areas upon the educational aspirations of the mothers. The aspirations for years of education to be completed by their children is markedly depressed among the husbandless mothers in Park project. (See Table 7.) The husbandless mothers in the other three projects, however, are likely to have high aspirations. Furthermore, in comparison with married mothers, the husbandless in Park are much less likely to have high aspirations; but the husbandless mothers in the other three projects are somewhat more likely to have high aspirations.[12] Considering the mothers living in all the surrounding neighborhoods, a high proportion of the married mothers, but only a moderate proportion of the husbandless, are high aspirers. This is in large part due to the fact that only about

---

[12]In this sample, nonwhites are less likely than whites to aspire for more than a high school education for their sons. Since Park is predominately nonwhite, one has to consider the possibility that the area differences are attributable to the racial composition of the areas. The data in Table 7 show that married mothers in Park are not particularly likely to have low aspirations; therefore, the depression of aspirations among the husbandless mothers in Park cannot be attributable simply to race.

If one controls for race, the pattern seems to be maintained, though the number of white husbandless mothers in Park is very small, and nonwhites in Evans and Grant are few. None of the three white, husbandless mothers in Park aspires for more than a high school education for a son. Among the nonwhites, of the ten husbandless mothers living in Stern, three aspire to at least some college; of the 13 living in the neighborhoods, only one aspires for more than a high school education; of the 32 in Park, only one aspires for more than a high school education for a son. In Evans and Grant, however, the nonwhites may be even less likely than those in Park to have high aspirations; the one nonwhite in Evans does not have high aspirations, nor do the six in Grant.

one-fifth of the complete families in the sample live in Park neighborhood while about one-half of the fatherless families live there.

As noted earlier, aspirations about marks in school are not as dependent upon environmental circumstances as are aspirations about years of school to be completed. Consequently, aspirations about school marks are not affected by residential area in the same degree or way as aspirations about years of schooling. Thus, in each area, husbandless mothers are more likely than married mothers to be disappointed if their children earn less than B's. (See Table 8.) Even the husbandless mothers in Park are as likely to have high aspirations as are those in all the other areas except Evans, in which most husbandless mothers are high aspirers.

All these findings indicate that husbandless mothers who live in handicapping circumstances are likely to depress aspirations depending upon such circumstances for realization. But, in circumstances which are not handicapping, aspirations are likely to be high. These findings also help account for the previously cited finding: working-class children in middle-class schools tend to have higher aspirations than their counterparts in predominantly working-class schools. Apparently, parents of the latter group are influenced by the opportunities and realities of the schools and the prevailing student efforts. Faced with an interrelated set of obstacles, the parents restrict aspirations for their children, reinforcing the children's own peer influences.

CONDUCT REGARDING CHILDREN'S EDUCATION

Husbandless mothers, at least under favorable circumstances, are somewhat more likely than married mothers to value education for their children and to have high educational aspirations. But implementing these wishes and desires is likely to pose greater difficulties for husbandless than married mothers.

Parental effort in regard to the children's school work is not a simple matter. It is impossible to say that one line of action will always have certain consequences. The child's own interests and abilities in school affect which line of action is most appropriate. Sometimes attempts at direct control and intervention may be most effective in promoting the child's best efforts. At other times, indirect control or simply indications of interest and support may be more appropriate. Given the husbandless mothers' concerns about their children, the danger to their children's educational achievement may not be lack of interest and support but too great direct control and too little general and indirect support.

The mothers' reports about whether the parents or the children decide upon the amount of time the children spend on schoolwork provide one indicator of parental control.[13] The respondents were asked to report about one child, the "study child." If the parent decides and the study child is older than the age at which most parents decide, this is considered "over-control." If the child decides and he is much younger than the usual age at which parents allow the child to decide, this is called "under control." If the child is only a year or two younger than the usual age, it is called "early independence." In other cases, control is at the usual age. In the aggregate, there is no difference between husbandless and married mothers in the proportion who report different kinds of control.

I suggested that the appropriate parental action in regard to a child's schoolwork varies with the interests and abilities of the students. It is possible that the husbandless mother's concern for the well-being and educational achievement of her child results in less responsiveness to the peculiarities of his school position than is true of married mothers. As a matter of fact, this study finds that married mothers who are satisfied with their children's marks are unlikely to report controlling the child over the usual age; while those who are not satisfied do tend to report over-control. Among the husbandless mothers, there is no relationship.[14] The point is made clearer if we look at parental control among mothers with students who are reported to have high marks (A's or B's) and among those whose children have low marks (C's or D's). In the latter case, there is no difference between husbandless and married mothers in parental control. But, among mothers of children with high marks, husbandless mothers are much less likely to report

---

[13]In asking about actual conduct, the questions were phrased as specifically as possible. Also one child was selected as the "study child" about whom questions were asked; this also increased the specificity of the questions.

Control of time spent on schoolwork is considered only for mothers with study children eight to 18 years old. Under-control refers to cases in which the parent does not decide and the study child is eight to ten years old. Early independence refers to cases in which the parent does not decide and the child is 11 to 13. Usual control refers to cases where the parent decides and the child is eight to 13, or the parent does not decide and the child is 14 to 18. Over-control refers to cases in which the parent decides and the child is 14 to 18.

Fifty percent of the mothers of 13-year-olds decide, and 32 percent of the mothers of 14-year-old study children report the parents decide the amount of time the study child spends on his or her schoolwork.

[14]Satisfaction with the study child's schoolwork was trichotomized: very satisfied, fairly satisfied, and somewhat or very dissatisfied. Among the married mothers, the relationship between satisfaction with schoolwork and control of time spent on schoolwork is high: Kendall Tau C is $+.24$, based upon 197 cases, $p=.001$ (Chi-square is 20.27, 6 df, $p=.01$); among the husbandless mothers, the Kendall Tau C is $+.05$.

under-control.[15] At least some husbandless mothers do not relax their pressure for educational achievement when a married mother would.

What the mothers report doing or saying to the child is also significant. As mentioned earlier, the mothers were asked whether or not they were satisfied with the school marks of the study child. If the mother said she was satisfied, she was asked if the study child ever had a mark which she thought was too low. If the mother was dissatisfied *or* if the child ever received a low mark, she was asked if she (or her husband) did or said anything to the child and what that was. Although the husbandless mothers seem to be more likely than married mothers to be concerned about the child's schoolwork and more demanding, they are more likely only to urge the child on, while married mothers are more likely to aid the child directly in school work or intervene with the school.

Parental support of children's educational efforts may also be given by the demonstration of interest in those efforts. One form of demonstration is participation in school affairs. The mothers were asked: Since last September, did you (or your husband) —

(1) Go to school on parent's day to visit a class or a program put on by the children?

(2) Attend PTA and/or Mothers' Club meetings?

(3) Go to a neighborhood meeting about school problems?

By asking married mothers about their own and their husbands' conduct, comparisons between married and husbandless mothers actually are comparing husbandless mothers to married parents. This turns out to be of limited importance, however, since husbands rarely go to the school on parents' days without their wives and practically never go to PTA meetings without their wives.[16]

---

[15]Among the mothers with study children usually earning A's or B's, married mothers are more likely to under-control than are husbandless mothers. Chi-square is 9.45, 3 df, based upon 190 cases, p=.05; Kendall Tau C is +.14, p=.01.

Control is related to marks among married mothers but not among husbandless mothers. This is similar to the findings on the relationship between type of control and satisfaction with schoolwork.

[16]Responses to another series of questions suggest an additional complication. After the questions about formal involvement in school affairs, the mothers were asked, "Besides any of those things, during the past school year, did you (or your husband) ever go to school to see any of your child(ren)'s teachers or counselors?" If a mother responded affirmatively, she was also asked, "Did the teacher ask that you (or your husband) come or did you (or your husband) go on your own?" More than half of the husbandless and the married mothers answered yes to the first question; but the married mothers were more likely to say that they went on their own than did the husbandless mothers. Among those who said they did see a teacher or counselor, about one-third of the husbandless mothers and fewer than ten percent of the married mothers said they were asked to come. This should be taken into consideration in examining the responses to the question about what action the parents take if they are dissatisfied with the schoolwork of their study children.

TABLE 9

TYPE OF PARENTAL CONTROL OF TIME WHICH STUDY CHILD SPENDS ON SCHOOL-WORK, BY AREA AMONG HUSBANDLESS AND MARRIED MOTHERS

Type of Control	A. HUSBANDLESS MOTHERS				
	Area				
	Evans	Grant	Park	Stern	Neighborhood
Under control Parent does not decide and child is 8-10	0.0	9.5	3.7	5.0	8.3
Early independence Parent does not decide and child is 11-13	30.0	19.1	25.9	5.0	16.7
Usual control Parent decides and child is 8-13 or parent does not decide and child is 14-18	70.0	57.1	70.4	75.0	58.3
Over-control Parent decides and child is 14-18	0.0	14.3	0.0	15.0	16.7
Total %	100.0	100.0	100.0	100.0	100.0
(N)	(10)	(21)	(27)	(20)	(12)

Type of Control	B. MARRIED MOTHERS				
	Area				
	Evans	Grant	Park	Stern	Neighborhood
Under-control Parent does not decide and child is 8-10	15.0	19.4	10.0	17.4	14.1
Early independence Parent does not decide and child is 11-13	10.0	19.4	15.0	8.7	16.2
Usual control Parent decides and child is 8-13, or parent does not decide and child is 14-18	65.0	55.6	75.0	60.9	64.7
Over-control Parent decides and child is 14-18	10.0	5.6	0.0	13.0	5.1
Total %	100.0	100.0	100.0	100.0	100.1
(N)	(20)	(36)	(20)	(23)	(99)

Parental participation in parents' day events is most common, followed by PTA meetings; neighborhood meetings are least likely to obtain participation. The three items of parental involvement in the schools are related so that they form a scale. That is, mothers going to neighborhood meetings about schools also go to PTA meetings and visit the school on parents' days; if they go to PTA meetings and do not go to neighborhood meetings, they still go to school on parents' days. A scale of involvement in school affairs was constructed of four scale types: (1) not involved at all; (2) visit school on parents' days only; (3) visit school and attend PTA meetings only; and (4) visit school, attend PTA, and attend neighborhood meetings.[17] Usually, involvement is dichotomized into low (scale types 1 or 2) or high (scale types 3 or 4) parental involvement. Husbandless mothers are slightly less likely to report parental involvement in the schools.

In addition to the direct involvement of parents in the educational efforts of their children, the intellectual climate of the home is an important condition affecting the educational achievement of children. On the whole, husbandless mothers are just as likely or unlikely to say that reading — to read books or to read magazines — is their most preferred leisure-time activity. Husbandless mothers are slightly more likely to have an encyclopedia at home, compared to married mothers in each housing project; but they are less likely to go to concerts, plays, and museums.

Neighborhood

Now one needs to consider to what extent, if any, residence in different kinds of neighborhoods affects the educationally relevant conduct of the mothers. First, I wish to examine parental control of the time the study child spends on schoolwork. It appears that such control is affected by the area of residence. (See Table 9.) In Grant the husbandless mothers are likely to report under- or over-control while the married mothers report allowing early independence. In Park neither husbandless nor married mothers report over-control, but neither do they report under-control more frequently than do mothers in other areas. Apparently, the more severe circumstances of Park result in the husbandless mothers trying to maintain control when the children are still young; but, when the children are older, the competition of the peers is too great and control is not maintained.

In Evans married mothers are particularly likely to report over-control, but the husbandless mothers report early independence. The husbandless mothers in Evans act as if the children's peers and schools are adequate and there is little need for parental control beyond the usual age. In Stern project both married and husbandless mothers disproportionally

---

[17]The coefficient of reproducibility is .88, using the methods suggested by W. H. Goodenough, as described in Allen L. Edwards, *Techniques of Attitude Scale Construction*, New York: Appleton-Century-Crofts, 1957, pp. 184-188. The minimal marginal reproducibility for the set of items is .77; see Edwards, pp. 191-193.

report over-control rather than control at the usual age. It seems that the great contrast between Stern tenants and Stern neighborhood residents constitutes a challenge to the mothers in the project. The response in the educational sphere is competitive and not retreatist.

What the parents do if they are dissatisfied or disappointed by the grades their children receive in school also differs by residential area. Husbandless mothers in Stern and Evans are least likely to be dissatisfied with the study children's marks or, if satisfied, to think the child received too low a mark. Furthermore, if the husbandless mothers in Evans do say or do anything, it is usually only to tell the child to study more, to urge him on, or to talk to him about his difficulties. The husbandless mothers in Stern, compared to those in the other projects, are particularly likely to report helping the child with his schoolwork. Husbandless mothers in Park and Grant are particularly likely to intervene with the school.

Apparently the Evans' husbandless mothers are most likely to be content and, if action is felt necessary, to take the minimal kind. The husbandless in Stern, even when they feel action is necessary, are not likely to talk with the teacher or otherwise intervene. The finding that both husbandless and married mothers in Park and Grant are particularly likely to intervene in the schools calls for special notice. One might expect that "better" schools would be more receptive to parental intervention than "poorer" schools. This overlooks two other considerations. Parents of children in schools which the parents do not consider good may be more likely to feel the school and its teachers are at fault if their children do not do well. They have general and specific reasons for thinking it appropriate to complain. Secondly, parents in low-income public housing projects may well feel at a disadvantage in complaining and intervening in schools with a predominantly middle-class student and parent constituency. Parents in Stern project would feel particularly out of place in relationship to the schools their children attend.

Participation in school affairs varies by residential area, particularly among husbandless mothers. (See Table 10.) Thus, husbandless mothers in Stern tend to have high formal involvement in school affairs. The characteristics of the neighborhood around the project and the relationship of the project tenants to the neighborhood apparently account for this. Involvement in school affairs among Stern neighborhood parents is high. This means that there are more opportunities for parents to participate in school affairs, more examples of other parents doing so, and even pressure from children to have their parents participate. The mothers in Stern project and particularly the husbandless mothers usually respond by trying to keep up with this pattern. Although the

TABLE 10

PERCENT OF FAMILIES WITH HIGH PARENTAL INVOLVEMENT IN SCHOOL AFFAIRS, BY
AREA AMONG FATHERLESS AND COMPLETE FAMILIES

	AREA				
Family Type	Evans	Grant	Park	Stern	Neighborhood
Husbandless	18.8 (16)	14.3 (21)	39.4 (33)	40.9 (22)	17.7 (17)
Complete	17.2 (35)	24.5 (53)	25.1 (28)	31.3 (32)	42.7 (110)

TABLE 11

PERCENT OF FAMILIES WHICH HAVE HIGH PARENTAL INVOLVEMENT IN SCHOOL
AFFAIRS BY MOTHER'S WORK STATUS AMONG FATHERLESS AND
COMPLETE FAMILIES

	WORK STATUS		
Family	Work Full Time	Work Part Time	Not Working
Fatherless	20.6 (29)	28.0 (25)	33.3 (54)
Complete	30.3 (43)	35.7 (70)	31.7 (142)

socioeconomic differences between project and neighborhood residents
may inhibit informal direct confrontations with the school teachers and
officials, apparently it does not inhibit most mothers from formal, if
passive, involvement. Mothers from Stern project sit at the back of the
meeting room and do not participate in the discussions. More than one-
third of the husbandless mothers in Stern project, however, withdraw
from *any* involvement. The stimulus of Stern neighborhood is a challenge
which many husbandless mothers meet while others are defeated by it.

A different explanation is needed for the relatively large proportion
of mothers, particularly husbandless mothers, in Park project who show
high involvement in school affairs. On the whole, involvement tends to
be low in the neighborhood around Park. The mothers of Park project
believe that the neighborhood education influences are not good, but
they are not particularly likely to try to compensate for this by dealing
directly with their children. Apparently, informal and formal involvement with the schools is their way of expressing their concern and desire

for the educational achievement of their children. Again, however, more than one-third of the husbandless mothers apparently do not attempt this kind of compensation.

One other point must be noted in regard to Park. At the time of the survey, a special educational program was underway in the schools serving the area around Park. This special program, in addition to trying to improve the education of the students in the area, also made attempts to involve parents. This does not fully expain the high participation of many husbandless mothers in Park project, however, since the involvement was not generally high in the neighborhood. It could mean that the interest and concern of husbandless mothers were more readily accepted by the schools or that husbandless mothers were particularly responsive to the appeals.

In Grant project, high involvement in school affairs is relatively rare. The stimulus for involvement from the outside is not as great as in Stern neighborhood, nor are project and neighborhood influences viewed as unfavorably as in Park project; thus, compensating for the project and neighborhood influences seems less necessary. They can take the position that the people in charge of the school know best how to administer it.

High involvement is also relatively uncommon in Evans project. Most parents in the surrounding neighborhood, although of moderate socioeconomic status, are not highly involved in school affairs. Even more than in the case of Grant, the Evans mothers believe that the area influences are not unfavorable to the educational achievement of their children — they need not compensate for it by extra effort.

Finally, I wish to note briefly any variations in indicators of the cultural level at home among the different residential areas. Having an encyclopedia in the home varies little by area among the husbandless mothers except that husbandless mothers in Stern project are most likely to report having one. In each project, however, husbandless mothers are slightly more likely than married mothers to have encyclopedias; but in the neighborhoods the situation is reversed. Going to concerts, plays, and museums does not vary much by area among husbandless mothers; although, again, it is slightly higher in Stern project than in the other areas. The proportion of mothers who read books and magazines and read books of a relatively serious nature is particularly high in Evans.

Income and Employment

Employment is unrelated to degree of control among husbandless mothers. Income, too, is generally unrelated to control over the time the child spends on schoolwork. Only among the husbandless is there a tendency for those who are not poor to over-control rather than exercise control at the usual age.

Income has a surprising lack of effect upon participation in school affairs. It is true that, among married mothers, low income is strongly associated with low involvement. Among the husbandless mothers, however, this is not the case. Low income does not denote low social status to the same degree for husbandless mothers as it does for married mothers. Husbandless mothers with low incomes, particularly if they live in public housing, are not as likely as married mothers to feel stigmatized and therefore inhibited from participation in neighborhood or community affairs.

Low income among husbandless mothers is highly associated with nonemployment. Full-time employment interferes with the husbandless mothers' high involvement in school affairs. (See Table 11.) Although employed husbandless mothers are particularly likely to have high educational aspirations for their children and to value education, they are less likely to be highly involved in school affairs, compared to nonemployed husbandless mothers.

TABLE 12

PERCENT OF FAMILIES HAVING HIGH PARENTAL INVOLVEMENT IN SCHOOL AFFAIRS, BY MOTHER'S ASPIRATIONS FOR YEARS OF EDUCATION FOR SON AMONG FATHERLESS AND COMPLETE FAMILIES

Family	EDUCATIONAL ASPIRATIONS	
	12 Years or Less	13 Years or More
Husbandless	28.6 (91)	27.8 (18)
Complete	29.1 (179)	40.3 (77)

CONCLUSIONS

On the whole, the husbandless mothers are very concerned about the educational achievement of their children. The analysis of the relationship between control of study time and school marks of the study child shows that husbandless mothers do not relax the pressure for academic achievement when married mothers might. Lacking some of the indirect and informal supports and influences upon their children and also lacking the secure base for future support and encouragement, husbandless mothers try to push hard where they can. This pressure may sometimes be excessive.[18]

In regard to the effects of income and employment, the patterns among married mothers are familiar ones. Those who are poor have lower aspirations and are less likely to participate in school affairs; their children do not do as well in school as the children of married mothers of higher income; and maternal employment does not make any real difference. Among the husbandless mothers, however, the relationships are not so obvious. Low income does depress aspirations for years of education, but it does not affect how well the child does in school nor the mothers' involvement in school affairs. Maternal employment is associated with higher aspirations and marks, but it seems to depress involvement in school affairs. In short, among married mothers the several aspects of educationally relevant attitudes and conduct are mutually consistent and even consistent with the academic achievement of the child. This is not as true among the husbandless mothers. (See Table 12.) It is as if they cling to what they can and even compensate for difficulties, but some obstacles are so great that they affect particular attitudes and actions. The subjective result must be considerable tension.

Residential areas have interesting and complex effects. In Stern project, many husbandless mothers are particularly likely to engage in behavior which is supportive and conducive to their children's achievement. Neither the values nor aspirations of the Stern mothers seem to explain this. Normative pressures from inside or outside the project do not seem to account for this conduct, since there is generally a low degree of normative consensus and social integration. It appears that responding to the models available in the surrounding neighborhood, perhaps communicated by the children in the schools, is one of the major processes by which the effect occurs. In addition, accommodation probably plays a major role. The surrounding neighborhood imposes a dual challenge: the schools have a student composition and personnel style that fosters some academic competitiveness, but the surrounding area also includes children and parents who are not part of this academic competition. For example, observations of a group of adolescents from

---

[18]Direct pressure may not have the desired consequences. One study of dropouts concluded that families of in-school students "seemed to focus their efforts on inculcating in the child the desire to do what was expected of him. . . . Families of the dropouts . . . seemed to rely more on overt pressures in the form of coaxing and persuading. . . . Many of these families spoke of their children having a mind of their own, apparently implying that they were unable to influence them in their decision to leave school, in spite of a desire to do so." Fortune V. Mannino, "Family Patterns Related to School Persistence," *Journal of Educational Sociology*, 35 (January, 1962), pp. 193-202.

Stern and the surrounding neighborhood revealed that nearly all the members of the group were uninterested in academic subjects and had only vague aspirations even about employment.[19] In such circumstances, a concerned parent might be expected to put extra pressure upon the child or otherwise try to structure his situation to encourage school achievement and fend off possible adverse peer influences. In some cases, of course, and particularly as the child becomes older, such efforts may be abandoned as futile.

In Park the husbandless mothers face much more severe educational obstacles for their children. Those who try to overcome these obstacles do so by various supportive activities rather than by direct control or aid. Again, neither the values nor aspirations of Park husbandless mothers seem to account for this. Although normative pressure is relatively high in Park project and neighborhood, it is in an absolute sense not very great. The conduct of the husbandless mothers is probably an accommodation to the difficulties of the area, an attempt at differentiating themselves and overcoming the obstacles. This is quite a different kind of challenge, and the models are not positive but negative. There is also less consistency and faith in the outcome — witness the low aspirations.

In Grant the husbandless mothers feel less educationally challenged by the neighborhood either positively or negatively. They can feel more relaxed. The area has almost as high a juvenile delinquency rate and therefore is almost as likely to be viewed as a source of certain undesired influences upon their children as is Park. But the mothers are not likely to see educational obstacles arising from widespread academic disinterest among parents and their children. The children can be allowed freer rein than in Park. Some husbandless mothers in Grant respond to the threat of delinquency by over-controlling the decision about the time their children can spend with friends.

Finally, in Evans the challenge is least threatening, and the husbandless mothers can most easily relax efforts to push their children. But they are also not stimulated to exert themselves in efforts which are educationally relevant for their children. Nevertheless, the generally supportive educational climate of the schools, neighbors, and the chil-

---

[19]The observations of David Cumming are summarized in Helen Icken Safa, "A Case Study of Adolescent Boys in Public Housing," *Social Mobility and Housing Case Studies in Participant Observation #1*, Syracuse University Youth Development Center, 1965, mimeographed; and in David Cumming and Elaine Cumming, "The Everyday Life of Delinquent Boys," in *Among the People: Studies of the Urban Poor*, ed. by Irwin Deutscher and Elizabeth J. Thompson, New York: Basic Books, Inc., forthcoming.

dren's peers, as well as the general level of educationally relevant activities, makes compensating parental effort unnecessary.

The findings suggest that, given supportive environmental conditions, the concern of husbandless mothers for the well-being of their children will be appropriate. But, given the harsh conditions too often associated with poor fatherless families, that concern is often expressed in ways which do not aid the children's educational achievement. Depending upon the social policies implemented, the findings can have hopeful or worrisome implications.

The Absent Father in Negro Families: Cause or Symptom?

HERBERT L. WASSERMAN

. . .

STUDY DESIGN

THE PRESENT STUDY FOCUSED ON THE FAMILY STRUCTURE IN A LOWER class Negro population as a presumed causal factor in the school achievement of boys within these families. It was undertaken to probe beneath the glossary of terms — such as unstable, disorganized, hard-core, multi-problem — to try and locate a diagnostic conceptualization that could in turn offer some insight into what programs of action might be significant.

In a subsample of lower class Negro families, we have attempted to compare the school performance of boys who are systematically selected in terms of their external characteristics but who have had contrasting parental experiences. In one set of families the father was present, in the other he was absent.

The sample consisted of 117 Negro families, living in a low income housing development and including at least one son in school who would already have reached age ten but not yet sixteen at the time of the data collection. The lower limit of age ten was chosen in order to allow for at least three years of school experience prior to the study. An upper limit of sixteen was necessary to preclude the possibility that boys over sixteen would no longer be enrolled in school and easy access to their school records might be difficult.

By limiting the sample to Negro families of low socioeconomic status living in housing projects, our attempt was to disentangle the causal variables from those that are linked to race, socioeconomic status, and

Paper presented at the National Conference on Social Welfare, San Francisco, California, May 24, 1968.

geographic location, as well as the experience of living in a housing project. By holding these socio-cultural variables constant we are not eliminating their effect but are attempting to set their impact aside momentarily in order more effectively to examine the relative significance of the family's internal structural qualities.

As the study progressed, it became clear that any definition of fatherless families would be subject to serious ambiguities unless one considered the circumstances of the father's loss, the duration and persistence of his absence, as well as the extent to which other male adults such as step-fathers had acted as consistent replacements. The father absent category was therefore defined as, "Absence of the boy's natural father as a result of marital disruption without any male replacement during the most recent three year period." Families with variations of these characteristics were examined separately in a mixed category. The breakdown included 45 father present, 46 father absent and 26 in the mixed category. We are here presenting only the first two, or so-called "pure" groups though our findings were substantially the same using the larger groups.

Data was collected from mothers using pre-coded and open-ended questions. Information on school performance for each of the boys during the prior three year period was obtained by inspection of school records.

CHARACTERISTICS OF THE SAMPLE

Approximately 60% of mothers studied were born in one of the southern states while only 21% were born in the Greater Boston area. Almost half had lived in the housing projects for five years or longer.

Income limits for families in the federally subsidized housing developments included in the study ranged from under $3,600 for those with one or two children to under $6,000 for families with eight or more children.

There is almost no social class differentiation as indicated by standard vocational indices. About a third of the women in the sample had fathers with occupations above the level of semi-skilled labor.

Reviewing the data from our sample, mothers in complete and fatherless families do not appear to differ markedly in their overall characteristics or style of life. No statistically significant differences were found in a group of background variables which included geographic area of birth and residence, educational level, number of siblings, respondents' ordinal positions, or the work history of the respondents' mother.

There is, however, a statistically significant relationship between the natal families of respondents and current marital status. Women who were brought up within intact families are more likely to be living in one. . . . Other distinctions between intact and broken families appear to be those inherently associated with the absence of the father or those related to different stages in the family life cycle. Husbandless mothers as a group have somewhat smaller families, are more likely to receive public welfare and to have full-time employment outside the home. The fact that more of the youngest and oldest boys ages ten to fifteen are found in the father present groups is consistent with the finding that mothers with intact families tend to be somewhat older and to have been married longer. They are also more likely to have continued having children during the most recent years than women who have been without husbands in the home.

An additional finding should also be noted. Women in this sample do not live with their mothers in tri-generational families. They have not developed their close adult relationships with mother nor do they depend on mother either for instrumental supplies or for emotional support. One implication of this is that commonly held stereotypes about the nature of "matriarchal" patterns in Negro families may obscure the true quality of the relationship between Negro mothers and their daughters.

SCHOOL PERFORMANCE

The analysis of the school performance for each of 117 boys in the sample took place only after each of their mothers had been interviewed and authorizations were obtained to enter the 15 different schools in which academic records were examined. Boys were enrolled in grades three through ten with a median number of seven school years completed. For the total sample, the median age range for the boys is 13 years with no significant differences between the groups.

A school achievement index was developed by first combining letter mark ratings in five major subjects areas over the past three years and deriving a mean score for each boy. Secondly, comparable measures for boys at different grade levels were accomplished by use of an age appropriate scale. Finally, an index was constructed by means of additive scores for age appropriate grade levels with the average of all grades available in major subjects over the most recent three year period.

When the school performance index is examined for differences between boys from families in which the father was present and those from which he was absent, only minor variations are found. Although a slightly higher percentage of pupils at the highest achievement level are found within the intact families, the differences are not statistically significant. Moreover, at each level within the range of school achievement, boys from broken and complete families are closely matched.

. . .

In addition to school performance, two other characteristics of the boys were also examined as outcome variables: namely, the incidence of behavior problems and/or symptoms of nervousness or internalized emotional conflict. Mothers were asked whether and to what extent their sons had shown evidence of groups of symptoms including eneuresis, fearfulness, speech problems, facial tics or tremors, etc. Items were included in a scale and boys were compared according to high and low scores.

The results for the total sample showed 62% of the boys in the high group and 38% scoring low. The father-absent boys included 74% with a high incidence of symptoms as compared with 50% of boys from intact families. This difference is statistically significant at beyond the .02 probability level.

The fact that this finding was not coincident with that of school performance may reflect the fact that fearful, overprotected, or withdrawn youngsters or those with problems of sexual identity are not only those who are highly conforming but may often be among the students with higher grades.

. . .

With regard to behavior problems, mothers questioned about their son's conduct both inside and outside the school reported far greater behavioral difficulty at school than in the general community. For the total sample, 87% of the boys were reported rarely or never in trouble outside school, while within school, only 61% were considered well-behaved. School records, including conduct marks, truancy figures, and other data largely validated the mother's reports.

In view of an earlier finding that boys whose fathers are present receive more discipline than fatherless boys, it is of note to find more behavioral problems reported for the latter group. Some behavioral difficulty is reported for 49% of fatherless boys, according to school records, and for 58% according to their mothers. For the father present group, 25% received poor conduct marks at school, again closely validating mothers who, for this group, report that 40% were problems.

. . .

The relationship between social background and school performance is not simple. There is convincing evidence of the influence of background variables on patterns of perceptual, language and cognitive development, and subsequent diffusion of such patterns into all areas of the child's academic performance. An understanding of these problems requires not only delineating the underlying skills in which these children are not proficient but what is perhaps most important, the specific aspects of their family background which are most influential in producing various kinds of deficits. As yet, we have no external criterion for evaluating the characteristics of family life in terms of how well it fosters educational achievement.

. . .

The Ordeal of the Negro Family

DANIEL PATRICK MOYNIHAN

. . .

THE CUMULATIVE RESULT OF UNEMPLOYMENT AND LOW INCOME, AND probably also of excessive dependence upon the income of women, has produced an unmistakable crisis in the Negro family, and raises the serious question of whether or not this crisis is beginning to create conditions which tend to reinforce the cycle that produced it in the first instance. The crisis would probably exist in any event, but it becomes acute in the context of the extraordinary rise in Negro population in recent years.

At the time of the founding of the nation, one American in five was a Negro. The proportion declined steadily until it was only one in ten by 1920, where it held until the 1950's when it began to rise. Since 1950 the nonwhite population has grown at a rate of 2.4 per cent per year, compared with 1.7 per cent for the total population. One American in nine is nonwhite today. If the rates of growth between 1950 and 1964 continue, one in eight will be nonwhite by 1972. In 1964 among children under the age of fourteen, 15 per cent were nonwhite. Under one year of age, 16.4 per cent were nonwhite: one in six. Although white and nonwhite fertility rates have declined somewhat since 1959, the non-white/white ratio of 1.42 has not narrowed. Between 1950 and 1960 the size of the white family changed very little, while that of nonwhites increased from 4.07 persons to 4.30 persons.

Perhaps most significantly, the gap between what might be called the generation rate between white and nonwhites is particularly wide. Negro women not only have more children, but have them earlier. Thus in 1960, there were 1,247 children ever born per thousand ever-married nonwhite women fifteen to nineteen years of age, as against only 725 for white women, a ratio of 1.7. The effect of this burgeoning population on family life is accentuated by its concentration among the poor.

Reprinted by permission of the publisher and author from *Daedalus* (Fall 1965), pp. 758-70.

In 1960 nonwhite mothers age thirty-five to thirty-nine with family incomes over $10,000 had 2.9 children; those with less than $2,000 had 5.3. A peculiar, and possibly important phenomenon, which might be termed the Frazier effect, after the distinguished author of *Black Bourgeoisie,* is that Negro upper-class families have fewer children than their white counterparts, while lower-class families have more. In 1960 nonwhite women (married once, husband present) age thirty-five to forty-four married early to undereducated laborers had 4.7 children, as against 3.8 for white women in the same situation. But nonwhite women in that age bracket, married at twenty-two or over to professional or technical workers with a year or more of college, had only 1.9 children, as against 2.4 for whites.

The impact of family size on the life chances of children and the strength of the family can be measured by a number of statistics. The Task Force on Manpower Conservation (1963) studied the nation's young men who failed to pass the Selective Service written test. A passing score on this test indicates the achievement of a seventh- or eighth-grade education. Three out of four of the nonwhite young men failing the test came from families with four or more children. One out of two came from families with six or more children.

A Negro child born to a large family is more likely to be reared in a broken family. Such are the strains of rearing large families with marginal incomes and unemployed fathers. In the urban U. S. in 1960 there were 154,000 one-child nonwhite families headed by married men age twenty to twenty-four with wives present. There were 19,000 such families headed by women separated from their husbands, one-eighth as many as whole families. There were a similar number of such husband-wife families with four or more children, 152,000, but there were 39,000 headed by married women separated from their husbands — one-fourth the number with both husband and wife. Poor families break under the responsibilities imposed by a large number of children. Children from these families become the nation's draft rejectees, because — among other reasons — they have spent a basic learning period in an institution too large for its resources and often with one of the instructors missing.

Poverty is both the cause and the result. In 1963 the median income of nonwhite families was $3,465, about half the $6,548 median of whites. The magnitude of the income gap is illustrated by the fact that incomes were lower in nonwhite families with employed heads than in white families with unemployed heads. What the long trend of the gap will be is not, of course, clear, but from 1960 to 1963 the nonwhite median family income as a per cent of white declined from 55 to 53.

In March 1964 nearly 20 million persons fourteen years and over were living in families with annual incomes under $3,000. Nonwhite persons accounted for a quarter of those living in such families. But nearly half of all nonwhite youths under fourteen are living in families with incomes under $3,000. Nonwhites make up 40 per cent of the children living in such families. Using a flexible scale that relates required family income to family size, the Department of Health, Education and Welfare has estimated that 60 per cent of the Negro children in America today are growing up in poverty-stricken families. In these circumstances the stability of the Negro family, still grievously impaired by the heritage of slavery and segregation, would seem to have been weakened still further.

The fundamental problem is the position of the male. To begin with, the Negro father tends to hold jobs with a minimum either of prestige or income. In 1963, fully one-third of the nonwhite family heads who worked at all had their longest (or only) job in farming, domestic service, or laboring occupations. For these persons, income was well under half that of all families with working heads. In addition to low income and low prestige, the Negro father is burdened with savage rates of unemployment at precisely that moment in his life when family responsibilities are most heavy. The ratio of nonwhite to white unemployment is highest among men between the ages of twenty-five and thirty-four — 2.57. This compares with a ratio of 2.17 for all men fourteen and over. The next highest ratio for men was 2.48, at thirty-five to forty-four years of age. In 1963, 29 per cent of nonwhite males in the work force were unemployed at one time or another. Three out of ten nonwhite men who were unemployed in 1963 had three or more periods of unemployment; one-fifth of all unemployed nonwhites were out of work half the year or more.

A measure of the distress of Negro men in their middle years is that they disappear — literally. In 1964 for every 100 white and nonwhite women age thirty to thirty-four years, there were 99.4 white, but only 86.7 nonwhite, men. The Negroes had not died — they begin to reappear after forty — they had simply become invisible. (An interesting question is whether an accurate enumeration of those missing males would not significantly increase current unemployment rates for Negro males.)

It is in the perspective of the underemployment of the Negro father that we must regard the Negro mother as being overemployed. From 1957 to 1964 the civilian labor-force participation rate of nonwhite men dropped from 80.8 per cent to 75.6 per cent. The ratio of nonwhite to white labor-force participation rates *dropped* from .99 to .97.

During this period, the civilian labor force participation of nonwhite women *rose* somewhat over-all. It rose particularly in ages twenty to twenty-four, from 46.6 per cent in 1957 to 53.6 per cent in 1964; in ages twenty-five to thirty-four years, from 50.4 per cent in 1957 to 52.8 per cent in 1964; and in ages forty-five to fifty-four where it reached 62.3 per cent in that year. Typically, the nonwhite/white ratio of labor-force participation for women is highest in the middle years, reaching 1.50 for age twenty-five to thirty-four, a stark contrast with the male situation. Strikingly, also, is the fact that the unemployment ratio of nonwhite to white women is *lower* than average in just those middle years when it is highest for nonwhite males. In 1964 it was only 1.73 for women thirty-five to forty-four years of age, compared with 2.48 for men of the same age and 1.96 for all women.

Inevitably, the underemployment of the Negro father has led to the break-up of the Negro family. In 1964, among unemployed white men twenty years and over there were 859,000 married with wife present and only 147,000 of "other marital status" (excluding men never married), the former group being six times the size of the latter. But among nonwhites, for 168,000 unemployed males with wives present, there were 76,000 of "other marital status." Nonwhites made up 34.1 per cent of all unemployed males of "other marital status." These are the men who first lose their jobs and then lose their families.

The first effect is simply that of broken homes. Nearly a quarter of Negro women living in cities who have ever married are divorced, separated, or living apart from their husbands. These rates have been steadily rising and are approaching one-third in, for example, New York City. Almost one-quarter of nonwhite families are headed by a woman, a rate that also continues to rise. At any given moment some 38 per cent of Negro children are living in homes where one or both parents are missing. It is probable that not much more than one-third of Negro youth reach eighteen having lived all their lives with both their parents. The second effect of the deterioration of the position of the Negro male worker has been a sharp increase in welfare dependency among Negro families. It would appear that a majority of Negro youth sooner or later are supported by the Aid to Families of Dependent Children program. In 1961 not quite half of all children receiving AFDC aid were Negro (1,112,106) and half of these were in cities of 250,000 population, where they made up three-quarters of the AFDC recipients. Nonwhites account for almost two-thirds of the increase in AFDC families between 1948 and 1961. The third effect that must be associated with the deteriorating position of the Negro male is the phenomenon Kenneth Clark has described as the tangle of pathology — the complex of interrelated disabilities and disadvantages that feed on each other and seem to make matters steadily worse for the individuals and communities caught up in it.

The cycle begins and ends with the children. A disastrous number begin their lives with no fathers present. Many, in some communities nearly half or more, are illegitimate. In 1963, 24 per cent of all non-white births in the nation were illegitimate. Too few live their early years in the presence of a respected and responsible male figure. The mothers, as often as not magnificent women, go to work too soon, if indeed they ever stop. This situation is getting worse, not better. In March 1959, 29.3 per cent of nonwhite women with children under six years of age were in the work force. By March 1964 this pro-portion had increased to 36.1 per cent! At that moment 56.7 per cent of nonwhite women with children six to seventeen years of age were in the work force — a higher percentage than that of nonwhite women with *no* children under eighteen years of age, which was 50.5 per cent. Although these movements were matched among white women, they clearly have gotten out of proportion among Negroes.

Negro children are going to school in nearly the same proportions as whites in the years from seven to nineteen, when free education is available more or less everywhere in the United States. But after having once closed the gap also in the crucial years on either side of that age span, they have begun to fall back again when education often is not free. In 1953, 18.1 per cent more of the white population than of the nonwhite were in school between the ages of five and six. By 1958 this gap had narrowed to 7.5. By 1963 it had widened again to 13.1. The conclusion must be that Negroes are falling behind once more in terms of the number of students who enter the main grades with advance preparation. Similarly the gap in population enrolled in school age twenty to twenty-four narrowed from 6.5 points in 1953 to 5.4 in 1958, but spread to 8.1 in 1963.

As they go through school, the economic pressures begin to mount. In a survey made in February 1963, half of the white male dropouts, but only one-third of the nonwhite, attributed their leaving school before graduation from high school to school-connected reasons, such as lack of interest in school, poor grades, or difficulties with school authorities. In contrast, more nonwhite males than white gave economic reasons for leaving school.[1]

To be sure, the gap between Negro and white education, however it may fluctuate within a decade, is now very narrow indeed — in formal terms. What has happened in real terms of the quality of education is not clear. Batchelder has suggested that "for the decade of the 1950's that although nonwhites (and surely Negroes too) gained on whites in median years of school completed, in the country as a whole, the average quality of a year of school completed by Negroes living in the North and West was reduced. . . . In educational attainment, quality dilution exceeded quantitative gains for Negroes in the North and West.[2]

Surely there are few developments in the area of employment, where improved education presumedly ought to produce better results, to indicate that the position of the Negro youth entering the labor force at present is improved over the past. Since 1961 the federal government has been engaged in a serious and sustained effort to improve the employment position of the American Negro by breaking down the barriers of discrimination. The President's Committee on Equal Employment has had unprecedented support both within the government and from the business and labor community. Results are slow to come, and the Committee has been loath to proclaim them when they have not existed — one break with the past that does honor to all concerned.

The Committee studies have provided considerable evidence that the position of the Negro worker is certainly not improving much in the normal course of events. Evidence has appeared that in large segments of American industry the number of Negro craftsmen is, if anything, proportionately greater than the number of Negro apprentices. Efforts to increase the number of apprentices have produced steady results, but at a pace and at a level which suggest fashioning a social revolution for twenty million souls one lad at a time.

Nor is it so obvious that middle-class Negroes are finding in ever-more-abundant supply the resources — family, financial, and other — required to pass through the lengthy apprenticeships demanded by the American professions. In 1965 after a decade of splendidly militant legal and political action by the civil rights movement, Clyde Ferguson, Jr., Dean of the Howard Law School, reported that of the 54,265 law students in the entire United States, there were only 543 Negroes.

Obviously, the most pressing question for American social policy is whether the essential first step for resolving the problem of the Negro American is to provide such a measure of full employment of Negro workers that the impact of unemployment on family structure is removed. The assumption would be that only then will the wide and increasing range and level of social services available to the Negro American have their full effect, and only then will there be a Negro

CASES OPENED UNDER AFDC (EXCLUDING UNEMPLOYED PARENT SEGMENT)
COMPARED WITH UNEMPLOYMENT RATE OF NONWHITE MALES

Year	AFDC Cases Opened[1]	Nonwhite Male Unemployment Rate
1964	429,048	9.1
1963	380,985	10.6
1962	370,008	11.0
1961	391,238	12.9
1960	338,730	10.7
1959	329,815	11.5
1958	345,950	13.7
1957	294,032	8.4
1956	261,663	7.3
1955	256,881	8.2
1954	275,054	9.2
1953	222,498	4.4
1952	234,074	4.5
1951	225,957	4.4
1950	291,273	8.9
1949	278,252	8.8
1948	210,193	5.1

[1]Does not include cases opened under program which commenced in some States in 1961 of assistance to children whose fathers are present but unemployed. There were 70,846 such cases opened in 1961, 81,192 in 1962, 80,728 in 1963, and 105,094 in 1964.

Source: ADFC cases opened from HEW; nonwhite male unemployment rates from Department of Labor.

population that not only has equal opportunities in the American economy, but is equal to those opportunities.

This, of course, is not an inconsiderable assumption. No one knows whether it is justified or not. The relation between economic phenomena, such as employment, and social phenomena, such as family structure, has hardly begun to be traced in the United States. An association between rising economic and social distress in the world of the Negro American can be seen readily enough in data, but proof of a causal relationship is a more complex matter. Such is the extent to which science has taught us to be skeptical of what our common senses tell us.[3]

A more sophisticated but not less pressing question is whether the impact of economic disadvantage on the Negro community has gone on so long that genuine structural damage has occurred, so that a reversal in the course of economic events will no longer produce the expected response in social areas. There are several combinations of social and economic data which make it reasonable to ask both of these questions. They prove little, but they suggest a great deal. More importantly, they raise questions researchers should attempt to answer, for many of the answers we are looking for will, in my opinion, be

Cases Opened Under AFDC Compared with
Unemployment Rate for Nonwhite Males

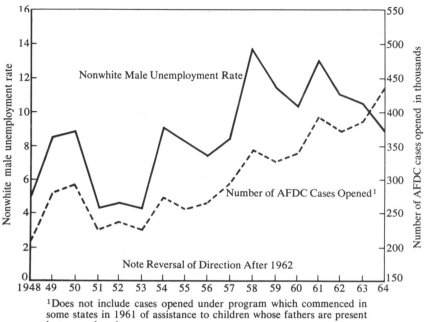

¹Does not include cases opened under program which commenced in
some states in 1961 of assistance to children whose fathers are present
but unemployed.

found in the interplay between the economic environment and the
social structure.

The relationship between the nonwhite male unemployment rate and
the number of *new* AFDC cases opened each year since 1948 (excluding cases under the program begun in some states since 1961
under which fathers may be present but unemployed) is one example.
The curves rise and fall together. Between 1948 (when, it will be
recalled, the nonwhite unemployment rate first became available) and
1962 they have the remarkable correlation of 91.[4] Between 1955 and
1956, however, the unemployment rate dropped, but the number of
new cases went up slightly, from 256,881 to 261,663. Unemployment
in 1960 was lower than in 1959, but new cases were higher, 338,730
as compared to 329,815. (Note the rising level of new cases.) In
1963 unemployment was down, but new cases were up. In 1964 it
went down, but new cases went up again — sharply now, reaching
the highest point ever: 429,000.

While the two lines on the chart go hand in hand, the situation is
more complex than it first appears. Some of the increase in AFDC

cases is the result of white dependency, not Negro. However, almost two-thirds of the increase in the AFDC rolls between 1948 and 1961 is attributable to nonwhite families. While the unemployment rate for nonwhite males it used for comparison, the unemployment rate for all males would show similar changes. Some of the changes in AFDC families among nonwhites are also due to unemployment problems among families headed by females, families broken long ago. At present, these components cannot be isolated completely, and we look to corroboration from additional approaches.

The statistics are available by which we can observe the year-to-year changes in the per cent of nonwhite married women who are separated

PER CENT OF NONWHITE MARRIED WOMEN SEPARATED FROM HUSBANDS AND UNEMPLOYMENT RATES OF NONWHITE MALES AGED 20 AND OVER

Year	NONWHITE MARRIED WOMEN SEPARATED FROM THEIR HUSBANDS MARCH OF EACH YEAR		UNEMPLOYMENT RATE OF NONWHITE MALES 20 AND OVER, 9 MONTHS PRIOR TO APRIL OF EACH YEAR	
	Per Cent	Deviation from Linear Trend	Per Cent	Deviation from Linear Trend
1953	10.6	−2.4	4.1	−2.1
1954	12.7	−0.6	5.6	−1.1
1955	15.1	+1.6	9.3	+2.2
1956	14.2	+0.5	6.8	+0.8
1957	13.1	−0.9	6.8	−1.3
1958	16.0	+1.8	9.8	+1.3
1959	17.6	+3.2	12.3	+3.3
1960	13.8	−0.9	10.2	+0.7
1961	14.3	−0.6	10.7	+0.8
1962	14.9	−0.2	11.2	+0.8
1963	14.6	−0.7	9.8	−1.1
1964	14.8	−0.8	8.6	−2.7

Source: Bureau of Labor Statistics.

from their husbands. The period from 1953 to 1964 was one of generally rising unemployment for Negro men with marked fluctuations corresponding to the rise and fall of the nation's economic activity in this period. This was also a period when the number of broken Negro families was rising, with fluctuations up and down.

The upper half of the chart shows the per cent of nonwhite married women separated from their husbands (as of March of each year) and the unemployment rate (for the nine months preceding separation rate) of nonwhite men twenty years of age and over. The two lines rise and fall together, with both having an upward trend. The bottom half of the chart shows the yearly fluctuations from the trend, and again, the lines rise and fall together. The correlation between the deviations of the two series from their respective trends is .81.

As in the comparison of AFDC cases and unemployment, the strength of the relationship between unemployment and separation is considerably less after 1959 than it was before, at least in the limited period of time we are able to examine it. After 1962, unemployment dropped sharply, but the increase in employment opportunities for Negro men was not accompanied by a decline in broken marriages.

Per Cent of Nonwhite Married Women Separated from Their Husbands and
Unemployment Rate of Nonwhite Men Aged 20 and Over

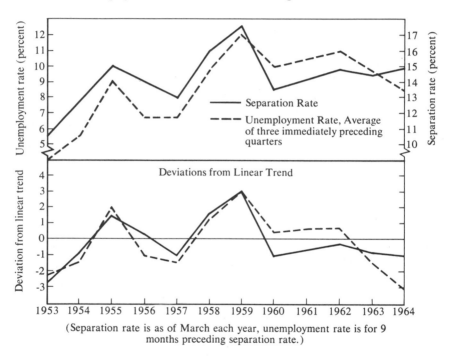

(Separation rate is as of March each year, unemployment rate is for 9 months preceding separation rate.)

It would be troubling indeed to learn that until several years ago employment opportunity made a great deal of difference in the rate of Negro dependency and family disorganization, but that the situation has so deteriorated that the problem is now feeding on itself — that measures which once would have worked will henceforth not work so well, or work at all.

The important point is not that we do not know whether this is or this is not the case. It is rather that until now we have never seriously asked such a question. Obviously an answer, or set of answers, can be had, and public policy can be guided accordingly. Time, not method, is our enemy. In the next six years the nonwhite work force will increase by 20 per cent, about twice the rate of the past decade and the rate for the whites in the coming same six years. The crisis of commitment is at hand.

REFERENCES

[1] The pinch of poverty is felt early. Negro families can save very little. In 1960-61 Negro families and single consumers living in cities average $23 in savings. White groups saved almost nine times that much.

[2] Alan B. Batchelder, "Decline in the Relative Income of Negro Men," *Quarterly Journal of Economics,* Vol. 78 (November, 1967), p. 538.

[3] There have been few attempts to examine the impact of unemployment on the survival of the family. It has been more than a quarter of a century since researchers addressed themselves to such questions in America, and, where investigation occurred, it was of white families, not Negro. An example is *Citizens Without Work* (1940), by Edward Wight Bakke. The most comprehensive analysis of the interrelationships between the ability of the Negro male to perform his expected economic role and the stability of the Negro family is still the work of E. Franklin Frazier. Anthropologists have investigated matrifocal families in search of some universal explanation of why they predominate in some societies. For a recent report, see "A Survey of the Consanguine or Matrifocal Family," by Peter Kunstadter in *American Anthropologist* (February 1963). Kunstadter concludes that the common feature of such societies is a division of labor which results in a physical separation of the male from the family over long periods of time. He reports that several investigators have pointed to the inability of males to fulfill their family economic roles successfully as the predominant feature of matrifocal societies. Kunstadter does not examine Negro American society in any detail which, of course, is quite mixed in this regard. However, the Negro American does not face a problem of a division of labor which results in physical separation. A recent investigation of the differences between white and Negro families with regard to the relative "power" of men and women is that of Robert Blood and Donald Wolfe, *Husbands and Wives: The Dynamics of Married Living* (New York, 1963).

[4] A correlation was also computed for the deviations from the linear trends of the two series. With the trend removed, the correlation was .82, thereby ruling out the possibility that a similar but unrelated trend was responsible for the high correlation.

The Negro Family: Dilemmas and Struggles of the Middle Class

ROBERT COLES

THE FATHER OF ONE SOUTHERN NEGRO YOUTH WHO WAS AMONG THE first and very few to enter the white schools of his state is a college graduate who majored in sociology, then went on to be a minister. He is an unusual father, the head of a very strong and stable family; perhaps when all things are considered the very strongest that I studied. His concern for his family is apparent, and has been successfully transmitted to his children, all of whom are at once sturdy and sensitive.

Yet the son who went to a white high school fared rather poorly compared to several others whom I frankly expected not to last at all. They did last, and so did the minister's boy; but he was more visibly upset than they, and often he openly talked of calling an end to the entire struggle. He resented leaving a well-protected, well-appointed home. He missed what he left because there was so much to it. He himself once described his dilemma this way: "I wasn't brought up to face all this kind of trouble. Some of the others, yes; they've been fighting all their lives just to keep going, but not me. My mother and daddy, they brought us up to work and study, and get along nice and easy with people — the way they do. So it's a shock, leaving home to find people swearing at you, and not even being able to talk to them, to ask them why they're saying what they are."

The minister lives in a very respectable and dignified neighborhood; I suppose it could be described as anything from "Negro upper middle-class" to "black bourgeoisie." He is a forceful man, and a frank talker. In time he admitted to me that he turned to the ministry to make a living: "I studied sociology because I was interested in it, but I didn't think I could get a job as a sociologist. When I was in college there weren't that many things a Negro *could* become. Teaching and the ministry were the two big fields, or the post office. I decided on the

Reprinted by permission of the publisher and author from *Children of Crisis* (New York: Dell Publishing Co., 1968), pp. 139-46.

ministry because I was interested in moral problems, and I knew I could find work as a preacher."

He is a Methodist, a "socially concerned" one he says, in the tradition of his church. For years he has sponsored a summer retreat for young couples, dedicated to family life and called "The Family As a Career." In 1961, when I first met him, he told me something about its purposes: "We try to strengthen the confidence of young husbands and wives. They are mostly religious people, but they don't know how to put their faith, their beliefs to work. Even though they come from good homes, they're not sure how to *start* a good home themselves. We have discussions, and we bring in outsiders — other ministers, professors from Atlanta University, like sociologists or experts in education and child development. There aren't too many around, but we get everyone who *is*, and we've even had one or two whites come talk to us, the liberal kind that aren't afraid to do so. (You never know when the police might hear of it and decide to intervene. They take a chance, those whites, and we're especially grateful to them.)

"I think our retreats have been a good thing. We've done it long enough to hear people talk about the effects. They feel they become better parents, better fathers and mothers. We've strengthened family life around here, and that's as important as desegregation or anything else."

The next year, 1962, I was a good deal more comfortable with him. His son's troubles had become a major problem for him — and in a way for me, too. More than with any other child I was then seeing I had to lend what support I could to the boy and encourage him to talk about the hard time he was having. In a curious way, the very favorable influences in his life had ill prepared him for the stresses he was encountering every day. His parents had most of all taught him to speak his mind, to talk with others and share his feelings with them. He had gone to good camps — one of them up North and interracial — where he met like-minded children from somewhat similar families. Now he was also at school with middle-class children — presumably the kind he would be able to approach with some ease. Instead they were grim-faced and unfriendly, while he was becoming fearful and unable to study. What is more, the Negro girl who was his ally appeared to be stronger — or tougher — than he.

"I don't know. She gets it as bad as I do, but she's a fighter, and she doesn't let things bother her. She won't even *talk* about what's happening. She tells me that she doesn't want to hear about it; there's enough to do just getting by the next class. I don't know why I'm going through this, voluntarily. It can't be right to put up with pain, when you can avoid it."

We talked, and talked. He was afraid to confide in his parents. He knew that they were hopelessly conflicted. They wanted him to last it through — as parents, as Negroes, as ordinary, decent citizens. They also felt guilty and afraid — that he was doing it all on their account, that he would be hurt in body or mind, even that they would also be hurt, by gunshot or dynamite. Here was one situation where I could stand in their stead, and help a boy by talking with him; because for him such conversation was a very familiar and necessary way to handle tensions from within — and now, without.

In 1962 I was invited to talk at the minister's summer retreat, and and I reluctantly did so. I recall two days of discussion on the family— this time, for the first time, on the Negro family. In his initial address the minister had an explanation: "You may wonder why we're talking about the *Negro* family, and not family life in general, as before. I think we have gone through a real crisis these past months, all of us in the South and in Georgia. The Negro has seen that he cannot overlook his race anywhere, even in the public schools. I think that also goes for the home."

At the time I thought much of the talk empty and boring, saturated with clichés and pieties that seemed to lead nowhere. Yet later in reading over the typed tapescript of the minister's concluding remarks I found the following comment: "Our homes have been vulnerable the way no other people's have been. We were never even allowed homes until a very few years ago. All of us have pictures of our slave ancestors. How can we compare *their* lives to the lives of other American grandparents or great-grandparents? Those of us here have overcome all those obstacles. We have somehow built a tradition for family life where none existed before, and none was allowed before. However, most of our people are still too poor, too confused to know where to begin, or how. We need help in helping them. We need the government, and the good will of white people; but most of all we need ourselves, especially people like us. The strong among our race must give to the weak; and what we must give is our strength, so that their families will be able to take that strength from us and build with it, and most of all hand it down to their children."

It was rhetoric, I suppose; a minister's rhetoric. Certainly I didn't pay much attention to it then. In later years, during my follow-up visits, I saw more of the son than the father. I watched a boy become a man, and develop a strong interest in his race's origins. (He is now studying in Africa.) I last met the father in 1965, and quite by accident we stumbled into the following conversation, which I put down here almost word for word.

The minister had asked me whether I was finding any difference in the new Negro and white children I was starting to observe in the North. "No, not yet. They seem to be very much like others I've met down here."

"I would have thought there might be some difference," he responded, a bit wearily. "It's such a diffcrent world for our Negro children from year to year. I can barely recognize it myself. This year we've even stopped our summer retreat. We don't think it's right to go *off* and contemplate, when what is needed is our presence among those who can't contemplate because thcy can barely stay alive from day to day."

"I guess you're doing what the President said has to bc done: trying to strengthen the Negro family, rather than talk about it."

"Yes, in a way that's what we're doing. But I don't like that talk about 'the Negro family.' It singles us out unfairly. Look at the white middle-class, and all its divorces and instability."

"I agree, but do you think the President or Mr. Moynihan wanted to single out the Negro that way, or for that reason? Weren't they simply saying what you've always said, what all the civil rights leaders have said—that the Negro has been oppressed, and paid a price for it?"

"I don't know what they meant to say, but most Negroes I know took it the other way around. They want what is *due* them, rather than pity and sympathy. They think that if you have to make people look *bad* or broken up before you can get the country to give them what they should have by right, then that's the same old racism and segregation at work."

"Yes, again I agree, but there has to be a *political* solution, some approach or plan that will catch the interest and concern of the nation. Most people are too comfortable to care about a lot of things that need doing. Don't you think that the Moynihan Report was done in order to collect all the important facts together, and offer them to Congress, to the courts, in a manner that would get action, get results?"

"No, I don't. I rely on what my son says more than my own thinking, to tell the truth. He's the coming generation, the next father of a family in *our* family. He feels insulted. He says all our worst points were brought up, and so once again the country has the image of the poor, shiftless Negro—or nigger."

"I'd like to ask your son whether the issue is what *image* the Negro has among certain people or what *facts* the Moynihan Report essentially wanted to stress: unemployment, faulty welfare practices, the disorganized home life that goes with social and economic insecurity?"

"That's not what we're arguing about. We know Negroes have suffered, and we know how a lot of our children have to grow up. We just don't believe that our *family* troubles should be emphasized;

particularly when everyone has family problems, and the divorce rate among whites is almost thirty-three per cent. We want the *causes* of our troubles licked, not the symptoms paraded up and down — which always happens to us, anyway. You yourself told us many times that you were seeing a lot of strength in our children. Look at what some of our Atlanta families went through; and in Little Rock and New Orleans it was much worse. Is that a sign of a weak family?"

"No; but I never meant to say that because some Negro children and their families acquitted themselves well under fire, the Negro family as a rule is strong. As you know, some of these children have lived very sad and upsetting lives, family lives. They survived a crisis — a lot was going for them in *that* crisis — but in many ways they are still hurt, or limited, or whatever word you want to use. (I think any word used will get *someone* in trouble, and get somebody angry, because tempers are short during a time of change, like now.) Perhaps that is it: the Moynihan Report with its emphasis on the Negro family's disintegration (or 'deterioration' or whatever) struck close enough to a painful truth to arouse protest, particularly when it didn't seem likely that the report would be followed by action — the action you feel is necessary."

"I agree. I think if we knew that the Congress was going to vote the billions we need to clear up slums, or even would give us more protection against snipers down here and slum landlords up North — then we could have overlooked a few people seeing us in a bad light. We're used to unfair treatment, but we're tired of it, too; and each time we get it now, we're going to yell, or know why we're not yelling."

"Then you don't object to what Mr. Moynihan said, but what you were afraid would — or in this case would *not* — come of what he said?" . . .

"Well, I object to the way some of our politicians treat one of the most serious moral problems in our history. They always talk like ministers, like me, but they behave like heathens. They don't lead us, they try to manipulate us. I think that if the President told the people what he wants and what the Negro needs, rather than what's wrong with the Negro family, then he could get it."

"I'm not so sure. American politics doesn't work that way. I think the President's advisers were trying to do just what you say they should do — and you see to what effect."

"I don't know what they were trying to do, but they sure put salt on open wounds, instead of coming to us with the first aid we need."

"I guess I'm defending them and their purposes. I suppose to some extent I can do that, not being a Negro and not feeling as sensitive about some of these matters."

"You beat me to the punch. I think we have to be sensitive. First of all, we *are*. Second of all, it's about time we were *more* sensitive. When I think of all I didn't worry about years ago, including the Negro family, I feel ashamed. We used to have those summer retreats, but did we ever worry about the Negro family then? Not really, only about ourselves, as individuals."

"Then Mr. Moynihan may have helped you do some thinking, just as the whole civil rights movement has helped you — and him."

"Yes. To be honest though, we need action. I have a friend who teaches sociology up North, and he wrote me the other day, asking why we always *discuss* the Negro, and do so little to change things. Now that's from a man who has discussed the Negro all his life."

"The Moynihan Report was a call for action."

"It was a call to white people. It didn't speak to Negroes."

"I disagree. It spoke to Americans. It was written by a politician, in the best sense of the word; in *your* sense of a good politician. He wanted change, or action."

"You don't see how we feel, reading those headlines, about our badness, our weakness — again."

"I disagree. I see how you feel, but I guess I can't feel as you do. We keep on coming back to that."

"Yes. We do; and all over the country people will, for a long while, I think."

Intergenerational Poverty

CHARLES V. WILLIE

WHETHER OR NOT THERE IS INTERGENERATIONAL TRANSMISSION OF poverty is an issue in need of more sociological analysis; there are many assertions but little supporting evidence. Actually, there has been an increase in wealth among all people in the United States and the proportion of the total population below the poverty income level has decreased over the years. Herman Miller pointed out that in 1962 dollars, the average income of families and individuals increased from $3,700 in 1935 to $6,400 in 1962.[1] Again using constant dollars, he found that the proportion of families with incomes below the $3,000 poverty level decreased from 51 percent in 1929 to 21 percent in 1962. Clearly, some families moved up the stratification hierarchy during the decades included in the Miller study. Many of the families and individual households which were poor 30 to 35 years ago no longer fit into this category today. At the upper end of the income range, Miller found that the proportion of people, in 1962 dollars, with incomes over $10,000 increased from five percent just before the Great Depression to 19 percent in 1962.[2] These changes have occurred largely because of continued growth and expansion of the American economy.

Several years ago, I conducted an ecological investigation of the distribution of the Syracuse, New York, population by age and discovered that "a significant number of adults in all socioeconomic areas moved at least once in 20 years to a neighborhood of higher status." This finding indicated that a tendency toward upward social mobility existed in all segments of the population.[3] There seems to be a natural tendency for families and individual households to improve their circumstances in time.

Yet poverty has not been eliminated in the United States. Why the nation has been unable to eradicate poverty is the issue about which

---

Reprinted by permission of the publisher and author from *Poverty and Human Resources Abstracts*, IV (Jan.-Feb. 1969), 1-13.

there is much conjecture. Some analysts argue that the upward social mobility described above was largely a function of the motivation, value-orientation, and social organization of immigrant communities which fought their way up as ethnic groups from the bottom of the economic ladder.[4] This same style of reasoning is used to explain why lower-class Negroes remain impoverished. The circumstances of many Negro Americans are frequently explained as a function of the inter-generational transmission of poverty.

POVERTY AMONG NEGROES: MOYNIHAN THESIS

In the United States Labor Department report on *The Negro Family,* Daniel Patrick Moynihan maintained that "a national effort towards the problems of Negro Americans must be directed towards the question of family structure." He looked upon the weakness of the family struc-ture as "the principal source of most of the aberrant, inadequate, or antisocial behavior that . . . perpetuates the cycle of poverty and de-privation." He concluded that "the present tangle of pathology (among lower-class Negroes) is capable of perpetuating itself."[5] In effect, Moynihan is saying that motivation, value-orientation and family organi-zation of ethnic group members contribute to the perpetuation or elimination of poverty within that population. The implication is that the family organization and cultural values of Negroes differ from those of other ethnic groups and that these account for the persistence of poverty among the members of this racial category. This assertion has been advanced as a basis for social action as if it were supported by empirical evidence. In fact, assertions about the intergenerational transmission of poverty among Negroes, such as Moynihan's, are in-adequately documented.

In particular, there is little information about the characteristics of affluent people who were once poor, and almost no comparitive data between these kinds of families and those that continue in poverty over a number of years. It could very well be that factors other than cultural heritage are associated with the presence or absence of social mobility among some low-income families. It could be that the per-sistence of poverty among some populations is a function of external forces in the society at large. It could be that the persistence of poverty is due to factors originating both inside and outside a population group.

TRENDS IN THE PROPORTION OF POOR PEOPLE

The evidence shows that the proportion of the total United States population which is poor today is less than half of the proportion which was poor three decades ago. Clearly, some Americans have escaped the poverty which their parents experienced only one generation ago. Whether people who are poor today are poor (1) because of external forces such as discrimination, oppression, and injustice which tend to block upward social mobility; or (2) because of insufficient motivation, low aspiration, and a fatalistic orientation which tend to inhibit upward social mobility is a complicated problem in need of much more objective analysis.

Research into the circumstances associated with poverty has not kept pace with the need because too many policy-makers have been more interested in justifying the presence or absence of poverty among "their people" or "those people" rather than explaining it. Thus, the search for solutions to poverty has proceeded within the context of varying ideological orientations. The two most prominent ideologies have been those which assert that the presence or absence of poverty either is a function of strengths or deficiencies in the person, family, and clan (ethnic group), or is a function of strengths or deficiencies in institutional arrangements and the opportunity system of the total community. Probably, there is an interaction effect between these two explanations of poverty. Some might argue that these theories are not mutually exclusive and that proposals for the reduction of poverty may derive from both of them equally and thus follow a middle course. But the fact is that proposals for action are usually representative of one of these orientations or the other. Research is needed to determine the relative contributions of forces both external and internal to particular populations in the perpetuation of poverty among nearly one-fifth of the people in this nation. It might be helpful to free these orientations from their doctrinal underpinning and to examine them as hypotheses, determining which might yield the most fruitful programs of research for explaining poverty and its prevention.

Moynihan has been identified publicly with the hypothesis that poverty is perpetuated intergenerationally largely because of deficiencies in the family structure. In the United States Labor Department report, he asserted that "employment . . . reflects educational achievement which depends in large part on family stability."[6] This trinitarian association, however, must be understood for what it is — an assertion and not a conclusion based on evidence. In fact, the evidence appears to point in another direction.

Mollie Orshansky raised a serious question about the strength of the association assumed to exist between poverty and family instability when she pointed out that "two-thirds of all children in the families called poor do live in a home with a man at the head" and that "more than half of all poor families report that the head currently has a job."[7] It would seem on the basis of the Orshansky analysis that many poor families are like affluent families. Thus, family instability cannot be considered to be the chief factor associated with poverty.

POVERTY AND FAMILY CHARACTERISTICS

A study of income and welfare conducted by the Survey Research Center of the University of Michigan found that characteristics of parents did have a substantial effect on the amount of education their children completed, but that this effect accounted for less than half — 41 percent — of the variance in years of school completed.[8] The contribution of a combination of nonfamily factors to the amount of schooling received by children, therefore, was found to be more important than variables pertaining to the structure and process of the kinship system.

The 1960 Census revealed that "six out of every ten college students in the United States were receiving higher education despite the fact that their fathers did not have this opportunity."[9] It is true that youth from higher-income families that have college trained heads are more likely to complete school than poorer youths. Yet it must be stated also that college youths come from all levels of American society. These data mean that no definitive answer is available concerning the extent to which insufficient education received by parents results in limited education and consequently low earning power for their children.

Since family characteristics have some association with the economic status of households, it might be helpful to consider characteristics that could have a significant intergenerational effect. The presence of one or both parents in the household is easily observed and usually is pounced upon as a quick and easy explanation. But since most low-income families are two-parent households, other variables should be considered. A more subtle, but possibly influential, variable is the education of the wife and mother in the family. The University of Michigan study discovered that "average education attained by children is also influenced by the educational achievement of the mother. The more education the wife has relative to her husband, the more education the children attain . . . . Where the wife has less education than the head, achievement of the children is impeded but not so much as they are advanced when the wife has more education than the head."[10]

WORKING WIVES AMONG THE POOR

In a study of the employed poor in Washington, D.C., I also found an association between the social mobility of a two-parent family and the education and employment of the wife. While my study did not focus on intergenerational social mobility, it did shed light in a cross-sectional way on why families headed by unskilled workers remain poor or become marginally affluent. In both poor and marginally affluent families, the head earned about $50 a week, but family income was above the poverty level among the marginals. The most striking difference between these households of different income levels with heads making wages similar was this:

> The wife in the marginal household is much more likely to be employed than the wife in the poor households. Three out of every four wives in marginal families are employed, and better than half are employed full time. The converse is true of the other group. Three out of every four wives in poor families are not gainfully employed. . . . Most of the wives in marginal families are engaged in service work. Of the few wives in poor families who are gainfully employed, most are service workers too. However, the median weekly income for marginals of $51 is about $11 higher than the median for working wives in poor families. This may be because seven out of every ten employed marginal wives render a service other than that of private household work, as compared with five out of every ten employed wives in poor families. Interestingly, the median weekly income of working wives in marginal families is one dollar higher than the median weekly earnings of their employed husbands. The few working wives in poor families tend to earn less than their menfolk. . . . A marked difference between poor and marginal households [also] is in the formal schooling of spouses in two-parent families: 46 percent of the wives in marginal households are high school graduates, compared with 27 percent among the poor. Wives in two-parent marginal households also tend to be high school graduates more frequently than [their] husbands. This may account for the fact that they also tend to earn as much or more than their husbands. In poor families, the median earnings of the few working wives is nearly ten dollars a week less than that of their spouses, and they also tend to have less education than their husbands.[11]

From the data presented in these two studies, it is clear that much more attention needs to be given to understanding the effects of education and employment of wives and mothers, as compared with the education and employment of husbands and fathers, upon the social mobility of low-income families. It is possible that many of the injunctions against the employment of mothers which predict unfortunate consequences are not based on verifiable facts at all, but are merely assertions derived from the writers' value systems. More research is needed to clarify the issue of working wives and their contributions to the integration or disintegration of family life in households of varying income levels.

PROMISCUITY, ILLEGITIMACY, AND POVERTY

Probably the behavior which has caught the attention of the public more than any other, and which is believed to be eminently responsible for the intergenerational transmission of poverty among Negroes, is illegitimacy. The Labor Department report authored by Moynihan stated that "the number of illegitimate children per 1,000 live births increased by 11 among whites in the period 1940-1963, but by 68 among nonwhites." The report further stated that there were 1.8 million nonwhite illegitimate children in the nation in 1961. Whether or not they received welfare was the only basis the author had for inferring the economic status of these illegitimate children. The report pointed out that 1.3 million were not receiving welfare aid in 1961. Nevertheless, illegitimacy was used as one of several indications of the family breakdown among Negroes which was assumed to be associated with the perpetuation of poverty. Why illegitimacy among whites was not declared to be a circumstance indicative of family breakdown was never clarified. The report stated that "the white family, despite many variants, remains a powerful agency not only for transmitting property from one generation to the next, but also for transmitting no less valuable contacts with the world of education and work. . . . White children without fathers at least perceive all about them the pattern of men working. Negro children without fathers flounder."[12]

Again, a series of assertions have been presented with little evidential base. The implication of these assertions is that part of the source of intergenerational poverty among Negroes could be eliminated if illegitimate births could be prevented. In a comparative analysis of problem and stable families in a low-income population in Syracuse, I pointed out that neither early marriage, nor the tendency to marry more than once . . . nor the tendency to give birth to children out of wedlock causes . . . instability among low-income families. These appear to be effects or consequences of their instability, rather than causes."[13] The conception of children out of wedlock is often described as a way of life for low-income women, a cultural expectation. William Goode believes that many low-income girls have few attributes other than sex at their disposal in the process of bargaining for husbands.

He arrives at this conclusion based on his study of illegitimacy in the Caribbean Islands.[14] It should go without saying that lower-class girls often are exploited by men who have no intention of marrying. But the fact remains that the illegitimate child is frequently a by-product of the girl's search for a husband. Viewed in this perspective, out-of-wedlock conceptions reflect not so much a breakdown in family structure as a broken promise. The girl submitted as one way of getting her man. All too frequently, he is the man who got away. Thus, sexual activity which may appear to be promiscuous may in fact be goal directed. And a major goal is to induce the suitor to marry and establish a two-parent household. In many cases, the girl misunderstands the paramour and miscalculates, with tragic results.

THE CULTURE OF THE POOR

In general, persons who hypothesize that poverty is intergenerationally transmitted due to deficiencies in the person, family, and clan believe that there is a "culture of the poor."[15] This concept which may help organize one's thoughts about the poor also may tend to inhibit the perception of the great variations in behavior among poor people. Their behavior is both similar to and different from the behavior of affluent people in any society. A range of behavior patterns exists among poor people just as a range of behavior patterns exists among the nonpoor. Thus, it is inappropriate to look upon the poor as constituting a subculture which reinforces and perpetuated itself, including the condition of poverty. Based on his studies of child-rearing in low-income families in Washington, D. C., Hylan Lewis rejected the concept of a lower-class cultural system which generates deviant behavior.[16] My studies, which revealed diversified behavior in rent payment practices and in family activities among households in a low-rent public housing project in Syracuse, New York, also cast doubt upon the concept of a culture of the poor.[17] Of course, there are deficiencies in the life style of some poor people as there are deficiencies in the life style of others in the society. But these deficiencies should not be interpreted as an internally integrated pattern of expectations or as a system of beliefs that guide and give direction to behavior which perpetuates poverty.

POVERTY AND THE SOCIAL SYSTEM

The hypothesis in opposition to the one discussed above is not formulated to explain whether or not poverty is transmitted intergenerationally. However, it does focus upon deficiencies in social systems and in the community at large. This alternative hypothesis is that change in social organization tends to be associated with change in individual behavior. According to this hypothesis, poverty is a function of inadequacies in the operations of social systems; thus, systemic changes are necessary to eliminate poverty among individuals. By implication, then, this hypothesis is relevant to the debate about intergenerational transmission of poverty. The background for this hypothesis is what has happened in this nation, as well as what is known to date about the intergenerational transmission of poverty.

The significant reduction in the proportion of low-income families during the past three decades has occurred largely because of change in the economic system. It has continued to grow and expand, increasing in productivity and efficiency, and has brought more income to people through the years. Thus, much of the poverty that might have been perpetuated intergenerationally was eliminated as a consequence of systemic change — the growth and expansion of the economy.

Certain specific studies of intergenerational poverty also cast doubt on its transmission through families. One, for example, conducted by Lawrence Podell in New York City, discovered that only "15 percent of a citywide sampling of mothers on welfare rolls . . . [in 1966] had parents who also had been relief recipients." Moreover, Podell found that "eight out of ten believed their children would not become dependent adults." In the light of the experience of the mothers included in this study, there is reason to believe that their predictions might be realized; less than two out of ten of the current recipients came from families that received welfare assistance.[18] (Failure to receive welfare, however, does not indicate automatically that 85 percent of the mothers came from nonpoor families. In spite of public concern about increasing welfare rolls, it is a well known fact that a large majority of poor families do not receive needed assistance.) Limiting the analysis to welfare families, one finds little evidence to support the contention that poverty is transmitted intergenerationally. The evidence indicates that intergenerational transmission is experienced in only a few families.

EDUCATION: PRO AND CON

Many analysts who subscribe to the system-change hypothesis as a more fruitful approach to an adequate explanation of poverty believe that the best way to eliminate it is to move in on the educational system. For instance, a report issued by the Upjohn Institute for Employment Research stated that "the keystone of any attempt to broaden the employment possibilities for Negroes is obviously education — not only the formal programs of kindergarten through high school but also education that is now available in the form of training programs financed by various federal agencies."[19] However, psychiatrists Abram Kardiner and Lionel Ovesey have not held much hope for manipulation of the educational system as a way of dealing with poverty, especially among Negroes, unless there is also a corresponding change in the education of white people. They state that "the psychosocial expressions of the Negro personality are the . . . end products of the process of oppression. . . . They can never be eradicated without removing the forces that create and perpetuate them. . . . What is needed by the Negro is not education but re-integration. It is the white man who requires the education." "There is only one way that the products of oppression can be dissolved," according to Kardiner and Ovesey, "and that is to stop the oppression."[20] These two psychiatrists consider the inadequate education of Negroes — and whatever association may exist between their poverty and education — [to be] the result of anti-Negro prejudice and discrimination among whites.

Robert Merton, in his essay, "The Self-Fulfilling Prophecy," supports this view in an illustration of the mechanism at work: whites who prophesy that Negroes are incompetent and incapable of benefiting from formal education withhold support from Negro schools (making them inferior) and then point to the smaller number of Negro high school or college graduates (which the inferior schools produce) as justification for not providing greater support for the education of Negroes.[21] In his commentary on schools in metropolitan areas, James B. Conant observed that "we now recognize so plainly but so belatedly [that] a caste system finds its clearest manifestation in an educational system."[22]

If the educational system in this country is to change so that it serves the needs of Negro people better, those people who established and continue to maintain a system of inferior education for Negroes must change. They must support an educational system which equips Negroes with the skills to participate productively in the mainstream of a technology-dominated economy. This, however, is not likely to occur unless whites are reoriented in their education and general socialization to relate to Negroes as human beings. Kardiner and Ovesey point out that Negroes were subjected to pure utilitarian use during the period of slavery in this country. "Once you degrade someone in that way," they remind us, "the sense of guilt makes it imperative to degrade the object further to justify the entire procedure."[23] Merton doubts the efficacy of education as a way of dealing with the prevailing patterns of race relations. His belief is that "education may serve as an operational adjunct but not as the chief basis for any but excruciating slow change in the prevailing patterns of race relations."[24] What is likely to be more effective, according to Merton, is "deliberate institutional change" designed to destroy discrimination.[25]

RACIAL DISCRIMINATION AND POVERTY

Economist Herman Miller, who also subscribes to the hypothesis of institutional change as a way of dealing with poverty among disadvantaged minority groups, maintains that "racial discrimination is a key cause" of the Negro's perpetually low estate. He refers to a study of the Council of Economic Advisers which estimated that $13 billion more would have been placed in the hands of Negroes in 1961 had there not been any racial discrimination in employment. He points out that Negro people with the same amount of education as whites usually earn less money. In an analysis of the 1960 Census, Miller discovered that "nonwhite men earn about three-fourths as much as whites with the same amount of schooling," and that "Negroes who have completed four years of college education can expect to earn only as much in a lifetime as whites who have gone beyond the eighth grade." Thus, Miller concludes, "there is some justification for the feeling by Puerto Ricans, Negroes, and other minority groups that education does not do as much for them, financially, as it does for others."[27]

It would appear that racial and ethnic discrimination more than inadequate education is one of the chief factors contributing to the low-income status of many Negroes. For example, among whites of limited education (with eight or fewer years of schooling), 50 percent are likely to have jobs as service workers or laborers at the bottom of the heap, while nearly 80 percent of the nonwhite workers with limited education are likely to find work only in these kinds of jobs.[28]

That racial discrimination is one of the major factors contributing to economic deprivation among Negroes is illustrated by an interview which one of the field workers in Hylan Lewis' Child Rearing Study conducted with a 50-year-old white painter who was also a foreman for a construction company. A part of the interview record, arranged in dialogue form, follows:

> Interviewer: Do you have any Negroes working under you?
> Foreman: No. Right now we are building a house for an Army colonel. We never use Negroes on jobs in Maryland and Virginia because that would hurt the company's reputation.
> Interviewer: Do you ever use Negroes?

Foreman:	When we have a job in Washington, we hire a large number of Negroes.
Interviewer:	Why?
Foreman:	The white painter gets $28 a day. The Negro is able and willing to do the same job for only $14. Give me a crew of six niggers and we'll knock out a five-story office building in a week. They all got families and $14 a day is damn good money for a nigger.[29]

James Tobin has pointed out that the low earning capacity of Negroes and their inferior education "both reflect discrimination."[30] The point I continue to emphasize, however, is that even when earning capacity and education are equal to those of whites, discrimination still persists and results in a lower family income for Negroes. The Moynihan thesis that the lack of improvement in opportunities for a large mass of Negro workers is correlated with a serious weakening of the Negro family, therefore, obscures the issue of discrimination and white racism in America, and so does his statement that "equality, as a fundamental democratic disposition, goes beyond equal opportunity to the issue of equal results."[31] The Census data analyzed by Miller indicated that equal opportunity has not yet been realized for Negro Americans and that discussion of equal results is indeed premature.

We know that "the rise in income in the past 20 years has been shared by nonwhite and white families," and that "the percent of nonwhite and white families with less than $3,000 purchasing power has been cut in half," according to the Bureau of Labor Statistics.[32] The two populations, however, started from a different base. Sixty-five percent of nonwhite families received less than $3,000 a year in 1947, compared with only 27 percent of white families. In 1966, the proportions had changed radically, but the relative incomes of the two racial populations remained the same. Thus, 32 percent of nonwhites received family incomes under $4,000 twenty years later, but only 13 percent of whites received income at this low level. The proportion of Negroes in poverty was almost two and one-half times greater than the proportion of poor whites 20 years ago, and this ratio has remained constant over the years.[33]

DIFFERENT APPROACHES FOR ELIMINATING POVERTY AMONG WHITES AND NONWHITES

Because there are twice as many poor nonwhites proportionately as there are poor whites, and because racial discrimination has been identified as a key cause which keeps Negroes at the bottom (an experience which they do not share with poor whites), it could very well be that different hypotheses are needed for explaining the continuation of poverty in the two racial populations. Failure to explore the possibility that different explanations of poverty may be required for different racial populations, which have had essentially different experiences, may have contributed to the contemporary controversy. It is conceivable, for example, that the hypothesis which may contribute to a better understanding of poverty among whites is one which seeks to determine the association, if any, between low-income status on one hand, and motivation, aspiration, life-orientation, and the presence or absence of primary group supports on the other. For nonwhites, however, a more powerful explanation of poverty might proceed from an examination of the hypothesis which seeks to determine the association, if any, between low-income status and discrimination, oppression, injustice, and the institutional controls that govern these phenomena.

The findings of another study which I conducted in Washington, D.C. are the basis for suggesting the possibility of differential explanations of poverty in white and Negro populations. The study dealt with juvenile delinquency among whites and nonwhites. I discovered that reducing family instability would probably contribute to a greater reduction in delinquency among whites than among Negroes, and that increasing economic opportunities would very likely contribute to a greater reduction in delinquency among Negroes than whites. While a good deal of family instability existed within the Negro population in Washington, economic insecurity was overwhelming. It appeared, according to the data collected, that one could not get at the family instability factor and its association with delinquency without first dealing with economic insecurity and its association with delinquency. Because a higher proportion of whites were not poor, family instability was their outstanding problem. But economic insecurity was the salient problem for Negroes, and it could not be circumvented in favor of family instability.[34]

The same principal may apply to the issue of poverty. Institutional changes during the past three to four decades have resulted in a substantial reduction in the proportion of whites who are poor. External changes in social organization have upgraded 87 percent of the white population beyond the poverty level. The 13 percent who remain poor probably have problems which are more personal and less susceptible to mass amelioration through institutional manipulation. These whites may be the individuals with insufficient motivation, low aspiration, and a fatalistic orientation unreached thus far by changes in the institutional systems of society which create new opportunities. The proportion of poor Negroes, however, remains at a high level and may still be amenable to ameliorative mass efforts. Apparently, the kinds of institutional changes needed to upgrade the Negro population are somewhat different from those required to upgrade the white population. In addition to deliberate institutional changes which may increase opportunities in an expanding economy, Negroes require deliberate institutional changes which will prevent racial discrimination. Until these are put into effect, we cannot know how large the residual proportion of nonwhite poor people might be who need such individualized attention as the 13 percent of poor whites may now require. To date, only 68 percent of the nonwhite population has been upgraded beyond poverty. There is every reason to believe that more can and must be done.

Problem with Moynihan Proposal

In the light of this discussion, it would seem that one problem with the Moynihan proposal for dealing with poverty is that it projects a solution more appropriate for the white than for the Negro poor. Projecting has been going on for a long time. Whites tend to project upon nonwhites solutions to social problems that are of value for whites, without understanding that experiences and conditions for nonwhites may be different. One essential difference with reference to poverty is that nonwhites also experience a great deal of discrimination and that the institutional changes which helped pull nearly 9 out of every ten whites above the poverty line have not run their full course for Negroes, especially those institutional changes and social controls which prohibit discrimination. This is why the Moynihan concern about equal results is premature until there are equal opportunities.

Conclusions

On the basis of the foregoing analysis, I conclude the following:

1. There is some intergenerational transmission of poverty, though not as much as is generally assumed.

2. Upward social mobility is a more common experience in the United States than the continuation of intergenerational poverty.

3. The perpetuation of poverty from one generation to the next is likely to be a function of personal and family-connected circumstances as well as patterns of institutional organization.

4. Personal and family-connected circumstances are likely to be more powerful explanations of poverty among whites than among nonwhites.

5. Institutional arrangements and patterns of social organization are likely to be more powerful explanations of the presence of poverty among nonwhite than among white people in the United States.

The latter two conclusions are stated tentatively and should be further tested as hypotheses. The reason for suggesting a differential explanation for the continuation of poverty by race is the fact that whites and non-whites have dissimilar patterns of participation in the economic system of the United Sttaes. As stated by Louis Kriesberg in "Inter-generational Patterns of Poverty," "generational changes in the proportion of the population which is poor is largely determined by economic developments and public policies regarding income maintenance and distribution."[35] Racial discrimination has prevented Negroes and other nonwhite minorities from participating fully in the benefits of an expanding economy. Even the income maintenance programs available to nonwhites have been encumbered with punitive restrictions so that their full value has not been experienced. Changes in institutional arrangements have been largely responsible for preventing poverty among whites, and there is reason to believe that such changes will aid in the prevention of poverty among nonwhites if the benefits of these changes are made available to all sectors of society.

Because whites, in general, have had free access to the opportunities produced by institutional change, the residual number of poor people in this racial category might well be a function of personal and family-connected deficiencies. It is not concluded that poverty among whites cannot be further reduced by more changes in the institutional systems of society. Rather, it is suggested that new manipulations of social institutions will probably net a smaller rate of change in the proportion of poor whites as compared with poor nonwhites, since most whites who could benefit from these major institutional changes have already taken advantage of them.

NOTES

[1]Herman Miller, *Rich Man, Poor Man* (New York: Thomas Y. Crowell Co., 1964), p. 26.

[2]*Ibid.*, p. 29.

[3]Charles V. Willie, "Age Status and Residential Stratification," *American Sociological Review*, 25 (April 1960), p. 264.

[4]Nathan Glazer and Daniel Patrick Moynihan, *Beyond the Melting Pot* (Cambridge: The M.I.T. Press and Harvard University Press, 1964).

[5]United States Department of Labor, *The Negro Family, A Case for National Action* (Washington: U.S. Government Printing Office, March 1965), pp. 47, 30.

[6]*Ibid.*

[7]Mollie Orshansky, "Consumption, Work and Poverty," Ben B. Seligman (ed.), *Poverty as a Public Issue* (New York: The Free Press, 1965), pp. 55-56.

[8]James N. Morgan, *et al.*, *Income and Welfare in the United States* (New York: McGraw-Hill Book Co., 1962), p. 383.

[9]Miller, *op. cit.*, pp. 162-163.

[10]Morgan, *op. cit.*, pp. 374-375.

[11]Charles V. Willie and Walter E. Riddick, "The Employed Poor: A Case Study," Ben B. Seligman (ed.), *op. cit.*, pp. 142-145.

[12]United States Department of Labor, *op. cit.*, pp. 8, 12, 34.

[13]Charles V. Willie and Janet Weinandy, "The Structure and Composition of 'Problem' and 'Stable' Families in a Low-Income Population," *Marriage and Family Living*, 25 (November 1963), p. 443.

[14]William J. Goode, "Illegitimacy in the Caribbean Social Structure," *American Sociological Review*, 25 (February 1960), pp. 20-30.

[15]Oscar Lewis, *Five Families* (New York: Science Editions, 1962), p. 2.

[16]Hylan Lewis, *Child Rearing Among Low Income Families* (Washington: Washington Center for Metropolitan Studies, 1961), pp. 10-11.

[17]Charles V. Willie, Morton O. Wagenfeld, and Lee J. Cary, "Patterns of Rent Payment Among Problem Families," *Social Casework*, 45 (October 1964), pp. 465-470.

[18]*The New York Times*, "Survey of Relief Shows Tie to Past," March 24, 1968.

[19]Harold L. Sheppard and Herbert E. Striner, *Civil Rights, Employment and the Social Status of American Negroes* (Kalamazoo: The W.E. Upjohn Institute for Employment Research, 1966), p. 22.

[20]Abram Kardiner and Lionel Ovesey, *The Mark of Oppression* (Cleveland: Meridian Books, 1962), p. 387.

[21]Robert K. Merton, *Social Structure and Social Theory* (New York: The Free Press, 1949), pp. 179-195.

[22]James B. Conant, *Slums and Suburbs* (New York: McGraw-Hill Book Co., 1961), pp. 11-12.

[23]Kardiner and Ovesey, *op. cit.*, p. 379.

[24]Merton, *op. cit.*, p. 183.

[25]*Ibid.*, p. 193.

[26]Herman Miller, "The Dimensions of Poverty, "Ben B. Seligman (ed.), *op. cit.*, p. 32.

[27]Miller, *Rich Man, Poor Man*, pp. 140-153.

[28]*Ibid.*

[29]Luther P. Jackson (ed.), *Poverty's Children (The Child Rearing Study of Low Income Families in the District of Columbia)*, (Washington: Health and Welfare Council of National Capital Area, 1966), p. 29.

[30]James Tobin, "On Improving the Economic Status of the Negro," *Daedalus*, 94 (Fall 1965), p. 887.

[31]Moynihan, "Employment, Income, and the Ordeal of the Negro Family," *Daedalus*, 94 (Fall 1965), pp. 746-747.

[32]Bureau of Labor Statistics and Bureau of the Census, *Social and Economic Conditions of Negroes in the United States* (Washington: U.S. Government Printing Office, October 1967, BLS Report No. 332, Current Population Reports, Series P-23, No. 24), p. 18.

[33]*Ibid.*

[34]Charles V. Willie, "Family Status and Economic Status in Juvenile Delinquency," *Social Problems*, 14 (Winter 1967), pp. 326-335.

[35]Louis Kriesberg, "Inter-Generational Patterns of Poverty," (paper presented at the annual meeting of the Eastern Sociological Society, Boston, Mass., April 6, 1968), pp. 5-6.

Is There a "Breakdown" of the Negro Family?

ELIZABETH HERZOG

MUCH HAS BEEN SAID OF LATE — AND OFTEN WITH GREAT HEAT — about the Negro family. Despite prevailing consensus on a number of points, controversy has been generated with regard to other points because one man's fact is another man's fiction. Some points of consensus deserve mention before points of controversy. First, it is generally agreed that a harmonious two-parent home is better for children than a one-parent home — and better for parents, too, in this society. It is agreed also that fatherless homes are far more frequent among Negroes than among whites and that in both groups their frequency rises as income falls.

Another point of firm consensus is that strong action is needed to remedy adverse conditions that have existed far too long, especially for low-income Negroes; and that these conditions bear especially on the low-income Negro man, whose disadvantaged situation takes heavy toll of himself, his children, their mother, and the family unit as a whole. All these statements have long been accepted by serious students of Negro family life.[1]

The controversy centers mainly on the following points: (1) whether "the" Negro family is "crumbling" at a disastrous rate, (2) whether the amount of breakdown that exists is primarily due to poverty, or to cultural inheritance, or to a cycle of self-perpetuating pathology,

---

[1] St. Clair Drake and Horace R. Cayton, *Black Metropolis* (New York: Harcourt, Brace, and Co., 1945); E. Franklin Frazier, *The Negro Family in the United States* (Chicago: University of Chicago Press, 1939); Hylan Lewis, "The Changing Negro Family," in Eli Ginzberg, ed., *The Nation's Children, Vol. 1: The Family and Social Change* (New York: Columbia University Press, 1960); Thomas F. Pettigrew, *A Profile of the Negro American* (Princeton, N.J.: D. Van Nostrand Co., 1964).

Reprinted by permission of the publisher and the author from *Social Work*, XI (January 1966), 3-10.

(3) whether the remedy is to be sought primarily through improving the economic, social, and legal status of Negroes or primarily through conducting a remedial campaign aimed directly at the Negro family.

THE MOYNIHAN REPORT

Impetus has been give to these and related questions by the much-discussed "Moynihan report."[2] Released to the general public in the late fall of 1965, this publication presents census figures and findings from some special studies to document the grim effects of poverty and discrimination and their impact on Negro families. It brings together all-too-familiar evidence that the frequency of broken marriage, female-headed families, births out of wedlock, and dependence on public assistance are much higher among Negroes than among whites. In doing so, it recognizes that these problems are most acute among the very poor and least acute at the middle- and upper-income levels. It points out also that they are more acute in cities than in rural areas and thus are intensified by continuing urbanization.

The report further documents the higher unemployment rates and lower wage rates among Negroes than among whites. It states, as others have done, the 2 to 1 white-Negro unemployment ratio that has persisted for years, the lower wages available to Negroes, and the fact that the median nonwhite family income is little more than half the median for white families. To this discrepancy is added the fact that the families of the poor tend to be larger than middle-class families. "Families of six or more children have median incomes 24 percent below families with three."[3] Other sources tell how heavily this fertility differential bears on Negro families: in 1963, according to the Social Security Administration Index, 60 percent of nonwhite children under 18 lived in poverty as compared with 16 percent of white children.[4]

The effect on marital and family stability of the man's economic instability is also discussed. The sad cycle has become familiar in the professional literature: the man who cannot command a stable job at adequate wages cannot be an adequate family provider; the man who cannot provide for his family is likely to lose status and respect in his own eyes and in the eyes of others — including his family. His inability to provide drains him of the will to struggle with continuing and insuperable family responsibilities. It is an incentive to desertion, especially if his family can receive public assistance only when he is gone.

---

[2]*The Negro Family: The Case for National Action* (Washington, D.C.: Department of Labor, Office of Planning and Research, 1965).

[3]*Ibid.*, p. 24.

[4]Mollie Orshansky, "Who's Who Among the Poor: A Demographic View of Poverty," *Social Security Bulletin*, Vol. 28, No. 7 (July 1965), pp. 3-32.

A good deal of the Moynihan report is devoted to interpretation of the documented figures and, quite naturally, it is on the interpretation that opinions diverge.[5] It is not the purpose of this paper to summarize fully, to concur with, or to take issue with the report as such, but rather to consider some propositions that were in circulation before it was published and to which it has given increased currency. With regard to the report itself, its factual summary has shocked some Americans into new recognition of old and unpalatable facts about the toll exacted by poverty coupled with discrimination; and its interpretive sections have challenged us to an assessment of evidence — two substantial services. Some of the propositions attributed to it may be misinterpretations of the author's intended meaning. In any case, they have taken on a life of their own and are met frequently in other current writings. Accordingly, they will be considered here on their own merits, without reference to any particular document.

FATHERLESS FAMILIES

One recurrent proposition concerns the "rapid deterioration" of the Negro family, often referred to as "crumbling" and presumably near dissolution. The incidence of fatherless families is used as the primary index of family breakdown. Although questions can be — and have been — raised about this index, such questions do not dominate the mainstream of the argument and will be disregarded here. But if one accepts the proportion of fatherless homes as a primary index of family breakdown, does it then follow, on the basis of the evidence, that the Negro family is rapidly deteriorating?

It is important to differentiate between sudden acceleration of family crisis and relatively sudden perception of a long-chronic situation, since the diagnosis of a social condition influences the prescription for relieving it and the context in which the prescription is filled.

Actually, census figures do not justify any such alarmist interpretation. It seems worth while to review these figures, not because there is no urgent need for remedial action — the need is urgent, especially in the area of jobs for low-income Negro men. Rather it is important to keep the problem in perspective and to avoid feeding prejudices that can

---

[5]Midway between statistical report and interpretation is discussion of a "startling increase in welfare dependency," described as occurring at a time when employment was increasing. *See* U.S. Department of Labor, *The Negro Family: The Case for National Action, op. cit.*, p. 12. It would require extensive and sophisticated analysis to determine the extent to which this upswing in AFDC recipients related to changes in families, or to liberalization of AFDC policies following new legislation, or to changes in population distribution. Similarly, differentials in rates of juvenile delinquency would need to be controlled for income and analyzed in light of differential rates of apprehension and treatment of presumed offenders, white or nonwhite.

all too readily seize upon statistical misconceptions as reason to delay rather than to speed such action.

As already noted, census figures do show much higher rates of fatherless families for Negroes than for whites. The 1964 figures show almost 9 percent of white families headed by a women as compared with 23 percent of nonwhite families; a difference of this order has persisted for years.[6] The figures do not, however, document a rapid increase in those rates during recent years. On the contrary — and this is a point curiously slighted by commentators on both sides of the argument — they show a gradual increase from 1949 (19 percent) to 1959 (24 percent). Moreover, from 1960 to 1964 the proportion of female-headed families among Negroes showed no net rise at all, standing at 23 percent in 1964. The total rise from 1949 to 1964 was about 5 percentage points, that is, about one-third of a percentage point a year. In 1940, the proportion was 18 percent.[7] Thus, an accurate description would be that during the past twenty-five years there has been a gradual rise, preceded and followed by a plateau, but not an acute increase in the over-all proportion of broken homes among Negroes. (Table 1)

ILLEGITIMACY

Another generalization also related to family breakdown is met so often that by now it threatens to attain the status of "fact," namely, that there has been an "alarming rise" in illegitimacy. It is true that the number of births out of wedlock has soared. In 1964 the number was 276,000 as compared with 176,600 in 1954.[8] This is a tremendous number, and the more distressing since there has been no services explosion to keep pace with the population explosion. However, in terms of people's behavior, the only relevant index of increase in

---

[6]These figures are available for white and nonwhite rather than for white and Negro families. However, most of the nonwhite (about 92 percent) are Negroes.

[7]Percentages have been rounded. The exact rise was from 18.8 percent to 23.6 percent, or 4.4 percentage points. The 1940 figure was 17.8 percent, as recomputed according to the definition of "family" introduced in 1947. Bureau of the Census, *Current Population Reports*, Series P-20, Nos. 125, 116, 106, 100, 88, 83, 75, 67, 53, 44, 33, and 26 (Washington, D.C.: U.S. Department of Commerce); Bureau of Labor Statistics, *The Negroes in the United States: Their Economic and Social Situation* (Washington, D.C.: U.S. Department of Labor, 1965); Bureau of the Census, *16th Census of the U.S. 1940. Population—Families—Types of Families* (Washington, D.C.: U.S. Department of Commerce, 1940).

[8]*Monthly Vital Statistics Reports, Advance Report, Final Natality Statistics, 1964* (Washington, D.C.: U.S. Department of Health, Education, and Welfare, National Center for Health Statistics, Public Health Service, October 22, 1965); *Vital Statistics of the United States, 1963. Volume I—Natality* (Washington, D.C.: National Center for Health Statistics, Public Health Service, Department of Health, Education, and Welfare, 1964).

illegitimacy is *rate,* that is, the number of births out of wedlock per 1,000 unmarried women of child-bearing age.

The rise in rate (as differentiated from numbers) was relatively steady over several decades. This rise represents a long-term trend and not a sudden upsurge. Moreover, in the last seven years reported (1957-1964) the rate has oscillated within about two points, at about the same level, rising or falling one point or less annually, but in effect representing a seven-year plateau. Since all national illegitimacy figures are based on estimates, with a number of states not reporting, very slight changes should not be regarded as significant. Thus, the current picture is a large rise in *numbers* and a leveling off in the *rate* of nonwedlock births.[9] Rates for teen-agers have increased less than for other groups, and for those under fifteen the rate has not increased since 1947.[10] (The ratio — the proportion of live births that are out of wedlock — has risen for both whites and nonwhites. However, *ratio* is far less meaningful than *rate* as an index of change.)

TABLE 1

FAMILIES HEADED BY A WOMAN AS PERCENT OF ALL FAMILIES BY COLOR
SELECTED PERIODS, 1949-1964

	FAMILIES HEADED BY A WOMAN AS PERCENT OF TOTAL	
Year	White	Nonwhite
1964	8.8	23.4
1963	8.6	23.3
1962	8.6	23.2
1961	8.9	21.6
1960	8.7	22.4
1959	8.4	23.6
1958	8.6	22.4
1957	8.9	21.9
1956	8.8	20.5
1955	9.0	20.7
1954	8.3	19.2
1953	8.4	18.1
1952	9.2	17.9
1950	8.4	19.1
1949	8.8	18.8

Source: U.S. Department of Commerce, Bureau of the Census: Current Population Reports, P-20, No. 125, 116, 106, 100, 88, 83, 75, 67, 53, 44, 33, and 26. Figures for 1963 and 1964 are drawn from Bureau of Labor Statistics, *The Negroes in the United States: Their Economic and Social Situation* (Washington, D.C., U.S. Department of Labor) Table IV, a, I.

[9] Elizabeth Herzog, "The Chronic Revolution: Births Out of Wedlock." Paper presented at meeting of American Orthopsychiatric Association, March 1965. To be published in a forthcoming issue of *Clinical Pediatrics.*

[10] Rates are not available by color except for a few years.

The recent relative stability of rate does not diminish the problems caused by nonwedlock births but it should affect the conclusions drawn from the statistics, the measures taken to act on those conclusions, and the attitudes of those who ponder the meaning of the figures.

Over half the children born out of wedlock are nonwhite, although only 12 percent of the population are nonwhite. The reasons for this difference have been much discussed and need only be mentioned here. They include (1) less use of contraception, (2) less use of abortion, (3) differences in reporting, (4) reluctance to lose a public assistance grant by admitting to a man in the house, (5) the expense of divorce and legal separation. It seems probable that, even if discount could be made for these and other factors, a difference would remain. It would be a much smaller difference, however, and conceivably could still relate more to income than to color.[11]

If further evidence were needed on this virtually unchallenged relation between income and illegitimacy rates, figures on rates in high- and low-income tracts should be sufficient. Pakter and associates, for example, found that the proportion of births out-of-wedlock in relation to total nonwhite births varied from a high of 38 percent in the Central Harlem district to a comparative low of 9 percent in the Pelham Bay District.[12]

Attitudes toward illegitimacy and toward marriage are clearly linked with the economic position of the Negro male. A male head of house who is not a breadwinner and provider is a hazard to the happiness of the marriage, and his loss of economic status is so great a hazard to his intrafamily status that he may decamp, either to protect his own ego or to make his family eligible for support from AFDC. Recent changes in the AFDC program are aimed against the latter reason for family desertion.

SLAVERY IS NOT THE EXPLANATION

Among the most frequent and most challenged generalizations relating to low-income Negro families is the assumption that their present characteristics are influenced more by the legacy of slavery than by postslavery discriminations and deprivations. The challenge rests chiefly

---

[11] Elizabeth Herzog, "Unmarried Mothers: Some Questions To Be Answered and Some Answers To Be Questioned," *Child Welfare*, Vol. 41, No. 8 (October 1962), pp. 339-350.

[12] Jean Parker, Henry J. Rosner, Harold Jacobziner, and Frieda Greenstein, "Out-of-Wedlock Births in New York City. I—Sociologic Aspects," *American Journal of Public Health*, Vol. 51, No. 5 (May 1961), pp. 683-696.

on (1) the similarity between very poor Negro families and very poor white families, and (2) the fact that slavery ended a hundred years ago while the postslavery situation is contemporary and appalling. Adequately controlled comparisons within different income levels show that the differences associated with income outweigh those associated with color. Family structure, for example, differs more between different income levels than between Negro and white families. The same is true of differences between Negro and white children in educational achievement, and — when income is controlled — the relative position of men with respect to women, economically and educationally, is the same for whites as for nonwhites.[13]

Descriptions of white families at the very low income levels read very much like current descriptions of poor Negro families, with high incidence of broken homes, "mother dominance," births out of wedlock, educational deficit, crowded living, three-generation households, and failure to observe the norms of middle-class behavior.[14] Such families are described by Hollingshead and Redlich:

> Doctors, nurses, and public officials who know these families best estimate from one-fifth to one-fourth of all births are illegitimate.

> Death, desertion, separation, or divorce has broken more than half the families (56%). The burden of child care, as well as support, falls on the mother more often than on the father when the family is broken. The mother-child relation is the strongest and most enduring family tie.

> Here we find a conglomerate of broken homes where two or three generations live together, where boarders and roomers, in-laws and common-law liaisons share living quarters. Laws may be broken and the moral standards of the higher classes flouted before the children's eyes day after day.[15]

These are descriptions of white families in the North, with no heritage of slavery to explain their way of life. It seems unlikely that the

---

[13]Myron J. Lefcowitz, "Poverty and Negro-White Family Structures." Unpublished background paper for White House Conference on Civil Rights, Washington, D.C., November 1965.

[14]Walter B. Miller, "Implications of Urban Lower-Class Culture for Social Work," *Social Service Review*, Vol. 33, No. 3 (September 1959), pp. 219-236; W. Lloyd Warner and Paul S. Lunt, *The Social Life of a Modern Community* (New Haven: Yale University Press, 1941); James West, *Plainville, USA* (New York: Columbia University Press, 1945).

[15]August B. Hollingshead, *Elmtown's Youth* (New York: John Wiley & Sons, 1949), pp. 116, 117; Hollingshead and Frederick C. Redlich, *Social Class and Mental Illness: A Community Study* (New York: John Wiley & Sons, 1958), p. 125.

slavery-specific thesis is needed to explain the occurrence among Negroes of patterns so similar to those produced in other groups merely by poverty, and so often described in other contexts as "the culture of poverty."[16]

It is difficult to be sure how much — if any — difference would remain in proportions of female-headed families if really sensitive comparisons were made between Negroes and whites on the same income level. Available income breakdowns employ rather broad groupings, and Negroes tend to be overrepresented at the lower layers of each grouping. It seems reasonable to assume that some differences between white and nonwhite would remain even with a more sensitive income classification. Yet it does not necessarily follow that they might be ascribed primarily to the legacy of slavery rather than to the hundred years since slavery. It seems more likely that differences between low-income white and Negro families, beyond that explained by income alone, may be attributed primarily to postslavery factors of deprivation and discrimination affecting every facet of life: occupation, education, income, housing, nutrition, health and mortality, social status, self-respect — the documented list is long and the documenting references myriad.[17]

The habit of analyzing data by color rather than by income encourages the tendency to attribute to race-related factors differences that may in fact be due to income level. Studies of prenatal care, for example, indicate that in effect one is comparing the prosperous with the poor in all three of the following comparisons: white mothers with nonwhite mothers; married mothers with unmarried mothers; all mothers who do, with all mothers who do not, obtain prenatal care.[18]

All the points mentioned here, and some not mentioned, are important. However, the emphasis on rapid deterioration is so central to current discussion of the low-income Negro family and to means proposed for alleviating its current problems that it deserves major emphasis — along with the slavery-specific thesis to which it is so often linked.

---

[16]Oscar Lewis, *The Children of Sanchez: Autobiography of a Mexican Family* (New York: Random House, 1961).

[17]Dorothy K. Newman, "Economic Status of the Negro." Unpublished background paper for White House Conference on Civil Rights, Washington, D.C., November 1965; Alvin L. Schorr, *Slums and Social Insecurity*, Research Report No. 1 (Washington, D.C.: Department of Health, Education, and Welfare, Social Security Administration, 1963).

[18]Elizabeth Herzog and Rose Bernstein, *Health Services for Unmarried Mothers*, Children's Bureau Publication No. 425 (Washington, D.C.: Department of Health, Education, and Welfare, Welfare Administration, 1964).

There has been little disposition to challenge the ample evidence that family structure and functioning in our society are strongly linked with social and economic status. The questions raised, as Robert Coles put it, have to do with which is the cart and which is the horse.[19] The alleged rapid acceleration of family breakdown has been cited as evidence that among low-income Negroes the family is the horse. Therefore it is important to recognize that, according to the chief index used by proponents of this view, no rapid acceleration of family breakdown is evident.

If there has been no substantial change in family structure during the past two decades, then there are no grounds for claiming that a new "tangle of pathology" has set up a degenerative process from within, over and above response to the long continued impact of social and economic forces from without; and that this process is specific to a Negro "culture" inherited from days of slavery.

Two Views — and Two Remedies

Both sides of the controversy agree that there is urgent need for strong action to increase the proportion of sound, harmonious two-parent homes among low-income Negroes. They disagree on whether that action should be focused primarily on intra-family or extra-family problems. The acute-crisis view suggests that primary attention be given to the family as such. The other view suggests that the best way to strengthen low-income families, as families, is to give primary attention to building up the economic and social status of Negro men.

According to this view, a number of noneconomic supports can and should be given to low-income Negro families, pending the time when fewer of them are fatherless. Such helps should include, among other things, (1) aids for the over-burdened mother in her multiple role as homemaker, child-rearer, and breadwinner; and (2) effective male models introduced into the lives of children — girls as well as boys. A number of new ways for providing both kinds of support have been proposed. In the long run, however, according to this view, what these families need most is jobs for Negro men — jobs with status, with stability, with future, and with fair wages. No one claims that this can be achieved easily, quickly, or cheaply; but many believe it can and must be done.

---

[19]Robert Coles, "There's Sinew in the Negro Family." Background paper for White House Conference on Civil Rights, Washington, D.C., November 1965. Reprinted from the *Washington Post*, October 10, 1965, p. E 1.

What is new for the white majority is not that it is suddenly faced with an explosive breakdown of "the" Negro family. What is new is the recognition of a long-standing situation, plus the determination to do something about it. If we are able to achieve that recognition and determination, however belatedly, then surely we must be able to act on this basis rather than to galvanize ourselves into action by believing that suddenly the Negro family is a bomb or a mine which will explode in our faces if it is not quickly defused. Surely we are able to act, not because of panic but because action is long overdue, and inaction flies in the face of decency.

What is new for the Negro minority is not a sudden acceleration of family breakdown. What is new is an injection of hope that attacks apathy and fatalism and sparks insistence on full justice. It is not increased family breakdown that activates outbreaks such as occurred in Harlem, Watts, and elsewhere. It is the recognition that the families of the "dark ghetto" no longer need to continue to accept the ghetto and what it does to them.

It must, of course, be recognized that "the" Negro family is itself a fiction. Different family forms prevail at different class and income levels throughout our society. In addition, at any given level a wide variety of families are found, each with its individual characteristics — some of which are and some of which are not class linked. When the great diversity among low-income families is ignored, there is danger that the deplored characteristics of some will be imputed to all.[20] At the same time, most writers — including the present one — find it almost impossible to avoid falling into the oversimplified form of reference to "the" Negro family that constantly risks oversimplified thinking.

It is necessary also to caution one's self and others that, while problems must be discussed and attacked, strengths must not be forgotten. Problem-focused discussions, however necessary and constructive, also invite distortion. Not all fathers are absent fathers among the poor — in fact, about two-thirds of them are present among low-income Negro families. And, as Erik Erikson reminds us, there are impressive strengths in many Negro mothers.[21] Robert Coles, after living among low-income Negroes for months, wrote:

---

[20]Hylan Lewis, *Culture, "Class and the Behavior of Low Income Families."* Unpublished background paper for White House Conference on Civil Rights, Washington, D.C., November 1965; Elizabeth Herzog, "Some Assumptions About the Poor,"*Social Service Review*, Vol. 37, No. 4 (December 1963), pp. 389-402.

[21]Erik H. Erikson, "The Concept of Identity in Race Relations: Notes and Queries." Published in December 1965 issue of *Daedalus*.

I was constantly surprised at the endurance shown by children we would all call poor or, in the current fashion, "culturally disadvantaged." . . . What enabled such children from such families to survive, emotionally and educationally, ordeals I feel sure many white middle-class boys and girls would find impossible? What has been the source of strength shown by the sit-in students, many of whom do not come from comfortable homes but, quite the contrary, from rural cabins or slum tenements?[22]

One may go on to speculate: What are the sources of strength and self-discipline that make possible a Montgomery bus boycott or a March on Washington, conducted without violence? We do well to ponder such questions, for we shall have to mobilize the strengths of families in poverty as well as the wisdom of others who ponder their problems, if we are at last "to fulfill these rights."

---

[22]Robert Coles, *op. cit.*, p. E 1 (Washington Post).